WRITERS AT WORK

Sixth Series

D0101617

Previously Published

WRITERS AT WORK
The *Paris Review* Interviews

FIRST SERIES

Edited, and with an Introduction, by MALCOLM COWLEY

E. M. Forster	Frank O'Connor
François Mauriac	Robert Penn Warren
Joyce Cary	Alberto Moravia
Dorothy Parker	Nelson Algren
James Thurber	Angus Wilson
Thornton Wilder	William Styron
William Faulkner	Truman Capote
Georges Simenon	Françoise Sagan

SECOND SERIES

Edited by GEORGE PLIMPTON and introduced by
VAN WYCK BROOKS

Robert Frost	Aldous Huxley
Ezra Pound	Ernest Hemingway
Marianne Moore	S. J. Perelman
T. S. Eliot	Lawrence Durrell
Boris Pasternak	Mary McCarthy
Katherine Anne Porter	Ralph Ellison
Henry Miller	Robert Lowell

THIRD SERIES

Edited by GEORGE PLIMPTON and introduced by ALFRED KAZIN

William Carlos Williams	Saul Bellow
Blaise Cendrars	Arthur Miller
Jean Cocteau	James Jones
Louis-Ferdinand Céline	Norman Mailer
Evelyn Waugh	Allen Ginsberg
Lillian Hellman	Edward Albee
William Burroughs	Harold Pinter

FOURTH SERIES

Edited by GEORGE PLIMPTON and introduced by WILFRID SHEED

Isak Dinesen	John Dos Passos
Conrad Aiken	Vladimir Nabokov
Robert Graves	Jorge Luis Borges
George Seferis	John Berryman
John Steinbeck	Anthony Burgess
Christopher Isherwood	Jack Kerouac
W. H. Auden	Anne Sexton
Eudora Welty	John Updike

FIFTH SERIES

Edited by GEORGE PLIMPTON and introduced by
FRANCINE DU PLESSIX GRAY

P. G. Wodehouse	Joyce Carol Oates
Pablo Neruda	Archibald MacLeish
Henry Green	Isaac Bashevis Singer
Irwin Shaw	John Cheever
James Dickey	Kingsley Amis
William Gass	Joseph Heller
Jerzy Kosinski	Gore Vidal
Joan Didion	

Writers at Work

The *Paris Review* Interviews

SIXTH SERIES

Edited by George Plimpton
Introduction by Frank Kermode

THE VIKING PRESS   NEW YORK

VIKING

Viking Penguin Inc., 40 West 23rd Street
New York, NY 10010 U.S.A.
Penguin Books Ltd, Harmondsworth,
Middlesex, England
Penguin Books Australia Ltd, Ringwood
Victoria, Australia
Penguin Books Canada Limited, 2801 John Street
Markham, Ontario, Canada L3R 1B4
Penguin Books (N.Z.) Ltd, 182–190 Wairau Road,
Auckland 10, New Zealand

First published in 1984 by Viking Penguin Inc.
Published simultaneously in Canada

ISBN 0-670-79099-0

Library of Congress Catalog Card Number: 83-40255 (CIP data available)

Printed in the United States of America
by R. R. Donnelley & Sons Company, Harrisonburg, Virginia

Contents

Introduction by Frank Kermode   ix

1. REBECCA WEST   1

2. STEPHEN SPENDER   39

3. TENNESSEE WILLIAMS   75

4. ELIZABETH BISHOP   123

5. BERNARD MALAMUD   149

6. WILLIAM GOYEN   169

7. KURT VONNEGUT, JR.   205

8. NADINE GORDIMER   239

9. JAMES MERRILL   281

10. GABRIEL GARCÍA MÁRQUEZ   313

11. CARLOS FUENTES   341

12. JOHN GARDNER   375

Notes on the Contributors   411

Introduction

B ETWEEN THE BIRTHS OF the oldest and the youngest of the
writers interviewed in this collection forty-one years
elapsed, and a lot of literary history. If we want to extend the
time span we can work on Rebecca West's remark that she was
kissed by the brother of the soprano Malibran, who died in
1836, and whose sister, Pauline Viardot, was the mistress of
Turgenev ("I think the duties were light," says Dame
Rebecca). No need to go into the question of who kissed
Malibran; we can move forward instead. There is a very reason-
able expectation that some of the seven writers of this dozen
who are still with us will be writing, submitting to interviews
and kisses, well into the next century.

The geographical spread, if not quite so generous as the
chronological, is still impressive. The seven Americans come
from the South, the Southwest, the Midwest, as well as from
the East; and there are two Latin Americans and a South
African, as well as two English writers. It is a coverage suffi-
ciently international to encourage some cautious generaliza-
tions about national, if not regional, styles.

The interview is not a medium that is natural to writers; it
requires of the script-bound a venture into naked orality. I
remember from my own experience how difficult it was to get

Graham Greene to say anything at all; what he did say was so unexpected (he would like to be able to write a novel like *Tom Jones*) that one wondered how much should be discounted as the involuntary product of boredom or embarrassment. Iris Murdoch, on the other hand, talked seriously but carefully rewrote everything she said before publication. Other writers prepare for the ordeal by deciding in advance what they will say, and again the sense of privileged talk is lost, and it becomes impossible for conversation to produce discoveries, as it should.

The Paris Review knows very well what chancy things interviews are, and takes or permits various precautions. So Mr. Vonnegut virtually interviews himself; others are put through it three times, with only the best takes getting into print. Yet we still find some writers apprehensive of the dreadful little machine. Gabriel García Márquez, indeed, begins by referring to the problem of the tape recorder, that modern third ear. There can be a touch of antagonism, purely formal of course, in the relations between its manipulator and its victim. The attitude of the interviewed one changes as soon as the tape begins to roll. When the interviewer remarks that this makes him feel guilty, Márquez craftily explains that it was meant to, that he wanted to put the fellow on the defensive. This may be an understandable reaction on the part of a writer who lives in Mexico City, a jostling conurbation described by Carlos Fuentes, perhaps a shade extravagantly, as a city drowning in shit. But it is true all the same that for many writers, such interviews as these are something of a test.

As to the topics upon which they think it proper to express themselves for the benefit of the public, there are certainly national differences between American and other writers. Some of the Americans feel threatened; but to outsiders it can appear that they are under no particular menace. Nadine Gordimer is a South African, and speaks with impressive sobriety of a life of permanent opposition, not to fate or death or any other abstract idea, but to an actual and oppressive régime;

and, for the time being at any rate, those of us who live in more comfortable countries have lost the power to imagine what that must be like (unless, of course, we happen to be at the bottom of our heap). "It amazes me," says Gordimer. "I come to America, I go to England, I go to France . . . nobody's at risk. They're afraid of getting cancer, losing a lover, losing their jobs, being insecure. It's either something you have no control over, like death—the atom bomb—or it's something with which you'll be able to cope anyway, and that is not the end of the world; you'll get another job or you'll go on state relief or something of this nature. It's only in my country that I find people who voluntarily choose to put everything at risk—in their personal life."

As her remarks on the censorship and its effect on black writing in South Africa show, Gordimer isn't saying that being in opposition or even "putting everything at risk" will make you a better writer. But it will certainly make you look rather differently at what appear to be horrifying problems. Gordimer remarks that "Commitment is not merely a political thing. It's part of the whole ontological problem in life"; and when she speaks them the words do not sound old-fashioned, though they imply an estimate of what really matters that may seem so in the U.S. or in England or France today. Gordimer, we note, doesn't think that she suffers as a writer by being a woman: "It doesn't matter a damn what sex a writer is." She does not seem to spend much time thinking about alcohol, or critics, or editors or writer's block.

However, these are some of the favorite topics of American writers. There is nothing factitious about this, and there is nothing inauthentic about the anxiety and suffering they describe. To survive is their preoccupation, exactly as it would be if they had a palpable external enemy. Not all of them talk about these matters, and not all of them suffer the same afflictions, but it is nevertheless possible for Tennessee Williams to generalize about "the terrible indignities, humiliations, privations, shocks that attend the life of an American writer." One important agent of these ills is booze. Think of O'Neill, he says. "There's a great deal of tension involved in writing," especially as you get older; then you have to have alcohol. And a writer may well be an unusually vulnerable figure to begin with; Williams certainly was. He had a respectable father who got his ear bitten off in a fight about poker; his mother thought the blacks of St. Louis were planning an uprising and signaling to one another by rattling garbage pails, and Williams remembers her screaming during sex and insisting that a horse had moved in with her. In some of this story of a happy family Williams may be exploiting the possibilities of farce; not so in his account of his own sojourn in the violent ward, or his encounter with the rough trade. Even to die is somehow to be different from other people who do the same: "Towards the end of an American writer's life it's just dreadful." The writer knows about death in advance—William Goyen, speaking of Carson McCullers, calls writer's block a sort of death, and attributes to its pains the persistence of remedies worse than the disease: "That's why so many of us become alcoholics or suicides or insane— or just no-good philanderers. It's amazing that we survive." And he adds that in some instances it is also a pity that we do.

Now it is a matter of observation, if not of record, that not all American novelists and playwrights lead such spectacularly awful lives. For example, many of them are teachers at colleges and universities—indeed, that vocation or avocation, life-support system or *violon d'Ingres,* is one of the peculiarities that distinguishes them most clearly from writers of other cultures. Occasionally they teach straight academic subjects, as John Gardner did; but usually they teach "writing." On the question whether "writing" should be taught, and the question whether it can be taught, opinion is deeply divided. It is hard to imagine Henry James or Hawthorne in a creative writing class: the whole idea is rather modern, and there is as yet little evidence that it produces remarkable writers. Rebecca West would have called it self-evidently absurd, but she was old and English. Yet even Elizabeth Bishop gently surmises that the students would be better off learning something learnable, a language perhaps.

All the same, there is much to be said in favor of the writing course. It is decently democratic—why shouldn't everybody who wants to be helped to write a bit? More important, it helps, as Bernard Malamud says, to create "a community of serious readers." He argues that teaching writing is teaching literature; occasionally the instructor may help a genuine writer, but the real justification is not that; it is that one adds to the number of people who have some skill in recognizing good writing, who have been taught to read books that do more than merely confirm the view of the world already laid on them by the society. They will know something of what it is in writing that, to borrow James's expression, makes interest, makes importance. That knowledge has to be acquired somewhere, and to get it from Malamud seems a pretty good idea. He is less confident of the creative writing powers of his students than Gardner, but his real point is that he can teach creative reading, and that is something serious writers have to count on. And if they don't make enough money from their books, their courses have the further value that they keep writers alive. They may even delay the onset of despair, booze, sleeping pills.

Novelists historically have a larger constituency than poets; and their work more closely resembles that of writers whose works sell by the million. They are that much nearer to general fame and great riches, and in a society that puts so high a value on success it hurts to be a near miss. Perhaps that is why the pain of the *romancier maudit* seems especially acute. Of course one doesn't forget the exemplary agonies of Berryman and Lowell, but these were poets who assumed that they, exceptionally, had a claim to universal celebrity. Other poets don't assume that, and the two in this collection are, it appears, relatively immune to what Conrad called *les stérilités des*

écrivains nerveux. Each is movingly because unquestioningly
sure of his or her vocation. Bishop is even a bit apologetic:
"There's nothing more embarrassing than being a poet, really,"
and she wonders not whether she is one, but whether it is not
some kind of moral defect, "an awful core of ego . . . I've never
felt it, but it must be there."

This charming scrupulousness also causes her to wonder if
she is being weighty enough in the interview, when what she
is admirably doing is giving a precious insight into the way her
kind of poetry occurs, as the ordering of perceptions imposed
upon her as if fortuitously; what Aristotle rightly said about
women's teeth, how it was fun to be at Yaddo because of the
Saratoga racetrack and the sales, where grooms with brass
dustpans and brooms with brass handles swept up after the
yearlings; with dozens of other little visions that make such a
world as hers. "I'm afraid everything in my life has just *happened* . . ." The word is closely related to "happiness," and
Shakespeare in *Hamlet* calls an uncanny aptness of discourse
"happiness," though Polonius is surprised because he thinks
Hamlet mad. We, however, may use it of the wholly sane to
whom poetry happily happens. There is a serenity in Merrill,
too; inveterately a poet, he experienced, he says, the common
transition from the jubilant ease of youthful composition to the
harder work of middle age without feeling the pain, or treating
himself for it, as some others have done. It is touching that the
Auden who communicates with him by Ouija board should
again be young and jubilant. As a young man Auden enjoyed
an utter certainty of vocation even before he discovered verse
forms and, as Spender tells us, called a poem a sonnet "because
it only has eleven lines." But later, when he knew pretty well
all there was to know about verse forms, he came to think of
poetry as prone to falsehood, which, since he had a fanatical
love of truth, made him, I think, sad in his vocation. So it is
good to think of him young and again jubilant.

Many writers agree that when the first easy gush is exhausted, only hard labor and sure technique can keep them going and keep them faithful to that early calling. You get a strong sense of this from Goyen and from Malamud, the one stitching at his poetic quilts, the other a little reserved, a little gnomic, but as certain as the torrential Gardner that the preservation of the personal voice and vision requires endless renewals and accumulations of art and craft. Vonnegut, more professionally flip, would nevertheless agree. And it may be, in the seriousness with which they are willing to speak of their vocation as a fate and a burden and also a privilege, that the Americans distinguish themselves from their British contemporaries, whose literary conversation tends to be less structured and less clearly serious—not very different indeed from gossip, with its revelations and concealments, its unconsidered judgments and its preference for the oblique over the straight.

The presence of the tape recorder is much less likely to make such subjects speak solemnly about their beliefs and aims, and of all the writers in this collection it is surely Rebecca West who cares least about it. She is throughout at her conversational ease, no respecter of persons, dead or alive—Tolstoy, Eliot, Iris Murdoch, Ian McEwan, the Virgin Mary (about whom her interviewer wrote a big book), and "that man, David Mitchell" are all put down with the same casual zest. Such candor and irreverence are perhaps unattainable by younger persons, who could not in any case claim the chic of having had pneumonia in the left ear, perceptively reviewed *The Good Soldier* on its first appearance, lived with H. G. Wells, and written the first book about Henry James. Her gossip has a sort of cordial testiness, but is, in its way, highly informative: on de Maistre, on sex and the advent of four-footed animals used for food, on Mark Twain as prophet of fascism, on not knowing Greek because upper-class French girls in the eighteenth century were forbidden it, lest they fall into the toils of the wicked Greek Orthodox Church, on Ivy Compton-Burnett as the apotheosis of the nanny, on George Washington Cable and the scandal of the modern American failure to read him, on the Booker Prize. (She says being on the committee of judges nearly drove her mad, but having served with her I can testify that she enjoyed it more than anybody and virtually dictated the decision.)

You get a strong impression that Dame Rebecca *knows* more than anybody else, having the facts about, say, Thomas Lake Harris or Christabel Pankhurst at her fingertips. Lacking this knowledge, few of us would dare to venture such casual judgments on whatever comes up, like Joan of Arc or Princess Anne. Her epigrams have a pre–World War I flavor, as when, referring to Malcolm Muggeridge, she says she "can never think Christ is grateful for being alluded to as if he were a lost cause." She is feminist—men are "awful rubbish"—but not quite in the modern manner, for her time was the time of the suffragettes. A wonderful survivor! Even the locution "do you know" ("That was, do you know, very disagreeable") sets her apart. The only other person I know who uses it regularly is William Golding, now in his seventies.

Stephen Spender is like West in that he regards gossip and informative talk as a continuum, and since he has known everybody in literature over the past six decades he is treated as a sort of cultural memory and is often required to talk less of himself than of Auden, Eliot, Yeats, Pound, Hemingway, Frost, Lowell, and so forth. "For myself," he says, meditating on the performances of Pound and Eliot, "I can't imagine inventing a persona," but his persona is precisely his candor; and now I am using the word in a way that requires one to remember not only the current sense but also the older, the sense that would have been primary for Dr. Johnson or Jane Austen. Fortunate readers in the distant future will have Spender's journals to document this happy shrewdness, this truth in gossip. I think of the remark that in a certain sense Auden's death has been a release to him; of the excellence of his memory, his recall of truths forgotten or, to the young, unknown: for example, his passing remark on the war, which constituted "a suspension of every other activity which makes life interesting." Note the word *other*. War, unfortunately, is interesting.

Márquez, so conscious of the tape recorder and of his "millions" of readers, is not a gossip, but he is not "American" either. He deplores critics and commentary, which the Americans pay great heed to and even fear. Yet he thinks that the "boom" in the Latin American novel, though sparked by the Cuban revolution, is really the product of cultural colonialism, and that Latin Americans didn't dare believe they were any good until the U.S.A. ordained that they were. This seems quite realistic as well as fantastic, much in the Márquez manner, the manner of the Caribbean realist who has to be a fantasist. Fuentes has a different tone but is as un-American as West, for instance, in his scorn for the gringo practice of submitting to the intervention of editors; though she simply says they're no good, whereas he thinks of them as menials with whom a true hidalgo would not dream of cooperating. Fuentes indeed makes good his claim that the European intellect now survives in Latin America, where the novelists are a sort of collective prince waking, after four centuries of silence, that sleeping beauty, the Spanish language. The position of those who write English is different, he says; the language never slept, and if it seemed to be dozing off, some Irishman would happen along and disturb it. He is splendid, too, on the persistence, in those countries, of the baroque, a specimen of which he gives in his paranomasia of mirror and asshole, *speculum* and *culo*. And when he tells us of the advantages of writing under an Eastern European régime, we think again of Gordimer and what she says about America, where "nobody's at risk" except from their own demons.

He who writes an introduction such as this must always seek patterns, resemblances, significant differences; but the reader may well rejoice in randomness, in the diversity of these talents. Some answer like Malamud, "truthfully but with cunning," shaping their responses as they do their fictions, cultivating and praising *mesure*; others are fluent or devious, irresponsible or world-considering. Goyen says he is not prone to talk about writing, but talk he does, and in a rather Wordsworthian way. For quite personal reasons I enjoyed his account of that chilly night when *The House of Breath* presented itself to him, an epiphany occurring in a very unlikely situation, the flightdeck of a baby flattop. He hated that ship; "I wanted to die because I couldn't endure what looked like an endless way of life with which I had nothing to do—the war, the ship, the water . . . I have been terrified of water all my life. . . ." I served in a ship as like to Goyen's as peas in a pod, am terrified of water, and thought the war would never end. I spent a lot of time breathing the night air on that flightdeck. No epiphany, I'm afraid, just some glimmer of an understanding of what it might be to have one. Good books can happen to good writers anywhere, just as they can find themselves among their kind without planning it, as Goyen dropped into the Lawrentian circle at Taos. Even American writers have good as well as bad luck. That is why sometimes, to adapt Malamud's remark about Dreyfus as a subject, they not only endure well but suffer well.

Here then are a dozen writers, looking, I suppose, much as they wanted to look, having posed before the machine with the sort of patience they might have needed in Hawthorne's time for a daguerreotype portrait; and they are for the most part only a little retouched. We should be grateful to them for offering themselves to the curiosity, the conjectures and the gossip, of their lesser contemporaries.

FRANK KERMODE

1. Rebecca West

A literary presence over more than half a century, Rebecca West was born Cicily Isabel Fairfield in County Kerry, Ireland, in December 1892. She changed her name to that of the heroine of Ibsen's play *Rosmersholm*, who is characterized by a passionate will. As "Rebecca West" she began in journalism and literary criticism, and continued to write throughout the traumatic years when she was alone bringing up her only child, Anthony Panther West, born to her and H. G. Wells in 1914. She published her first book in 1916 and her first novel, *The Return of the Soldier*, in 1918. She wrote novels throughout the twenties (*The Judge*, 1922; *Harriet Hume, A London Fantasy*, 1929), and in 1928 collected her criticism in *The Strange Necessity*. The subject of the title essay is the touchstone of Rebecca West's philosophy: the unquenchable and healing need of human beings for art and literature. More essays followed in *Ending in Earnest: A Literary Log* (1931), in which, notably, she acclaimed the genius of D. H. Lawrence. Two years later, she published her biographical masterwork, *St. Augustine*.

In the late thirties, she travelled widely with her husband, Henry Maxwell Andrews, in the Balkans, and from these experiences she built her formidable analysis of the origins of World War II, *Black Lamb and Grey Falcon* (1941), the book generally considered her masterpiece. The marked political and historical character of this work led naturally to *The New Meaning of Treason* (1947) and *A Train of Powder* (1955) West's matchless account of the Nuremburg trials.

Honored with the French Legion of Honor and an award from the Women's Press Club for Journalism, Dame Rebecca West was still writing book reviews up until her death on March 16, 1983.

Since sunrise it had died and been reborn.

Its rebirth, I calculated rapidly, was likely to be followed by an agonising existence. I knew at once, as everybody must who had any knowledge of international affairs, what foreign powers had combined to kill this man. It appeared to me ~~then~~, as I lay in bed in the nursing-home, inevitable that war must follow; and indeed it must have done, had not the Yugoslavian Government exercised an iron control over its population, then and thereafter, and abstained from the smallest provocative action against its enemies. On that forbearance, which is indeed one of the most extraordinary feats of statesmanship ~~performed~~ in post-war Europe, I could not be expected to rely. So I saw myself widowed and childless, which was another instance of the archaic outlook of the back of the mind; for in the next war we women will have hardly any reason to fear bereavement, as bombardments unpreceded by declarations of war will send us and our loved ones to the next world in the breathless unity of scrambled eggs. That thought did not then occur to me, so I rang for my nurse, and when she came I cried to her, "Get me a telephone quickly! I must speak to my husband at once. A most terrible thing has happened. The King of Yugoslavia has been assassinated." "Oh, dear!" she replied. "Did you know him?" "No," I said. "Then why," she said, "do you think it is so terrible?"

Her words made me realise that the word 'idiot' comes from a Greek root meaning a private person. She was certainly intelligent in her work and was probably so in her ~~personal~~ life, but her unawareness of the bonds that linked her to strangers made her ~~follow her fate in a~~ ~~~~ darkness deep as that cast by malformed cells in the brain. It might be argued that she was happier so; but that is true only in the most limited sense. She would not be happy long. A population which does not know that the assassination of the King of Yugoslavia might precipitate a European war is a perpetual temptation to its governors; it will believe any lies, it can be seduced into supporting unnecessary wars and peace treaties that favour class interests. But it might be

A Rebecca West manuscript page from *Black Lamb and Grey Falcon*.

Rebecca West

*In Rebecca West's hallway hangs a drawing of her by Wynd-
ham Lewis, done in the thirties, "before the ruin," as she puts
it. In fact, in person, there is no ruin, not of her brilliant,
penetrating brown eyes, the energy of her voice, and her attention to all things. She was wearing a bright and patterned caftan
when we first met, a loose blouse over trousers the second time.
Cataracts mean she has two pairs of spectacles, on chains like
necklaces; arthritis has made a stick necessary. Her hair is white
and short; she wears beautiful rings. Her voice has kept some of
the vowel sounds of the Edwardian period, and some of its turns
of phrase: "I can't see someone or something" meaning "I can't
tolerate." She says words of foreign derivation, like "memoirs,"
with the accent of the parent language. We sat in her sitting
room, a room filled with drawings and paintings with a wide bay
window on to some of London's tall trees. Their leaves, which*

were turning when we met, almost brushed against the window panes.

INTERVIEWER: In your novel, *The Fountain Overflows*, you describe the poverty of the educated class very beautifully. Was that your background?

WEST: Oh, yes. I'll tell you what the position was. We had lots of pleasant furniture that had belonged to my father's family, none that had belonged to my mother's family, because they didn't die—the whole family all went on to their eighties, nineties—but we had furniture and we had masses of books, and we had a very good piano my mother played on. We were poor because my father's father died, when he and his three brothers were schoolboys. Their mother was a member of the Plymouth Brethren and a religious fanatic with a conscience that should have been held down and, you know, been eunuchized or castrated. She refused to keep on, to accept any longer, an annuity, which she was given by the Royal Family. And nobody knew why she was given it, and she found out the reason and she didn't approve of it, and she refused it, and they were poor forever after. The maddening thing was nobody ever knows why she said to Queen Victoria, "I cannot accept this allowance." It was hard on my father, who was in the army, because you needed money to be an officer. He was a ballistics expert. He did quite well in various things.

INTERVIEWER: He was a professional soldier?

WEST: No. Not all his life. He left the army after he got his captaincy. He went out to America and he ran a mine and wrote a certain amount, mostly on political science. He wrote well. He had a great mechanical mind and he drew very well. He did all sorts of things, and he'd had a fairly good training at Woolwich, a military academy. We were the children of his second marriage and he could no longer make much money. He went out to Africa and just got ill there. He came back and died in Liverpool when I was twelve or thirteen.

INTERVIEWER: Was he a remote and admirable figure, as the father is in *The Fountain Overflows?*

WEST: Oh, he wasn't so cracked as the father and he didn't sell furniture that didn't belong to him and all that sort of thing. That was rather a remembrance of another strange character.

INTERVIEWER: You've written very movingly, in several of your books, on how cruel natural death is, how it is the greatest hardship as opposed to some of the more violent deaths that you've also written about. Was it a very traumatic experience for you, as a child, when you lost your father?

WEST: Oh, yes, it was terrible. . . . The whole of life was extremely uncomfortable for us at that time. We had really got into terrible financial straits, not through anybody's fault. My mother had had to work very hard, and though she was a very good pianist, she was out of the running by then, and when she realized that my father was old and wasn't going to be able to go on with things, she very nobly went and learnt typewriting. Do you know people are always writing in the papers and saying that typists started in the last war, but they've been going on since the eighties and the nineties and 1900. Well, my mother did some typing for American evangelists called Torry and Alexander and she took over their music. They toured in England and my mother whacked the "Glory Song," a famous hymn—you still hear it whistled in the streets—out on the grand piano on the platform. It was a very noble thing to do. She wasn't well and she wasn't young, and then we came up to Scotland. My sister was studying medicine. My other sister had a scholarship at Cheltenham, which was rather useless to her; she was very brilliant indeed, and amusing as well.

INTERVIEWER: Which sister was that?

WEST: That's Winifred, who was more or less like Mary in *The Fountain Overflows.* Then there was myself, who had to go and try to get scholarships, which I usually did, at the local school. My mother ran a typing business, and I assisted her, which was amusing and which gave me a quickness of eye, which has been quite useful. She used to type manuscripts, particularly for the music faculty in Edinburgh. There was a German professor she'd known all her life. He used to send along pieces and I remember still with horror and amusement an enormous German book of his on program music with sentences like, "If the hearer turns his attention to the flutes and the piccolos, surely there will come to his mind the dawn rising over the bronze horses of Venice." There is a lot of rather good idiom of writing I can summon up, if necessary, about music in the post-Wagnerian period, which was very, very lush.

INTERVIEWER: Were you brought up to play yourself?

WEST: I played, but not well. From an early age—but it was not detected for many, many years—I've had difficulty about hearing. Finally, I lost my hearing almost entirely in this ear. I got pneumonia in it, which I think is rather chic. Then I thought I'd got my hearing back slowly, but really I'd learnt to lip-read and, it's an extraordinary thing, young people—if they lose their hearing young—learn lip-reading unconsciously, lots of them. It's quite common. I did that without knowing when I got double cataracts, I suddenly found my hearing going and I said, "Goodness, I've gone deaf at the same time as my eyes are going wrong," but my aurist, who's a very nice man, said, "No, you haven't. Your lip-reading power is breaking down," which was very disappointing, but, on the other hand, I was amazed at the ingenuity of the human animal. It did strike me as an extraordinary thing.

INTERVIEWER: In your home, was the atmosphere for women very emancipated because you were left alone?

WEST: Oh, yes. We were left alone. We had an uncle, who was very preoccupied. He was president of the Royal Academy of Music, Sir Alexander McKenzie, and he didn't really think anything of any woman but his wife. He was very thoughtless about his own daughter, who was an actress who acted very well in the early Chekhov plays. He treated her very inconsiderately and made her come back and nurse her mother and leave her husband in Paris, and the husband, after six years, lost heart and went off with someone else. We were very feminist altogether, and it was a very inspiring thing. Who is that man, David Mitchell, who writes silly hysterical books about Christabel Pankhurst? What is he? Who is he?

INTERVIEWER: He's now writing a book about the Jesuits.

WEST: The Jesuits? How does he know about the Jesuits?

INTERVIEWER: You thought his book on Christabel was hysterical, did you?

WEST: Absolute rubbish and nonsense. He writes about how she went to Paris and how she didn't go down to the cafés and meet the young revolutionaries. But how on earth was she to find out where they were? Because, you see, the Bolshevik generation was not yet identifiable. How would she find out any of the people, who hadn't really made their mark? It was an obscure time in the history of revolution. It was a time when very remarkable people were coming up, but they weren't visible yet. She did know the people like Henri de Rochefort very well. Mitchell also says she took a flat and had a housekeeper, who was also a very good cook, and didn't that show great luxury? Well, if he'd asked anybody, he would have found that, in those days, you couldn't take a furnished flat or house in Paris, nor, so far as I know, in most parts of France, unless you took a servant, who was left by the owner. All the furnished houses I ever had in France, modest as they were, had somebody that I had to take with the house.

INTERVIEWER: But you yourself broke with the suffragette movement.

WEST: I was too young and unimportant for that to mean much. I admired them enormously, but all that business about venereal disease, which was supposed to be round every corner, seemed to me excessive. I wasn't in a position to judge, but it did seem a bit silly. [Christabel Pankhurst headed a chastity campaign for women.]

INTERVIEWER: Christabel, in her later phase, became the

equivalent of a misogynist. She became very, what would the word be, misanthropic against men only, didn't she?

WEST: It wasn't quite that. She fell curiously into a sort of transatlantic form of mysticism, where there is a sort of repudiation of sex. Do you ever read anything about Thomas Lake Harris? He was an American mystic. Curious thing—you repudiated sex but you had a "counterpart," and you usually could get a counterpart by getting into bed with somebody else, with whom your relations were supposed to be chaste, but when you lay in his arms, you were really lying in the counterpart's arms, and . . . isn't it a convenient arrangement? That was one sort of pattern of American mysticism and dottyism. Christabel got caught up with that vagueness—though not with counterparts. If you read Harris's sermons—somebody took them down and I had a look at them—they were all very queer like that, disguised sexuality, but I wouldn't say the worse for that.

INTERVIEWER: You have written that there is a great difference between a male sensibility and a female sensibility, and you have a marvelous phrase for it in *Black Lamb and Grey Falcon.*

WEST: Idiots and lunatics. It's a perfectly good division. [The Greek root of "idiot" means "private person"; men "see the world as if by moonlight, which shows the outlines of every object but not the details indicative of their nature."] It seems to me in any assembly where you get people, who are male and female, in a crisis, the women are apt to get up and, with a big wave of the hand, say: "It's all very well talking about the defenses of the country, but there are thirty-six thousand houses in whatever—wherever they're living—that have no bathrooms. Surely it's more important to have clean children for the future." Silly stuff, when the enemy's at the gate. But men are just as silly. Even when there are no enemies at the gate, they won't attend to the bathrooms, because they say defense is more important. It's mental deficiency in both cases.

INTERVIEWER: But do you think it's innate or do you think it's produced by culture?

WEST: Oh, I really can't tell you that. It's awfully hard. You can't imagine what maleness and femaleness would be if you got back to them in pure laboratory state, can you? I suspect the political imbecility is very great on both sides.

I've never gone anywhere where the men have come up to my infantile expectations. I always have gone through life constantly being surprised by the extreme, marvelous qualities of a small minority of men. But I can't see the rest of them. They seem awful rubbish.

INTERVIEWER: In many of the political things that you've written, it would be impossible to tell that you were a woman, except that here and there you sometimes produce a comparison to do with a child or something, which may betray a certain feminine stance, but, in fact, you have overcome completely this division between idiot and lunatic. You're not an "idiot" at all. You don't only think of the personal angle.

WEST: I think that probably comes of isolation, that I grew up just as I was without much interference from social images except at my school.

INTERVIEWER: What were they at school?

WEST: We had large classes, which was an ineffable benefit, because the teachers really hadn't time to muck about with our characters. You see, the people who wanted to learn, sat and learnt, and the people who didn't, didn't learn, but there was no time, you know, for bringing out the best in us, thank God. I had some magnificent teachers, actually, a Miss MacDonald, who taught me Latin irregular verbs.

INTERVIEWER: Did you have a classical training?

WEST: No, no. I had no Greek. They didn't teach any Greek for the reason that our school took on from a very early school, at which they had followed Madame de Maintenon's school at St. Cyr, where the children were taught Latin but not Greek. Why do you think I wasn't taught Greek?—Because Madame de Maintenon thought girls shouldn't learn Greek in case they fell into the toils of the heretical Eastern Orthodox Church, which is rather funny, considering we were all good girls at Edinburgh. Very curious bit of history, that.

INTERVIEWER: And this tradition reached as far as Scotland?

WEST: Well, you see, the man who was the begetter of our school had been to St. Cyr, and he just took the whole thing on.

INTERVIEWER: What did your mother expect you to be? What images did she set up for you?

WEST: There was a great idea that I should be an actress because a woman called Rosina Fillipi had seen me act in a play and she thought I was terribly good as a comedian, as a sort of low-comedy character, and she said, "If you come to the Royal Academy of Dramatic Art, I will look after you and you can get a job." I'm the only person I ever heard of who wanted to go on the stage not because I was stagestruck but it just seemed to be the thing to do. I loved the theatre. I still love it, but I had no stagestruck feeling. I felt how nice if people would give me a part. I went to the Royal Academy of Art, where there was a man called Kenneth Barnes, who ran it, who had got his job because he was the brother of the Vanbrughs, Irene and Violet Vanbrugh, if that means anything to you. He couldn't understand what Rosina Fillipi had seen in me and he made me very uncomfortable. I didn't stay out the course.

INTERVIEWER: But you chose the name of a dramatic character—Rebecca West.

WEST: Yes. Not really for any profound reason. It was just to get a pseudonym.

INTERVIEWER: It really wasn't profound? You don't think unconsciously it was?

WEST: People have always been putting me down in any role that was convenient but it would not, I think, naturally have been my own idea. I've aroused hostility in an extraordinary lot of people. I've never known why. I don't think I'm formidable.

INTERVIEWER: I think that your hallmark is that you have always disliked people who wanted approval. You like the heterodox.

WEST: I should like to be approved of. Oh, yes. I blench. I hate being disapproved of. I've had rather a lot of it.

INTERVIEWER: And yet, in your writing, there is quite a strong strain of impatience with people who do things because society approves of it.

WEST: Oh, yes. I think I see what you mean. Oh, that's Scotch, I think, yes, Scotch, because . . . oh, yes, and it's also a bit of my mother and my father. My father was educated by Elisée and Eli Reclus, two famous French brothers, early geographers; my cracked grandmother, the religious maniac who refused the family fortune, had hired them because they were refugees in England; she thought that, as young Frenchmen in England, they must be Protestants who had escaped from the wicked Catholics' persecution. They were actually anarchists and they'd escaped, run away from France because they'd seized the town hall—I can't remember which town it was—in the course of an émeute against Louis Napoleon. They were very sweet. They said, when they found out the mistake, "Oh, well, we must be careful about teaching the children." They taught them awfully well. My father was a very, very well educated man, and so were all his brothers.

INTERVIEWER: What did you read at home as a child? Who were the early formative influences?

WEST: Oh, pretty well everything. We read a terrific lot of Shakespeare, which my mother knew by heart and so did my father . . . and a lot of George Borrow. Funny thing to read, but . . . really early Victorian England was quite familiar to me because of that. Oh, lots . . . I can't think. My mother and my sister, Winifred, who was much the cleverest of us, she read frightfully good poetry. She taught me a lot of poetry, which I've all forgotten now, but you know, if I see the first line, I can go on.

INTERVIEWER: Would you acknowledge Conrad or anyone else as an influence on you?

WEST: Well, I longed, when I was young, to write as well as Mark Twain. It's beautiful stuff and I always liked him. If I wanted to write anything that attacked anybody, I used to have a look at his attack on Christian Science, which is beautifully written. He was a man of very great shrewdness. The earliest article on the Nazis, on Nazism, a sort of first foretaste, a prophetic view of the war, was an article by Mark Twain in *Harper's* in, I should think, the nineties. He went to listen to the Parliament in Vienna and he describes an awful row and what the point of view of Luger, the Lord Mayor, was, and the man called George Schwartz, I think, who started the first Nazi paper, and what it must all lead to. It's beautifully done. It's the very first notice that I've ever found of the Austrian Nazi Party, that started it all.

INTERVIEWER: What was your first conscious encounter with fascism?

WEST: A lot of boys, who stopped my sister and myself and took her hockey stick away from her. The thing was they weren't doing it as robbery but it was fun and good fellowship, and they were the boys together. That was the first. They were just street children. We had a brick wall and an alley behind it and we used to come up half the alley, if we were going into the house of some neighbors, and there these boys caught us in the alley and they took it away; but we fought them and screamed and shouted and got back the hockey stick.

INTERVIEWER: That was when?

WEST: That must have been—I was born in 1892—about 1903, or, no earlier than that, just in this century perhaps.

INTERVIEWER: Yes, so, before the First World War, you saw the seeds of fascism.

WEST: No, no. I just saw violence. There was the race thing and sacred Germanism and all that, but the enemy before the First World War you can't really compare with fascism. It was the imperialism of Germany and the supremacy of the army, but that isn't exactly fascism. I think you could say, there was more fascism, but of an intellectualized kind, in France. The crux of the Dreyfus case was that it didn't matter whether Dreyfus was guilty or not, you musn't spoil the image of the army. That was more or less fascist.

INTERVIEWER: But do you feel, with your strong sense of justice and of pity, that our wars have remained as terrible, or do you feel that we have learned?

WEST: I don't know what *you've* learnt. I'll tell you I think the Second World War was much more comfortable because in the First World War women's position was so terrible, because there you were, not in danger. Men were going out and getting killed for you and you'd much prefer they weren't. My father was always very tender about armies, having been a soldier. The awful feeling for a small professional army was that they were recruited from poor people who went out and got killed. That was, do you know, very disagreeable. There was a genuine humanitarian feeling of guilt about that in the first war. It was very curious, you see. There I sat on my balcony in Leigh-on-Sea and heard guns going in France. It was a most peculiar war. It was really better, in the Second World War, when the people at home got bombed. I found it a relief. You were taking your chance and you might be killed and you weren't in that pampered sort of unnatural state. I find the whole idea of a professional army very disgusting still. Lacking a normal life, they turn into scoundrels. As Wellington said, they're despised for being scoundrels and it's not their fault and they die like flies and have the worst discomforts.

INTERVIEWER: And yet a conscripted army, as fought in Vietnam . . . You laugh?

WEST: Well, I can't help thinking that the whole of the Vietnam War was the blackest comedy that ever was, because it showed the way you can't teach humanity anything. We'd all learnt in the rest of the world that you can't now go round and put out your hand and, across seas, exercise power; but the poor Americans had not learned that and they tried to do it. The remoteness of America from German attack had made them feel confident. They didn't really believe that anything could reach out and kill them. Americans are quite unconscious now that we look on them as just as much beaten as we are. They're quite unconscious of that. They always have talked of Vietnam as if by getting out they were surrendering the prospect of victory, as if they were being noble by renouncing the possibility of victory. But they couldn't have had a victory. They couldn't possibly have won.

INTERVIEWER: But when you say they're beaten as we are, in what way do you mean we are beaten?

WEST: Only as regards world power. We can't put our hands out and order things to happen a long way away. Oh, I think we're also beaten in other ways—in industry. I think the war between the public and the unions is very difficult and I don't see where its solution lies.

INTERVIEWER: Have you ever seen a society about which you really felt: Here is society that works for the benefit of its citizens without harming others?

WEST: No, I think the earth itself is slightly resistant to routine. You might come to a place which was favorable, because of a discovery of minerals that could be mined more easily, you know, "place mines," as they call the ones on the surface, and you'd think that was very nice and they would get on with it. Then round the corner you'd find there was a dispute about water rights. Humanity wasn't obviously a made-to-order thing. It's a continual struggle, isn't it?

INTERVIEWER: Have you ever been tempted at all to any religious belief?

WEST: Oh, yes. It all seems so damned silly and incomprehensible, there might as well be a silly and incomprehensible solution, don't you think? I'd be quite prepared for anything to happen, but not very respectfully, I think.

INTERVIEWER: I think you might stand up to God.

WEST: No, not exactly that, but I don't think there would be a God who would really demand it. If there is a God, I don't think He would demand that anybody bow down or stand up to Him. I have often a suspicion God is still trying to work things out and hasn't finished.

INTERVIEWER: Were your parents at all believing?

WEST: My mother was, in a sort of musical way, and I think my father accepted it as part of the structure, but didn't do anything. We always went to church and enjoyed it. I don't feel the slightest resistance to the church except when it's a bad landlord or something like that. I don't see why people feel any *écrasez l'infâme.* I know much infâm-er things than religion, much more worthy of being écraséd.

INTERVIEWER: What can you remember as being a moment of great happiness?

WEST: Extremely few. I had a very unhappy time with H. G. Wells, because I was a victim of a sort of sadist situation. Partly people disapproved of H. G. so much less than they did of me, and they were very horrible to me, and it was very hard. It was particularly hard later, people being horrid to me because I was living with H. G., when I was trying as hard as I could to leave him. It was really absurd, and now I think it's rather funny, but it wasn't funny at the time. Then I had a short time of happiness on my own and a time of happiness with my marriage [R. W. married Henry Andrews in 1930], but then my husband got ill, very ill. He had meningitis, this thing that's always struck at people near me, when he was young and then he got cerebral arteriosclerosis, and after years it came down on him. He was in a very unhappy state of illness for a good many years before he died, but we had a great many good years together. I was very happy.

INTERVIEWER: Have any of the men you've known helped you?

WEST: The men near you always hinder you because they

always want you to do the traditional female things and they take a lot of time. My mother helped me to work because she always talked to me as if I were grown-up.

INTERVIEWER: Do you feel men did not want to help you as a writer?

WEST: Oh, yes! So many men hate you. When my husband was dying I had some very strange dialogues. People were very rude just because they'd heard I was a woman writer. That kind of rudeness is as bad as ever.

INTERVIEWER: Would it have been easier to have been a man?

WEST: It certainly would have been.

INTERVIEWER: Are there any advantages at all in being a woman and a writer?

WEST: None whatsoever. You could have a good time as a woman, but you'd have a much better time as a man. If in the course of some process, people turn up a card with a man's name on it and then a card with a woman's, they feel much softer towards the man, even though he might be a convicted criminal. They'd treat the man's card with greater tenderness.

INTERVIEWER: You don't think there's been an improvement?

WEST: Not very much.

INTERVIEWER: Everyone is still very curious about your love affair with H. G. Wells.

WEST: Why, I can't see why. It was a very long time ago, and it wasn't interesting. Why would I have brought it to an end if it had been interesting? It wasn't.

INTERVIEWER: What did your husband, Henry Andrews, do?

WEST: He was unfortunately put into a bank. He should have been an art historian. He got out of the bank in the end because he was too ill. He did a bit in the war where he was in the Ministry of Economic Warfare and very good. He was a delightfully funny man. He said very funny things, and he was very scholarly and he was very generous and he was very kind. There were all sorts of pleasant things about him.

INTERVIEWER: You could talk to him.

WEST: We talked a very great deal, but it's extraordinary the really tragic and dreadful things there are in marriage which are funny. I've never known anybody to write about this. My husband would insist on going and driving a car, and he'd never been a good driver. Like all bad drivers, he thought he was the best driver in the world and he couldn't drive at all at the end and it was terrible. I'm one of the few women who has been driven on the left side of a bus queue, on the *near* side of the pavement. It was awful. Well, that really made my life poisoned for years. All the time I never thought I would live to the end of the year. I thought he would be sure to kill me here or there. And he meant no harm.

INTERVIEWER: You weren't able to tell him this?

WEST: I told him and he wouldn't believe me. Two doctors said to me it could be so bad for his ego values, if he was not allowed to drive a car. Doctors tend to be chumps. I have had two or three marvelous doctors. I have a marvelous doctor now, who's very nice, very funny and very clever, but some of my worst enemies have been doctors, I can assure you.

INTERVIEWER: You have actually been quite ill yourself, haven't you?

WEST: Well, I had an attack of TB when I was a schoolgirl. Everybody did in those days. It simply meant that you got a shot of TB in your youth and you didn't get it later on. It was rather dramatic. What was awful was that I got it at the same time as my great friend, Flora Duncan, who was at school with me and whom I liked enormously; she died of it years afterwards in the most dreary way. She went with her aunt to stay in a hotel from which she was coming to lunch with me—this was just after I was married—and she pulled down the window and the bit where her left lung had gone thin started to hemorrhage; and she was dead in a few hours. They couldn't stop the hemorrhage. It has sometimes inconvenienced me, but as I've lived to be eighty-eight, I can't say I've really suffered very much from it. At the time it gave me a lot of time to read.

INTERVIEWER: When you look back on all the books that you've written, is there one that you like best?

WEST: Oh, no. They don't seem to me as good as they might be. But I really write to find out what I know about something and what is to be known about something. And I'm more or less experimental. I wish I could have written very much more but, to be absolutely frank, for twenty-five years, you see, I've had this disastrous personal trouble. You don't easily get over it if someone near to you is constantly attacking you in public. Do you know Anthony [West]?

INTERVIEWER: I've met him once. He's writing about Joan of Arc, he told me.

WEST: What on earth about Joan of Arc?

INTERVIEWER: He believes that she was a princess, a bastard princess.

WEST: Why? What an extraordinary idea.

INTERVIEWER: A lot of people do.

WEST: What! This is new to me. Who might she be?

INTERVIEWER: She's meant to be the result of an incestuous adulterous match, the Queen and the Queen's brother-in-law, Louis d'Orléans.

WEST: I wish he'd turn his mind to other problems than bastardy. Alas. He's writing about six books, he told me. But I wonder why this. Whose theory is this? I never heard of it.

INTERVIEWER: Oh, it's a very old one. It was produced in 1810 by Pierre Caze in a play. Instead of accepting that Joan of Arc was exciting for spiritual reasons, you say she was exciting because she was a royal princess—which is a practical solution.

WEST: Nonsense. Have you seen Princess Anne? Can you imagine, if she appeared and said, "Save England," or whatever, that it would work? What a wonderful idea.

INTERVIEWER: What are you working on now?

WEST: I've been looking at old photographs . . . Rangoon in the last century. Goodness, some are absolutely beautiful. It's funny how photographs were better in the past than they are now.

INTERVIEWER: Why are you looking at Rangoon?

WEST: In what I'm writing now, I'm describing my husband's mother's life. She went out to Rangoon and lived there in vast, great big rooms each the size of a gymnasium, and full of cluttered little tables.

INTERVIEWER: She was the wife of an official, was she?

WEST: No, she was the wife of a man who had a job in Wallace Export-Import. They exported Burmese teak and they imported machinery. I've got masses of photographs I have to give to the Institute of Machinery but I never get round to it, showing the machines, as they came in. They had the largest army of elephants ever. There are beautiful photographs in this book of things like a lot of elephants crossing a wide river in a sort of floating island. She was a lady of very mixed ancestry, my husband's mother, and after Rangoon, she came back to Hamburg. Her mother was a Miss Chapman, who was related to the Chapman family that T. E. Lawrence belonged to. They lived in Lancashire, and then she married a local alien, a member of the hereditary Teutonic knights of Lithuania. She had various children in Lithuania, and then her daughter came to live in Hamburg and married Lewis Andrews, who was working in this firm in Rangoon, and ultimately became my mother-in-law.

INTERVIEWER: What are you writing about her?

WEST: It comes into my memoirs. Poor widow. She took her son [Henry Andrews] out with her to Hamburg and kept him too long. It was 1914 and the war came. Eventually she was sent back to England, but he was sent into a camp. He was there all through the war, in Rubleden [the civilian POW camp at Spandau]. It was very sad. It did spoil his life, really.

He was nineteen. It was very tough. But these young creatures were highly educated; he wrote quite clever letters to Romain Rolland.

INTERVIEWER: How far have you got with your memoirs?

WEST: I've nearly got my father and mother to the end of their respective careers. It's been supernatural, which is always encouraging. Do you know, my mother was always saying that the scenery in Australia was so extraordinarily beautiful, and my father did some very nice pictures of Australian landscapes. Suddenly, a man started sending me picture books of Australia. He said, "I've always liked your books, and I wanted to send these to you." So extraordinarily dead-on: pictures of what Australia was like when my parents were there in the last century.

INTERVIEWER: Are you taking only a section of your life in your memoirs?

WEST: Well, I hope to cover most of it, but still, I've only just begun it really and I must really get on with it. I haven't read anybody's memoirs for ages except Coulton's [medieval historian, author of *Five Centuries of Religion*], which I liked very much. He wrote a life called *Four Score*. Hated Catholics. When did you read him?

INTERVIEWER: I read him on the Virgin Mary.

WEST: You know, I don't really appreciate the Virgin Mary. She always looks so dull. I particularly hate Raphael, Raphael's Madonnas. They are awful, aren't they?

INTERVIEWER: Are you working on anything else?

WEST: I'm doing a book for Weidenfeld on the 1900s, but it's not a long book. I'm not approaching the 1900s chronologically. I've started by doing a lot with the paintings of Sargent, and with some beautiful photographs. But that period in America has been done and done and done, and it's hard to be fresh. They've really dealt with nostalgia too fiercely. I begin with the death of Gladstone in 1898, and more I cannot tell you.

INTERVIEWER: You have lots of paintings. Have you written about them?

WEST: To a certain extent, yes. My husband bought the ones over there, but these I bought. It was lovely that I could buy them when they were cheap. They didn't cost me very much, even the Bonnard, and I think that's the best picture that Dufy ever painted. I have a passion, too, for Carol Weight, the man who painted this one, because I think he paints the contours of the land so beautifully. And that's by Vuillard, the woman over there, Madame Marchand. She committed suicide in the war, alas. She was a Polish Jewess, a friend of Colette's and a lot of other people.

INTERVIEWER: You have a high opinion of Colette, don't you?

WEST: Yes. I didn't like her very much as a person and I think she was repetitive and I hate all her knowing nudges about men, but I think she was a good writer on the whole and she was very good on landscape. She did a wonderful book called *Trio*. She was really more egotistical than you could possibly imagine, and she was outside a lot of experiences in a most curious way. I was taken to see her in Paris with a man who was a judge at Nuremburg. She didn't pick it up at all.

INTERVIEWER: You were in Paris again recently, I believe?

WEST: To film *The Birds Fall Down*, yes, for the B.B.C. It was quite fun. It was uncomfortable in many ways and I was so horrified by the cheap food in Paris. It was so bad. Terribly bad. The film turned out to be visually very beautiful. Sometimes it seemed to me a little slow. Some of the dresses are lovely.

INTERVIEWER: Have you had other books adapted?

WEST: No, people always buy them and then find they can't do them, so that I've gained financially but otherwise hardly ever. A man called Van Druten, who's forgotten now, did *The Return of the Soldier* as a play and it wasn't really good, though some of his plays were. I can't remember who acted it, or indeed anything about it.

INTERVIEWER: You've never written for the stage yourself?

WEST: I've had so little time to write. Also, theatrical people can't be bothered with me. I wrote a play in the twenties which I think had lovely stuff in it, *Goodbye Nicholas*, and fourteen copies were lost by managers, fourteen, that's really true, and I just gave up. One of them, who lost three, was a man called Barry Jackson, who was at the Birmingham Repertory Theatre; after we'd had a terrific apologies and that kind of thing, about a year later he met me in the bar of some theatre and said, Rebecca, why have you never written a play? They are like that.

INTERVIEWER: What was the play about?

WEST: Oh, it was about Kruger, the financier, who committed suicide. It just showed you how they did the fraud and what they thought about it. It was sound enough, but nobody was interested in it at all. Then I lent it to an old friend of mine. I'm sorry to say he used a lot of it, without acknowledgement, in a play of his, an American man.

INTERVIEWER: Who was that?

WEST: I won't tell you, but it was very naughty. But never mind. His play died a death too. I would like to write old-fashioned plays like de Musset's. I think they're lovely. I think de Musset's essay on Rachel and Malibran is one of the loveliest things in the world. It's lovely about acting and romanticism. It's beautifully written and it's quite wonderful.

INTERVIEWER: Rachel is quite important to you, because you wrote a beautiful thing in your lecture on McLuhan about her.

WEST: Oh, not *my* beauty, not *my* beauty, it's Valéry's, who wrote the beautiful thing and who loved Rachel. Isn't it a beautiful thing? The ear of the lover took down what his beloved Rachel was saying and commemorated the secret of it. It's really wonderful. It's about as nice a form of immortality as anyone could have, isn't it? I fell on the essay, when I was quite young, and then I read it again because Malibran [Maria-Felicia García, d. 1836] was the sister of Madame Viardot [Pauline García, d. 1910] who is, you know, the lady who is supposed to have been the mistress—but I think the duties were light—of Turgenev. Turgenev lived in the house of Madame Viardot nearly all his life, and she brought up his illegitimate daughter. She was an opera singer but she had a dreadful time getting jobs at the opera because she and her husband were anti-Bonapartist and the Bonapartists had command of the opera. She was a great girl, and it's a very terrible thing: all her life she wrote compositions but nobody has ever played them. She was terribly busy. There's a description of her as "*too* busy" in the letters of Brahms and Clara Schumann. The Garcías were people who had two odd genetic streaks: one was for longevity, the other was for music. The first García bumped his family all over the Americas and all over Europe as a musical troupe. There were several in the family; the brother taught at the Royal Academy of Music in London, where my uncle was principal, and he used to give children's parties. I remember going to a children's party and being kissed by the old gentleman who was the brother of Malibran. He lived to be a hundred and one. I think his descendants transplanted themselves to somewhere in the north of England. The life of the family has all sorts of odd things embedded in it. You know how in du Maurier's books, how in *Trilby*, she vocalised to the music of Chopin's Nocturnes and people say that's so absurd. But Viardot did it and it apparently came off and Chopin himself liked it.

INTERVIEWER: Did you used to go to concerts a lot?

WEST: Yes, I used to and I used to listen on the radio. I can't do even the radio any longer. It doesn't seem to *respond*, as the Americans say.

INTERVIEWER: You said once that all your intelligence is in your hands.

WEST: Yes, a lot, I think. Isn't yours? My memory is certainly in my hands. I can remember things only if I have a pencil and I can write with it and I can play with it.

INTERVIEWER: You use a pencil, do you, when you write?

WEST: When anything important has to be written, yes. I

think your hand concentrates for you. I don't know why it should be so.

INTERVIEWER: You never typed?

WEST: I did, but not now. I can't see in front and behind a typewriter now with cataract-operated eyes. If you have the spectacles for the front thing, you can't see the back, and I can't do with bifocals. I just get like a distracted hen. I can't do it. Hens must wear bifocals, if one looks closely. It explains it all. It's so difficult dealing with ribbons too. I can only write by hand now. I used to do a rough draft longhand and then another on the typewriter. I'm a very quick typist. When I had mumps I was shut up in a bedroom, because both my sisters had to sit examinations. When I came out, I could type.

INTERVIEWER: Do you do many drafts?

WEST: I fiddle away a lot at them. Particularly if it's a fairly elaborate thing. I've never been able to do just one draft. That seems a wonderful thing. Do you know anyone who can?

INTERVIEWER: I think D. H. Lawrence did.

WEST: You could often tell.

INTERVIEWER: How many hours a day do you write?

WEST: I don't manage much. When I write uninterrupted, I *can* write all day, straight through.

INTERVIEWER: Did you find any of your books especially easy to write?

WEST: No. It's a nauseous process. They're none of them easy.

INTERVIEWER: Have you ever abandoned a book before it was finished?

WEST: I've abandoned work because I've not had time. I've had a worrisome family thinking up monkey tricks to prevent me finishing books, and I had a terrible time when I was young and in the country, because I had no money, and no reference books, and I couldn't get up to London and to the London Library, where I had a subscription.

INTERVIEWER: There is a great diversity in your work. Did

you find it difficult to combine criticism and journalism and history and fiction?

WEST: I did, really. My life has been dictated to and broken up by forces beyond my control. I couldn't control the two wars! The second war had a lot of personal consequences for me, both before and after. But I had enough money at that time, because I had a large herd of cows and a milk contract. I had to take some part in looking after the cows, but the dear things worked for me industriously. At one time I had to write articles because I had to put up a lot of money for family reasons. Everyone has to pay for their families every now and then.

INTERVIEWER: Who are the writers you admire? You commented recently that Tolstoy was most overrated.

WEST: I'm a heretic about Tolstoy. I really don't see *War and Peace* as a great novel because it seems constantly to be trying to prove that nobody who was in the war knew what was going on. Well, I don't know whoever thought they would . . . that if you put somebody down in the wildest sort of mess they understand what's happening. The point's very much better done, I think, by Joseph de Maistre. He wrote a very interesting essay in the late eighteenth century, saying how more and more people would not be able to know what was happening to them in wartime because it was all too complicated. He was in a very complicated state himself because he came from Aspramonte, which is a village on a hill near Nice. The people of Aspramonte were of the original Mediterranean population. They wore long hair all through the centuries, the conservative hippies. He was descended from a family who went round getting mulberry leaves for the silk worms. He got into the service of the King of Sardinia. He was sent as an ambassador to St. Petersburg. He wrote *Les Soirées de St.-Pétersbourg,* which is marvelous descriptive writing. He did a very good thing about hanging. He was for it, but his essay demonstrates the painfulness of ever considering whether you do hang people or not. I don't know how he became a diplomat for the King of Sardinia. I'm very often curious about people in history; they turn up in the oddest places. They strayed like goats in a road, but from class to class.

INTERVIEWER: Do you admire E. M. Forster?

WEST: No. I think the Indian one [*A Passage to India*] is very funny because it's all about people making a fuss about nothing, which isn't really enough. I can never understand how people read Proust at the same time. But they did. You can read Proust all the time. There is a book of that period that I do like very much, and that is *They Went* by Norman Douglas. It's about the king of a legendary country. I've read it several times and I've always found it beautiful.

INTERVIEWER: Are you interested in T. S. Eliot's writing?

WEST: Goodness! T. S. Eliot, whom I didn't like a bit? He was a poseur. He was married to this woman who was very pretty. My husband and I were asked to see them, and my husband roamed around the flat and there were endless photographs of T. S. Eliot and bits of his poetry done in embroidery by pious American ladies, and only one picture of his wife, and that was when she was getting married. Henry pointed it out to me and said, "I don't think I like that man."

INTERVIEWER: What about the work of Somerset Maugham, whom you also knew?

WEST: He couldn't write for toffee, bless his heart. He wrote conventional short stories, much inferior to the work of other people. But they were much better than his plays, which were too frightful. He was an extremely interesting man, though, not a bit clever or cold or cynical. I know of many affectionate things he did. He had a great capacity for falling in love with the wrong people. His taste seemed to give way under him so extraordinarily sometimes. He fascinated me by his appearance; he was so neatly made, like a swordstick that fits just so. Occasionally his conversation was beautifully funny and quite unmalicious. I object strongly to pictures of Maugham as if he were a second-rate Hollywood producer in the lavish age. His house was very pleasant and quiet and agreeable.

INTERVIEWER: Some critics think that sex is still written about with great awkwardness. Why is this?

WEST: I would have thought that was completely true of Kafka, who couldn't write about sex or value its place in life. I think there's an awful lot of nonsense in Lawrence when he writes about Mexican sacrifices and sexual violence. Their only relevance was to the Mexicans' lack of protein, as in the South Sea Islands. Funny, that's a wonderful thing. I don't know why more people don't write about it: how the whole of life must have been different when four-footed animals came in. They had just a few deer before, but not enough to go round, and so they prevented the deer from becoming extinct by making them sacred to the kings. It's much more interesting to write about that than about sex, which most of your audience knows about.

INTERVIEWER: Have you ever worked closely with a publisher who has suggested ideas to you?

WEST: No. I write books to find out about things. I wrote *Saint Augustine* because, believe it or not, there was no complete life in English at the time.

INTERVIEWER: Have you never had a close relationship with an editor, who has helped you after the books were written?

WEST: No. I never met anybody with whom I could have discussed books before or after. One doesn't have people on one's wavelength as completely as that. And I very rarely found the *New Yorker* editors any good.

INTERVIEWER: They have a tremendous reputation.

WEST: I don't know why.

INTERVIEWER: When you read, do you just follow your imagination completely?

WEST: Well, I've had eighty-five years to read in.

INTERVIEWER: I wondered whether you made book lists?

WEST: Yes, I do, but I'm often disappointed. I do think

modern novels are boring on the whole. Somebody told me I ought to read a wonderful thing about how a family of children buried Mum in a cellar under concrete and she began to smell. But that's the sole point of the story. Mum just smells. That's all that happens. It is not enough.

INTERVIEWER: This is a new Ian McEwan, isn't it? I thought you, in your book on Augustine, made a marvelous comment which applies to him and to some of the other fashionable novelists now. You say that Augustinianism is "the ring-fence, in which the modern mind is still prisoner." I think that Ian McEwan is very Augustinian in his sense of unmovable evil in human life.

WEST: Yes, but he doesn't really do very much with it, does he? This thing just presents you with the hairs along people's groins and the smell, and very little else.

INTERVIEWER: Do you feel this relates to your feeling about the will to die in people, that this kind of very black outlook on the human body and human emotions is part of the suicidal streak that you've written about in both individuals and in society?

WEST: Oh, I suppose it is. It's very farfetched, isn't it? One rarely recognises the smell of Mum under the concrete, does one? I don't know. I cannot see the abysmal silliness of a lot of novels. Did you read a book called *The Honey Tree*? By Janice Elliott. If you didn't read it, it's no use talking about it. It's all about people who take a house and fornicate all over it, and they all have children, and their swollen bodies are a great source of satisfaction to Mrs. Elliott, and paternity does all sorts of thing to men which I doubt, don't you?

INTERVIEWER: Perhaps. I believe you admire A. L. Barker.

WEST: Enormously, but I'm the only person who does, so far as I can make out. I think she's the best novelist now writing, not always, but I think *The Middling* is a magnificent novel. And *A Source of Embarrassment*, about the woman who knew she was going to die. This last book, *The Heavy Feather*, is so good I can't believe it, and nobody likes it. And they are wrong. I am exaggerating, of course. Lots of people do admire her, but not enough.

INTERVIEWER: What are the particular qualities that you think she has that others at the moment haven't?

WEST: She really tells you what people do, the extraordinary things that people think, how extraordinary circumstances are, and how unexpected the effect of various incidents. There's a terribly good thing in *The Heavy Feather*, where a woman goes home and there's a railway accident. The train is just jarred and the poor woman is sitting with a suitcase over her head. The suitcase falls on top of the woman sitting opposite her and kills her. This woman has been saying how happy she is and how all her children love her and how ideal her life is. Then the other, when she gets home, finds she's taken the woman's suitcase instead of her own, and it's got the address and she goes to take back the suitcase and try and get her own from the husband, who turns out to be Hindustani. The woman was white, and he's living there with a Hindustani girl and they're both terrified because they have been waiting for this white woman, who had no children and wasn't adored and was utterly miserable. The people come off the page to tell you what this would be like. You feel: Now I understand this better. And she also has in the book very good heterosexuals and very good homosexuals . . . with the different quality quite marked.

INTERVIEWER: Yes. Would you place her as high as the women writers that you have said overcome the problem of being female in their writing? I am thinking of Madame de Sévigné, Madame de La Fayette, Jane Austen, Willa Cather, Virginia Woolf, Colette.

WEST: Oh, she's almost better than anybody, I think. She's much better than Iris Murdoch, I think. But then Iris Murdoch I like enormously except when she begins to clown and be funny, because I don't think she ever is very funny. She writes curious books on goodness. Have you read her philosophic works? I can't make head or tail of them. They're better written than anything else she writes. They are so strange. She says that one has to study what goodness is by looking at good people. She says that the trouble with good people is that, if they're men, usually very little is known about them because they're so obscure, and, as for women, goodness is rarely found in women except in the inarticulate mothers of large families, which is just such an idiotic remark, you can't believe it. Is she pulling one's leg? One hopes so. But even so, why?

INTERVIEWER: Do you have a high opinion of Ivy Compton-Burnett?

WEST: She had her own stereotype, and wrote too many books exactly like each other in form. But it was a damn good form. At the time of a rising in South Africa, when it seemed that the colored races were going to burst forth and one was afraid that the white suburbs were being set on fire, I managed to get in happy nights reading the novels of Ivy Compton-Burnett. But it was very funny that people believed in her story of herself. She was a nanny, and you had only to meet her to see it; all her stories are nanny stories, about how awful the family is. She was very, very clever. You'd have to be very tasteless not to see she had something unique to give her age. . . .

INTERVIEWER: How do you feel about Doris Lessing?

WEST: I wish I knew her. I think she's a marvelous writer. There's a peculiar book about European refugees in Africa, but it fascinates. It's beautifully done, the play side of philosophy. They were talking about all their ideas and it was as if the children were trying to go into a shop and buy things not with coins but with butterscotch or toffee apples. It's very curious. Yes, she's the only person who absolutely gets the mood of today right, I think. An absolutely wonderful writer. She wrote a picaresque novel, *The Children of Violence*, I thought was very fine. Who got the Booker Prize? Does anybody know? [Iris Murdoch won it for *The Sea, The Sea*, after this meeting.]

INTERVIEWER: Do you follow prizes?

WEST: Not very much. I was on the Booker Prize Committee twice. It almost drove me mad. I think they give people prizes too late. This is a sad thought. They've been heard of as failures and they have become conditioned to failure, so it is rather wide of the point. It's nice for them, though.

INTERVIEWER: Do you feel that public taste has declined as expressed in things like prizes?

WEST: People in England read books. I have read Mr. Mc-Ewan, and I read new books all the time, whether I review them or not, but you see, most people in America are reading the same books over and over again. They read Scott Fitzgerald and Hemingway and James Joyce and Nabokov, and they haven't moved on anywhere for years.

INTERVIEWER: John Gross says in his book on the English man of letters that we are now as far from Joyce as Joyce was from George Eliot, but in terms of the progress of literature, we haven't moved at all.

WEST: Yes. It's curious. People have no desire to read anything new. It is bad that English is taught in universities. It's bad over here, where it's sometimes not badly taught, but over there, where it's horribly badly taught, it simply stops the thing in its traces.

INTERVIEWER: Because people always look back on the past?

WEST: They don't even look onto the past. They look onto the certified past. There really were beautiful writers in America like G. W. Cable, who wrote about the South in the middle of last century. It's very rich, rather Balzacian sort of stuff about the South, New Orleans and so on. But nobody reads him now.

INTERVIEWER: Why do you think English is so badly taught in America?

WEST: It's an absurd error to put modern English literature in the curriculum. You should read contemporary literature for pleasure or not read it at all. You shouldn't be taught to monkey with it. It's ghastly to think of all the little girls who are taught to read *To the Lighthouse*. It's not really substantial food for the young because there's such a strong feeling that Virginia Woolf was doing a set piece and it didn't really matter very much. She was putting on an act. Shakespeare didn't put on an act. But *Orlando* is a lovely original splash, a beautiful piece of fancy. Leonard Woolf had a tiresome mind. When you read his books about Malaya, and then the books of the cadets who went out there, he's so petty, and they have such an enthusiasm and such tolerance for the murderous habits of the natives. But he was certainly good to Virginia. I couldn't forgive Vanessa Bell for her awful muddy decorations and those awful pictures of Charlotte Brontë. And I hated Duncan Grant's pictures too. The best thing that was ever said about Bloomsbury was said by a lovely butler of mine. At dinner one evening, they began to talk of Faulkner's book in which someone uses a corncob for the purposes of rape. They were being terribly subtle, and doing this and that gesture over the table. The butler came in to my son Anthony's room and asked, "Do you know where they keep the Faulkners? It seems they're very saucy." . . . Virginia Woolf's criticism was much better than criticism others were writing then.

INTERVIEWER: Amongst critics, do you admire Cyril Connolly? Or Malcolm Muggeridge?

WEST: Connolly? What an extraordinary thing to ask! He was a very good editor of *Horizon,* but he wasn't an interesting person. As for writing, he was fond of it, as you might say. But he didn't know much about it, did he? I've got no opinion of Muggeridge. He's very nice and friendly. What ever have I read of his in the past? I can never think Christ is grateful for being alluded to as if He were a lost cause.

INTERVIEWER: Did you want to write about trials?

WEST: Not at all. I had done it once or twice, when I was very hard up, when I was young, just to get some money, and so I learnt how to do them, and then I used to sit and listen to William Joyce [Lord Haw-Haw, hanged 1945] when he was broadcasting. Then I arranged to go to his trial because I was interested in him. A man called Theo Matthew, who was director of public prosecutions, though not a prosecuting sort of person, said, "I wish you'd report a lot of these trials because otherwise they will go unnoticed because there is so little newsprint." He said, "Really, if you will consider it as war work, it would be extremely valuable." So I did that for one book [*The New Meaning of Treason*, 1947] and then I did it for another [*A Train of Powder*, 1955]. Most of the people in Intelligence didn't agree with my views. I don't know whether it had any effect on them at all. Someone asked me recently how did I think Intelligence had found out John Vassal? [British spy, jailed in 1963]. It seemed to me such a silly question. He had it tattooed on his forehead. I never know how people don't find out spies.

INTERVIEWER: Are you interested in espionage still?

WEST: I won't say I'm interested in spies, but they do turn up in my life in quite funny ways. There was a man called Sidney Reilly, who was a famous spy, a double agent. My mother-in-law was very upset because my husband married me instead of the daughter of a civil servant. My husband's mother thought she was a nice Catholic girl, who'd be so nice for my husband, and it always tickled me because it gradually emerged that this girl was the mistress of this *very* famous and very disreputable spy. It was a wonderful thing to have in your pocket against your mother-in-law. My mother-in-law was an enormous, huge woman, and extremely pathetic. She had had her life broken up so often. By the First World War, and then the Second. Between the wars she was perfectly happy going to tea at those old-fashioned tea places they had—Rumpelmayer's. But her other son was very ill and he went out to Australia and he had a weak lung, and she went to see him and she got caught by the war there. If you like Rumpelmayer's, you wouldn't want to be in Australia for six years.

INTERVIEWER: Do you enjoy reviewing for the *Sunday Telegraph?*

WEST: Yes, I do. I do. I would feel awfully cut off if I didn't review; I think it's such a good discipline. It makes you really open your mind to the book. Probably you wouldn't, if you just read it.

INTERVIEWER: Oh, yes. It concentrates one, yes. I thought your review of Christopher Isherwood's *Christopher and His Kind* was dazzling. You demolished him.

WEST: I was so horrified by the way he treated the little German pansy. Also I thought it must have been so disgusting for the people in the village on the Greek island. I know Greeks love money, but I think a lot of money would have to pass before you'd be reconciled to Isherwood making such a noise.

INTERVIEWER: When I read your review, I was completely convinced by your argument, that it was an extraordinary sort of obliviousness that comes from class privilege.

WEST: Well, I didn't want to make a butt of him. Do you know, a bookseller's assistant said to him, "What do you think of Rebecca West's review of your book?" and he is alleged to have said such a lovely thing: "I shall think of some way of turning it to my advantage." You can't think how bad reviewing was when I first started to review, so dull and so dreadful. Nobody good but Lady Robert Cecil, one of the Salisbury family.

INTERVIEWER: But your reviews were absolutely sparkling. I love the essay you wrote about *The Uncles.*

WEST: Oh, Bennett was horrible about it. He was a horrible mean-spirited hateful man. I hated Arnold Bennett.

INTERVIEWER: But you were very nice about him.

WEST: Well, I thought so, and I think he was sometimes a very good writer. I do think *The Old Wives' Tale* is very good, don't you? He was a horrible man.

INTERVIEWER: Was he in a position to make things difficult for you then?

WEST: Yes. He was not nice. He lived with these two women, the French woman to whom he was married and also the woman who was with him when he died. He was always telling other people how tiresome these women were. It was all very, as people say, unchivalrous.

INTERVIEWER: English writing hasn't really produced the kind of giants it produced in the twenties. The stagnation of English writing since then is extraordinary. Joyce, Virginia Woolf, Wells, Shaw: all these people were writing, and who have we got to compare now?

WEST: I find Tom Stoppard just as amusing as I ever found Shaw. Very amusing, both as a playwright and as himself. But I'm not now an admirer of Shaw. It was a poor mind, I think. I liked his wife so much better. He *was* conceited, but in an odd way. Usually, you know, it's people shouting to keep their spirits up, but he really did think he was better than most people. I thought that book on Yeats's postbag was so good, letters that people wrote to Yeats. Did you read that? It's absolutely delightful. It's got delightful things like a very nicely phrased letter from a farmer, saying that he understands Yeats writes about supernatural matters and can he recommend a reliable witch? You know, charming things like that.

INTERVIEWER: Did you meet Yeats?

WEST: Yes. He wasn't a bit impressive and he wasn't my sort of person at all. He boomed at you like a foghorn. He was there one time when Philip Guedalla and two or three of us were all very young, and were talking nonsense about murderers in Shakespeare and whether a third murderer ever became a first murderer by working hard or were they, sort of, hereditary slots? Were they like Japanese specialists and one did one kind of murder, another did another? It was really awfully funny. Philip was very funny to be with. Then we started talking about something on the Western Isles but Yeats wouldn't join in, until we fussed round and were nice to him. But we were all wrong; what he liked was solemnity and, if you were big enough, heavy enough, and strong enough, he loved you. He loved great big women. He would have been mad about Vanessa Redgrave.

INTERVIEWER: Is your Irish birth important to you?

WEST: Frightfully, yes. I loved my family. I have a great affiliation to relations of mine called Denny. The present man is an architect, Sir Anthony Denny. He's exactly like Holbein's drawing of his ancestor, Anthony Denny, which I think is a great testimonial. Anthony Denny lives up in the Cotswolds and he and his wife are most glamorous people in a very quiet way. They have two charming sons, one of them paints very well, and they adopted a child, a Vietnamese child. Tony went out to see his brother, who had fever there, and he was walking along a quay and one of the refugee babies, who was sitting about, suddenly ran up to him and clasped him round the knees and looked up in his face. So he just said, "I'll have this one" —and took him home. It was a most lovely reason. The Dennys did nice things like that. And then my father used to speak about this cousin in Ireland, in the west of Ireland, called Dickie Shoot. Dickie Shoot beggared himself by helping people.

INTERVIEWER: I always think it's astonishing how much literature Protestant Ireland has produced.

WEST: I don't thing they're very poetical people or sensitive people really, but what a lot of literature they've produced compared with the Scotch, who I think have really deeper emotions. It's most peculiar.

INTERVIEWER: Shaw. Wilde. Whatever one thinks of their quality, there they are. Samuel Beckett. All from Protestant Irish stock.

WEST: You know, an Irish priest said a most beautiful thing to me the other day, and I absolutely loved it. He looked at those books and said—a very old man he is, he's older than I am, he must be over ninety—and he said to me, "What are you doing with all your books, when you're dead? You must have planned for them." I said, "I'm giving those Oxford

dictionaries to the grandson of Oscar Wilde, Merlin Holland."
And he said, "Oh, how beautiful that makes it all. It's rather
as if it hadn't happened." I said, "What do you mean?" He
said, "Well, your family lives in Fitzwilliam Square and
Wilde's people lived in Merrion Square and it's such a natural
thing to do for a family in Fitzwilliam Square to give their
Oxford dictionary to the son of a family living in Merrion
Square." Almost as if it hadn't happened. He couldn't have
added a word to it. I love Merlin. I went to see him out in
Beirut with his mother, which was rather a trial. She's Australian in a big way but you know, it was so extraordinary, the
glimpse I had of her. He was very fond of a ballet dancer, and
we went out to lunch. We went up to her house, and after
dinner Mrs. Holland, who is plump and sixty-something, got
up and she turned on one of the records, *Swan Lake*, and
danced to it, as she'd learnt to, and she was quite beautiful.
Obviously she should have been a dancer.

INTERVIEWER: Do you think it has become easier for women
to follow their vocations?

WEST: I don't know. It's very hard. I've always found I've had
too many family duties to enable me to write enough. I would
have written much better and I would have written much
more. Oh, men, whatever they may say, don't really have any
barrier between them and their craft, and certainly I had.

INTERVIEWER: What inspired you later to write your great
book on Yugoslavia? Was it the contact with the people?

WEST: What I was interested in really was wandering about
with Henry. I wanted to write a book on Finland, which is a
wonderful case of a small nation with empires here and there,
so I learnt Finnish and I read a Finnish novel. It was all about
people riding bicycles. But then, when I went to Yugoslavia,
I saw it was much more exciting with Austria and Russia and
Turkey, and so I wrote that. I really did enjoy it terribly, loved
it. I loved writing about St. Augustine, too. I like writing about
heretics, anyway.

INTERVIEWER: You consider Augustine a heretic, do you?

WEST: Oh, no, he wasn't a heretic. Most of his life he wasn't at all a nice man, but that's quite a different thing. I like to think about people like the Donatists, who were really suffering agonies of one kind and another because the Roman Empire was splitting up and it was especially uncomfortable to be in Roman Africa. But they didn't know anything about economics, and did know about theology. Theology had taught them that if you suffered, it was usually because you'd offended God: so they invented an offense against God, which was that unworthy priests were celebrating the Sacraments. So that satisfied them and then they went round the country, looting and getting the food and the property they wanted because they said that they were punishing heretics. I think it's wonderful that in the past people overlooked things that now seem to us quite obvious, and thought they were doing things for the reasons they weren't, and tried to remedy them by actions. Perhaps there's some quite simple thing we'll think of some day, which will make us much happier.

MARINA WARNER
Summer 1981

2. Stephen Spender

Stephen Spender was born in London in February, 1909. Raised in an otherwise austere, post-Victorian family, he was encouraged to cultivate an interest in poetry from an early age by his maternal grandmother. At nineteen Spender entered Oxford University, where he met W. H. Auden, who served as his literary model and advisor. During his second year at Oxford, Spender joined "The Group," which included Auden, Louis MacNeice, C. Day Lewis, and Christopher Isherwood.

During the thirties Spender frequented the literary societies of London, and in particular the Bloomsbury circle of Leonard and Virginia Woolf. Like them, he situated himself politically to the left; in 1936 he joined the Communist Party and began reporting for *The New Statesman* and other leftist journals on the developing Spanish Civil War. He remained a member for only a short time and described his gradual disillusionment with the party in an essay published in *The God That Failed*.

His poetry, available in *The Collected Poems: 1928–53, Selected Poems,* and *The Generous Days,* has won him his reputation, but he has also written a novel, *The Backward Son,* plays, and many volumes of criticism, among them *The Destructive Element, The Struggle of the Modern, T. S. Eliot,* and *New Realism: A Discussion.* An authentic man of letters in the modern world, his autobiography, *World Within World,* is among the finest examples of the genre, a masterpiece of frankness and decorum.

Spender was the co-editor of *Horizon* magazine with Cyril Connolly (1939–41) and of *Encounter* magazine (1953–67). An accomplished artist, he is fond of painting. He has been married twice—to Inez Pearn in 1936, and to Natasha Litvin, a pianist, in 1941—and is the father of two children.

lay in   lay within
                                              a Grade
The gramophone which crackles a worn

                                              loooop
    Like all the rest   clod earth
    When my burial came I dropped the clod
    Picked from a heap a earth onto the great
    Brass- handled, oak old fashioned
                                    besides the grave onto
                         tall down coffin at
    And heard it thud upon the bed
    The horizontal door within — with a loud
                                              the knock

    Which you
    Against that horizontal door
    Behind which you had made you
                              roomhome
    Beyond which was your home within that city
    I those who who walked with us
    where those who stood vertical upon the rim
    Lie down suddenly under the ground

        Hearing it knock against the wood, I saw
        Suddenly your body under
                                   utter
        The It's covering in the dark, as I thought

Self-portrait

Stephen Spender

The strength of Mr. Spender's literary reputation, which is international in scope, has made him something of a nomad as scholar and poet. His homes are in St. John's Wood, London, and Maussane-Les-Alpieles, France, where he spends his summers; but he is often on the road, giving readings and lectures and serving as writer-in-residence at various American universities. This interview took place in May, 1978, at the end of Mr. Spender's stint as visiting professor of English at the University of Houston.

Mr. Spender's domicile in Houston was a penthouse apartment atop a high-rise dormitory on the university campus. The walls of the apartment are glass and afforded the poet a 270° view of America's self-proclaimed twenty-first-century city. His fellow residents in the dorm were mostly athletes, a fact which especially delighted Mr. Spender at breakfast, for with them he was served steaks, sausage, ham, eggs, biscuits, and grits.

At the time of the interview, Mr. Spender was busy with several projects; besides preparing for his imminent departure and saying goodbye to his many friends, he was completing the text for Henry Moore: Sculptures and Landscape, *which was published in 1979. He had also been invited by the university to deliver its commencement address, an event that took place on the afternoon of May 13, just hours after our last taping session. "I've never even been to a commencement before. What does one say?" he had asked. "I suppose I will tell them to read books all their lives and to make a lot of money and give it to the university."*

INTERVIEWER: I'd like to begin by asking about some people you may have known. Were you at all close to William Butler Yeats?

SPENDER: I met Yeats, I think probably in 1935 or 1936, at Lady Ottoline Morrell's. Ottoline asked me to tea alone with Yeats. He was very blind and—I don't know whether he was deaf, but he was very sort of remote, he seemed tremendously old. He was only about the age I am now, but he seemed tremendously old and remote. He looked at me and then he said, "Young man, what do you think of the Sayers?" I hadn't the faintest idea what he was talking about—I thought perhaps he meant Dorothy Sayers' crime stories or something—I became flustered. What he meant was a group of young ladies who chanted poems in chorus. Ottoline got very alarmed and rushed out of the room and telephoned to Virginia Woolf, who was just around the corner, and asked her to come save the situation. Virginia arrived in about ten minutes' time, tremendously amused, and Yeats was very pleased to meet her because he'd just been reading *The Waves.* He also read quite a lot of science—I think he read Eddington and Rutherford and all those kinds of things—and so he told her that *The Waves* was a marvelous novel, that it was entirely up to date in scientific theory because light moved in waves, and time, and so on. Of course Virginia, who hadn't thought of all this, was terribly pleased and flattered. And then I remember he started telling her a story in which he said, "And as I went down the stairs there was a marble statue of a baby and it started talking in Greek to me"—that sort of thing. Virginia adored it all, of course.

Ottoline had what she called her Thursday parties, at which you met a lot of writers. Yeats was often there. He loosened up a great deal if he could tell malicious stories, and so he talked about George Moore. Yeats particularly disliked George Moore because of what he wrote in his book *Ave, Salve, Vale,* which is in three volumes, and which describes Yeats in a rather absurd way. Moore thought Yeats looked very much like a black crow or a rook as he walked by the lake on Lady Gregory's estate at Coole. He also told how Yeats would spend the whole morning writing five lines of poetry and then he'd be sent up strawberries and cream by Lady Gregory, and so Yeats would have to get his own back on George Moore. Another thing which amused Yeats very much for some reason was Robert Graves and the whole saga of his life with Laura Riding. He told how Laura Riding threw herself out of a window without breaking her spine, or breaking it but being cured very rapidly. All that pleased Yeats tremendously.

I remember his telling the story of his trip to Rapallo to show the manuscript of *The Tower* to Ezra Pound. He stayed at the hotel and then went around and left the manuscript in a packet for Pound, accompanied by a letter saying I am an old man, this may be the last poetry I'll ever write, it is very different from my other work—all that kind of thing—and what do you think of it? Next day he received a post card from Ezra Pound with on it the one word "putrid." Yeats was rather amused by that. Apparently Pound had a tremendous collection of cats, and Yeats used to say that Pound couldn't possibly be a nasty man because he fed all the cats of Rapallo. I once asked him how he came to be a modern poet, and he told me that it took him thirty years to modernize his style. He said he didn't really like the modern poetry of Eliot and Pound. He thought it was static, that it didn't have any movement, and for him poetry had always to have the romantic movement. He said, "For me poetry always means 'For we'll go no more a-roving/By the light o' the moon.' " So the problem was how to keep the movement of the Byron lines but at the same time enlarge it so that it could include the kind of material that he was interested in, which was to do with everyday life—politics, quarrels between people, sexual love, and not just the frustrated love he had with Maud Gonne.

INTERVIEWER: I believe you were an early admirer of Dylan Thomas.

SPENDER: I knew Dylan from very early on. In fact, I was the first literary person he met in London. Edith Sitwell made the absurd claim that she'd discovered Dylan Thomas, which is rubbish. All she did was write a favorable review of his first book. There was a Sunday newspaper called *Reynolds' News* at that time, and it had a poetry column which was edited by a man called Victor Neuberg. He would publish poems sent in by readers. I always read this column, being very sympathetic with the idea of ordinary people writing poetry. And then in one issue I saw a poem which I thought was absolutely marvelous—it was about a train going through a valley. I was very moved by this poem, so I wrote to the writer in care of the column, and the writer wrote back. It was Dylan Thomas, and in his letter he said first of all that he admired my work, something which he never said again. Then he said he wanted to come up to London and that he wanted to make money—he was always rather obsessed by money. So I invited him to London, and may have sent him his fare. I felt nervous about meeting him alone, which is what I should have done, so I invited my good friend William Plomer to have lunch with us. We took him to a restaurant in Soho. He was very pale and intense and nervous, and Plomer and I talked a lot of London gossip to prevent the meal from going in complete silence.

I think he probably stayed in London—he was a friend of Pamela Hansford Johnson, who became Lady Snow. Then, right at the end of his life, Dylan wrote me a letter saying he'd never forgotten that I was the first poet of my generation who met him. He was thanking me for some review I'd written—this was the most appreciative review he'd had in his life, I think he said, something like that. Mind you, he probably wrote a dozen letters like that to people every day. And he certainly said extremely mean things behind my back, of that I'm quite sure. I don't hold that against him at all—it was just his style. We all enjoy doing things like that. After those very early days I didn't see Dylan often; one reason is that I never get on well with alcoholics. Also he liked to surround himself with a kind of court which moved from pub to pub. And Dylan was expected to pay for everyone, which he always did, and he was expected to be "Dylan." Of course when I was at *Horizon* with Cyril Connolly, Dylan was always coming in, usually to borrow money. Richard Burton was funny telling me about Dylan. He was a young actor and absolutely without money. He would be playing somewhere and Dylan would turn up to borrow a pound. When he left, Burton would always hear a taxi carrying the pauper away.

INTERVIEWER: How well did you know Ernest Hemingway?

SPENDER: Hemingway I knew during the Spanish Civil War. He often turned up in Valencia and Madrid and other places where I happened to be. We would go for walks together, and then he'd talk about literature. He was marvelous as long as he didn't realize that he was talking about literature—I mean he'd say how the opening chapter of Stendhal's *La Chartreuse de Parme* was the best description of war in literature—when Fabrizio gets lost, doesn't know where he is at all in the battle of Waterloo. Then I'd say, "Well, what do you think about *Henry IV*, do you think Shakespeare writes well about war?"

"Oh, I've never read Shakespeare," he'd say. "What are you talking about—you seem to imagine I'm a professor or something. I don't read literature, I'm not a literary man"—that kind of thing.

He was very nice when one was alone with him, but the public Hemingway could be troublesome. On one occasion I remember we went into a bar where there were girls. Hemingway immediately took up a guitar and started strumming, being "Hemingway." One of the girls standing with him pointed at me and said, *"Tu amigo es muy guapo"*—your friend is very handsome. Hemingway became absolutely furious, bashed down the guitar and left in a rage. He was very like that. Another time, my first wife and I met him and Marty Gellhorn in Paris. They invited us to lunch, someplace where there were steaks and chips, things like that, but my wife ordered sweetbread. Also she wouldn't drink. So Hemingway said, "Your wife is yellow, that's what she is, she's yellow. Marty was like that, and do you know what I did? I used to take her to the morgue in Madrid every morning before breakfast." Well, the morgue in Madrid before breakfast really must have been something.

Hemingway always said of me, "You're O.K. All that's wrong with you is you're too squeamish." So he would describe modern war. He'd say, "If you think of modern war from the point of view of a pilot, the city that he's bombing isn't all these people whom you like to worry about, people who are going to suffer—it's just a mathematical problem. It's like shading in a circle with dark areas where you drop your bombs. You mustn't think of it in a sentimental way at all." At that same meeting in Paris, he told me again I was squeamish, and then he said, "This is something you ought to look at, it will do you good." He produced a packet of about thirty photographs of the most horrible murders, which he carried around in his pockets. This toughened one up in some way. He told me that what motivated him really, while he was in Spain, wasn't so much enthusiasm about the Republic, but to test his own courage. He said, "Only if you actually go into battle and bullets are screeching all around you, can you know whether you're a coward or not." He had to prove to himself that he wasn't a coward. And he said, "Mind, you shit in your pants with fear. Everyone does that, but that isn't what counts." I don't remember quite what it is that counts—but he always wanted to test his own courage. Physical courage to him was a kind of absolute value.

INTERVIEWER: Given Auden's general air of superiority, a quality that seems to come through over and over, was it possible really to feel close to him as a human being?

SPENDER: Yes, because there was a kind of nonseriousness about Wystan, a kind of buffoonery, which undercut the superiority. He wasn't intellectually arrogant. He was extremely clever and quite demanding, I should say, and he criticized one's work with authority, but he never had the air of a critic. He really was a born teacher. He would say, "If I were you, I wouldn't put in the word 'like' here," for instance. Or, "That line's marvelous, but the rest is absolute trash." He'd talk like that, but he wouldn't give you the feeling that he was preaching at you. Of course I was a bit in awe of him, being two or three years younger than he was. But still there was a great deal of fun, of playfulness in all that he said. In fact his whole relationship with a person like Isherwood seemed one long farcical dialogue. If you'd heard our kind of conversation, it would probably have seemed quite frivolous. In fact, there always was a strong strain of frivolity, which one cannot imagine in a conversation, say, between F. R. Leavis and Mrs. Leavis about literature. He always had a deep-down desire not to be taken seriously. For instance, after the war, quite late on, he once gave me a terrific lecture about my behavior and my life. I was quite impressed by this, and so I said, "Oh, you are quite right Wystan, I think I'll change my whole life." He buried his head in his hands and said, "Please. What are you talking about? Don't you realize I'm not serious? I don't in the least want you to be any different from what you are. The thing that I can't bear about America is that everyone always takes me seriously."

There was a constant streak of absurdity about him. I stayed the night with him once in Greenwich Village, and when I got up in the morning, I naturally pulled the curtain. Immediately the whole thing—curtains, rods, everything—clattered to the floor. Auden said, "Why on earth did you draw the curtain?" And I said, "Well, because I wanted the daylight." And he said, "I never draw the curtain, I just always leave it closed." About two weeks later I returned, and the curtain was still on the floor, exactly where it had fallen. Auden always had a sort of Beatrix Potter quality to him, a sort of Mrs. Tickeltedemal. And that he was camp—I mean it is difficult to think of a serious critic who is camp, isn't it? Oscar Wilde, for instance, would not give you a serious lecture on first principles of literary criticism. You'd have to take yourself so seriously.

Another interesting thing about Auden is he didn't like seeing people in twos and threes. He'd put up with a party, quite enjoy it, as a kind of ceremony. But otherwise he liked seeing one alone, and he really resented another person being introduced into the situation. On one occasion I was to have dinner with him in Greenwich Village. Well, I ran into an old friend of ours from Oxford, Rex Warner, so I rang up Auden and asked if I could bring him to dinner. Auden said, "Yes, of course, bring him along." This was about ten o'clock at night, when I rang him, and Auden was probably drunk. Anyhow, he forgot completely about it, and when I turned up with Rex Warner, he just looked at him and said, "Why are you here?" So I said, "You invited Rex." "No I didn't. I never invited Rex. I expected you." Then he said, "Anyhow there's nothing for Rex to eat. There's only enough for Stephen and me." Then he recovered himself a bit and said, "Well, never mind, I'll eat some hamburger or something. Stephen and you can have the two chops I've prepared." He did this in a very ostentatious way. Poor Rex was deeply hurt.

INTERVIEWER: I've heard Auden could be selfish or miserly in small ways.

SPENDER: An important thing to remember is that most people who are famous have a kind of public relations side to their character; they are careful to hide certain things about themselves. But Auden didn't care. For instance, one of the things he most detested was people taking his cigarettes. On one occasion he was staying on Ischia when a yacht I was travelling on called there. In the course of the afternoon which I spent with him, I happened to take one of his cigarettes. He said, "Why don't you have cigarettes of your own?" And I said, "As a matter of fact, I would have bought some but I don't have any Italian money—I have just English money with me." "Well," he said, "I'd be happy to change some for you. Give me a pound." Then he looked up the rate of exchange in the *Herald-Tribune*, and he said, "Well, my dear, I am afraid the pound's doing very badly. I can only give you a hundred lira, but now you can go downstairs and buy some cigarettes." If you wanted to make up a story to show the utter stinginess of someone, you could not do better than that. But then a few months later, Auden was staying with us in the country, in England. Our daughter at that time was always talking about having a horse. But we couldn't quite afford it, so Auden said, "Well, look, Stephen, what Lizzie wants most in this world is a horse. Here's fifty pounds towards buying her one." This was the same person. I don't think it is so odd, what he did. What is odd is that he made no attempt to conceal the odd quirk of meanness.

INTERVIEWER: In your new book, you speak of Herbert Read describing Eliot as lacking in affection for perhaps everyone. Did you find him to be this cold a person?

SPENDER: No. He was extremely discriminating and mannered, I should say, and his life was very much governed by conventions of behavior. One would never ring him and say, "May I come round and see you?" Everything had to be elaborate and courteous. But I think that he was quite affectionate, in a rather remote way, towards people. I think probably Herbert Read felt like a junior partner to Eliot all his life. He seemed to resent the fact that Eliot had a greater reputation than he did, that people read Eliot's poems but not Herbert Read's. He didn't seem to understand that Eliot was much better than he was. I was in a rather similar position in regard to Auden, but in my case I did have a very clear idea that Auden was much better than I, which prevented me from resenting him. Eliot himself, to some extent, didn't understand his own reputation and thought of it as a bit unfair. He once told me that he felt Conrad Aiken had all his own qualities, that he was as serious and as dedicated, and that all of his life he'd felt it an injustice that he'd got so much attention while Conrad Aiken had been so neglected. But I don't think he felt that about Herbert Read.

I think Eliot was fond of me and of other people, but he was always rather distant. I mean if one gets on fairly good terms with someone, you immediately feel that you know them well. There is a kind of break-in period, after which, instead of just being an acquaintance, you somehow feel that you know the person completely. Well, Eliot never allowed one to have that feeling. There was nothing casual in his relationships. Of course, he had confidantes—Geoffrey Faber, who was his closest friend and his partner in Faber and Faber, probably knew him better than anyone. He certainly knew more about Eliot and his troubles with his first wife than anyone else did. Yet it was Geoffrey Faber who drew my attention to a story of Richard Aldington's which is obviously about Eliot. It describes a man who has a completely spurious reputation but who manipulates it very adroitly. He has a wife whom he treats with extreme correctitude but without any sort of warmth or passion; he freezes the relationship between them through his conventionality and his perfect manners. It is an odious portrait, really; and Aldington was a man of no talent. The funny thing is that Faber said, "If you really want to understand

Eliot, read that story—there's a streak of truth about that." He said that early on, certainly before Eliot's second marriage. Eliot changed greatly with his second marriage. But of course one has also to remember that Faber himself was a rather stuffy, correct man with strangely repressed passions. I think another important thing about Eliot is that he was one of those people who is always acting himself, his own role, whatever he is at a given moment. The poet who is a bank clerk, the perfect gentleman, all that sort of thing. And I think this element of acting was inseparable from the irony and made other people conscious of the irony.

INTERVIEWER: That sounds like trying to "put on a face to meet the faces that you meet."

SPENDER: That's it exactly, yes.

INTERVIEWER: Eliot made such a point of the impersonality of poetry, especially of his own poetry, and yet there seems to be a resemblance between the character of Eliot and that personality, even neurotic personality, which is projected in "Prufrock," *The Waste Land,* and some of his other early poems. Do you think that maybe he was violating his own rule, that actually there is more of his own personality in those poems than he would let on?

SPENDER: Yes. I think he indicated as much really when he later described *The Waste Land* as "one man's grouse." But at the same time one has to remember that nearly all of Eliot's early criticism is extremely polemical, and so if he says that poetry has to be impersonal it's because he's thinking of the Georgian poets, who made a cult of self-expression. They were all wearing their hearts on their sleeves; their poetry was written to show that you were a poet in your whole being. When I was young, if you talked to those people about a poem, they'd say, "Oh, yes, the poet is there, the poet is in those lines." A poem like, say, "The Lake Isle of Innisfree" is exactly that, really. It's the poet being The Poet in the poem and the poem being inseparable from the poet and the reader liking the poem because he's put in contact with the poet. I think it's that view of poetry which Eliot is really reacting against. In fact, what he's always saying is that a poem ought to be made objectively, with tools and technique, as a carpenter turns a table leg with a lathe. And of course when he talks about the impersonality of the poet, if you'll remember, he puts in an escape clause at the end. He says, "But, of course, only those who have personality and emotions know what it means to want to escape from these things"—which is very sly, and shows in a way that he has his tongue in his cheek.

This also has to do with the international movement towards modernism, which goes back to the 1890s. In English poetry, this means a strong French influence through such things as Arthur Symons's book on the symbolists. From all this comes the idea of the persona or the mask, the idea that the poet must never be himself in his poetry, but must invent an artificial self, must be a mysterious person whom other people don't understand. Laforgue had this idea, and Eliot completely identified with Laforgue. In fact, his second marriage was held in the same church in London where Laforgue had been married. For myself, I can't imagine inventing a persona. I think it was very much something that generation did. Of course, the most elaborate mask of all is Pound's Hugh Selwyn Mauberly. It is elaborate to the point of confusion, and one wonders whether it doesn't really show a kind of mental confusion on Pound's part.

INTERVIEWER: You say that Eliot was the most approachable and helpful poet of his generation to younger poets. Was he helpful to you when you were a younger poet?

SPENDER: Yes, he was. The letters he wrote to me when he was a young man—they were the letters of a person with real affection and real concern. He was also a bit of a taskmaster, saying "You ought to discipline yourself," and so on. But he was always very kind to us, always helpful. Occasionally one got upset about things the critics wrote about one's work. Eliot always stood by one, and said, "Why do you worry about that? Just ignore them. This work will add to your reputation." In a rather unobtrusive way, he couldn't have been more encouraging.

INTERVIEWER: I take it that the editors of *Scrutiny* were not similarly encouraging.

SPENDER: No, they weren't. When I was in the London Fire Service, there was a fellow fireman who would never really look at me. And then one day he said, "Don't you realize who I am?" His name was Peacock. Then he said, "Well, I'm the person who wrote that terrible attack on your first book in *Scrutiny.*" And he said, "The reason I did it was because I was instructed by Leavis to do it, and told exactly what to say." So it was a very different kind of thing. I think that Eliot might have given us a bit more criticism, as a matter of fact. No one knows to this day what Eliot really thought about Auden's poetry. Well, of course he admired it, and he published it, but he never really said anything about it. He was rather mysterious about it.

INTERVIEWER: Why do you think Leavis would have that kind of attitude? Was he just the kind of person who loves to attack young poets?

SPENDER: A great difficulty about criticism is that critics really form their judgments on the basis of past work, don't they? You may be an extremely good critic of past work but totally incapable of judging modern or contemporary work. A critic always feels that his knowledge, which may be vast, and the critical standards which he has derived from a study of past work, ought to apply. And so he will only like the kind of work by living writers in which they do apply. This argument is obviously based on a false logic. One may be an extremely good judge of art, say, up to 1910, but be incapable of judging later work because it contains an element which is unprecedented in the art which one is able to judge. When I was editing *Encounter,* I once asked Auden whether I shouldn't write to

Leavis and ask him to write a column in which he'd be completely free to say whatever he liked. And Auden said, "That would be extremely irresponsible of you, because, although he is a very good judge of what he likes, Leavis is quite incapable of judging what he doesn't like. So you'd get good criticism of the things that he liked and then you'd get savage attacks on things that don't happen to come within his conspectus."

INTERVIEWER: You mentioned your critic, Mr. Peacock of the Fire Brigade. Did you not know who he was because you'd never met him before or because you hadn't paid any particular attention to his attack on your work?

SPENDER: No, I'd been very upset by it. I think one has to remember that attacking writers, especially when they are young, may be extremely damaging to them. I myself was very discouraged by the attacks of *Scrutiny* and other things like that. Of course it is difficult to decide, because on the other hand I think that criticism has to be centered, you have to have standards, don't you? My own experience of criticism is that of course one sometimes attacks something because one thinks the work criticized may be very bad. But there's always an element of pleasure in doing this. I think an attack is never really objective. What you say may be objective, your standards may be objective, but there is actually a kind of pleasure nevertheless, which is a strongly subjective element. Of course critics pretend that this isn't so, but I think it is so, and it is very difficult for a critic to resist that.

INTERVIEWER: Doing frank reviews, and especially having negative things to say about people who were your friends, did that ever cause you trouble? Did you ever find that a difficult thing to do?

SPENDER: Well, it probably annoyed them on occasion, but my friends always behaved very nicely to me; they never held it against me and very rarely showed their annoyance. Auden himself had total self-confidence, of course. He just thought that he was cleverer than anyone else, but without arrogance, really, just out of his own judgment, which may or may not have been right, but which nevertheless was never arrogant. He knew exactly what he was doing, and he was totally indifferent to what anyone said about it. And then being a "psychoanalyst" helped him a great deal. For instance, when he was so attacked by Randall Jarrell in 1947 or so, he said, "He must be in love with me; I can't think of any other explanation." Well, that isn't what one usually thinks about being attacked in print. He was genuinely puzzled. He didn't think it was a damaging attack in any way.

INTERVIEWER: You have been an editor yourself, especially well known for your years at *Encounter,* from which you resigned in some heat.

SPENDER: *Encounter* was supported by an organization called the Congress for Cultural Freedom, which was funded by about forty different foundations. Irving Kristol and I were the first editors of the magazine, then Irving went back to America and I stayed on with another American editor. In 1968, with all the exposure about the CIA, it was revealed that these foundations were simply channeling money for the CIA. So the two English editors, Frank Kermode and I, we both resigned. *Encounter* was a good magazine, and we editors had a free hand with what we published. So lots of people used to ask, "What was wrong with the CIA connection?" What was wrong with it was that we ought to have known.

INTERVIEWER: To get back to the people that you've known, did you have much contact with Ezra Pound?

SPENDER: In around 1936, I was in Rapallo, so I wrote to Pound saying I wanted to come and see him, but I never got any reply. There may have been hundreds of reasons for that —probably it was because he thought I was a hopeless case of leftism and he didn't like my poetry anyhow. But I saw him when he was in St. Elizabeth's Hospital, and he was then always extremely friendly. Then I used to see him every year for some years at the Spoleto Festival. He recognized in Gian

Carlo Menotti a person who really patronized the arts in a quite sacrificial way. He practically never said anything, but on one occasion did say something which moved me very much. About five or seven poets, two of whom were Ezra and myself, all read their poems, and at the end of the reading, as we moved off the platform, Ezra Pound took my arm and said, "Why do you and I do this? We realize it's all vanity and useless." Then he said, "Oh, for a touch of real sincerity." I was rather touched that he said that to me.

INTERVIEWER: But of the Pound who directed the course of modern poetry for so many years, or supposedly did, you did not see that side of Pound?

SPENDER: No. I think Pound had very little influence on the English poets of my generation. He did not mean much to Auden, I know. Auden really just couldn't be bothered with *The Cantos*, I think. I've grown to admire Pound, but only in patches. I've been reading *The Cantos* again recently, and to me they are unrelated lyric poems of very great beauty—marvelous language and also this marvelous feeling for light in the Mediterranean. I think what does come through is his wonderful reverence for civilization—Mediterranean civilization. I once asked him about *The Cantos*. I said, "Will there be a complete edition of *The Cantos*?" This was in the 1950s. And he said, "Forget about them, just forget about them."

INTERVIEWER: Do you think he was turning his back on them?

SPENDER: I think that Pound, when he became silent, was undergoing some kind of remorse, and I think he probably felt that his whole political career and his arrogance had been a terrible mistake. Perhaps as a result of that he condemned everything that he wrote during that period. That's a possible explanation. Of course it may have been a result of mental illness. And it may have been both.

INTERVIEWER: I want to ask you about the politics of Yeats, Eliot, and Pound. Do you think that there is possibly an incred-

ible level of naïveté in their politics, as though for them politics
was a game or a symbolic or even aesthetic activity, in which
they ignored the realities of fascism?

SPENDER: Yes. I think you might call their politics the politics of civilization, or of their concept of civilization. They
connected the idea of civilization with the idea of tradition.
The logic of this position, which is a cultural position, is that,
if challenged, you have to extend it into politics. If you extend
it into politics, the only people whom you can admire are the
reactionaries. It is very much this way with T. S. Eliot. His
attitude towards the external world of society originally was
taken from Baudelaire. What he got from Baudelaire was a
hatred of the idea of progress and industrialization and a hatred
of the materialism of middle-class society. Baudelaire was also
a classicist writing in a modern idiom—writing the poetry of
the city in the language of Racine. So in these respects, Baudelaire was the model for Eliot, who in any case looked very
largely to France for his view of civilization and politics.

So when Eliot, Yeats, and Pound looked around in the
contemporary world for leaders to admire, they found such
guardians of the tradition as Mussolini, Franco, and General
O'Duffy. But from our point of view, it wasn't serious. I think
we would have felt antagonistic to the politics of Eliot and
Pound and Yeats if we'd regarded them seriously as Fascists,
but we couldn't do so, even today, although Pound in particular
considerably incriminated himself by supporting Mussolini and
being very anti-Semitic. But we admired these writers so much
as writers. And even from the cultural point of view, one could
admire their attitude. It was simply the extension of it into
political action that we didn't agree with. One thing we used
to discuss in the 1930s was whether a fascist could be a good
writer. We always decided that he couldn't because fascism
was stupid and inhuman. So by definition a person who was a
good writer might call himself a fascist, but couldn't really be
one.

INTERVIEWER: Didn't you also later decide that a programmatic Communist could not be a good writer?

SPENDER: Yes. In the early days, though, before the nature of Stalinism became apparent, there was a lot we admired about Soviet art. We admired Soviet movies extremely, and I think they had a great influence on my work, perhaps also on Isherwood's work. Christopher Isherwood and I used to study the Berlin newspapers to see what Russian movies there were, and we'd always go and see them. Their imagery, using industrial machinery as a kind of poetic symbolism, like the tractor, the railway engine, factory chimneys, that kind of thing, to us was rather heroic.

The language used by the government itself, on the other hand, was so consistently stilted. A friend of mine in the Spanish Civil War, a Communist in the International Brigade, used to laugh about the Communists for their hackneyed propaganda. He said that on one occasion someone got up at a meeting and said, "Comrades, let's send a spontaneous telegram to Stalin."

INTERVIEWER: With respect to Communist literature and the rather hard words you have had for some of it, would you revise this at all in view of more contemporary writers like Yevtushenko, Voznesensky, and perhaps even Pablo Neruda?

SPENDER: Well, I cannot really consider Pablo Neruda a Communist at all. His kind of Communism was almost entirely rhetorical; he was a sort of highly privileged propagandist. He was banqueted all the time by the Russians, was given all sorts of awards in Russia, and so on. I refused to review his autobiography because he treats all this so casually. As for the others, I've never been able to admire Yevtushenko. I consider him to be an operator. On the other hand, it may be that, in a devious way, he is working for greater freedom in Russia. Of course, the same applies to Voznesensky, whom I prefer to Yevtushenko, but I'm not a Russian scholar. Then there is Joseph Brodsky, whom I'm very fond of and admire greatly. He holds extreme anti-Soviet views which I would hold if I were in his position. I think it is a tragedy that the Russian defectors turn out to be so anti-Communist that they consider the Western anti-Communists as comparative weaklings.

INTERVIEWER: As a poet with a passionate interest in world politics, does it seem to you that poetry can have any real effect on society or its direction?

SPENDER: I think only in certain situations. For instance, always at the beginning of a war there is a demand from editors that poets should write war poetry. This comes from a recognition that, in a situation in which patriotic feelings are required, poetry may stimulate those feelings. I imagine the sonnets of Rupert Brooke at the beginning of the First World War probably did make some people join up to fight the Germans. During the Spanish Civil War, the poetry that was written probably helped the International Brigade. Then in a much wider sense poetry can be politically effective as well. Surely one can trace the sources of the movement for Italian unity to the fact that Dante decided to write *The Divine Comedy* in idiomatic Italian and not in Latin, which would have been the correct thing for him to have done. And Goethe, who created, really all by himself, modern German literature, also contributed greatly to the idea of German unity through doing this. He created a German culture and taught Germans that they could respect themselves in relation to France, especially, and other countries.

But I think it is wrong to believe that poetry is really very effective in politics. And politics can certainly be very bad for poetry. I was discussing this with Denise Levertov when she was here. She read a political poem, which was based on her visiting Hanoi and being taken round by the North Vietnamese to see damage done to hospitals by American aircraft. Of course she had extremely strong feelings about this, and I don't want to call it just a propaganda operation on the part of the North Vietnamese, but somehow to enter almost as a tourist into that kind of suffering and to make propaganda out of it is not what a poet should be doing. For a journalist it's all right, but a poet has to go in for an act of the imagination, which is on a deeper level. I mean, if you penetrate to the depths of the suffering, you see that it is not just inflicted by one side; it's something that human beings do to one another. Also if you write what one has to call propaganda poetry, you lay yourself open to a kind of argument which is all right in politics but which oughtn't to occur in poetry. Someone will say, "Well, if the North Vietnamese had had airplanes, they'd have done the same thing," which you can't really dispute. I don't think that poets ought to get themselves into that kind of argument.

There are, of course, political situations so absolutely unspeakable that they become quite literally unimaginable. It would be impertinent, for example, to imagine what was happening in the concentration camps during the 1930s and 1940s. The only way to know that suffering was to be a part of it, but if you became a part of it, you were destroyed. As a matter of fact, at the end of the concentration camp era, when various poets, particularly in Poland, emerged from the camps, they hated poetry. They regarded poetry as the greatest betrayal because it always in some way offers pleasure. It would therefore have to extract some kind of comfort, something pleasurable, from all these horrors. And so they started writing what they called antipoetry.

INTERVIEWER: What about the effect of war on poets who were not as closely involved?

SPENDER: In some ways war is a suspension of every other activity which makes life interesting, like art and conversation. Also, war is a kind of dictatorship, one cannot say certain things. On the other hand, though, in London during the war there was a blackout; one saw the stars, and all that was very charming. Some of the descriptions which came out of the war had a sort of Surrealist effect. One felt during the war that Surrealism had come true.

INTERVIEWER: To turn to another subject, there was, in the 1920s, an intense migration of American writers to Europe. Then, in the 1940s and later, we find many English writers— Auden, Isherwood, Gunn, yourself—migrating from England to America. How does one account for this?

SPENDER: Well, I think in a Marxist way one ought to say that both migrations had some economic basis. The Americans went in large numbers because they could live very cheaply in Europe in the 1920s. Because of the tremendous inflation in France, the American writers could eat French food, enjoy French mistresses, and absorb French civilization at a very low price. Then for those of us who have come this way across the Atlantic, there again is a very strong economic reason. And that is that, for just being what we are, being poets and doing a little teaching and lecturing, we can make a living in America. In fact, we are rather handsomely rewarded in America. This simply did not happen before the war in England, where you'd be rather surprised to get even ten dollars for giving a lecture or reading. Today you get up to a hundred dollars for giving a reading, simply because the whole thing is subsidized by the Arts Council. That is one reason. Another is the excitement of America, the pleasure of finding oneself with American colleagues. I think I've talked much more about poetry and about things I care for with American colleagues than I ever have with English ones—whole generations of them. America is, among the poets, a place where everything is openly discussed, and it's really immensely more interesting than the scene in England.

INTERVIEWER: Is there a greater serious audience for poetry in America than in England?

SPENDER: The United States, when it takes it seriously, takes it deadly seriously. In England, on the other hand, no one would expect it to be taken seriously. An English poet writes, I think, just for people who are interested in poetry. An American poet writes, and feels that everyone ought to appreciate this. Then he has a deep sense of grievance, because he may only be appreciated by two thousand people.

One of my great surprises when I was in America was about twenty-five years ago in Harvard, hearing Randall Jarrell deliver a bitter attack on the way poets were neglected. Yet there were about two thousand people present, and he was being paid five hundred dollars for delivering this attack.

INTERVIEWER: Did you know Robert Frost?

SPENDER: I met him only two or three times. He had a number of sides to his nature, as we know, including a very black one. He showed me his vain side. I had to give a dinner party for him, and had someone bellow in his ear the names of all the other people and had all their place names written out very large so he could see them at the table. He sat next to E. M. Forster, and asked, "And what magazine do you write for?" He just didn't take these people seriously, and didn't bother to find out who they were.

INTERVIEWER: You have said that there is a strong American influence in the work of Ted Hughes, but also that there is a good deal of Englishness about his work. I'm not, in asking this question, particularly interested just in Hughes's work, but rather in the terms, the qualities you are talking about. What characteristics do you have in mind when you speak of American and English qualities in poetry?

SPENDER: The American to me would be the kind of turned-on, confessional aspect of Hughes, the violence really. The English would be that he is still very much a nature poet. He lives in Devonshire and writes poetry about the countryside, very beautiful I think, which I consider to be a very English kind of thing. Of course American poets write nature poetry, but not in the same way. English nature poetry has a more rooted quality, more the feeling that the poet lives in this landscape, has always lived in this landscape. But in quite a lot of recent American poetry about nature, say Gary Snyder's, you feel that he has only just arrived with his knapsack and tent. I suppose that Frost was much more like an English poet in this respect, and maybe this is why he was first published in England and was so very much admired in England.

INTERVIEWER: It has been said that, over the last twenty or thirty years, American poetry has been more lively than British poetry. What do you think of this hypothesis?

SPENDER: Well, there's been a great deal more of it. As material I should think it is more interesting to read, but that might be true of journalism also. On the whole, America since 1950 or so has been the place where things happen. America has, in the twentieth century, very much the role England had in the nineteenth. England in the nineteenth century was where the consequences of the industrial revolution were most acutely felt. Therefore all English literature of the nineteenth century, including poetry, contains a great deal of news about the problems of living with child labor and the destruction of the landscape and that kind of thing. This is essentially what you find in American poetry of this century—things like reacting to pollution and trying to heat up personal values through confession or drugs or any kind of stimulus in order to compete with the depersonalization caused by the industrial society. Of course it is interesting and exciting. I think as a matter of fact that some of the best English poets, particularly Philip Larkin, are making a virtue of the unexcitingness of England, insisting on the quietness of England.

INTERVIEWER: Speaking of Larkin, you have written of the insular type of English poetry, citing Betjeman and Larkin as examples, a type of poetry which Donald Davie speaks of in his book on the Hardy tradition. You've also said that you yourself are not of this type. How would you characterize yourself, your own work?

SPENDER: I think I'm international—I've always thought that I was. When I was young, the feeling for Englishness, for being English, was so strong that I inevitably felt like a foreigner. I'm one-quarter German-Jewish, a quarter German, and half English. In America this wouldn't mean anything, but in the England of the upper classes and middle classes when I grew up, before the 1930s, this made me feel like a foreigner. I was always very conscious of Englishness, as though it were something very beautiful, worthy of one's strongest admiration, but just a little apart from myself. I always felt twice as much alive the moment I left England. The excitement of just waking up in the morning and thinking, "This is foreign, I'm abroad," has always been very stimulating. I think that's why I've always been going abroad, getting away from England.

INTERVIEWER: Early in your life, Auden told you, apparently at Oxford, that you were essentially an autobiographer, as a writer. This is something that you have mentioned periodically throughout your career, accepting the characterization. I think that most readers, looking at your career, recognizing the many prose works that you have written, would still say that poetry is at the center of your achievement and is what holds it all together. What do you think of this; is it poetry or is it autobiography that lies at the heart of your career?

SPENDER: I don't at all regret having written autobiography, and hope to write more of it one day. What I do regret is that I've spent so much time writing criticism rather than writing more creative works. I am quite well qualified as a critic, and I suppose I have quite a lot of critical sensibility. I also have a rather inventive mind, and I keep on thinking of fascinating ideas for books. I ought to think them up for other people to write rather than me. *Love-Hate Relations* is a good example of this. It's a very good idea for a book, but, because I didn't really have the time to read all the matter, I found it a tremendous chore after having started it. Someone else could have done it so much more easily than I, and without sacrificing other work. What I really do reproach myself for is that I ever wrote a successful critical work as a young man; *The Destructive Element* was published when I was twenty-six, in 1936. I wish it had been so bad that I'd have had to stop, but it was sort of half-good and rather helped me along. Really, it all came from accepting advances. Publishers will offer you advances for a book of that kind, but not for other kinds of books. So what I really think is that I ought to have written novels, plays, stories, poems, anything that was creative. Writing autobiography is rather inhibiting in two ways. First of all, you are writing about yourself, and I've always felt the egotism is indecent, even though I have such quantities of it. I can't bear to read aloud poems of mine which are very autobiographical—some of them I think are my best poems, but I just can't read them aloud to an audience. And secondly, of course, autobiography tends to be self-consuming and repetitious. An autobiographical writer is constantly using up his material, or he is constantly wanting to use the same material again. The same anecdote will fit into thirty or forty different pieces, you see.

As regards poetry, I'm feeling very self-critical at this stage in my life. I feel that I understand my work much better than I did and my whole life much better than I did. I think that a lot of my poetry was spoiled by my not knowing how to write my own kind of poem. I think that I only really grasp it now. For instance, I recently looked again at a poem of mine called "The Marginal Field." It is about the theory of economics which describes something called "the margin of profit." There is a field somewhere, say, where it is just worth sowing corn because, although it is terribly stony and unproductive, you can just make a profit out of it. Somehow there are certain ideas in economics, and even in politics, which are true as economics but also true as poetic metaphors. So I wrote this poem, which is really quite beautiful in theory, in which I describe a field at the edge of cliffs. The person who is tilling it is sheeted in sweat and thinking about another field, which is very profitable, where the corn is waving and golden. Now looking at that poem, I thought, "Oh, I must write that poem." It's as though it wasn't written at all; I think perhaps I can still write that poem. The reason I couldn't write it then is because I was unable to draw a clear enough distinction between the abstract part of the poem and the imagistic richness of the poem. I just didn't know how to work at it really. I have always worked rather hard at my poems, and I feel now that I know how to work. I feel that if I'd written much more poetry without worrying whether it was good or bad, and been prepared to make many more mistakes, I'd have been much better off in the end. But I've always felt terribly sensitive to criticism, and I've suffered agonies from critical remarks. I've always felt that perhaps it's true, I oughtn't to do this, I'm not a poet. And that can be really inhibiting. There's a marvelous remark in *The Pisan Cantos,* where Pound, in his mood of contrition, talks about his arrogance, his pride, saying "Pull down thy vanity." But then he immediately answers himself with the opposite opinion, which says that if you accept a negative evaluation of yourself, then you will never accomplish anything: "Here the error is all in the not done, all in the diffidence that faltered." I felt tremendously the force of those lines when I first read them, and have had them in my mind ever since.

INTERVIEWER: You have said of many poets that you had the sense when you read their work, poets who were dead, at the end of their careers, that they hadn't started yet. Is this in the back of your mind as you talk about your own career?

SPENDER: Yes. I want to do another autobiography, revise *World Within World* and make it about twice as long. That's an important aim I have. And I want to do this play. Then I'd like to do a proper volume of collected poems, and write many more poems. That's about it. It would be nice just to have about three books which were really worthwhile.

INTERVIEWER: Robert Lowell, in a review of Stanley Kunitz's book *The Testing Tree,* spoke of the movement towards a more relaxed, more open, less formal verse as "the drift of our age." Do you feel that your work has evolved in this direction?

SPENDER: No, not at all. And if it is the drift of our age, then I am in favor of going against the age. I have a strong feeling that the interesting new poet would be formal and even artificial, someone who would push language always to the point where it has the fascination of artifice and is not just straightforward. If Lowell hadn't believed that, he probably would have written much better poetry in the last twenty years of his life. I think he suffered from a compulsion rather like Picasso towards the end of his life, to overproduce simply to prove to himself that he was the greatest poet producing the greatest quantity of poetry. I think he produced much of his best poetry when he was under pressure of his illness. But in later years he was getting drugs which kept him sort of half-ill, half-well the whole time, and so his poetry came to lack pressure. Then he should have written less and concentrated more on just a few poems. Some of his later poems are very good, but many are not, and someone is going to have to make a careful selection. He was one of the most distinguished and interesting poets of his time. However lax he became, there was still his tone of voice; you always hear him speaking, and this is exactly what lacks in the people who criticize him. A distinctive tone of voice is one of the rarest things in poetry; I think it is what makes the great poet.

INTERVIEWER: Many writers of your generation are now gone. John Berryman used to speak in his romantic way about being a "lone survivor." How do you feel about being, in a sense, the survivor of your generation?

SPENDER: I feel that I ought to do my best as representative of my generation. I have even thought that I oughtn't to write anything which is a waste of the reader's time any more. I often feel, in a mysterious way, that I am showing my work to members of my generation, writing it for them, particularly Auden, because I was closest to him. Perhaps I might just say something about the writers I am usually classified with. Cecil Day Lewis I liked very much, though I never quite understood why he wrote the kind of poetry he did. It always seemed to me that he was over-literary in some way, that he was somehow turning his experiences into literature as he lived them, long before actually writing about them.

Louis MacNeice was tremendously gifted, I think, a most marvelously gifted technician. I think it's significant that one

of his best works is his translation of *Faust*. It is a marvelous
English poem, very close to Goethe in language and even in
its shifts of meter, which is miraculous considering he didn't
know German. He did the translation with a friend who did
know German. I've always thought that MacNeice had limitations of temperament. He sometimes seems to be writing a
jazzy, crazy kind of poetry, but when you look closer you realize
that it's always perfectly controlled. Inside MacNeice there
was always an academic scholar pulling in the rein. He was
actually a very reticent man. In his autobiography, he reveals
that his mother went mad when he was very young, and I think
that the effect of this was to repress his emotional life and to
make him avoid at all costs the confessional.

Auden seemed the man of very real genius, very great talent.
It is curious that, when we were at Oxford together, he knew
almost nothing about form, so the poems he wrote then are
really free verse. I remember him once showing me a poem
which he said was a sonnet. I asked him why he called it a
sonnet, and he said, "Because it only has eleven lines." Then
he suddenly began to study form, to the point where he became
a virtuoso. I think his mastery of form is what allowed him to
incorporate ideology, his ideas, into his poetry so that he eventually became an intellectual, meditative poet. He was very
conscious of his own mental superiority. Once I happened to
remark to Auden how, when one is a child, one somehow
establishes one's position in relation to the other children by
knowing whether they are cleverer than you or not. Auden
looked at me in an odd way and said, "I always knew that I was
brighter than anyone else." I think he did always know that,
and it affected him greatly. I think that my relationship to him
was very much that of a less clever younger brother. I had two
elder brothers who have died. One was a scientist, an incredibly
competent person who knew all about machinery, engineering,
that kind of thing. As long as he was alive I couldn't do
anything, I couldn't even drive a car. And in some funny way,

the death of Auden has seemed a release to me. I never resented being overshadowed by Auden, but at the same time I think it held me back. Auden was also very preoccupying. When he went back to live in England, we saw a great deal of him, and if you saw Auden it was difficult to do anything else. He was rather temperamental and required quite a lot of attention, demanded great punctuality at meals, that kind of thing. So if Auden announced he was going to come and stay for three weeks, although I was delighted because it was nice to have him there, I also knew that I wouldn't be able to work for three weeks. He had that sort of effect on me—on everyone, in fact.

INTERVIEWER: There is a generation of American poets who seemed to feel that it was necessary to be unhappy to write poetry, to be alcoholic and even suicidal. How do you feel about that?

SPENDER: I should have said really quite the opposite. I think it's almost a duty to be happy. Unhappiness is something one can absolutely count on; one is bound to have a great many worries and one is bound to be very conscious of other people's unhappiness. To me it seems important to realize that other people's unhappiness is probably greater than one's own, that there's a scale of unhappiness in the world. To me it is the attitude of a very spoiled person even to say, "I'm unhappy." It seems really astonishing, in the age in which there've been concentration camps and seven million people asphyxiated, that people can seek unhappiness. Also I do see very much the point of Yeats. That if you're writing a tragic poetry, the unhappier it is, the more energetic and the more vitalizing you must make the language. You don't want to make the reader identify with your own unhappiness, but to make him enjoy the depiction of unhappiness in some way, perhaps to make it cathartic. I think this is one of the profoundest things in Yeats. It led him to rather brutal utterances sometimes, but I think that when you apply this say to Shakespeare, to Lear, it throws real light on the fact that one very much enjoys King Lear's misery. And the more miserable Lear is, the more magnificent the language, and the more enjoyable.

INTERVIEWER: Could you say something about the process of writing a poem? What comes first? A line? The intellectual concept?

SPENDER: Often, a very vivid memory, usually visual, which suggests that it could be realized in concentrated written language, in a form which is adumbrated dimly, not yet clear . . . to be discovered. Above all, the feeling that the poem is *there*—if only I can release it. When I write a poem I do not know consciously how it will develop, but I feel I know this unconsciously. Writing is the gradual revelation of a wholeness already felt when one has the idea for the poem.

INTERVIEWER: Can you give an example of this?

SPENDER: Well, there are two theories of inspiration. One idea is that poetry can actually be dictated to you, like it was to William Blake. You are in a hallucinated state, and you hear a voice or you are in communication with something outside, like James Merrill's poetry, which he says is sometimes dictated through the Ouija board by Auden and other people.

The other idea is Paul Valéry's, what he calls *une ligne donnée*, that you are given one line and you try to follow up this clue, pulling the whole poem out of it. My own experience is that a rhythm or something comes into my head which I feel I must do, I must write it, create it.

For example, I recall looking out of a railway window and seeing an industrial landscape, factories, slag heaps, and the line coming into my head, "A language of flesh and roses." The thought at the back of this was that the industrial landscape was a language, what people have made out of nature, the contrast of nature and the industrial, "A language of flesh and roses." The problem of the poem was to work this connection out, trying to go back to remember what you really thought at that instant, and trying to recreate it. If I think of a poem, I may spend six months writing, but what I am really trying to do is remember what I thought of at that instant.

INTERVIEWER: Can you finish a poem in a burst? Or is revising a large part of the creative process?

SPENDER: Occasionally, I can write a poem straight off. Usually I revise a great deal—a hundred or more rewritings. One good remark Virginia Woolf makes somewhere in her journals is that too much rewriting is symptomatic of a failure of imagination. *Mea culpa.* But if you put a poem aside, when you look at it again it tends to rewrite itself, because your remembered intention criticizes the failures of expression.

INTERVIEWER: What are the disciplines necessary to keep working on a poem for an extended period of time?

SPENDER: The poet Walter de la Mare said that if there is a leak of attention when you are trying to concentrate, the leak can be stifled by smoking a cigarette, or in Schiller's case, by inhaling the rotten apples which he kept in a drawer.

INTERVIEWER: Is a poem ever truly completed? Can you read over what you've done without wanting to worry it some more?

SPENDER: If poems have been anthologized a lot, I feel they probably should not be touched—they do not belong to me. Other poems I want to change if I feel that things in them are a false or incompletely expressed memory of what I intended to write. A poem may, if one is happy with it, lay a ghost to rest by one's expressing objectively something which one needs to express subjectively.

INTERVIEWER: What do you make of Virginia Woolf's somewhat peremptory insistence that one should not publish before the age of thirty?

SPENDER: I think all she meant was that she hadn't published before she was thirty, so she didn't think anyone else should do so.

INTERVIEWER: I wonder if you could say what the most common faults of experienced poets might be?

SPENDER: The most common fault of experienced poets is

that they acquire facility, which reduces tension in their art. Tension usually comes from the sense of difficulty—that the poet has to struggle with language and form.

INTERVIEWER: Do you have to bother with any rituals?

SPENDER: The only important ritual for me is to write in such a way that I shut out all consciousness of my public. Journalism is for the public; poetry is a kind of secret vice. If someone asks me what I am writing, I hate to say "a poem."

INTERVIEWER: Robert Lowell once said that it is harder to be a good man than a great poet. He seemed to feel that there is something about being a poet that makes leading a normal life unusually difficult. What do you think of this notion?

SPENDER: Well, it is hard to be a good man, of course, and a poet is perhaps especially conscious of this. The great poet or writer is faced by the dilemma that in order to accomplish his art he must be a selfish person. Think how James Joyce, for instance, sacrificed his family. The poet may feel he is justified in doing something because his art demands it. On the whole, artists take this attitude, and perhaps this attitude is right. You feel, perhaps, that you must fall in love, and if other people suffer for it, well, it is justified by your poetry. So the artist says something quite arrogantly which the ordinary man probably would not say. I don't think even an automobile manufacturer would say, "I must be unfaithful to my wife for the good of General Motors," whereas a poet is a person who does say that kind of thing. A poet like Lowell is conscious of this dilemma. He may have felt that his imagination offered him a choice— he could have been a good man, in which case he may not have written poetry. But he chose to write poetry, and seems to have felt he had to justify doing things which he probably wouldn't morally have approved in people who weren't poets. Lowell caused quite a lot of suffering to other people, and he was a good man. His poetry is really just one long justification for the pattern of his life. At the same time, he was really very self-aware; he was a good and kind and generous man, who never turned on his attackers, who never said anything mean, except in gossip and amusement, about anyone. A particularly good man, I would say.

INTERVIEWER: I see that our time is about up. Is there anything we haven't covered that you would particularly like to say?

SPENDER: I have recently been amused and taken by surprise several times at my poetry readings. For instance, a woman in Dallas asked me, "Mr. Spender, how will your gossamer dreams help to save the world?" And on another occasion, a man asked, "How many movies have been made of your poems?" Alas, there've been none, none at all.

PETER STITT
Summer 1978

3. Tennessee Williams

Tennessee Williams (Thomas Lanier Williams) drew much of the material for his plays from the South, and in particular from Columbus, Mississippi, where he was born in March, 1911. Prone to illness from a very young age, he found writing to be a tonic. He began his college education at Washington University in St. Louis, later attended the University of Missouri, and ultimately received a degree from the University of Iowa in 1938. He worked at a variety of odd jobs, among them as a poet/waiter at a Greenwich Village restaurant and as a movie theatre usher. The first recognition of his literary skill came in 1940, when he received a Rockefeller Fellowship for his first play, *Battle of Angels*. In 1943 he signed a six-month contract with Metro-Goldwyn-Mayer, which was cancelled when he submitted a script that was eventually to become *The Glass Menagerie*. The play, which in 1945 earned him the New York Drama Critics' Circle Award, introduced him as an important American playwright. Awarded the Pulitzer Prize in 1948 for *A Streetcar Named Desire*, and again in 1955 for *Cat on a Hot Tin Roof*, he earned the Gold Medal for Literature in 1969 from both the American Academy of Arts & Letters and the National Institute of Arts & Letters.

In addition to his plays, which fill at least seven volumes, Williams published collections of poetry (*The Summer Belvedere* [1944], *Winter of Cities* [1956]) and short stories (*Hard Candy* [1954], *Eight Mortal Ladies Possessed* [1974], and *It Happened the Day the Sun Rose* [1982]). A memoir, *Where I Live: Selected Essays*, appeared in 1978.

During his latter years, Tennessee Williams lived mainly in Key West, making occasional trips to New York. He died there, alone, on February 25, 1983.

Hotel Elysée

60 EAST 54TH STREET NEW YORK 22, N.Y.
TELEPHONE PLAZA 3-1066

Girl (Cont'd)

- it's **important** - the truth... '

Leona

—Man cannot live by Pepperonis alone, but —

(SHE has torn a couple of cellophane-wrapped sausages from over the bar and hands them to the YOUTH.)

You mistify me, you care for each other, bring a new life in a world over-populated.

Out with me. Down the walk's a blue neon sigh- sign. - "Rooms Vacant." I donate the price of a clean bed for this girl for a night's rest and the ~~truth~~ underground is not going to go out on you if it's there.

(SHE shepherds them out: pauses a moment for a a farewell salute to the sailfish.)

'Meglior solo', huh, ducks?

(Exits.)

FOLLOW THROUGH SCENE BETWEEN MONK AND VIOLET AND MONK'S SOLILOQUY AT CURTAIN - with ~~possible~~ excision of line relating to the underground paper.)

probable

Think we should give this a " Sunday try" — it can be removed, if it doesn't work, ~~before~~ pre-views. ~~or during~~ during

A Tennessee Williams manuscript page from a draft of his play *Small Craft Warnings* written on the back of a piece of thin onion-skin hotel stationery.

Don Bachardy

Tennessee Williams

The Paris Review *interview with Tennessee Williams took place over several weeks, first in Chicago, and then in New York.*

In Chicago, Williams was hard at work on the production of a new play being done at the Goodman Theater. It was a humorous and moving work called A House Not Meant to Stand, *the title of which was his comment on the state of American civilization.*

I interviewed Williams in his suite at the Radisson Hotel on North Michigan Avenue in Chicago. It was a huge, four bedroom penthouse decorated in a 1930s mock Moroccan style: fake stone walls, iron chandeliers, a massive fireplace, a staircase and balcony, all of it reminiscent of the interior design especially popular about the time, 1943, that Williams had been a contract writer at the film studios in Hollywood. For that reason he had dubbed the place "The Norma Desmond Suite," after the role played by Gloria Swanson in Sunset Boulevard.

It was Williams's seventieth birthday, and he followed the routine he has adhered to most of his adult life. He got up at dawn and went to his typewriter and worked. Then he swam in the hotel's pool. He returned to his suite and glanced through a pile of mail, mostly birthday greetings from friends. He opened several presents and a box containing a literary prize just presented to him by Italy for The Roman Spring of Mrs. Stone. *He found this somewhat puzzling because, he explained, when the novel and movie first appeared the Italians were angered by his story of a Roman gigolo romancing an older woman.*

He finally sat down and talked with me for several hours. Williams was dressed in a loose embroidered shirt, beige slacks, and soft canvas shoes. He was tanned, having spent most of the winter at his home in Key West, Florida. He looked ten years younger than his age. He was in an unusually happy mood, in part because the play was going well, but also because he had around him a number of close friends, among them Jane Smith, the actress and widow of artist Tony Smith. Also in Chicago was Williams's brother Dakin, with his wife and two adopted daughters.

Three weeks later, after flying to Key West from Chicago, Williams came to New York. While he kept an apartment in the city, he rarely used it. Instead, as was his habit for many years, he stayed at the Hotel Elysée on East 54th Street. He had come to New York to visit his sister Rose, who is a resident at a private sanitarium upstate, near West Point. He was also in New York to conduct some business. He consulted with his editors about three forthcoming books: a collection of short fiction tentatively entitled It Happened the Day the Sun Rose; *a volume of five of his screenplays, among them* The Loss of a Teardrop Diamond, Boom!, One Arm, *and* All Gaul Is Divided; *and an autobiographical work,* My Life in the American Theater: An Interpretive World. *Additionally, Williams had three full-length plays in various preproduction stages, and was*

*contending with movie producers on a possible remake of the
film version of* A Streetcar Named Desire.

*The night before I interviewed him in New York, Williams,
along with the painter Vassilis Voglis and myself, spent a night
on the town. We had an early dinner at an Italian restaurant,
and then went to see the Paul Taylor Dance Company perform
at City Center. We ended at a bar called Rounds, which boasts
a somewhat piss-elegant decor and a clientele consisting largely
of male hustlers and those who employ them.*

*Around noon the next day, I completed the interview with
Tennessee Williams in his suite at the Elysée. He was tired from
the night before, and perhaps because of that he was more
subdued than he had been in Chicago, and the interview was
more reflective. Williams very much disliked talking about his
work and the process through which he created his art. But in
New York, on that dreary, gray day, he was open to it and told
me what he could about how he writes.*

THE GENESIS OF WRITING

I was a born writer, I think. Yes, I think that I was. At least
when I had this curious disease affecting my heart at the age
of eight. I was more or less bedridden for half a year. My
mother exaggerated the cause. She said I swallowed my tonsils!
Years later, when I had the *Time* cover story, and she was
quoted, doctors looked it up and said, "A medical impossi-
bility!"

But I do think there was a night when I nearly died, or
possibly *did* die. I had a strange, mystical feeling, as if I were
seeing a golden light. Elizabeth Taylor had the same experience. But I survived that night. That was a turning point, and
I gradually pulled out of it. But I was never the same physically.
It changed my entire personality. I'd been an aggressive tom-
boy until that illness. I used to beat up all the kids on the block.
I used to confiscate their marbles, snatch them up!

Then that illness came upon me, and my personality changed. I became a shut-in. I think my mother encouraged me to be more of a shut-in than I needed to be. Anyway, I took to playing solitary games, amusing myself. I don't mean masturbation. I mean I began to live an intensely imaginative life. And it persisted that way. That's how I turned into a writer, I guess. By the age of twelve, I started writing.

MOTHER AND MISS ROSE

My mother—everyone calls her Miss Edwina—was essentially more psychotic than my sister Rose. Mother was put away once, you know. She was put away long before she was old, in the early part of the decade of the fifties. I was on St. Thomas in the Virgin Islands, and she called me up.

"Tom, guess where I am?" she said.

"Why, Mother, aren't you at home?"

"No, Tom, they put me away!"

She was living alone, and I guess her fantasies got the best of her. She thought the blacks were planning an uprising in St. Louis, and they were exchanging signals by rattling the garbage pails. She called the family doctor over to tell him about these threatening aspects of life, and he took her right to the bughouse! So I left St. Thomas and sprung her.

Later, when I was in St. Louis, the phone rang and she picked it up. There was no one at the other end. After a while, she said, "*I* know who you are! I'm here waiting! *Unafraid!*"

Mother chose to have Rose's lobotomy done. My father didn't want it. In fact, he cried. It's the only time I saw him cry. He was in a state of sorrow when he learned that the operation had been performed.

I was at the University of Iowa, and they just wrote me what happened. I didn't know anything about the operation. I'd never heard of a lobotomy. Mother was saying that it was bound to be a great success. Now, of course, it's been exposed as a very bad procedure that isn't practiced anymore. But it didn't embitter me against my mother. It saddened me a great deal because my sister and I cared for each other. I cared for her more than I did my mother. But it didn't embitter me against Miss Edwina. No, I just thought she was an almost criminally foolish woman.

Why was the operation performed? Well, Miss Rose expressed herself with great eloquence, but she said things that shocked Mother. I remember when I went to visit her at Farmington, where the state sanitarium was. Rose loved to shock Mother. She had great inner resentment towards her, because Mother had imposed this monolithic puritanism on her during adolescence. Rose said, "Mother, you know we girls at All Saints College, we used to abuse ourselves with altar candles we stole from the chapel." And Mother screamed like a peacock! She rushed to the head doctor, and she said, "Do anything, *anything* to shut her up!" Just like Mrs. Venable, you know, except that Mother wasn't as cruel as Mrs. Venable, poor bitch. Whatever Mother did, she didn't know what she was doing.

She was terrified of sex. She used to scream every time she had sex with my father. And we children were terrified. We'd run out in the streets and the neighbors would take us in.

A year or so before Mother died, she believed she had a horse living with her in her room. She didn't like its presence at all, and she complained bitterly about this imaginary horse that moved into the place with her. She'd always wanted a horse as a child. And now that she finally had one, she didn't like it one bit.

At the end, she changed her name. Miss Edwina dropped the "a" from her name and became Edwin Williams. That's how she signed herself. It's strange to have a mother who at ninety-four decides to call herself Edwin.

Miss Rose smokes too much. She enters a restaurant and asks, "How many packs of Chesterfields do you have? *I'll take them all!*" Or she'll ask in a store, "How many bars of Ivory soap do you have? That all you got? Well, I need at least twenty!"

One night Rose went with me to Mrs. Murray Crane's as a dinner guest. She had a huge reticule with her. Do you know what that is? It's a huge embroidered bag. Rose was very sly, as schizophrenics often are. All during dinner, after each course, or even while people were eating, she would turn to Mrs. Crane, this stately dowager to her right, and say, "Have a cigarette, dear?" And Mrs. Crane would reply, "Oh, I don't smoke, Miss Williams. I do not smoke! And I fear that you're smoking too *much*, Miss Williams!"

Well, Miss Rose took umbrage at that. So after dinner she excused herself. There were four or five lavatories in this duplex apartment, and Rose was gone for a *remarkably* long time. When she came back her reticule was absolutely packed like Santa Claus's bag. She'd cleared the house completely out of soap and toilet paper! It was the biggest haul since the James Brothers. Needless to say, we didn't get a return engagement there.

She's very nervous, you know. When she was in Key West while you were there, she was trying not to smoke so she tried to keep herself busy. She took it upon herself to water all the trees and plants, and there are a great many. Rose would take a glass of water from the house, water a plant with it, return and fill the glass, and go out again, all day long. I find that touching, how she tried to occupy her time.

She has curious misapprehensions about things. Richard Zoerink was so kind to her. They would go walking in Key West along the water. He'd buy her an ice-cream cone, something she loves. One day, I asked Rose where she'd been that afternoon, and she said that she and Richard had taken a walk along the Mediterranean Sea, and she had enjoyed the view of Italy. Lovely Miss Rose. She thinks she's Queen of England, you know. She once signed a photograph of herself to me, "Rose of England."

I love her, you know. For a person like Rose who spent many years in a state asylum, as she had to do before I got any money, living is constantly a defensive existence. The stubbornness, the saying "No!" flatly to things is almost an instinctive response. If I say to Rose, "Don't you think it's time for you to get some rest?," her instinct is just to say "No!"

Once in Key West some people dropped by, and they began telling some very bawdy jokes. Rose didn't approve. So she got up and stood in a corner with her hands clasped in prayer. My cousin Stell, who was taking care of her, said, "Rose, why are you standing like that?"

Rose replied, "I'm praying for their redemption!"

SUCCESS

It all began for me in Chicago in 1944. I've had some of the happiest times of my life here. We were in Chicago for three and a half months with *The Glass Menagerie*. We opened in late December, and played until mid-March. And I had a lovely time. I knew a lot of university students, you know?

So I associate the success of *Menagerie* with the Chicago critics Claudia Cassidy and Ashton Stevens. They really put it over. The opening night audience had never seen this kind of theater before, and their response was puzzlement. And I suppose the play would have died here if Claudia Cassidy and Ashton Stevens hadn't kept pushing and pushing and pushing. They compared Laurette Taylor to Duse, which was a good comparison, I think. Miss Cassidy is very elderly now, but her mind's as sharp as a whistle!

Menagerie got to New York in 1945. It was sold out three and a half months before it opened. People would stop off in New York to see it because they knew it was a new kind of theater, and they knew about Laurette's incredible performance, though the rest of the cast was pretty run-of-the-mill.

The sudden success? Oh, it was terrible! I just didn't like it. If you study photographs taken of me the morning after the huge reception it got in New York, you'll see I was very depressed.

I'd had one eye operation, and I went into the hospital for another one I needed. Lying in the hospital, unable to move for several days, people came over and read to me, and I recovered some sense of reality.

Then, after *Menagerie*, I went to Mexico and had a marvelously happy time. I went alone. Leonard Bernstein was there. He introduced me to Winchell Mount, who gave weekly Saturday night dances. All male. And I learned how to follow! I was the belle of the ball because I could always dance well, but I gave up that career for writing.

Before the success of *Menagerie* I'd reached the very, very bottom. I would have died without the money. I couldn't have gone on any further, baby, without money, when suddenly, *providentially, The Glass Menagerie* made it when I was thirty-four. I couldn't have gone on with these hand-to-mouth jobs, these jobs for which I had no aptitude, like waiting on tables, running elevators, and even being a teletype operator. None of this stuff was anything I could have held for long. I started writing at twelve, as I said. By the time I was in my late teens I was writing every day, I guess, even after I was in the shoe business for three years. I wrecked my health, what there was of it. I drank black coffee so much, so I could stay up nearly all night and write, that it exhausted me physically and nervously. So if I suddenly hadn't had this dispensation from Providence with *Menagerie*, I couldn't have made it for another year, I don't think.

WHERE PLAYS COME FROM

The process by which the idea for a play comes to me has always been something I really couldn't pinpoint. A play just seems to materialize; like an apparition, it gets clearer and clearer and clearer. It's very vague at first, as in the case of

Streetcar, which came after *Menagerie.* I simply had the vision of a woman in her late youth. She was sitting in a chair all alone by a window with the moonlight streaming in on her desolate face, and she'd been stood up by the man she planned to marry.

I believe I was thinking of my sister, because she was madly in love with some young man at the International Shoe Company who paid her court. He was extremely handsome, and she was profoundly in love with him. Whenever the phone would ring, she'd nearly faint. She'd think it was he calling for a date, you know? They saw each other every other night, and then one time he just didn't call anymore. That was when Rose first began to go into a mental decline. From that vision *Streetcar* evolved. I called it at the time *Blanche's Chair in the Moon,* which is a very bad title. But it was from that image, you know, of a woman sitting by a window, that *Streetcar* came to me.

Of course, the young man who courted my sister was nothing like Stanley. He was a young executive from an Ivy League school. He had every apparent advantage. It was during the Depression years, however, and he was extremely ambitious. My father had an executive position at the time with the shoe company, and the young man had thought perhaps a marriage to Rose would be to his advantage. Then, unfortunately, my father was involved in a terrible scandal and nearly lost his job. At any rate, he was no longer a candidate for the Board of Directors. He had his ear bit off in a poker fight! It had to be restored. They had to take cartilage from his ribs, and skin off his ass, and they reproduced something that looked like a small cauliflower attached to the side of his head! So any time anybody would get into the elevator with my father, he'd scowl, and people would start giggling. That was when the young man stopped calling on Rose. He knew the giggling had gone too far and gotten into the newspapers.

The idea for *The Glass Menagerie* came very slowly, much more slowly than *Streetcar,* for example. I think I worked on

Menagerie longer than any other play. I didn't think it'd ever be produced. I wasn't writing it for that purpose. I wrote it first as a short story called "Portrait of a Girl in Glass," which is, I believe, one of my best stories. I guess *Menagerie* grew out of the intense emotions I felt seeing my sister's mind begin to go.

INFLUENCES

What writers influenced me as a young man? *Chekhov!*
As a dramatist? Chekhov!
As a story writer? Chekhov!
D. H. Lawrence, too, for his spirit, of course, for his understanding of sexuality, of life in general.

EFFECTS

When I write I don't aim to shock people, and I'm surprised when I do. But I don't think that anything that occurs in life should be omitted from art, though the artist should present it in a fashion that is artistic and not ugly.

I set out to tell the truth. And sometimes the *truth* is shocking.

LOOKING BACK

I now look back at periods of my life, and I think, Was that really *me*? Was I doing those things? I don't feel any continuity in my life. It is as if my life were segments that are separate and do not connect. From one period to another it has all happened behind the curtain of work. And I just peek out from behind the curtain now and then and find myself on totally different terrain.

The first period was from the age of eleven until I left the university and went into the shoe business. I was madly in love with a girl named Hazel who was frigid. And that period in my life was marked by extreme shyness. I couldn't look at people in the face without blushing. In high school, I couldn't verbally answer questions. I could only give written answers. I couldn't produce my voice. It sounded like grunting, you know? *That* shy. I supposed it was caused by an unconscious clash in me between my sexual drives and the puritanism imposed by my mother, and the great fear my father inspired in me. He was a terrifying man. He was so unhappy that he couldn't help but be tyrannical at home. That was one period.

The next period was happy. It was after I came out in the gay world. I didn't think of it as coming out. I thought of it as a new world, a world in which I seemed to fit for the first time, and where life was full of adventure that satisfied the libido. I felt comfortable at last. And that was a happy time, but *The Glass Menagerie* ended that period and new problems developed with success.

From then through the sixties, because even during the sixties I was working more or less steadily, that was another period different from the rest. But at the end of the sixties I ended up in the bughouse because I violated Dr. Max Jacobson's instructions not to drink when I took the speed injections. Toward the end, this combination produced paranoia and affected my memory and my health. When I went to New York, I couldn't remember having met my producers before, although they'd had daily meetings with me in Key West. Finally, after Ann Meechem and I fled to Tokyo after the terrible reception of *In the Bar of a Tokyo Hotel*, I became more and more ill. I had to be assisted up stairs. When I returned home alone to Key West I was *very* ill. They were building a new kitchen on my house, and the stove was in the patio. It was still operating there while the builders worked. I was stumbling around with a Silex pan, totally disoriented, trying to get it on the stove. And I just sat down on the stove! It was an electric stove, and I inflicted third-degree burns on my body! I think Marion Vicarro called my brother, and Dakin came down to Key West. He called Audrey Wood, and she said, "Well, put him in a hospital." But she didn't bother to say which one.

Dakin, thinking I was going to die anyway, I was in such terrible condition, had me immediately converted to Roman Catholicism so I'd be saved from hell, and then he just threw me into Barnes Hospital (St. Louis), right into the psychiatric ward, which was *incredibly* awful. They suddenly snatched away every pill I had! The injections went too. So I blacked out. It was cold turkey, baby. They tell me I had three brain concussions in the course of one long day, and a coronary. How I survived, I don't know. I think there were homicidal intentions at work there. I was in that place for three and a half months. The first month I was in the violent ward, although I was not violent. I was terrified and I crouched in a corner trying to read. The patients would have terrible fights over the one television set. Someone would put on the news, and another patient would jump up, yelling, and turn on cartoons. No wonder they were violent.

CHRISTIANITY

I was born a Catholic, really. I'm a Catholic by nature. My grandfather was an English Catholic (Anglican), very, very high church. He was higher church than the Pope. However, my "conversion" to the Catholic church was rather a joke because it occurred while I was taking Dr. Jacobson's miracle shots. I couldn't learn anything about the tenets of the Roman Catholic church, which are ridiculous anyway. I just loved the beauty of the ritual in the Mass. But Dakin found a Jesuit father who was very lovely and all, and he said, "Mr. Williams is not in a condition to learn anything. I'll give him extreme unction and just pronounce him a Catholic."

I was held up in the Roman Catholic church, with people

supporting me on both sides, and I was declared a Catholic. What do you think of that? Does that make me a Catholic? No, I was whatever I was before.

And yet my work is full of Christian symbols. Deeply, deeply Christian. But it's the image of Christ, His beauty and purity, and His teachings, yes . . . but I've never subscribed to the idea that life as we know it, what we're living now, is resumed after our death. No. I think we're absorbed back into, what do they call it? The eternal flux? The eternal shit, that's what I was thinking.

POETRY

I'm a poet. And then I put the poetry in the drama. I put it in short stories, and I put it in the plays. Poetry's poetry. It doesn't have to be called a poem, you know.

YOUNG WRITERS

If they're meant to be writers, they will write. There's nothing that can stop them. It may kill them. They may not be able to stand the terrible indignities, humiliations, privations, shocks that attend the life of an American writer. They may not. Yet they may have some sense of humor about it, and manage to survive.

WRITING

When I write, everything is visual, as brilliantly as if it were on a lit stage. And I talk out the lines as I write.

When I was in Rome, my landlady thought I was demented. She told Frank [Merlo], "Oh, Mr. Williams has lost his mind! He stalks about the room talking out loud!"

Frank said, "Oh, he's just writing." She didn't understand *that*.

REWRITING

In writing a play, I can get started on the wrong tangent, go off somewhere and then have to make great deletions and begin over, not *all* the way over, but just back to where I went off on that particular tangent. This is particularly true of the surrealist play that I'm currently writing. I'm dedicating it to the memory of Joe Orton. *The Everlasting Ticket*, it's called. It's about the poet laureate of Three Mile Island. I'm in the third revision of *Ticket* at the moment.

I do an enormous amount of rewriting. And when I finally let a play go, when I know it's complete and as it should be, is when I see a production of it that satisfies me. Of course, even when *I'm* satisfied with a production, the critics are not, usually. In New York, especially. The critics feel I'm basically anarchistic, and dangerous as a writer.

AUDIENCE

I don't have an audience in mind when I write. I'm writing mainly for myself. After a long devotion to playwriting I have a good inner ear. I know pretty well how a thing is going to sound on the stage, and how it will play. I write to satisfy this inner ear and its perceptions. That's the audience I write for.

DIRECTORS

Sometimes I write for someone specifically in mind. You know, I always used to write for [Elia] Kazan, although he no longer works as a director. What made him a great director was that he had an infinite understanding of people on an incredible level.

At one point Kazan and José Quintero were rather equal in talent. That was when Quintero began at the Circle in the Square downtown and did things like *Summer and Smoke* and

A Long Day's Journey Into Night. Those early things. Then he took heavily to drink.

He was living at a very fashionable address, the penthouse apartment at One Fifth Avenue. I remember walking with Quintero out on the terrace. I said to him, "Why are you killing yourself like this with liquor? Because you are, you know. You're drinking much too heavily." He always liked me very much. He was an extremely kind and sweet person. He said, "I know. I know. It's just that all of a sudden I got all this attention, and it made me self-conscious. It scared me. I didn't know how my work was *done.* I simply worked through intuition. Then suddenly it seemed to me as if secrets of mine were being exposed." And so he drank excessively, and now he can't drink at all.

During *The Seven Descents of Myrtle,* as they called it, although it was actually *The Kingdom of Earth,* Quintero was drinking so heavily that Estelle Parsons said she couldn't take direction from him. David Merrick was producing, and he came to town. He said, "I have to fire this man. He's destroying the play." And I said, "Mr. Merrick, if you fire poor José I'm going to withdraw the play." So he let it come in.

You know, in those days David Merrick was a lovely man. He's been around the bend some since, but he was so nice in those days. We both went to Washington University. We were in the same drama class, I believe. In the sixties he used to come to my apartment at the Mayfair when I wouldn't go out ever. He came over there to tell me he wanted to do *Kingdom of Earth.* And I just slurred something in reply. That's how I talked in those days. He said, "It's a very funny play!" And I went *grrrowwww* . . . I didn't give a shit whether he put it on or not, or whether I lived through the night.

TITLES

Sometimes I'll come up with a title that doesn't sound good in itself, but it's the only title that really fits the meaning of the play. Like *A House Not Meant to Stand* isn't a beautiful title. But the house it refers to in the play is in a terrible state of disrepair, virtually leaking rain water everywhere. That house, and therefore the title, is a metaphor for society in our times. And, of course, the critics don't like that sort of thing, nor do they dare to openly approve of it. They know who butters their bread.

Some titles come from dialogue as I write a play, or from the setting itself. Some come from poetry I've read. When I need a title I'll usually reread the poetry of Hart Crane. I take a copy of Crane's work with me when I travel. A phrase will catch my eye and seem right for what I'm writing. But there's no system to it. Sometimes a line from the play will serve as its title. I often change titles a number of times until I find one that seems right.

There is a Catholic church in Key West named "Mary, Star of the Sea." That would make a lovely title for a play.

LINE CHANGES

Performers can be enormously valuable in suggesting line changes in a play, I mean if they're intelligent performers. For instance, Geraldine Page. She's very intelligent, and she's a genius at acting. Being a genius at acting and being intelligent aren't always the same thing. She'd suggest line changes. She'd say, "I find this line difficult to read." I think most of her suggestions were good, although she's not a writer. So I'd make the changes to satisfy her. I often do that with actors, if they're intelligent and care about the play.

MARLON BRANDO

Brando came up to the Cape when I was there. There was no point in discovering him, it was so obvious. I never saw such raw talent in an individual, except for Laurette Taylor, whose talent was hardly raw. Then, before he was famous, Brando was a gentle, lovely guy, a man of extraordinary beauty when I first met him. He was very natural and helpful. He repaired the plumbing that had gone on the whack, and he repaired the lights that had gone off. And then he just sat calmly down and began to read. After five minutes, Margo Jones, who was staying with us, said, "Oh, this is the greatest reading I've ever heard, even in *Texas!*" And that's how he was cast in *Streetcar.*

WARREN BEATTY

I didn't know of Warren's work, and I thought the role in *The Roman Spring of Mrs. Stone* should be played by a Latin type, since the role's a Roman gigolo. I happened to be in Puerto Rico with Marion Vicarro, you know, the banana queen? She and I were gambling. She was playing blackjack, and I was playing roulette. All of a sudden a waiter came up to me with a little glass of milk, on a silver platter, and said, "A gentleman has sent this to you." I said, "I don't appreciate this kind of sarcasm!" So I went on playing roulette.

After I'd lost the amount of money I allow myself to lose, I started to leave. And there standing grinning at the door was Warren Beatty.

"Tennessee, I've come to read for you," he said. He was very young then, a really handsome boy.

I said, "But why, Warren? You're not the type to play a Roman gigolo."

And he said, "I'm going to read with an accent, and without it. I've come all the way from Hollywood to read for you."

"Well, that's lovely of you." And Marion and I went to his room, and he read fabulously. With an accent, and without.

Warren has no embarrassment about anything. Whenever he sees me he always embraces me. What an affectionate, warm, lovely man. I've found actors to be lovely people, although there are a few of them who have been otherwise.

AUDREY WOOD

Ever since my split with Audrey Wood [his longtime agent] there's been a holding pattern. I think she's the dominant figure in this. I think she has stock in the concern, ICM, and she won't allow anything to happen until I'm dead, baby.

Why did I break with her? I didn't. Just the usual thing happened. An opening night. My nerves always go like spitfire then. We had a very good first preview [of *A Two Character Play*]. The second preview we had a bunch of old, sour dames. They didn't get anything, and they hated it. It enraged me. I always lose my mind slightly when I get angry. Audrey was used to this. It happened time and time again. It shouldn't have surprised her at all. And I just turned to her after the performance and said, "You must have been pleased by this audience," because she hadn't been pleased by the enthusiastic, younger audience the night before. She got angry, and left town immediately, with the greatest amount of publicity. And I realized that she had neglected me so totally during my seven years of terrible depression that any kind of professional relationship with her was no longer tenable.

I don't hold grudges. So when I encountered her some time later in the Algonquin Hotel, I stretched out my hand to touch hers. There was no way of avoiding her. She hissed like a snake! and drew back her hands as if I were a leper. Well, since then I know this woman hates me! She'd lost interest in me. I don't think you should lose interest in a person who is in deep depression. That's when your interest and concern should be most, if you're a true friend.

And I think I had a great deal to do with making her career. She'd only sold *Room Service* to the Marx Brothers before I came along and got her Bill Inge and Carson McCullers and . . . this sounds bitter, and I hold no animosity toward people. I hope I don't.

BEST FRIENDS

Carson McCullers and Jane Bowles were my best friends as writers. I think if poor Carson had not suffered this very early stroke when she'd barely turned thirty, she would have been the greatest American writer. She had recurrent illnesses, of course, each diminishing her power. It was a tragic thing to watch. It went on for ten years. I met her in Nantucket. I'd written her a fan letter about *Member of the Wedding*, I thought it was so lovely. I knew cousins of hers. And at my invitation, she came to the island to be my guest. Such an enchanting person! This was the last year before she had a stroke, the year Carson lived at 31 Pine Street in Nantucket with Pancho and me.

My other great writer friend, Jane Bowles, I first met in Acapulco in the summer of 1940, after I'd broken up with Kip. I took a trip to Mexico on one of these share-the-expense plan tours. I went down with a Mexican boy who'd married an American hooker, you know? He met her at the World's Fair. The poor girl was terrified. She was a sweet girl, but she was a hooker and he didn't know it. And she'd come to my room at night and tell me they were having terrible problems sexually. I think he was gay, you know, because all the *other* men in the car were. That's a pretty good indication! She said she wasn't getting any sex, and she thought I'd provide her with some.

I said, "I'm afraid, honey, it's not quite what I do anymore because, frankly, I'm homosexual."

"Oh, that's all right," she said, "I know female hygiene is a lot more complicated!" God, I thought that was a funny answer!

Apparently, their marriage worked out somehow. I left some of my gear in the trunk of the car, and several years later, after I'd become known, after *The Glass Menagerie,* she shipped it all back to me with a very lovely note.

It was that summer in Mexico when I met Jane Bowles. I knew she was there with Paul. Poor Paul was always sick. He couldn't eat anything in Mexico. But there's very little in Mexico you *can* eat, at least not in those days. They were such a charmingly odd couple, I loved them both. Jane produced such a small body of work, but it was tremendous work. And Paul's work? I guess it's about as good as anything is now.

FRANK MERLO

I met Frankie by accident at the Atlantic House in Province-town one summer, the summer of 1947 when I was finishing *Streetcar.* I was in the Atlantic House, and Pancho was there, Margo Jones, and Joanna Albers. We were all living in a cottage. Stella Brooks was singing at the Atlantic House, and I'd gone out on the porch at the Atlantic House to breathe the fresh air and the lovely sea mist coming in. And Frankie came out behind me, and leaned against the balcony, and I observed that beautifully sculptured body in Levis, you know? I was rather bold, as I am at certain moments. And I just said, "Would you like to take a drive?" He grinned, and said yes. He'd come there with John Latouche, you know, the songwriter.

So we drove out to the beach and made love. It was ecstatic, even though it was in the sand.

I didn't see him again until accidentally I ran into him in a delicatessen on Third Avenue. I was living in an apartment designed by Tony Smith on East 58th Street. Frankie was with a young war buddy of his. And I said, "Why, Frank!" And he said, "Hi, Tenn." I said, "Why haven't you called me?" And he replied, "I read about your great success, and I didn't want to seem like I was trying to hop on the bandwagon."

He and his buddy came home with me to this lovely apartment. And Frankie just stayed on. He was so close to life! I was never that close, you know. He gave me the connection to day-to-day and night-to-night living. To reality. He tied me down to earth. And I had that for fourteen years, until he died. And that was the happy period of my adult life.

TRAVEL

I'm restless. I like traveling. When Frank Merlo was living, he being Sicilian, we spent four or five, sometimes six months out of the year in Rome.

I was once asked why I travel so much, and I said, "Because it's harder to hit a moving target!"

THE COMPETITION

I don't compete with Eugene O'Neill or anyone else. My work is totally in its own category. It's more esoteric than anyone else's, except Joe Orton's. And I don't compete with Joe Orton. I love him too much.*

EUGENE O'NEILL

Now O'Neill is not as good a playwright as, for instance, Albee. I don't think he's even as good as Lanford Wilson. I could give you quite a list.

I liked O'Neill's writing. He had a great spirit, and a great sense of drama, yes. But most of all it was his spirit, his *passion*, that moved me. And when *The Iceman Cometh* opened to very bad notices, very mixed notices at best in New York, I wrote him a letter. I said, in reading your play, at first I found it too long, then I gradually realized that its length, and the ponderosity of it, are what gave it a lot of its power. I was deeply moved by it, finally.

He wrote me a very nice reply and said he was always deeply

---

*Among his plays are *What the Butler Saw, Entertaining Mr. Sloane, Loot,* and *Funeral Games.* In 1967 Joe Orton was murdered in his sleep by his longtime lover Kenneth Halliwell. Later that night Halliwell committed suicide. Joe Orton was thirty-five at the time of his death.

depressed after an opening and that he appreciated my letter particularly. But that letter has disappeared like most of my letters.

LIQUOR

O'Neill had a terrible problem with alcohol. Most writers do. American writers nearly all have problems with alcohol because there's a great deal of tension involved in writing, you know that. And it's all right up to a certain age, and then you begin to need a little nervous support that you get from drinking. Now my drinking has to be moderate. Just look at the liver spots I've got on me!

OPENING NIGHTS

On opening nights in the old days, when I really could drink —I can't drink heavily now because of this pancreatitis I developed from over-drinking—but when I *could* drink, on opening nights I'd either have a flask on me and keep myself drunk and stand at attention in the theater, or else I'd dart out to the nearest bar and sit there until nearly before the curtain came down, and then I'd head back into the theater.

Now I take openings much more calmly. If they're giving a good performance, and they usually do on opening night, I just sit and enjoy it. After the curtain, I take a red-eye flight out of town. I have a car waiting for me with the luggage in it, and scoot out to LaGuardia or Kennedy and take the red-eye to Key West.

KEY WEST

It's delightful. When I first went there in 1941 it was still more delightful than it is now. I have one-quarter of a city block there now, you know. A swimming pool. My studio with a skylight. I have a little guest house in the form of a ship's cabin, with a double-decker bunk in it. And I have my gazebo, the Jane Bowles Summer House. Everything I need for a life. It's a charming, comfortable place.

HABITS OF WORK

In Key West I get up just before daybreak, as a rule. I like being completely alone in the house in the kitchen when I have my coffee and ruminate on what I'm going to work on. I usually have two or three pieces of work going at the same time, and then I decide which to work on that day.

I go to my studio. I usually have some wine there. And then I carefully go over what I wrote the day before. You see, baby, after a glass or two of wine I'm inclined to extravagance. I'm inclined to excesses because I drink while I'm writing, so I'll blue pencil a lot the next day. Then I sit down, and I begin to write.

My work is *emotionally* autobiographical. It has no relationship to the actual events of my life, but it reflects the emotional currents of my life. I try to work every day, because you have no refuge but writing. When you're going through a period of unhappiness, a broken love affair, the death of someone you love, or some other disorder in your life, then you have no refuge but writing. However, when depression comes on of a near-clinical nature, then you're paralyzed even at work. Immediately after the death of Frank Merlo, I was paralyzed, unable to write, and it wasn't until I began taking the speed shots that I came out of it. Then I was able to work like a demon. Could you live without writing, baby? I couldn't.

Because it's so important, if my work is interrupted I'm like a raging tiger. It angers me so. You see, I have to reach a high emotional pitch in order to work if the scene is dramatic.

I've heard that Norman Mailer has said that a playwright only writes in short bursts of inspiration while a novelist has to write six or seven hours a day. Bull! Now Mr. Mailer is more involved in the novel form, and I'm more involved in the play form. In the play form I work steadily and hard. If a play grips me I'll continue to work on it until I reach a point where I can no longer decide what to do with it. Then I'll discontinue work on it.

DRUGS

There was a very lovely young guy at New Directions named Robert MacGregor, who's dead now. He'd been a patient of Dr. Max Jacobson. He only took little pills that Jacobson gave him. I was in a state of such profound depression that he thought anything was worth trying, so he took me to Jacobson. It was through this Robert MacGregor that I had those three years of Jacobson shots that he mailed to me in the various parts of the country.

I did find Max Jacobson's shots marvelously stimulating to me as a writer. And during those last three years of the sixties, before my collapse, I did some of my best writing. People don't know it yet, but I did.

My collapse was related to the fact that I continued to drink while taking the shots. I was not supposed to. I had a bad heart. Dr. Max Jacobson never listened to my heart. Never took my pulse. Never took my blood pressure. He would just look at me. He was really sort of an alchemist. He would look at me for a long time. He had all these little vials in front of him. He'd take a drop from one, and a drop from another, and then look at me again, and take another drop or two. . . . Of course, the primary element was speed. And after I had a shot, I'd get into a taxi and my heart would begin to pound, and I'd immediately have to have a drink or I wouldn't be able to get home. I'd have died in the cab otherwise.

ON BEING SINGLE

I think it made it possible for me to practice my profession as a writer. You know what happened to poor Norman Mailer. One wife after another, and all that alimony. I've been spared all that. I give people money, yes. But I couldn't have afforded alimony, not to all those wives. I would've had to behead them! Being single made it possible for me to work.

HOMOSEXUALITY

I never found it necessary to deal with it in my work. It was never a preoccupation of mine, except in my intimate, private life. In my work, I've had a great affinity with the female psyche. Her personality, her emotions, what she suffers and feels. People who say I create transvestite women are full of shit. Frankly. Just vicious shit. Personally, I like women more than men. They respond to me more than men do, and they always have. The people who have loved me, the ratio of women to men is about five to one, I would say.

I know there's a right-wing backlash against homosexuals. But at the age of seventy I no longer consider it a matter of primary concern. Not that I want anything bad to happen to other homosexuals. God knows, enough has.

I always thought homosexual writers were in the minority of writers. Nobody's yet made a correct census of the actual number of homosexuals in the population of America. And they never will be able to because there are still too many closets, some of them rather securely locked. And it's also still dangerous to be openly homosexual.

CRUISING

I enjoyed cruising, more for Donald Windham's company, than for the pickups that were made. After all, pickups are just pickups. But Windham was a delightful friend to be with. I always realized that he had a streak of bitchery in him. And that's why my letters to him had a great deal of malicious humor in them. I knew he liked that. And since I was writing to a person who enjoyed that sort of thing I tried to amuse him with those things. Of course, I didn't know he was *collecting* my letters! And I didn't know I was signing away the copyright. I'm happy the letters were published because they're beautiful, I think. I'm very unhappy that he may have shut down *London Magazine* with that lawsuit.*

There used to be a place in Times Square called the Crossroads Tavern, right near a place called Diamond Jim Brady's. The place was closing down, and on this occasion these big, drunk sailors came and picked us up. We didn't pick *them* up. I wasn't attracted to them. I didn't want to, and I felt really uneasy about the situation. But Windham was always attracted to rough sailor types.

As it happened, Windham was staying at the Claridge Hotel, which doesn't exist now, in the Times Square area. He had been living with a painter, Paul Cadmus. He was occupying a room with Paul Cadmus, and it was through Paul Cadmus that he met Sandy Campbell.** It had been inconvenient for Cadmus to have Donald Windham at his place one night,

---

*When Donald Windham published *Tennessee Williams' Letters to Donald Windham: 1940–1965* (Holt, Rinehart and Winston, New York, 1977), Dotson Rader wrote an essay for *London Magazine* reviewing the letters. The piece was critical of Windham. Mr. Windham responded with a lawsuit.

**Sandy Campbell is Windham's friend and companion.

and so he'd gotten him a room at the Claridge. And Donald had taken the two sailors and me into Claridge's.

I got more and more suspicious because in the lobby the sailors said, "We'll go up the elevator, and you wait ten minutes, and we'll meet you in the corridor. . . ." Or something like that. It seemed suspicious, but I was a little high, and so was Donald.

We got up to the room, and it was really a bestial occurrence. I hated every minute of it. Finally, after they ripped the phones out of the wall, they stood me against a wall with a switchblade knife while they beat Windham, knocking a tooth out, blackening both his eyes, beating him almost to death. I kept saying, "Oh, don't do that, don't hit him anymore! He's *tubercular!*"

Then they said, "Now it's your turn!" So they stood poor, bloody Windham against the wall while they beat me nearly to death. I had a concussion from the beating. Next thing I knew I was at the emergency Red Cross station at the YMCA where I lived.

KIP

Kip was very honest, and I loved him and I think he loved me. He was a draft-dodger from Canada. He had a passion to be a dancer, and he knew he couldn't if he went into the war. It'd be too late, he felt, when it was over, for him to study dancing. You see, he was a boy of twenty-one or twenty-two when the war happened.

I've written a play called *Something Cloudy, Something Clear* about Kip. The setting is very important in this play. It involves a bleached, unfurnished beach shack in which the writer, who represents me, but is called August, is working on a portable typewriter supported by an old crate. He sleeps on a mattress on the floor. Alongside that set is the floor of another beach house shack that's been blown away in a hurricane. This floor, however, forms a platform on which Kip used to dance, practicing dancing to my Victrola. The subtitle of the play is *The Silver Victrola.*

I prefer the title *Something Cloudy, Something Clear* because it refers to my eyes. My left eye was cloudy then because it was developing a cataract. But my right eye was clear. It was like the two sides of my nature. The side that was obsessively homosexual, compulsively interested in sexuality. And the side that in those days was gentle and understanding and contemplative. So it's a pertinent title.

Now this play is written from the vantage point of 1979, about a boy I loved and who is now dead. The author (August) knows it's 1979. He knows Kip is dead, and that the girl whom Kip dances with is dead. I've invented the girl. Occasionally during the play the author onstage will make references that puzzle the boy, Kip, and the girl. But the author is the only one who realizes that it's really forty years later, and the boy and girl are dead, and he survives, still he survives. It happened in the summer of 1940, and it's a very lyrical play, probably the most lyrical play I've done in a very long while.

Kip died at the age of twenty-six. It was just after I completed my professionally abortive connection with MGM. The phone rang one day and an hysterical lady said, "Kip has ten days to live." A year before I had been told that Kip had been successfully operated on for a benign brain tumor.

He was at the Polyclinic Hospital near Times Square. You know how love bursts back into your heart when you hear of the loved one's dying.

As I entered Kip's room he was being spoon-fed by a nurse: a dessert of sugary apricots. He had never looked more beautiful. Kip's mind seemed as clear as his Slavic blue eyes.

We spoke a while. Then I rose and reached for his hand and he couldn't find mine, I had to find his.

After Kip died his brother sent me, from Canada, snapshots of Kip posing for a sculptor and they remained in my wallet some twenty years. They disappeared mysteriously in the sixties. Well, Kip lives on in my leftover heart.

HEMINGWAY AND FITZGERALD

Hemingway had a remarkable interest in and understanding of homosexuality, for a man who wasn't a homosexual. I think both Hemingway and Fitzgerald had elements of homosexuality in them. I make quite a bit of that in my rewrite of *Clothes for a Summer Hotel.*

Have you ever read "A Simple Inquiry" by Hemingway? Well, it's about an Italian officer in the Alps during the First World War. And he's of course deprived of female companionship. He has an orderly, a very attractive young orderly. He desires the orderly. And he asks the boy, rather bluntly, "Are you interested in girls?" The boy panics for a moment, and says, "Oh, yes, I'm engaged to be married." And the boy goes out of the room, and the Italian officer says, "I wonder if that little sonofabitch was lying?"

The final line in Hemingway's *Islands in the Stream* is one man saying I love you to another. It didn't mean they'd had homosexual relations, although Gertrude Stein intimated that Hemingway had. But does it matter? I don't think it matters.

You know what he said about Fitzgerald? Hemingway said that "Fitzgerald was pretty. He had a mouth that troubled you when you first met him, and troubled you more later."

Fitzgerald played the female lead in the Princeton Triangle Club, and there's a picture of him as a woman that's more feminine than any woman could look. Fitzgerald never had an affair with anybody but his wife. There was Sheila Graham at the end, but did he sleep with her? I doubt it. Anyway, I don't think the sexuality of writers is all that interesting. It has no effect, I can tell you that. In very few instances does it have any effect on their ability to portray either sex. I am able to

write of men as well as women, and I always project myself
through whichever sex I'm writing about.

FIDEL CASTRO

I met Castro only once, and that was through Hemingway.
The time I met Hemingway was the time I met Castro. I was
in Havana during the first year of Castro's regime. Castro
would have remained a friend of the United States except for
that bastard John Foster Dulles, who had this phobia about
anything revolutionary. He apparently thought that Mr.
Batista—a sadist who tortured students to death—was great
fun.

I met Hemingway through Kenneth Tynan at the restaurant
Floridita in Havana. Hemingway and I had a very pleasant
meeting. He gave us both a letter of introduction to Castro.
Hemingway said this was a good revolution. And if Mr. Dulles
hadn't alienated Castro, it might have been.

Castro was a gentleman. An educated man. He introduced
me to all the Cuban cabinet. We'd been waiting three hours
on the steps for this emergency cabinet meeting to end. When
he introduced us, he turned to me and said, "Oh, that *cat!*"
and winked. He meant *Cat on a Hot Tin Roof*, of course. I
found that very engaging.

JOHN F. KENNEDY

I met President Kennedy through Gore Vidal, at the family
estate in Palm Beach before he was president. And then I met
him at the White House, where he gave a great dinner party
for André Malraux and invited all the literary people, the
theater people.

John Kennedy was a great gentleman, a really good, gentle
man. On the way to see him we were caught in terrible traffic.
Gore Vidal isn't a particularly good driver, though he's a good

writer at times. So we were an hour late for lunch with Mr. Kennedy, and he acted as if we were on time. His manners were so impeccable, and Jackie was a tremendous charmer, and still is, I presume, although I haven't seen her in a long time.

THE CARTER WHITE HOUSE

The first time I went there was some occasion when the film industry was being honored. At that time the Carters had not yet adjusted themselves to entertaining. He's rather abstemious, Mr. Carter, which is the one major fault I found with him. We were only allowed to have one very small glass of what was purported to be a California chablis. I downed my glass in one swallow, and then tried to figure out how to get some more. All there was was wine. No hard liquor. Nothing. But you could only have one glass. So I got ahold of Sam Spiegel, who is a very portly gentleman, and I said, "Sam, will you stand in front of the table and slip me another glass of wine surreptitiously?" So I hid behind Sam and he snuck me several small glasses, which helped to get me through the evening.

Later, when I went to the White House, the Carters had begun serving champagne. But they never did get around to hard liquor.

I think Jimmy Carter was a great humanitarian, and his second term might have been wonderful compared to what we got. I thought his human rights concern was right, and I am sorry that our government has abandoned it.

I don't think the big money people wanted Mr. Carter back in. He wasn't pliable enough.

JANE WYMAN

Jane Wyman was in the movie of *The Glass Menagerie.* She married Ronald Reagan. The no-nose girl married the no-brain man!

HOLLYWOOD

Most of my films were subjected to excessive censorship. Which is one of the reasons why I might be interested in seeing *Streetcar* done again as a film by Sidney Lumet, now that Kazan has stopped directing. But I'd have to have a great Stanley, and the only person they've mentioned so far is Sylvester Stallone, and so I'm not paying much attention to this project of remaking *Streetcar* until there's a suitable Stanley, and a really great actress to play Blanche.

In the 1940s I had a glorious time in Hollywood because I was fired almost at once from the project I was working on and they had to continue to pay me. That was in my contract. For six months they had to pay me $250 a week. This was in 1943, when $250 was equivalent to about $1000 now, I would guess. They had to pay me whether I had an assignment or not.

First they put me on *Marriage Is a Private Affair* for Lana Turner. Well, they expressed great delight with my dialogue, and I think it was good. But they said, "You give Miss Turner too many multi-syllable words!" So I said, "Well, some words *do* contain more than one syllable!" And Pandro Berman, who loved me very much—Lana Turner just happened to be his girlfriend at the time—he said to me, "Tennessee, Lana can tackle two syllables, but I'm afraid if you go into three you're taxing her vocabulary!"

Then they asked me if I'd like to write a screenplay for a child star, one named Margaret O'Brien. I said, "I'd sooner shoot myself!" By that time I knew I'd get the $250 regardless.

So I lived out in Santa Monica and had a ball until the money ran out.

ELIZABETH TAYLOR

Monty Clift was one of the great tragedies among actors, even more than Marilyn Monroe, I believe. One of the loveliest things about Elizabeth Taylor was her exceptional kindness to him. Many women were very kind to him. Katherine Hepburn. But Elizabeth particularly. She's a very dear person. She's the opposite of her public image. She's not a bitch, even though her life has been a very hell. Thirty-one operations, I believe. Pain and pain. She's so delicate—fragile, really.

I saw her in Fort Lauderdale at the opening of Lillian Hellman's *The Little Foxes,* and she held that stage as if she'd always been a stage actress. But she has a little deficiency of humor. I knew she would catch it, I hoped she would. And she opened so well in Washington that I think she must have caught the humor.

I know you think Lillian Hellman's a somewhat limited playwright. But *Hellman* doesn't think so, does she? No! After the opening, when I saw Liz Taylor could act on stage, there was a huge party, with great imported champagne, the works! The director was seated next to me at my table. He said he had to get up and call Hellman.

I said, "Well, tell her I want a piece of her royalties!"

So he gave her the message, and came back to the table grinning. "Hellman said to tell you the check is in the mail!"

She's a funny woman, and a skillful playwright. Several of her plays are enormously skillful. . . . I've heard she has emphysema. Who *isn't* sick! They're all sick and dying!

WILLIAM INGE

Bill Inge was a tragic person. *Tragic.* The critics treated him very cruelly. They're brutal. I always thought he wrote two wonderful plays. *Come Back, Little Sheba* was a brilliant play.

That's when I introduced him to Audrey Wood. And then he wrote a play in which a kid kills his mother, an enormously brilliant work. *Natural Affection*, or something like that.

I met him in St. Louis. I came back there during the run of *Menagerie* in Chicago, and he interviewed me for a paper called the St. Louis *Star-Times*. He was the drama and music critic for it. He entertained me quite a bit the week I was there. We became friends.

At the end of his life, Barbara Baxley, with whom he attempted to have a heterosexual affair, and who was very, very fond of him, called me and said that Inge was in a desperate situation in California. "He's sleeping with lots of barbiturates under his mattress. He only gets up to drink, and then he goes back to bed."

I said, "He's on a suicide course."

She said, "I know it. He commits himself voluntarily, and then lets himself out the next day."

"Who's he with?"

"His sister," she said. "I want you to call his sister and tell her that she's got to commit him."

So after consulting Maureen Stapleton, who said I should, I did call his sister and she said, "Yes, that's just how it is." She was talking in a whisper. I said, "I can hardly hear you. Why are you whispering like that?"

She answered, "Because I never know whether he's up or down."

I said, "Just listen then. Get him into a hospital. Don't have him commit himself. *You* commit him. Otherwise he's going to kill himself."

Well, a month later in Rome I read a headline in the Rome *Daily American* that Bill Inge was dead. He had asphyxiated himself by running the motor on his car in a closed garage.

Fitzgerald, Hemingway, Hart Crane, Inge . . . oh, the debris! The *wreckage!* Toward the end of an American writer's life it's just dreadful. Hemingway's last years were a nightmare. He tried to walk into the propeller of a plane. Fitzgerald's end was not much better, although it was less dramatic. . . . Once they become known, everybody wants a piece of them.

CHRISTOPHER ISHERWOOD

I met him in the forties in California. At the time he was into Vedanta, an Eastern religious thing. He was living in a monastery. They had periods of silence and meditation, you know. The night I met him, through a letter from Lincoln Kirstein, I arrived during one of these silent periods. The monk who opened the door handed me a pencil and paper to write what my business was and who I'd come to see. I wrote "Christopher Isherwood," and they regarded me with considerable suspicion from that point on.

In this big room in the monastery, everyone was sitting in . . . what do they call it? The lotus position? Including Christopher. All strictly observing the vow of silence. I didn't dig the scene.

I suddenly made some reference out loud about the Krishna. I didn't know who the hell he was, I was only trying to break the silence. Christopher got up, and wrote on a piece of paper, "I'll call you tomorrow." He was very polite, and he took me to the door.

He's a superb writer, and I haven't a clue why he went through this period in a monastery. I think it was a period of unhappiness in his life. I think his love affair with Bill Caskie was breaking up, or had broken up, and he had not yet found Don Bachardy. He was intensely lonely. So he went into this monastery that had this vow of silence and poverty.

I found Chris terribly attractive, not so much in a sexual way, but as a person. Charismatic. Brilliant. And one of the greatest gentlemen I've known. So, being attracted to him, I declared myself.

Then I found out that another one of the vows they took in

this place was sexual abstinence! Christopher said to me, "Tennessee, it's perfectly all right if I submit *passively* to oral intercourse, but I cannot perform it. I'd be breaking the vow!" I howled with laughter, and so did he. Then we cemented our friendship.

YEVTUSHENKO

What's happened to him? Is he still in favor with the Soviets?

When he was last in the States he asked me to have lunch with him. He ordered bottles of Château Lafite Rothschild. And the bill was so tremendous it occupied three pages! I was stuck with it, of course. I told him he was a fucking capitalist pig!

He was accompanied by this very fat gourmand of a translator who didn't translate anything. Yevtushenko spoke perfect English and he understood English perfectly. And the alleged translator didn't understand a damn thing except how to eat and drink like a rich capitalist!

I've heard a lot of people speak against Yevtushenko. I don't know how far he can be trusted, but he's charming in his way. If you can afford it.

TRUMAN CAPOTE

I met Truman in 1948, I guess. He'd just published *Other Voices, Other Rooms.* I thought he was quite cute, slim, with this marvelously witty, slightly malicious tongue. I got mad at him after awhile. He said something cruel about Frankie. Frank Merlo, Jack Dunphy, who was Truman's friend, and I, we were all traveling in my Buick Roadmaster convertible. We'd gotten as far as Naples. At a waterfront restaurant in Naples he said something quite cruel, and I said I'm not going on to Ischia with this man. After a couple of days, Frankie talked me into it. And we went anyway,

I never disliked Truman after that, I just realize that he has this impulse to be catty at times. I think it's because he's a little guy who's been picked on a lot, especially when he was growing up. You know, Truman makes the mistake of claiming he was born in New Orleans, and giving interviews, even points out the house he was born in. Everyone knows he was born in Huntsville, Alabama. Everyone in Huntsville claims him. They all know it, it's registered.

Now why does he do such things? I think it's because the poor little man likes mystery, likes to confuse people about himself. Well, Truman's a mythologist, baby, you know that. That's a polite way of saying he does fabricate. I love him too much to say he's a liar. That's part of his profession.

MY FUNNIEST ADVENTURE

I was alone in Miami. Frank [Merlo] hadn't arrived yet from New York. I was staying in Miami until he got there and took me to Key West.

It was night, and I was lonely. I walked out onto Biscayne Boulevard. There's a park along there. This young vagrant was lolling on a bench. I think he was mentally retarded, poor child. I struck up a conversation with him. He seemed not too bright, but personable. I said I was alone, would he like to accompany me to my hotel? He said he would. Well, once he got under a street light I saw he'd never be able to go through a hotel lobby because his clothes were so dilapidated. So I suggested that we go out by the pool where I had a cabana.

We got out there, and he suddenly jerked my wallet out of my pocket. I had only seven dollars in it, though. Then he tried to get my wristwatch off. It had a very simple clasp upon it, but he couldn't manage to get it unclasped. Finally he gave up on that. I wasn't frightened at all, for some reason. I was wearing a ring with three diamonds and he couldn't get that off either. It was a tight fit. So I said, "Now this is a very silly situation. I've got hundreds of dollars upstairs in my room. You sit down here and rest, and I'll be down in a little while with a large sum of money for you." I'd realized by this time that he was a moron.

Well, I went back to my room in the hotel, locked the door, and went to bed. And at half-hour intervals all night, the phone would ring and he'd say, "I'm still waiting!" I finally said, "Baby, go see a doctor. You really think I was coming back down with a hundred dollars for you?" I liked the poor kid by that time.

It's the funniest adventure I ever had. "I'm still waiting!" He might still be.

HUMOR

You know, with advancing age I find humor more and more interesting. Black humor, especially. My present play, the one I'm working on [*The Everlasting Ticket*], I call a Gothic comedy. My humor is Gothic in theater. I make some serious, even tragic observations about society, but I make them through the medium of comedy.

THE RICH

My feeling about the rich is not anger, really, but a feeling that they are emotionally restricted. They live in a very narrow, artificial world, like the world of Gloria Vanderbilt, who can be very unpleasant, you know. Or the Oscar de la Rentas, who are the most shocking of all. They are the Madame du Barrys of our time! You mention Oscar de la Renta to me and I turn purple with rage. They are basically very common people, you know. I know where he's from and how he started, and I know all about where she's from, too. Now they think they're the best thing since the invention of the wheel. I find them an outrageous symptom of our society, the shallowness and superficiality, the lack and fear of any depth that characterizes this age, this decade. It appalls me.

The sixties were a decade of great vitality. The civil rights movement, the movement against war and imperialism. When I said to Gore Vidal, "I slept through the sixties," I was making a bad joke. I was intensely aware of what was going on. Even in the violent ward I read the newspapers avidly. Then we had brave young people fighting against privilege and injustice. Now we have the de la Rentas.

TODAY'S COLLEGE KIDS

They aren't noticeable now. They seem to be totally reactionary, like the rich. The ones I've met rarely seem different from their parents in attitudes and values.

In the sixties, or even the early seventies, the kids I met seemed to be in revolt against the mores and social ideas of their parents. It may just be an illusion of mine, but it seems today that the children are frightened of deviating from their parents' way of life and thought. The ME-ME-ME Generation. Selfishness. A complete lack of interest in what's happening in the world. No interest in what's going on in El Salvador, this military junta supported by our government that rushes its troops into villages, pulls the peasants out and slaughters them! American kids don't care. In Guatemala, four hundred people a day being slaughtered, although no one mentions it much. Honduras. Don't they care, this generation? We know why Allende was assassinated, and how and why. All Latin America is in strife, and the ME-ME-ME Generation doesn't appear to care.

The sixties were intensely alive! We were really progressing toward a workable, just society. But then Nixon came along, and everything fell back into its old routine of plutocracy.

LECTURES

I don't give formal lectures, although they call them that. I just give formal readings. Once I went to the University of

Tennessee in Knoxville with a prepared lecture. When I got there I discovered I'd left the lecture at home. So I had to get up on stage and improvise, which infuriated the professors. They were outraged! Knoxville, like other academic places, is very reactionary.

THE STATE OF THE CULTURE

Literature has taken a back seat to the television, don't you think? It really has. We don't have a culture anymore that favors the creation of writers, or supports them very well. I mean, serious artists. On Broadway, what they want are cheap comedies and musicals and revivals. It's nearly impossible to get serious work even produced, and then it's lucky to have a run of a week. They knocked Albee's *Lolita* down horribly. I've never read such cruel reviews. But I felt it was a mistake for Albee to do adaptations. He's brilliant doing his own original work. But even so, I think there's a way of expressing one's critical displeasures with a play without being quite so hard, quite so cruel. The critics are literally killing writers.

REGRETS

Oh God, yes, baby! But I can't think about them now. So many things to regret. But there are, I believe, so very *few* things that one can change in one's life. There are very few acts of volition. I don't believe in individual guilt. I don't think people are responsible for what they do. We are products of circumstances that determine what we do. That's why I think capital punishment's an outrage. But then the population growth and the growth of crime have become so enormous there aren't enough prisons to put people in. Prisons. Killing. Yet I don't believe in individual guilt at all, and sometimes I wonder whether I even believe in collective guilt. And yet I do believe that the intelligent person, the moral individual, must avoid evil and cruelty and dishonesties. One can try to pursue a path of virtue. That remains to us, I hope.

THE NOBEL PRIZE

I'll tell you why I think I haven't gotten it.

I'd heard I'd been nominated for it several times in the fifties. But then suddenly a scandal happened. This lady, I call her the Crepe de Chine Gypsy, went to Stockholm. And she lured me to Stockholm by telling me she was living in a charming little hotel near the waterfront, and that I would have my own suite with a private entrance. And that I would have a fantastic time, if you know what I mean—I was at the height of my fame then—she used my name as an excuse to get all the people around that she'd wanted to meet but had no way of meeting. She later turned out to be a dominatrix! Well, she had all the press there. She was like a field marshal! "You over that way! You over there! You do not approach Mr. Williams until I give you the signal!" Barking out orders. Oh, it was just terrifying. The next morning the newspapers all came out saying Mr. Williams arrived in Stockholm preceded by a very powerful press agent! And my agent in Scandinavia, Lars Schmidt, who married Ingrid Bergman, said, "You know, you've been nominated for the Nobel Prize but now it's finished." The scandal was so awful, the press having been abused, and they associated me with this awful woman.

Well, after all, one doesn't *have* to get it. It'd be nice because it's a lot of money, isn't it? I could use that, if I could get it.

CURRENT WORK

I've been busy with the production of the new play, *A House Not Meant To Stand*. The production of a play is for me an event that eclipses everything else, even turning seventy. I love the Goodman Theater, and I'm going to work with them again. We're already making plans to move this play on to the main stage, and to do *Something Cloudy, Something Clear,* about the summer when I met Kip on the Cape, though I've added other characters besides Kip and me.

And I've got an important play, *In Masks Outrageous and Austere.* It's a line of Eleanor Wiley's, from a poem by her. It goes like this: "In masks outrageous and austere / the years go by in single file; / Yet none has merited my fear, / and none has quite escaped my smile."

It happens to fit the play, which has a great deal of poetry in it and yet at the same time the situation is bizarre as hell. It's about the richest woman on earth. Babe Foxworth is her name. She doesn't know where she is. She's been abducted to Canada, on the east coast. But they don't know where they are. A village has been constructed like a movie set to deceive them. Everything is done to confine and deceive them while her husband is being investigated. Babe is really an admirable person, besides her hypersexuality, though that can be admirable. I think it is! It's a torture to her because she's married to a gay husband who's brought along his boyfriends. I think it's an extremely funny play.

ADVICE TO YOUNG PLAYWRIGHTS

What shouldn't you do if you're a young playwright? *Don't bore the audience!* I mean, even if you have to resort to totally arbitrary killing on stage, or pointless gunfire, at least it'll catch their attention and keep them awake. Just keep the thing going any way you can.

THE MONEY PEOPLE

Do you know what the most difficult aspect of playwriting is? I'll tell you. *It's dealing with the money people.* The commercial end of it is the most appalling part. The demands for changes and rewrites don't bother me if they're made by the director, and I think they're intelligent demands. But when the money people get into the act, you're in trouble.

MY MOST DIFFICULT PLAY

I think *Clothes for a Summer Hotel* was the most difficult play to write, of all my plays. Because of the documentation I had to do. I had to spend four or five months reading everything there is about Fitzgerald and Zelda. There's a huge amount of material. Finally, when it was written I had to cut an hour out of the play on the road. José Quintero was in very fragile health, and after every opening, he had to flee. So I had to do it without any help or advice from anybody. To cut an hour out of it. And then I had to start rewriting it. The scene the critics objected to most violently was that between Hemingway and Fitzgerald. But that's an integral part of the play because each was a central figure in the life of the other. I thought the confrontation between them indispensable. Now I've rewritten the play again, and I've built up that scene, not so much in length of playing time, but in content, making it more pointed.

ZELDA FITZGERALD

Zelda's one great love affair was with this French aviator. It was her first infidelity to Scott, and probably her only one. It was aggressive because she was being liberated by infidelity from this very possessive love that Scott had for her. And for the first time she was experiencing erotic ecstasy. She'd never experienced that with Scott. She used to complain to poor Scott that he was sexually inadequate.

She frightened the aviator by the violence of her reactions. She went around the bend because of him. She tried to kill herself, swallowing the contents of a bottle of morphine or something. The aviator was frightened away.

Zelda was also terribly anti-Semitic, like most Southern women, and a touch of it goes into the play [*Clothes*]. I think I just couldn't leave it out and do a true portrait of her. I have her make a single anti-Semitic remark in the play, which is about Sheila Graham, whose real name is Lili Sheil.

In the theater you hardly dare use the word Jew, and it's really a detriment to a very fine people that they're so frightened of any criticism whatsoever, although after the Holocaust they certainly have reason to be frightened. I have no feelings of anti-Semitism, but those feelings do exist in other people, and it's difficult to present a picture of the world as it truly is without on occasion allowing a voice to those sentiments.

CHILDREN

I'm very happy I never had any children. There have been too many instances of extreme eccentricity and even lunacy in my family on all four sides for me to want to have children. I think it's fortunate I never did.

Rose, Dakin, and I are the last of two direct blood lines, the Dakin family and the Williams. And all three of us are childless.

HANDLING LONELINESS

It's not easy. I have a few close friends, though. And you can get by with a few. And as for sex? I don't feel I require it that much anymore. I miss having a companion very much. I'll never be without someone with me, although it'll just be someone who is fond of me and takes care of me, but it won't be a sexual thing anymore.

DEATH

Everyone's afraid of it, but I'm no more than most, I suppose. I'm beginning to reconcile myself to it. I'm *not* reconciled to dying before my work is finished, though. I have a very strong will. There were occasions in the last years or so when I might have gone out. But my will forces me to go on because I've got unfinished work.

DOTSON RADER
Fall 1981

4. Elizabeth Bishop

Elizabeth Bishop's father died eight months after her birth in April, 1911, and her mother spent long periods in mental institutions during Elizabeth's childhood. She was essentially juggled from relative to relative until her boarding-school years, a history which may explain the importance of travel to both her life and poetry. At Vassar College, from which she graduated in 1934, she met Marianne Moore, with whom she formed a life-long friendship. Though she majored in music composition and intended to become a composer, Bishop continued to write extensively; she published her first poems long before she earned her degree. Her first collection, *North & South,* which was published in 1946, won the Houghton Mifflin Poetry Award; the following year she was awarded a Guggenheim Fellowship, the first of two she was to be granted. In 1956 she won the Pulitzer Prize for her second volume, *Poems,* and in 1969 she won the National Book Award for *The Complete Poems,* a collection titled with characteristic irony. The recipient of many grants and fellowships, she became the first woman—in fact, the first American—to win the prestigious Books Abroad/Neustadt International Prize for Literature. *Geography III* was her last book before her sudden death in 1979.

Bishop's ties to South America were strong, and she translated much Brazilian literature, including *The Diary of "Helena Morley."* She served as consultant in poetry to the Library of Congress (1949–50) before accepting teaching posts at Harvard, New York University, and The Massachusetts Institute of Technology.

An indefatigable traveler, Elizabeth Bishop lived in New York and Key West, although from 1952 until 1971 she considered her home Rio de Janeiro.

A manuscript page from Elizabeth Bishop's "Sonnet," published in 1979.

Elizabeth Bishop

The interview took place at Lewis Wharf, Boston, on the afternoon of June 28, 1978, three days before Miss Bishop and two friends were to leave for North Haven, a Maine island in Penobscot Bay where she summered. Her living room, on the fourth floor of Lewis Wharf, had a spectacular view of Boston Harbor; when I arrived, she immediately took me out on the balcony to point out such Boston landmarks as Old North Church in the distance, mentioning that "Old Ironsides" was moored nearby.

Her living room was spacious and attractive, with wide-planked polished floors, a beamed ceiling, two old brick walls, and one wall of books. Besides some comfortable modern furniture, the room included a jacaranda rocker and other old pieces from Brazil, two paintings by Loren MacIver, a giant horse conch from Key West, and a Franklin stove with firewood in a donkey pannier, also from Brazil. The most conspicuous piece was a large carved figurehead of an unknown beast, open-mouthed, with horns and blue eyes, which hung on one wall below the ceiling.

Her study, a smaller room down the hall, was in a state of disorder. Literary magazines, books, and papers were piled everywhere. Photographs of Marianne Moore, Robert Lowell, and other friends hung on the walls; one of Dom Pedro, the last emperor of Brazil, she especially liked to show to her Brazilian visitors. "Most have no idea who he is," she said. "This is after he abdicated and shortly before he died—he looked very sad." Her desk was tucked in a far corner by the only window, also with a north view of the harbor.

At sixty-seven, Miss Bishop was easily and accurately described by the word "striking," her short, swept-back white hair setting off an unforgettably noble face. She was wearing a black tunic shirt, gold watch and earrings, gray slacks, and flat brown Japanese sandals which made her appear shorter than her actual height: five feet, four inches. Although she looked well and was in high spirits, she complained of having had a recent hay fever attack and declined to have her photograph taken with the wry comment, "Photographers, insurance salesmen, and funeral directors are the worst forms of life."

Seven or eight months later, after reading a profile I had written for The Vassar Quarterly (which had been based on this interview) and worrying that she sounded like "the soul of frivolity," she wrote me: "I once admired an interview with Fred Astaire in which he refused to discuss 'the dance,' his partners, or his 'career' and stuck determinedly to golf—so I hope that some readers will realize I do think about ART once in a while even if babbling along like a very shallow brook . . ."

Note: Though Miss Bishop did have the opportunity of correcting those portions of this interview incorporated in the Vassar Quarterly article, she never saw it in this form.

INTERVIEWER: Your living room seems to be a wonderful combination of the old and new. Is there a story behind any of the pieces, especially that figurehead? It's quite imposing.

BISHOP: I lived in an extremely modern house in Brazil. It was very beautiful and when I finally moved I brought back things I liked best. So it's just a kind of mixture. I really like modern things but while I was there I acquired so many other things I couldn't bear to give them up. This figurehead is from the São Francisco River. Some are more beautiful; this is a very ugly one.

INTERVIEWER: Is it supposed to ward off evil spirits?

BISHOP: Yes, I think so. They were used for about fifty years on one section, two or three hundred miles, of the river. It's nothing compared to the Amazon but it's the next biggest river in Brazil. This figurehead is primitive folk art. I think I even know who made it. There was a black man who carved twenty or thirty, and it's exactly his style. Some of them are made of much more beautiful wood. There's a famous one called "The Red Horse" made of jacaranda. It's beautiful, a great thing like this one, a horse with its mouth open, but for some reason they all just disappeared. I made a week-long trip on that river in 1967 and didn't see one. The riverboat, a sternwheeler, had been built in 1880—something for the Mississippi, and you can't believe how tiny it was. We splashed along slowly for days and days . . . a very funny trip.

INTERVIEWER: Did you spend so much of your life traveling because you were looking for a perfect place?

BISHOP: No, I don't think so. I really haven't traveled that much. It just happened that although I wasn't rich I had a very small income from my father, who died when I was eight months old, and it was enough when I got out of college to go places on. And I traveled extremely cheaply. I could get along in Brazil for some years but now I couldn't possibly live on it. But the biographical sketch in the first anthology I was in said, "Oh, she's been to Morocco, Spain, etc.," and this has been repeated for years even though I haven't been back to any of these places. But I never traveled the way students travel now. Compared to my students, who seem to go to Nepal every Easter vacation, I haven't been anywhere at all.

INTERVIEWER: Well, it always sounds as if you're very adventurous.

BISHOP: I want to do the Upper Amazon. Maybe I will. You start from Peru and go down—

INTERVIEWER: Do you write when you're actually traveling?

BISHOP: Yes, sometimes. It depends. I usually take notes but not always. And I keep a kind of diary. The two trips I've made that I liked best were the Amazon trip and one to the Galapagos Islands three or four years ago . . . I'd like very much to go back to Italy again because I haven't seen nearly enough of it. And Sicily. Venice is wonderful. Florence is rather strenuous, I think. I was last there in '64 with my Brazilian friend. We rented a car and did northern Italy for five or six weeks. We didn't go to Rome. I *must* go back. There are so many things I haven't seen yet. I like painting probably better than I like poetry. And I haven't been back to Paris for years. I don't like the prices!

INTERVIEWER: You mentioned earlier that you're leaving for North Haven in several days. Will this be a "working vacation"?

BISHOP: This summer I want to do a lot of work because I really haven't done anything for ages and there are a couple of things I'd like to finish before I die. Two or three poems and two long stories. Maybe three. I sometimes feel that I shouldn't keep going back to this place that I found just by chance through an ad in the Harvard *Crimson.* I should probably go to see some more art, cathedrals, and so on. But I'm so crazy about it that I keep going back. You can see the water, a great expanse of water and fields from the house. Islands are beautiful. Some of them come right up, granite, and then dark firs. North Haven isn't like that exactly, but it's very beautiful. The island is sparsely inhabited and a lot of the people who have homes there are fearfully rich. Probably if it weren't for these people the island would be deserted the way a great many Maine islands are, because the village is very tiny. But the inhabitants almost all work—they're lobstermen but they work as caretakers. . . . The electricity there is rather sketchy. Two summers ago it was one hour on, one hour off. There I was with *two* electric typewriters and I couldn't keep working. There was a cartoon in the grocery store—it's eighteen miles from the mainland—a man in a hardware store saying, "I want an extension cord eighteen miles long!" Last year they did plug into the mainland—they put in cables. But once in a while the power still goes off.

INTERVIEWER: So you compose on the typewriter?

BISHOP: I can write prose on a typewriter. Not poetry. Nobody can read my writing so I write letters on it. And I've finally trained myself so I can write prose on it and then correct a great deal. But for poetry I use a pen. About halfway through sometimes I'll type out a few lines to see how they look.

William Carlos Williams wrote entirely on the typewriter. Robert Lowell printed—he never learned to write. He printed everything.

INTERVIEWER: You've never been as prolific as many of your contemporaries. Do you start a lot of poems and finish very few?

BISHOP: Yes. Alas, yes. I begin lots of things and then I give up on them. The last few years I haven't written as much because of teaching. I'm hoping that now that I'm free and have a Guggenheim I'll do a lot more.

INTERVIEWER: How long did it take you to finish "The Moose"?

BISHOP: That was funny. I started that *years* ago—twenty years ago, at least—I had a stack of notes, the first two or three stanzas, and the last.

INTERVIEWER: It's such a dreamy poem. It seems to move the way a bus moves.

BISHOP: It was all true. The bus trip took place before I went to Brazil. I went up to visit my aunt. Actually, I was on the wrong bus. I went to the right place but it wasn't the express I was supposed to get. It went roundabout and it was all exactly the way I described it, except that I say "seven relatives." Well, they weren't really relatives, they were various stepsons and so on, but that's the only thing that isn't quite true. I wanted to finish it because I liked it, but I could never seem to get the middle part, to get from one place to the other. And then when I was still living in Cambridge I was asked to give the Phi Beta Kappa poem at Harvard. I was rather pleased and I remembered that I had another unfinished poem. It's about whales and it was written a long time ago, too. I'm afraid I'll never publish it because it looks as if I were just trying to be up-to-date now that whales are a "cause."

INTERVIEWER: But it's finished now?

BISHOP: I think I could finish it very easily. I'm going to take it to Maine with me. I think I'll date it or nobody will believe I started it so long ago. At the time, though, I couldn't find the one about whales—this was in '73 or '74, I think—so I dug out "The Moose" and thought, "Maybe I can finish it," and I did. The day of the ceremony for Phi Beta Kappa (which I'd never made in college) we were all sitting on the platform at Sanders Theater. And the man who had asked me to give the poem leaned across the president and said to me whispering, "What is the name of your poem?" I said, " 'The Moose,' M-o-o-s-e," and he got up and introduced me and said, "Miss Bishop will now read a poem called, 'The *Moos.* ' " Well, I choked and my hat was too big. And later the newspaper account read, "Miss Bishop read a poem called 'The Moose' and the tassle of her mortarboard swung back and forth over her face like a windshield wiper"!

The Glee Club was behind us and they sang rather badly, I thought, everybody thought. A friend of mine who couldn't come to this occasion but worked in one of the Harvard houses and knew some of the boys in the Glee Club asked one of them when they came back in their red jackets, "Well, how was it?" He said, "Oh, it was all right but we didn't sing well"—which was true—and then he said, "A woman read a poem." My friend said, "How was it?" And he said, "Well, as poems go, it wasn't bad"!

INTERVIEWER: Have you ever had any poems that were gifts? Poems that seemed to write themselves?

BISHOP: Oh yes. Once in awhile it happens. I wanted to write a villanelle all my life but I never could. I'd start them but for some reason I never could finish them. And one day I couldn't believe it—it was like writing a letter.* There was one rhyme I couldn't get that ended in e-n-t and a friend of mine, the poet Frank Bidart, came to see me and I said, "Frank, give me a rhyme." He gave me a word offhand and I put it in. But neither he nor I can remember which word it was. But that kind of thing doesn't happen very often. Maybe some poets always write that way. I don't know.

INTERVIEWER: Didn't you used to give Marianne Moore rhymes?

BISHOP: Yes, when she was doing the LaFontaine translations. She'd call me up and read me something when I was in New York—I was in Brazil most of that time—and say she needed a rhyme. She said that she admired rhymes and meters very much. It was hard to tell whether she was pulling your leg or not sometimes. She was Celtic enough to be somewhat mysterious about these things.

INTERVIEWER: Critics often talk about your more recent poems being less formal, more "open," so to speak. They point out that *Geography III* has more of "you" in it, a wider emotional range. Do you agree with these perceptions?

BISHOP: This is what critics say. I've never written the things I'd like to write that I've admired all my life. Maybe one never does. Critics say the most incredible things!

*The poem is "One Art," in *Geography III*.

INTERVIEWER: I've been reading a critical book about you that Anne Stevenson wrote. She said that in your poems nature was neutral.

BISHOP: Yes, I remember the word "neutral." I wasn't quite sure what she meant by that.

INTERVIEWER: I thought she might have meant that if nature is neutral there isn't any guiding spirit or force.

BISHOP: Somebody famous—I can't think who it was— somebody extremely famous was asked if he had one question to ask the Sphinx and get an answer, what would it be? And he said, "Is nature for us or against us?" Well, I've never really thought about it one way or the other. I like the country, the seashore especially, and if I could drive, I'd probably be living in the country. Unfortunately, I've never learned to drive. I bought two cars. At least. I had an MG I adored for some years in Brazil. We lived on top of a mountain peak, and it took an hour to get somewhere where I could practice. And nobody really had time to take an afternoon off and give me driving lessons. So I never got my license. And I *never* would have driven in Rio, anyway. But if you can't drive, you can't live in the country.

INTERVIEWER: Do you have the painting here that your uncle did? The one "about the size of an old-style dollar bill" that you wrote about in "Poem"?

BISHOP: Oh, sure. Do you want to see it? It's not good enough to hang. Actually, he was my great-uncle. I never met him.

INTERVIEWER: The cows in this really are just one or two brushstrokes!

BISHOP: I exaggerated a little bit. There's a detail in the poem that isn't in the painting. I can't remember what it is now. My uncle did another painting when he was fourteen or fifteen years old that I wrote about in an early poem ["Large Bad Picture"]. An aunt who lived in Montreal had both of these and they used to hang in her front hall. I was dying to get them and I went there once and tried to buy them, but she wouldn't sell them to me. She was rather stingy. She died some years ago. I don't know who has the large one now.

INTERVIEWER: When you were showing me your study, I noticed a shadow-box hanging in the hall. Is it by Joseph Cornell?

BISHOP: No, I did that one. That's one of my little works. It's about infant mortality in Brazil. It's called *anjinhos,* which means "little angels." That's what they call the babies and small children who die.

INTERVIEWER: What's the significance of the various objects?

BISHOP: I found the child's sandal on a beach wading east of Rio one Christmas and I finally decided to do something with it. The pacifier was bright red rubber. They sell them in big bottles and jars in drugstores in Brazil. I decided it couldn't be red, so I dyed it black with India ink. A nephew of my Brazilian friend, a very smart young man, came to call while I was doing this. He brought two American rock-and-roll musicians and we talked and talked and talked, and I never thought to explain in all the time they were there what I was doing. When they left, I thought, "My God, they must think I'm a witch or something!"

INTERVIEWER: What about the little bowls and skillets filled with rice?

BISHOP: Oh, they're just things children would be playing with. And of course rice and black beans are what Brazilians eat every day.

Cornell is superb. I first saw the *Medici Slot Machine* when I was in college. Oh, I loved it. To think one could have *bought* some of those things then. He was very strange. He got crushes on opera singers and ballet dancers. When I looked at his show in New York two years ago I nearly fainted, because one of my favorite books is a book he liked and used. It's a little book by an English scientist who wrote for children about soap bubbles

[*Soap Bubbles; their colours and the forces which mold them,* by Sir C. V. Boys, 1889].

His sister began writing me after she read Octavio Paz's poem for Cornell that I translated. (She doesn't read Spanish.) She sent me a German-French grammar that apparently he meant to do something with and never did. A lot of the pages were folded over and they're all made into star patterns with red ink around them. . . . He lived in what was called Elysian Park. That's an awfully strange address to have.

INTERVIEWER: Until recently, you were one of the few American poets who didn't make their living teaching or giving readings. What made you decide to start doing both?

BISHOP: I never wanted to teach in my life. I finally did because I wanted to leave Brazil and I needed the money. Since 1970 I've just been *swamped* with people sending me poems. They start to when they know you're in the country. I used to get them in Brazil, but not so much. They got lost in the mail quite often. I don't believe in teaching poetry at all, but that's what they want one to do. You see so many poems every week, you just lose all sense of judgment.

As for readings, I gave a reading in 1947 at Wellesley College two months after my first book appeared. And I was *sick* for days ahead of time. Oh, it was absurd. And then I did one in Washington in '49 and I was sick again and nobody could hear me. And then I didn't give any for twenty-six years. I don't mind reading now. I've gotten over my shyness a little bit. I think teaching helps. I've noticed that teachers aren't shy. They're rather aggressive. They get to be, finally.

INTERVIEWER: Did you ever take a writing course as a student?

BISHOP: When I went to Vassar I took sixteenth-century, seventeenth-century, and eighteenth-century literature, and then a course in the novel. The kind of courses where you have to do a lot of reading. I don't think I believe in writing courses at all. There weren't any when I was there. There was a poetry-writing course in the evening, but not for credit. A couple of my friends went to it, but I never did.

The word "creative" drives me crazy. I don't like to regard it as therapy. I was in the hospital several years ago and somebody gave me Kenneth Koch's book, *Rose, Where Did You Get That Red?* And it's true, children sometimes write wonderful things, paint wonderful pictures, but I think they should be *dis*couraged. From everything I've read and heard, the number of students in English departments taking literature courses has been falling off enormously. But at the same time the number of people who want to get in the writing classes seems to get bigger and bigger. There are usually two or three being given at Harvard every year. I'd get forty applicants for ten or twelve places. Fifty. It got bigger and bigger. I don't know if they do this to offset practical concerns, or what.

INTERVIEWER: I think people want to be able to say they do something creative like throw pots or write poems.

BISHOP: I just came back in March from reading in North Carolina and Arkansas, and I swear if I see any more handcrafts I'll go mad! I think we should go right straight back to the machine. You can only use so many leather belts, after all. I'm sorry. Maybe you do some of these things.

INTERVIEWER: Do many strangers send you poems?

BISHOP: Yes. It's very hard to know what to do. Sometimes I answer. I had a fan letter the other day, and it was adorable. It was in this childish handwriting. His name was Jimmy Sparks and he was in the sixth grade. He said his class was putting together a booklet of poems and he liked my poems very much—he mentioned three—because they rhymed and because they were about nature. His letter was so cute I did send him a postcard. I think he was supposed to ask me to send a handwritten poem or photograph—schools do this all the time—but he didn't say anything like that, and I'm sure he forgot his mission.

INTERVIEWER: What three poems did he like? "The Sandpiper"?

BISHOP: Yes, and the one about the mirror and the moon, "Insomnia," which Marianne Moore said was a cheap love poem.

INTERVIEWER: The one that ends, ". . . and you love me"?

BISHOP: Yes. I never liked that. I almost left it out. But last year it was put to music by Elliott Carter along with five other poems of mine* and it sounded much better as a song. Yes, Marianne was very opposed to that one.

INTERVIEWER: Maybe she didn't like the last line.

BISHOP: I don't think she ever believed in talking about the emotions much.

INTERVIEWER: Getting back to teaching, did you devise formal assignments when you taught at Harvard? For example, to write a villanelle?

BISHOP: Yes, I made out a whole list of weekly assignments that I gave the class; but every two or three weeks was a free assignment and they could hand in what they wanted. Some classes were so prolific that I'd declare a moratorium. I'd say, "Please, nobody write a poem for two weeks!"

INTERVIEWER: Do you think you can generalize that beginning writers write better in forms than not?

BISHOP: I don't know. We did a sestina—we started one in class by drawing words out of a hat—and I wish I'd never suggested it because it seemed to have *swept* Harvard. Later, in the applications for my class, I'd get dozens of sestinas. The students seemed to think it was my favorite form—which it isn't.

INTERVIEWER: I once tried a sestina about a woman who watches soap operas all day.

BISHOP: Did you watch them in college?

---

*"Anaphora," "The Sandpiper," "Argument," "O Breath," and "View of the Capitol from The Library of Congress."

INTERVIEWER: No.

BISHOP: Well, it seemed to be a fad at Harvard. Two or three years ago I taught a course in prose and discovered my students were watching the soap operas every morning and afternoon. I don't know when they studied. So I watched two or three just to see what was going on. They were *boring*. And the advertising! One student wrote a story about an old man who was getting ready to have an old lady to dinner (except she was really a ghost), and he polished a plate till he could see his face in it. It was quite well done, so I read some of it aloud, and said, "But look, this is impossible. You can never see your face in a plate." The whole class, in unison, said, "Joy!" I said, "What? What are you talking about?" Well, it seems there's an ad for Joy soap liquid in which a woman holds up a plate and sees— you know the one? Even so, you can't! I found this very disturbing. TV was *real* and no one had observed that it wasn't. Like when Aristotle was right and no one pointed out, for centuries, that women *don't* have fewer teeth than men.

I had a friend bring me a small TV, black and white, when I was living in Brazil. We gave it to the maid almost immediately because we only watched it when there were things like political speeches, or a revolution coming on. But she loved it. She slept with it in her bed! I think it meant so much to her because she couldn't read. There was a soap opera that year called "The Right to Life." It changed the whole schedule of Rio society's hours because it was on from eight to nine. The usual dinner hour's eight, so either you had to eat dinner before so that the maid could watch "The Right to Life" or eat much later, when it was over. We ate dinner about ten o'clock finally so that Joanna could watch this thing. I finally decided I had to see it, too. It became a chic thing to do and everybody was talking about it. It was absolutely ghastly! They got the programs from Mexico and dubbed them in Portuguese. They were very corny and always very lurid. Corpses lying in coffins, miracles, nuns, even incest.

I had friends in Belo Horizonte and the mother and their cook and a grandchild would watch the soap operas, the *novellas,* they're called, every night. The cook would get so excited she'd talk to the screen: "No! No! Don't do that! You know he's a bad man, Doña So-and-so!" They'd get so excited, they'd cry. And I knew of two old ladies, sisters, who got a TV. They'd knit and knit and watch it and cry and one of them would get up and say, "Excuse me, I have to go to the bathroom," to the television!

INTERVIEWER: You were living in Brazil, weren't you, when you won the Pulitzer Prize in 1956?

BISHOP: Yes, it was pretty funny. We lived on top of a mountain peak—really way up in the air. I was alone in the house with Maria, the cook. A friend had gone to market. The telephone rang. It was a newsman from the American Embassy and he asked me who it was in English, and of course it was very rare to hear someone speak in English. He said, "Do you know you've won the Pulitzer Prize?" Well, I thought it was a joke. I said, "Oh, come on." And he said, "Don't you hear me?" The telephone connection was very bad and he was shrieking. And I said, "Oh, it can't be." But he said it wasn't a joke. I couldn't make an impression on Maria with this news, but I felt I had to share it, so I hurried down the mountain a half mile or so to the next house, but no one was at home. I thought I should do something to celebrate, have a glass of wine or something. But all I could find in that house, a friend's, were some cookies from America, some awful chocolate cookies—Oreos, I think—so I ended up eating two of those. And that's how I celebrated winning the Pulitzer Prize.

The next day there was a picture in the afternoon paper— they take such things very seriously in Brazil—and the day after that my Brazilian friend went to market again. There was a big covered market with stalls for every kind of comestible, and there was one vegetable man we always went to. He said, "Wasn't that Doña Elizabetchy's picture in the paper yesterday?" She said, "Yes, it was. She won a prize." And he said, "You know, it's amazing! Last week Señora (Somebody) took a chance on a bicycle and *she* won! My customers are so lucky!" Isn't that marvelous?!

INTERVIEWER: I'd like to talk a little bit about your stories, especially "In the Village," which I've always admired. Do you see any connection, other than the obvious one of shared subject matter, between your stories and poems? In "method of attack," for example?

BISHOP: They're very closely related. I suspect that some of the stories I've written are actually prose poems and not very good stories. I have four about Nova Scotia. One came out last year in the *Southern Review*. I'm working on a long one now that I hope to finish this summer. . . . "In the Village" was funny. I had made notes for various bits of it and was given too much cortisone—I have very bad asthma from time to time—and you don't need any sleep. You feel wonderful while it's going on, but to get off it is awful. So I couldn't sleep much and I sat up all night in the tropical heat. The story came from a combination of cortisone, I think, and the gin and tonic I drank in the middle of the night. I wrote it in two nights.

INTERVIEWER. That's incredible! It's a long, long story.

BISHOP: Extraordinary. I wish I could do it again but I'll never take cortisone again, if I can possibly avoid it.

INTERVIEWER: I'm always interested in how different poets go about writing about their childhood.

BISHOP: Everybody does. You can't help it, I suppose. You are fearfully observant then. You notice all kinds of things, but there's no way of putting them all together. My memories of some of those days are so much clearer than things that happened in 1950, say. I don't think one should make a cult of writing about childhood, however. I've always tried to avoid it. I find I have written some, I must say. I went to an analyst for a couple of years off and on in the forties, a very nice woman who was especially interested in writers, writers and blacks. She said it was amazing that I would remember things that happened to me when I was two. It's very rare, but apparently writers often do.

INTERVIEWER: Do you know what your earliest memory is?

BISHOP: I think I remember learning to walk. My mother was away and my grandmother was trying to encourage me to walk. It was in Canada and she had lots of plants in the window the way all ladies do there. I can remember this blur of plants and my grandmother holding out her arms. I must have toddled. It seems to me it's a memory. It's very hazy. I told my grandmother years and years later and she said, "Yes, you did learn to walk while your mother was visiting someone." But you walk when you're one, don't you?

I remember my mother taking me for a ride on the swan boats here in Boston. I think I was three then. It was before we went back to Canada. Mother was dressed all in black—widows were in those days. She had a box of mixed peanuts and raisins. There were real swans floating around. I don't think they have them anymore. A swan came up and she fed it and it bit her finger. Maybe she just told me this, but I believed it because she showed me her black kid glove and said, "See." The finger was split. Well, I was thrilled to death! Robert Lowell put those swan boats in two or three of the *Lord Weary's Castle* poems.

INTERVIEWER: Your childhood was difficult, and yet in many of your stories and poems about that time there's a tremendously lyrical quality as well as a great sense of loss and tragedy.

BISHOP: My father died, my mother went crazy when I was four or five years old. My relatives, I think they all felt so sorry for this child that they tried to do their very best. And I think they did. I lived with my grandparents in Nova Scotia. Then I lived with the ones in Worcester, Massachusetts, very briefly, and got terribly sick. This was when I was six and seven. Then I lived with my mother's older sister in Boston. I used to go to Nova Scotia for the summer. When I was twelve or thirteen

I was improved enough to go to summer camp at Wellfleet until I went away to school when I was fifteen or sixteen. My aunt was devoted to me and she was awfully nice. She was married and had no children. But my relationship with my relatives—I was always a sort of a guest, and I think I've always felt like that.

INTERVIEWER: Was your adolescence a calmer time?

BISHOP: I was very romantic. I once walked from Nauset Light—I don't think it exists anymore—which is the beginning of the elbow [of Cape Cod], to the tip, Provincetown, all alone. It took me a night and a day. I went swimming from time to time but at that time the beach was absolutely deserted. There wasn't anything on the back shore, no buildings.

INTERVIEWER: How old would you have been?

BISHOP: Seventeen or eighteen. That's why I'd never go back —because I can't bear to think of the way it is now. . . . I haven't been to Nantucket since, well, I hate to say. My senior year at college I went there for Christmas with my then boyfriend. Nobody knew we were there. It was this wonderful, romantic trip. We went the day after Christmas and stayed for about a week. It was terribly cold but beautiful. We took long walks on the moors. We stayed at a very nice inn and we thought that probably the landlady would throw us out (we were very young and this kind of thing wasn't so common then). We had a bottle of sherry or something innocent like that. On New Year's Eve about ten o'clock there was a knock on the door. It was our landlady with a tray of hot grogs! She came in and we had the loveliest time. She knew the people who ran the museum and they opened it for us. There are a couple of wonderful museums there.

INTERVIEWER: I heard a story that you once spent a night in a tree at Vassar outside Cushing dormitory. Is it true?

BISHOP: Yes, it was me, me and a friend whose name I can't remember. We really were crazy and those trees were wonderful to climb. I used to be a great tree climber. Oh, we probably gave up about three in the morning. How did that ever get around? I can't imagine! We stopped being friends afterwards. Well, actually she had invited two boys from West Point for the weekend and I found myself *stuck* with this youth all in —[her hands draw an imagined cape and uniform in the air] —the dullest boy! I didn't know what to say! I nearly went mad. I think I sort of dropped the friend at that point. . . . I lived in a great big corner room on the top floor of Cushing and I apparently had registered a little late because I had a roommate whom I had never wanted to have. A strange girl named Constance. I remember her entire side of the room was furnished in Scotty dogs—pillows, pictures, engravings, and photographs. And mine was rather bare. Except that I probably wasn't a good roommate either, because I had a theory at that time that one should write down all one's dreams. That that was the way to write poetry. So I kept a notebook of my dreams and thought if you ate a lot of awful cheese at bedtime you'd have interesting dreams. I went to Vassar with a pot about this big—it did have a cover!—of Roquefort cheese that I kept in the bottom of my bookcase. . . . I think everyone's given to eccentricities at that age. I've heard that at Oxford Auden slept with a revolver under his pillow.

INTERVIEWER: As a young woman, did you have a sense of yourself as a writer?

BISHOP: No, it all just happens without your thinking about it. I never meant to go to Brazil. I never meant doing any of these things. I'm afraid in my life everything has just *happened*.

INTERVIEWER: You like to think there are reasons—

BISHOP: Yes, that people plan ahead, but I'm afraid I really didn't.

INTERVIEWER: But you'd always been interested in writing?

BISHOP: I'd written since I was a child but when I went to Vassar I was going to be a composer. I'd studied music at Walnut Hill and had a rather good teacher. I'd had a year of counterpoint and I also played the piano. At Vassar you had to perform in public once a month. Well, this terrified me. I really was sick. So I played once and then I gave up the piano because I couldn't bear it. I don't think I'd mind now, but I can't play the piano anymore. Then the next year I switched to English.

It was a very literary class. Mary McCarthy was a year ahead of me. Eleanor Clark was in my class. And Muriel Rukeyser, for freshman year. We started a magazine you may have heard of, *Con Spirito*. I think I was a junior then. There were six or seven of us—Mary, Eleanor Clark and her older sister, my friends Margaret Miller and Frani Blough, and a couple of others. It was during Prohibition and we used to go downtown to a speakeasy and drink wine out of teacups. That was our big vice. Ghastly stuff! Most of us had submitted things to the *Vassar Review* and they'd been turned down. It was very old-fashioned then. We were all rather put out because *we* thought we were good. So we thought, Well, we'll start our own magazine. We thought it would be nice to have it anonymous, which it was. After its third issue the *Vassar Review* came around and a couple of our editors became editors on it and then they published things by us. But we had a wonderful time doing it while it lasted.

INTERVIEWER: I read in another interview you gave that you had enrolled or were ready to enroll after college in Cornell Medical School.

BISHOP: I think I had all the forms. This was the year after I had graduated from Vassar. But then I discovered I would have to take German and I'd already given up on German once, I thought it was so difficult. And I would have had to take another year of chemistry. I'd already published a few things and I think Marianne [Moore] discouraged me, and I didn't go. I just went off to Europe instead.

INTERVIEWER: Did the Depression have much reality for college students in the thirties?

BISHOP: Everybody was frantic trying to get jobs. All the

intellectuals were Communist except me. I'm always very perverse so I went in for T. S. Eliot and Anglo-Catholicism. But the spirit was pretty radical. It's funny. The girl who was the biggest radical—she was a year ahead of me—has been married for years and years to one of the heads of Time-Life. I've forgotten his name. He's very famous and couldn't be more conservative. He writes shocking editorials. I can still see her standing outside the library with a tambourine collecting money for this cause and that cause.

INTERVIEWER: Wanting to be a composer, a doctor, or a writer—how do you account for it?

BISHOP: Oh, I was interested in all those things. I'd like to be a painter most, I think. I never really sat down and said to myself, "I'm going to be a poet." Never in my life. I'm still surprised that people think I am. . . . I started publishing things in my senior year, I think, and I remember my first check for thirty-five dollars and that was rather an exciting moment. It was from something called *The Magazine*, published in California. They took a poem, they took a story—oh, I wish those poems had never been published! They're terrible! I did show the check to my roommate. I was on the newspaper, *The Miscellany*—and I really was, I don't know, mysterious. On the newspaper board they used to sit around and talk about how they could get published and so on and so on. I'd just hold my tongue. I was embarrassed by it. And still am. There's nothing more embarrassing than being a poet, really.

INTERVIEWER: It's especially difficult to tell people you're meeting for the first time that that's what you do.

BISHOP: Just last week a friend and I went to visit a wonderful lady I know in Quebec. She's seventy-four or seventy-five. And she didn't say this to me but she said to my friend, Alice, "I'd like to ask my neighbor who has the big house next door to dinner, and she's so nice, but she'd be bound to ask Elizabeth what she does and if Elizabeth said she wrote poetry, the poor woman wouldn't say another word all evening!" This is awful, you know, and I think no matter how modest you think you feel or how minor you think you are, there must be an awful core of ego somewhere for you to set yourself up to write poetry. I've never *felt* it, but it must be there.

INTERVIEWER: In your letter to me, you sounded rather wary of interviewers. Do you feel you've been misrepresented in interviews? For example, that your refusal to appear in all-women poetry anthologies has been misunderstood as a kind of disapproval of the feminist movement.

BISHOP: I've always considered myself a strong feminist. Recently I was interviewed by a reporter from *The Chicago Tribune*. After I talked to the girl for a few minutes, I realized that she wanted to play me off as an "old-fashioned" against Erica Jong, and Adrienne [Rich], whom I like, and other violently feminist people. Which isn't true at all. I finally asked her if she'd ever read any of my poems. Well, it seemed she'd read *one* poem. I didn't see how she could interview me if she didn't know anything about me at all, and I told her so. She was nice enough to print a separate piece in *The Chicago Tribune* apart from the longer article on the others. I had said that I didn't believe in propaganda in poetry. That it rarely worked. What she had me saying was, "Miss Bishop does not believe that poetry should convey the poet's personal philosophy." Which made me sound like a complete dumbbell! Where she got that, I don't know. This is why one gets nervous about interviews.

INTERVIEWER: Do you generally agree with anthologists' choices? Do you have any poems that are personal favorites? Ones you'd like to see anthologized that aren't?

BISHOP: I'd rather have—well, anything except "The Fish"! I've declared a moratorium on that. Anthologists repeat each other so finally a few years ago I said nobody could reprint "The Fish" unless they reprinted three others because I got so sick of it.

INTERVIEWER: One or two more questions. You went to

Yaddo several times early in your career. Did you find the atmosphere at an artist's colony helpful to your writing?

BISHOP: I went to Yaddo twice, once in the summer for two weeks, and for several months the winter before I went to Brazil. Mrs. Ames was very much in evidence then. I didn't like it in the summer because of the incessant coming and going, but the winter was rather different. There were only six of us and just by luck we all liked each other and had a very good time. I wrote one poem, I think, in that whole stretch. The first time I liked the horse races, I'm afraid. In the summer—I think this still goes on—you can walk through the Whitney estate to the tracks. A friend and I used to walk there early in the morning and sit at the track and have coffee and blueberry muffins while they exercised the horses. I loved that. We went to a sale of yearlings in August and that was beautiful. The sale was in a big tent. The grooms had brass dustpans and brooms with brass handles and they'd go around after the little colts and sweep up the manure. That's what I remember best about Yaddo.

INTERVIEWER: It was around the time that you went to Yaddo, wasn't it, that you were consultant in poetry to the Library of Congress? Was that year in Washington more productive than your Yaddo experience?

BISHOP: I've suffered because I've been so shy all my life. A few years later I might have enjoyed it more but at the time I didn't like it much. I hated Washington. There were so many government buildings that looked like Moscow. There was a very nice secretary, Phyllis Armstrong, who got me through. I think she did most of the work. I'd write something and she'd say, "Oh, no, that isn't official," so then she'd take it and rewrite it in gobbledegook. We used to bet on the horses— Phyllis always bet the daily double. She and I would sit there reading the *Racing Form* and poets would come to call and Phyllis and I would be talking about our bets!

All the "survivors" of that job—a lot of them are dead—

were invited to read there recently. There were thirteen of us, unfortunately.

INTERVIEWER: A friend of mine tried to get into that reading and she said it was jammed.

BISHOP: It was *mobbed!* And I don't know why. It couldn't have been a duller, more awful occasion. I think we were supposedly limited to ten minutes. I *stuck* to it. But there's no stopping somebody like James Dickey. Stafford was good. I'd never heard him and never met him. He read one very short poem that really brought tears to my eyes, he read it so beautifully.

I'm not very fond of poetry readings. I'd much rather read the book. I know I'm wrong. I've only been to a few poetry readings I could *bear*. Of course, you're too young to have gone through the Dylan Thomas craze. . . .

When it was somebody like Cal Lowell or Marianne Moore, it's as if they were my children. I'd get terribly upset. I went to hear Marianne several times and finally I just couldn't go because I'd sit there with tears running down my face. I don't know, it's sort of embarrassing. You're so afraid they'll do something wrong.

Cal thought that the most important thing about readings was the remarks poets made in between the poems. The first time I heard him read was years ago at the New School for Social Research in a small, gray auditorium. It was with Allen Tate and Louise Bogan. Cal was very much younger than anybody else and had published just two books. He read a long, endless poem—I've forgotten its title*—about a Canadian nun in New Brunswick. I've forgotten what the point of the poem is, but it's very, very long and it's quite beautiful, particularly in the beginning. Well, he started, and he read very badly. He kind of droned and everybody was trying to get it. He had gotten about two-thirds of the way through when somebody

---

*"Mother Marie Therese" in *The Mills of the Kavanaughs*.

yelled, "Fire!" There was a small fire in the lobby, nothing much, that was put out in about five minutes and everybody went back to their seats. Poor Cal said, "I think I'd better begin over again," so he read the whole thing all over again! But his reading got much, much better in later years.

INTERVIEWER: He couldn't have done any better than the record the Poetry Center recently put out. It's wonderful. And very funny.

BISHOP: I haven't the courage to hear it.

ELIZABETH SPIRES
Summer 1978

5. Bernard Malamud

Bernard Malamud was born April 26, 1914, in Brooklyn, New York. He was educated in the New York public schools and graduated from the City College of New York in 1936, receiving a master's degree from Columbia University in 1942. He worked for nine years in the evening high schools in New York City. In 1945 he married Ann de Chiara, with whom he has two children. In 1961, he began to teach at Bennington College.

Considered one of the prominent American-Jewish writers to emerge after World War II, Bernard Malamud published his first novel, *The Natural,* in 1952. His second novel, *The Assistant,* appeared in 1956, winning the Rosenthal Award of the National Institute of Arts & Letters; the same year he was awarded a Partisan Review–Rockefeller grant. His short stories are collected in four volumes: *The Magic Barrel* (which won The National Book Award for fiction in 1959), *Idiots First, Rembrandt's Hat,* and *The Stories of Bernard Malamud.*

A member of the American Academy and Institute of Arts & Letters, and the American Academy of Arts & Sciences, Malamud served as president of PEN American Center from 1979 to 1981. In 1983, he won the Gold Medal for Fiction of the American Academy of Arts & Letters.

Other works by Bernard Malamud are: *A New Life,* 1961; *The Fixer,* 1966 (Pulitzer Prize and National Book Award); *Pictures of Fidelman,* 1969; *The Tenants,* 1971; *Dubin's Lives,* 1979; *God's Grace,* 1982.

For instance Freduced his wife?

Eorvas

Abramowitz, out for a walk ~~romp~~ in the fields, looks upon beauty bare? There is this naked lady lying asleep in the grass after a bath [and] instead of asking how wo been introduced, on at least who is this lady and is she married or not, if she was married or not. He drops his pants and gets on top; they both enjoy the comprising act; but when he gets off, wondering at his nerve, she too screams and he takes off, galloping, realizing before he has gone too very far, from his movements and the noise of his pounding hooves that he has been changed into a horse, and the lady is Mrs. Goldberg [~~a good friend~~] a priest's or the family.]

What happened to Abramowitz?

From the first draft of "Talking Horse" by Bernard Malamud.

Bernard Malamud

Bernard Malamud lives in a white clapboard house in Benning-
ton, Vermont. Spacious and comfortable, it sits on a gentle
downward slope, behind it the rise of the Green Mountains. To
this house on April 26, 1974, came friends, family, colleagues,
and the children of friends—to celebrate Malamud's sixtieth
birthday. It was a sunny weekend, the weather and ambience
benign, friendly.

There were about a half-dozen young people taking their rest
in sleeping bags in various bedrooms and in a home volunteered
by a friend and neighbor. Three of them, from nearby universi-
ties, were children of friends on the faculty of Oregon State
University more than a dozen years ago.

On Saturday night there was a birthday party, with cham-
pagne, birthday cake, and dancing. At the end of the evening
the young people drummed up a show of slides: scenes of past

travels; in particular, scenes of Corvallis, Oregon, where Mala-mud had lived and taught for twelve years before returning East.

Bernard Malamud is a slender man with a graying mustache and inquisitive brown eyes that search and hide a little at the same time. He is a quiet man who listens a lot, and responds freely. His wife, Ann, an attractive, articulate woman of Italian descent, had planned the party, assisted by the young people from Oregon and the Malamuds' son, Paul, and daughter, Janna.

The taping of the interview began late Friday morning, on the back porch, which overlooks a long, descending sweep of lawn and, in the distance, the encircling mountains. It was continued later in the book-filled study where Malamud writes. (He also writes in his office at Bennington College.) At first he was conscious of the tape recorder, but grew less so as the session —and the weekend—continued. He has a quick laugh and found it easy to discourse on the questions asked. An ironic humor would seem to be his mother tongue.

INTERVIEWER: Why sixty? I understand that when the *Paris Review* asked you to do an interview after the publication of *The Fixer*, you suggested doing it when you hit sixty?

MALAMUD: Right. It's a respectable round number, and when it becomes your age you look at it with both eyes. It's a good time to see from. In the past I sometimes resisted interviews because I had no desire to talk about myself in relation to my fiction. There are people who always want to make you a character in your stories and want you to confirm it. Of course there's some truth to it: Every character you invent takes his essence from you; therefore you're in them as Flaubert was in Emma—but, peace to him, you are not those you imagine. They are your fictions. And I don't like questions of explication: What did I mean by this or that? I want the books to speak for themselves. You can read? All right, tell me what my books mean. Astonish me.

INTERVIEWER: What about a little personal history? There's been little written about your life.

MALAMUD: That's how I wanted it—I like privacy, and as much as possible to stay out of my books. I know that's disadvantageous to certain legitimate kinds of criticism of literature, but my needs come first. Still, I have here and there talked a little about my life: My father was a grocer; my mother, who helped him, after a long illness, died young. I had a younger brother who lived a hard and lonely life and died in his fifties. My mother and father were gentle, honest, kindly people, and who they were and their affection for me to some degree made up for the cultural deprivation I felt as a child. They weren't educated, but their values were stable. Though my father always managed to make a living, they were comparatively poor, especially in the Depression, and yet I never heard a word in praise of the buck. On the other hand, there were no books that I remember in the house, no records, music, pictures on the wall. On Sundays I listened to somebody's piano through the window. At nine I caught pneumonia, and when I was convalescing my father bought me *The Book of Knowledge*, twenty volumes where there had been none. That was, considering the circumstances, an act of great generosity. When I was in high school he bought a radio. As a kid, for entertainment I turned to the movies and dime novels. Maybe *The Natural* derives from Frank Merriwell as well as the adventures of the Brooklyn Dodgers in Ebbets Field. Anyway, my parents stayed close to the store. Once in a while, on Jewish holidays, we went visiting, or saw a Jewish play—Sholem Aleichem, Peretz, and others. My mother's brother, Charles Fidelman, and their cousin, Isidore Cashier, were in the Yiddish theatre.

Around the neighborhood the kids played Chase the White Horse, Ringolevio, Buck-Buck, punchball and one o'cat. Occasionally we stole tomatoes from the Italian dirt farmers, gypped the El to ride to Coney Island, smoked in cellars, and played blackjack. I wore sneakers every summer. My education at home derived mostly from the presence and example of good, feelingful, hard-working people. They were worriers, with other faults I wasn't much conscious of until I recognized them in myself. I learned from books, in the public schools. I had some fine teachers in grammar school, Erasmus Hall High School, and later in City College, in New York. I took to literature and early wanted to be a writer.

INTERVIEWER: How early?

MALAMUD: At eight or nine I was writing little stories in school and feeling the glow. To anyone of my friends who'd listen I'd recapitulate at tedious length the story of the last movie I'd seen. The movies tickled my imagination. As a writer I learned from Charlie Chaplin.

INTERVIEWER: What in particular?

MALAMUD: Let's say the rhythm, the snap of comedy; the reserved comic presence—that beautiful distancing; the funny with sad; the surprise of surprise.

INTERVIEWER: Please go on about your life.

MALAMUD: Schools meant a lot to me, those I went to and taught at. You learn what you teach and you learn from those you teach. In 1942 I met my wife, and we were married in 1945. We have two children and have lived in Oregon, Rome, Bennington, Cambridge, London, New York, and have traveled a fair amount. In sum, once I was twenty and not so young, now I'm sixty inclined on the young side.

INTERVIEWER: Which means?

MALAMUD: Largely, the life of imagination, and doing pretty much what I set out to do. I made my mistakes, took my lumps, learned. I resisted my ignorance, limitations, obsessions. I'm freer than I was. I'd rather write it than talk. I love the privileges of form.

INTERVIEWER: You've taught during the time you were a professional writer?

MALAMUD: Thirty-five years—

INTERVIEWER: There are some who say teaching doesn't do

the writer much good; in fact it restricts life and homogenizes experience. Isn't a writer better off on the staff of *The New Yorker,* or working for the BBC? Faulkner fed a furnace and wrote for the movies.

MALAMUD: Doesn't it depend on the writer? People experience similar things differently. Sometimes I've regretted the time I've given to teaching, but not teaching itself. And a community of serious readers is a miraculous thing. Some of the most extraordinary people I've met were students of mine, or colleagues. Still, I ought to say I teach only a single class of prose fiction, one term a year. I've taught since I was twenty-five, and though I need more time for reading and writing, I also want to keep on doing what I can do well and enjoy doing.

INTERVIEWER: Do you teach literature?

MALAMUD: If you teach prose fiction, you are teaching literature. You teach those who want to write to read fiction, even their own work, with greater understanding. Sometimes they're surprised to find out how much they've said or not said that they didn't know they had.

INTERVIEWER: Can one, indeed, teach writing?

MALAMUD: You teach writers—assuming a talent. At the beginning young writers pour it out without much knowing the nature of their talent. What you try to do is hold a mirror up to their fiction so, in a sense, they can see what they're showing. Not all who come forth are fully armed. Some are gifted in narrative, some shun it. Some show a richness of metaphor, some have to dig for it. Some writers think language is all they need; they mistake it for subject matter. Some rely on whimsy. Some on gut feeling. Some of them don't make the effort to create a significant form. They do automatic writing and think they're probing themselves. The odd thing is, most young writers write traditional narrative until you introduce them to the experimental writers—not for experiment's sake, but to try something for size. Let the writer attempt whatever he can.

There's no telling where he will come out stronger than before. Art is in life, but the realm is endless.

INTERVIEWER: Experiment at the beginning?

MALAMUD: Sometimes a new technique excites a flood of fictional ideas. Some, after experimenting, realize their strength is in traditional modes. Some, after trying several things, may give up the thought of writing fiction—not a bad thing. Writing—the problems, the commitment, the effort, scares them. Some may decide to try poetry or criticism. Some turn to painting—why not? I have no kick against those who use writing, or another art, to test themselves, to find themselves. Sometimes I have to tell them their talents are thin— not to waste their lives writing third-rate fiction.

INTERVIEWER: Fidelman as a painter? The doubtful talent?

MALAMUD: Yes. Among other things, it is a book about finding a vocation. Forgive the soft impeachment.

INTERVIEWER: In *Fidelman* and *The Tenants* you deal with artists who can't produce, or produce badly. Why does the subject interest you so much? Have you ever been blocked?

MALAMUD: Never. Even in anxiety I've written, though anxiety, because it is monochromatic, may limit effects. I like the drama of nonproductivity, especially where there may be talent. It's an interesting ambiguity: the force of the creative versus the paralysis caused by the insults, the confusions of life.

INTERVIEWER: What about work habits? Some writers, especially at the beginning, have problems settling how to do it.

MALAMUD: There's no one way—there's so much drivel about this subject. You're who you are, not Fitzgerald or Thomas Wolfe. You write by sitting down and writing. There's no particular time or place—you suit yourself, your nature. How one works, assuming he's disciplined, doesn't matter. If he or she is not disciplined, no sympathetic magic will help. The trick is to make time—not steal it—and produce the fiction. If the stories come, you get them written, you're on the right track. Eventually everyone learns his or her own best way. The real mystery to crack is you.

INTERVIEWER: What about the number of drafts? Some writers write only one.

MALAMUD: They're cheating themselves. First drafts are for learning what your novel or story is about. Revision is working with that knowledge to enlarge and enhance an idea, to re-form it. D. H. Lawrence, for instance, did seven or eight drafts of *The Rainbow*. The first draft of a book is the most uncertain —where you need guts, the ability to accept the imperfect until it is better. Revision is one of the true pleasures of writing. "The men and things of today are wont to lie fairer and truer in tomorrow's memory," Thoreau said.

INTERVIEWER: Do you teach your own writing?

MALAMUD: No, I teach what I know about writing.

INTERVIEWER: What specific piece of advice would you give to young writers?

MALAMUD: Write your heart out.

INTERVIEWER: Anything else?

MALAMUD: Watch out for self-deceit in fiction. Write truthfully but with cunning.

INTERVIEWER: Anything special to more experienced types?

MALAMUD: To any writer: Teach yourself to work in uncertainty. Many writers are anxious when they begin, or try something new. Even Matisse painted some of his fauvist pictures in anxiety. Maybe that helped him to simplify. Character, discipline, negative capability count. Write, complete, revise. If it doesn't work, begin something else.

INTERVIEWER: And if it doesn't work twenty or thirty times?

MALAMUD: You live your life as best you can.

INTERVIEWER: I've heard you talk about the importance of subject matter?

MALAMUD: It's always a problem. Very young writers who don't know themselves obviously often don't know what they have to say. Sometimes by staying with it they write themselves into a fairly rich vein. Some, by the time they find what they're capable of writing about, no longer want to write. Some go through psychoanalysis or a job in a paint factory and begin to write again. One hopes they then have something worth saying. Nothing is guaranteed. Some writers have problems with subject matter not in their first book, which may mine childhood experience, or an obsession, or fantasy, or the story they've carried in their minds and imagination to this point, but after that—after this first yield—often they run into trouble with their next few books. Especially if the first book is unfortunately a best seller. And some writers run into difficulties at the end, particularly if they exclude important areas of personal experience from their writing. Hemingway would not touch his family beyond glimpses in short stories, mostly the Nick Adams pieces. He once wrote his brother that their mother was a bitch and father a suicide—who'd want to read about them? Obviously not all his experience is available to a writer for purposes of fiction, but I feel that if Hemingway had tried during his last five years, let's say, to write about his father rather than the bulls once more, or the big fish, he mightn't have committed suicide. Mailer, after *The Naked and the Dead*, ran into trouble he couldn't resolve until he invented his mirror-image, Aquarius, Prisoner of Sex, Doppelgänger, without whom he can't write. After he had invented "Norman Mailer" he produced *The Armies of the Night*, a beautiful feat of prestidigitation, if not fiction. He has still to write, Richard Poirier says, his *Moby Dick*. To write a good big novel he will have to invent other selves, richly felt selves. Roth, since *Portnoy*, has been hunting for a fruitful subject. He's tried various strategies to defeat the obsession of the hated wife he almost never ceases to write about. He'll have at last to bury her to come up with a new comedy.

INTERVIEWER: What about yourself?

MALAMUD: I say the same thing in different worlds.

INTERVIEWER: Anything else to say to writers—basic stuff?

MALAMUD: Take chances. "Dare to do," Eudora Welty says. She's right. One drags around a bag of fears he has to throw to the winds every so often if he expects to take off in his writing. I'm glad Virginia Woolf did *Orlando*, though it isn't my favorite of her books, and in essence she was avoiding a subject. Still, you don't have to tell everything you know. I like Updike's *Centaur*, Bellow's *Henderson*. Genius, after it has got itself together, may give out with a *Ulysses* or *Remembrance of Things Past*. One doesn't have to imitate the devices of Joyce or Proust, but if you're not a genius, imitate the daring. If you are a genius, assert yourself, in art and humanity.

INTERVIEWER: Humanity? Are you suggesting art is moral?

MALAMUD: It tends toward morality. It values life. Even when it doesn't, it tends to. My former colleague, Stanley Edgar Hyman, used to say that even the act of creating a form is a moral act. That leaves out something, but I understand and like what he was driving at. It's close to Frost's definition of a poem as "a momentary stay against confusion." Morality begins with an awareness of the sanctity of one's life, hence the lives of others—even Hitler's, to begin with—the sheer privilege of being, in this miraculous cosmos, and trying to figure out why. Art, in essence, celebrates life and gives us our measure.

INTERVIEWER: It changes the world?

MALAMUD: It changes me. It affirms me.

INTERVIEWER: Really?

MALAMUD: (*laughs*) It helps.

INTERVIEWER: Let's get to your books. In *The Natural*, why the baseball-mythology combination?

MALAMUD: Baseball flat is baseball flat. I had to do something else to enrich the subject. I love metaphor. It provides two loaves where there seems to be one. Sometimes it throws in a load of fish. The mythological analogy is a system of metaphor. It enriches the vision without resorting to montage. This guy gets up with his baseball bat and all at once he is, through the ages, a knight—somewhat battered—with a lance; not to mention a guy with a blackjack, or someone attempting murder with a flower. You relate to the past and predict the future. I'm not talented as a conceptual thinker but I am in the uses of metaphor. The mythological and symbolic excite my imagination. Incidentally, Keats said, "I am not a conceptual thinker, I am a man of ideas."

INTERVIEWER: Is *The Assistant* mythological?

MALAMUD: Some, I understand, find it so.

INTERVIEWER: Did you set it up as a mythology?

MALAMUD: No. If it's mythological to some readers I have no objection. You read the book and write your ticket. I can't tell you how the words fall, though I know what I mean. Your interpretation—*pace* S. Sontag—may enrich the book or denude it. All I ask is that it be consistent and make sense.

INTERVIEWER: Is it a moral allegory?

MALAMUD: You have to squeeze your brain to come up with that. The spirit is more than moral, and by the same token there's more than morality in a good man. One must make room in those he creates. So far as range is concerned, ultimately a writer's mind and heart, if any, are revealed in his fiction.

INTERVIEWER: What is the source of *The Assistant*?

MALAMUD: Source questions are piddling but you're my friend, so I'll tell you. Mostly my father's life as a grocer, though not necessarily my father. Plus three short stories, sort of annealed in a single narrative: "The Cost of Living" and "The First Seven Years"—both in *The Magic Barrel*. And a story I wrote in the forties, "The Place is Different Now," which I've not included in my story collections.

INTERVIEWER: Is *The Fixer* also related to your father's life?

MALAMUD: Indirectly. My father told me the Mendel Beilis story when I was a kid. I carried it around almost forty years and decided to use it after I gave up the idea of a Sacco and Vanzetti novel. When I began to read for the Sacco and

Vanzetti it had all the quality of a structured fiction, all the necessary elements of theme and narrative. I couldn't see any way of re-forming it. I was very much interested in the idea of prison as a source of the self's freedom and thought of Dreyfus next, but he was a dullish man, and though he endured well he did not suffer well. Neither did Beilis, for that matter, but his drama was more interesting—his experiences; so I invented Yakov Bok, with perhaps the thought of him as a potential Vanzetti. Beilis, incidentally, died a bitter man, in New York —after leaving Palestine, because he thought he hadn't been adequately reimbursed for his suffering.

INTERVIEWER: Some critics have commented on this prison motif in your work.

MALAMUD: Perhaps I use it as a metaphor for the dilemma of all men: necessity, whose bars we look through and try not to see. Social injustice, apathy, ignorance. The personal prison of entrapment in past experience, guilt, obsession—the somewhat blind or blinded self, in other words. A man has to construct, invent, his freedom. Imagination helps. A truly great man or woman extends it for others in the process of creating his/her own.

INTERVIEWER: Does this idea or theme, as you call it, come out of your experience as a Jew?

MALAMUD: That's probably in it—a heightened sense of prisoner of history, but there's more to it than that. I conceive this as the major battle in life, to transcend the self—extend one's realm of freedom.

INTERVIEWER: Not all your characters do.

MALAMUD: Obviously. But they're all more or less engaged in the enterprise.

INTERVIEWER: Humor is so much a part of your work. Is this an easy quality to deal with? Is one problem that the response to humor is so much a question of individual taste?

MALAMUD: The funny bone is universal. I doubt humorists think of individual taste when they're enticing the laugh. With me humor comes unexpectedly, usually in defense of a character, sometimes because I need cheering up. When something starts funny I can feel my imagination eating and running. I love the distancing—the guise of invention—that humor gives fiction. Comedy, I imagine, is harder to do consistently than tragedy, but I like it spiced in the wine of sadness.

INTERVIEWER: What about suffering? It's a subject much in your early work.

MALAMUD: I'm against it, but when it occurs, why waste the experience?

INTERVIEWER: Are you a Jewish writer?

MALAMUD: What is the question asking?

INTERVIEWER: One hears various definitions and insistences, for instance, that one is primarily a writer and any subject matter is secondary; or that one is an American-Jewish writer. There are qualifications, by Bellow, Roth, others.

MALAMUD: I'm an American, I'm a Jew, and I write for all men. A novelist has to, or he's built himself a cage. I write about Jews, when I write about Jews, because they set my imagination going. I know something about their history, the quality of their experience and belief, and of their literature, though not as much as I would like. Like many writers I'm influenced especially by the Bible, both Testaments. I respond in particular to the East European immigrants of my father's and mother's generation; many of them were Jews of the Pale as described by the classic Yiddish writers. And of course I've been deeply moved by the Jews of the concentration camps, and the refugees wandering from nowhere to nowhere. I'm concerned about Israel. Nevertheless, Jews like rabbis Kahane and Korrf set my teeth on edge. Sometimes I make characters Jewish because I think I will understand them better as people, not because I am out to prove anything. That's a qualification. Still another is that I know that, as a writer, I've been influenced by Hawthorne, James, Mark Twain, Hemingway, more than I have been by Sholem Aleichem and I. L. Peretz, whom I read with pleasure. Of course I admire and have been moved by other writers, Dostoyevsky and Chekhov, for instance, but the point I'm making is that I was born in America and respond, in American life, to more than Jewish experience. I wrote for those who read.

INTERVIEWER: Thus S. Levin is Jewish and not much is made of it?

MALAMUD: He was a gent who interested me in a place that interested me. He was out to be educated.

INTERVIEWER: Occasionally I see a remark to the effect that he has more than a spoonful of you in him.

MALAMUD: So have Roy Hobbs, Helen Bober, Willie Spearmint, and Talking Horse. More to the point—I prefer autobiographical essence to autobiographical history. Events from life may creep into the narrative, but it isn't necessarily my life history.

INTERVIEWER: How much of a book is set in your mind when you begin? Do you begin at the beginning? Does its course ever change markedly from what you had in the original concept?

MALAMUD: When I start I have a pretty well developed idea what the book is about and how it ought to go, because generally I've been thinking about it and making notes for months, if not years. Generally I have the ending in mind, usually the last paragraph almost verbatim. I begin at the beginning and stay close to the track, if it is a track and not a whalepath. If it turns out I'm in the open sea, my compass is my narrative instinct, with an assist by that astrolabe, theme. The destination, wherever it is, is, as I said, already defined. If I go astray it's not a long excursis, good for getting to know the ocean, if not the world. The original idea, altered but recognizable, on the whole remains.

INTERVIEWER: Do characters ever run away from you and take on identities you hadn't expected?

MALAMUD: My characters run away, but not far. Their guise is surprises.

INTERVIEWER: Let's go to Fidelman. You seem to like to write about painters?

MALAMUD: I know a few. I love painting.

INTERVIEWER: Rembrandt and who else?

MALAMUD: Too many to name, but Cézanne, Monet, and Matisse, very much, among modernists.

INTERVIEWER: Chagall?

MALAMUD: Not that much. He rides his nostalgic nag to death.

INTERVIEWER: Some have called you a Chagallean writer.

MALAMUD: Their problem. I used Chagallean imagery intentionally in one story, "The Magic Barrel," and that's it. My quality is not much like his.

INTERVIEWER: Fidelman first appears in "The Last Mohican," a short story. Did you already have in mind that there would be an extended work on him?

MALAMUD: After I wrote the story in Rome I jotted down ideas for several incidents in the form of a picaresque novel. I was out to loosen up—experiment a little—with narrative structure. And I wanted to see, if I wrote it at intervals—as I did from 1957 to 1968—whether the passing of time and mores would influence his life. I did not think of the narrative as merely a series of related stories, because almost at once I had the structure of a novel in mind and each part had to fit that form. Robert Scholes in *The Saturday Review* has best explained what I was up to in Fidelman.

INTERVIEWER: Did you use all the incidents you jotted down?

MALAMUD: No.

INTERVIEWER: Can you give me an example of one you left out?

MALAMUD: Yes, Fidelman administering to the dying Keats in Rome—doing Severn's job, one of the few times in his life our boy is engaged in a purely unselfish act, or acts. But I felt I had no need to predict a change in him, especially in a sort of dream sequence, so I dropped the idea. The painting element was to come in via some feverish watercolors of John Keats, dying.

INTERVIEWER: Fidelman is characterized by some critics as a schlemiel.

MALAMUD: Not accurately. Peter Schlemiel lost his shadow and suffered the consequences for all time. Not Fidelman. He does better. He escapes his worst fate. I dislike the schlemiel characterization as a taxonomical device. I said somewhere that it reduces to stereotypes people of complex motivations and fates. One can often behave like a schlemiel without being one.

INTERVIEWER: Do you read criticism of your work?

MALAMUD: When it hits me in the eye; even some reviews.

INTERVIEWER: Does it affect you?

MALAMUD: Some of it must. Not the crap, the self-serving pieces, but an occasional insightful criticism, favorable or unfavorable, that confirms my judgment of my work. While I'm on the subject, I dislike particularly those critics who preach their aesthetic or ideological doctrines at you. What's important to them is not what the writer has done but how it fits, or doesn't fit, the thesis they want to develop. Nobody can tell a writer what can or ought to be done, or not done, in his fiction. A living death if you fall for it.

INTERVIEWER: That narration, for instance, is dead or dying?

MALAMUD: It'll be dead when the penis is.

INTERVIEWER: What about the death of the novel?

MALAMUD: The novel could disappear, but it won't die.

INTERVIEWER: How does that go?

MALAMUD: I'm not saying it will disappear, just entertaining the idea. Assume it does; then someday a talented writer writes himself a long, heartfelt letter, and the form reappears. The human race needs the novel. We need all the experience we can get. Those who say the novel is dead can't write them.

INTERVIEWER: You've done two short stories and a novel about blacks. Where do you get your material?

MALAMUD: Experience and books. I lived on the edge of a

black neighborhood in Brooklyn when I was a boy. I played with blacks in the Flatbush Boys Club. I had a friend—Buster; we used to go to his house every so often. I swiped dimes so we could go to the movies together on a couple of Saturday afternoons. After I was married I taught for a year in a black evening high school in Harlem. The short stories derive from that period. I also read black fiction and history.

INTERVIEWER: What set off *The Tenants?*

MALAMUD: Jews and blacks, the period of the troubles in New York City; the teachers strike, the rise of black activism, the mix-up of cause and effect. I thought I'd say a word.

INTERVIEWER: Why the three endings?

MALAMUD: Because one wouldn't do.

INTERVIEWER: Will you predict how it will be between blacks and Jews in the future?

MALAMUD: How can one? All I know is that American blacks have been badly treated. We, as a society, have to redress the balance. Those who want for others must expect to give up something. What we get in return is the affirmation of what we believe in.

INTERVIEWER: You give a sense in your fiction that you try not to repeat yourself.

MALAMUD: Good. In my books I go along the same paths in different worlds.

INTERVIEWER: What's the path—theme?

MALAMUD: Derived from one's sense of values, it's a vision of life, a feeling for people—real qualities in imaginary worlds.

INTERVIEWER: Do you like writing short stories more than you do novels?

MALAMUD: Just as much, though the short story has its own pleasures. I like packing a self or two into a few pages, predicating lifetimes. The drama is terse, happens faster, and is often outlandish. A short story is a way of indicating the complexity of life in a few pages, producing the surprise and effect of a profound knowledge in a short time. There's, among other things, a drama, a resonance, of the reconciliation of opposites: much to say, little time to say it, something like the effect of a poem.

INTERVIEWER: You write them between novels?

MALAMUD: Yes, to breathe, and give myself time to think what's in the next book. Sometimes I'll try out a character or situation similar to that in a new novel.

INTERVIEWER: How many drafts do you usually do of a novel?

MALAMUD: Many more than I call three. Usually the last of the first puts it in place. The second focuses, develops, subtilizes. By the third most of the dross is gone. I work with language. I love the flowers of afterthought.

INTERVIEWER: Your style has always seemed so individual, so recognizable. Is this a natural gift, or is it contrived and honed?

MALAMUD: My style flows from the fingers. The eye and ear approve or amend.

INTERVIEWER: Let's wind up. Are you optimistic about the future?

MALAMUD: My nature is optimistic but not the evidence— population misery, famine, politics of desperation, the proliferation of the atom bomb. Mylai, one minute after Hiroshima in history, was ordained. We're going through long, involved transformations of world society, ongoing upheavals of colonialism, old modes of distribution, mores, overthrowing the slave mentality. With luck we may end up in a society with a larger share of the world's goods, opportunities for education, freedom going to the presently underprivileged. Without luck there may be a vast economic redistribution without political freedom. In the Soviet Union, as it is presently constituted, that's meant the kiss of death to freedom in art and literature. I worry that democracy, which has protected us from this indignity, especially in the United States, suffers from a terrifying inadequacy of leadership, and the apathy, unimaginativeness, and hard-core selfishness of too many of us. I worry about technology rampant. I fear those who are by nature beastly.

INTERVIEWER: What does one write novels about nowadays?

MALAMUD: Whatever wants to be written.

INTERVIEWER: Is there something I haven't asked you that you might want to comment on?

MALAMUD: No.

INTERVIEWER: For instance, what writing has meant to you?

MALAMUD: I'd be too moved to say.

DANIEL STERN
Spring 1974

6. William Goyen

William Goyen was born on April 24, 1915, to a working-class family in Trinity, Texas. A composer as well as a poet and prose writer, Goyen spoke always of writing as "singing," and his work resonates with a finely tuned lyricism.

Goyen received his bachelor's degree in 1932 and his master's degree in 1939 from Rice University. He spent five years in the U.S. Navy during World War II, and the sketches he wrote during that time became *The House of Breath* (1950), the book which won him the McMurray Award and which immediately established his reputation. He became associated with Frieda Lawrence and her circle of intellectuals, and later lived for a time in London, at Stephen Spender's urging. A recipient of Guggenheim fellowships in 1952 and 1954, he produced a collection of stories, *Ghost and Flesh,* and in 1955 a second novel, *In a Farther Country.* He published two additional novels, a book of poetry, and two nonfictional works before he died of leukemia in August, 1983; another novel, *Arcadio,* was published several months after his death.

William Goyen taught at the New School for Social Research in New York, Columbia University, Brown University, Princeton University, and the University of Southern California. An intensely private man, his publishing history was punctuated by the same silences as his conversations, and in discussing his ideal working conditions, he once remarked that his "lonesome times are best." In 1963 he was awarded a Ford Foundation grant, and he received the American Society of Composers, Authors and Publishers Award for musical composition in 1965, 1966, and 1968–70. He had been married to actress Doris Roberts since 1963.

Cobe Tongues of Men and of Angels

I started out to tell about what became of two cousins and their uncle who loved them, according to what the older cousin told me. But some of their kinfolks' lives would have to be told if you're going to talk at all about the cousins and their uncle. So what I have to tell about is first all one family, what I heard told to me and what I watched happen. I have been here in this family's town longer than any of the family, and have in my long time noted—and wonder if you have, ever—the turning around of some peoples' lives, as if some force moved in them against their will: runaways suddenly arrived back to the place they fled; berserk, possessed people come serene; apparently Godblessed people overnight fall under malediction.

4 Spaces

Joe Parrish

3 Spaces

Blanch, Louetta's mother, ran away —(Continue as written, p. 24)

A William Goyen manuscript page.

William Goyen

The interview with William Goyen took place on a sunny Saturday afternoon in June, 1975—the spring of Goyen's sixtieth birthday and also of the publication of the Twenty-fifth Anniversary Edition of his first novel, The House of Breath.

Taped over a three-hour period in the home of a friend in Katonah, New York, Mr. Goyen remained seated on a sofa throughout the interview, sipping a soft drink. He requested that baroque music be played over the stereo, "to break the silences." There were silences—long, considering pauses between thoughts.

William Goyen is slender and lanky, and a handsome figure at sixty. His aspect is intense and patrician, his manner gracious and courtly. Goyen's hair is silver; he speaks with a strong Southwestern accent.

INTERVIEWER: In the Introduction to your *Selected Writings,* you stated that you began writing at the age of sixteen, at a time when you were also interested in composing and dancing and other art forms. Why writing as a career rather than one of the other arts?

GOYEN: My foremost ambition, as a very young person, was to be a composer, but my father was strongly opposed to my studying music—that was for girls. He was from a sawmill family who made a strict division between a male's work and a female's. (The result was quite a confusion of sex roles in later life: incapable men and oversexed women among his own brothers and sisters.) He was so violently against my studying music that he would not allow me even to play the piano in our house. Only my sister was allowed to put a finger to the keyboard . . . the piano had been bought for her. My sister quickly tired of her instrument, and when my father was away from the house, I merrily played away, improving upon my sister's études—which I had learned by ear—and indulging in grand Mozartian fantasies. In the novel *The House of Breath,* Boy Ganchion secretly plays a "cardboard piano," a paper keyboard pasted on a piece of cardboard in a hidden corner. I actually did this as a boy. My mother secretly cut it out of the local newspaper and sent off a coupon for beginners' music lessons. I straightaway devised Liszt-like concerti and romantic overtures. And so silent arts were mine: I began writing. No one could hear that, or know that I was doing it, even as with the cardboard piano.

INTERVIEWER: You weren't having to write under the sheets with a flashlight, were you?

GOYEN: You know, I *was* playing my music under the quilt at night, quite literally. I had a little record player and I played what music I could under the quilt and later wrote that way. So I did write under the sheets.

INTERVIEWER: What was your father's reaction to writing?

GOYEN: Something of the same. He discovered it some years

later, when I was an undergraduate at Rice University in Houston. He found me writing plays, and to him the theatre, like the piano, was an engine of corruption which bred effeminate men (God knows he was generally right, I came to see), sexual libertines (right again!), and a band of gypsies flaunting their shadowed eyes and tinselled tights at reality. When my first novel was published, my father's fears and accusations were justified—despite the success of the book—and he was outraged to the point of not speaking to me for nearly a year.

This could, of course, have been because the book was mostly about his own family—the sawmill family I spoke of earlier. My father, his brothers, his father, everybody else were lumber people, around mills . . . and forests. I went around the sawmills with him, you see, and saw all that. He loved trees so! My God, he would . . . he'd just *touch* trees . . . they were human beings. He would smell wood and trees. He just loved them. He knew wood. He was really meant for that.

Poor beloved man, though, he later came around to my side and became the scourge of local bookstores, making weekly rounds to check their stock of my book. He must have bought a hundred copies for his lumbermen friends. God knows what *they* thought of it. Before he died he had become my ardent admirer, and my *Selected Writings* is dedicated to him.

INTERVIEWER: Do you agree with the theory that an unhappy childhood is essential to the formation of exceptional gifts? Were you genuinely unhappy?

GOYEN: How could it have been any other way? My own nature was one that would have made it that way. It was a melancholy childhood. It was a childhood that was searching for—or that *needed*—every kind of compensation it could get. I think that's what makes an artist. So that I looked for compensation to fulfill what was not there.

INTERVIEWER: How have the physical conditions of your writing changed over the years? What is the relation between the creative act and privacy for you, today? In your *Note* on the Twenty-fifth Anniversary Edition of *The House of Breath*, you stated that part of the novel was written on an aircraft carrier in the Pacific.

GOYEN: Since my writing began in the air of secrecy, indeed, of alienation—as the work had to be done without anyone's knowing it—forever after my work has had about it the air of someone in solitude having done it, alienated from the press of society and the everyday movements of life.

On the ship, where I continued working, I found that there are many hidden places on an aircraft carrier where one can hide out and do secret work. And this was easily achieved. Also on the night watches and so forth, there was a lot of time. There is a great deal of free time aboard a ship in wartime, ironically. This kind of tradition in my work has been mine all my life, and I have generally lived in hidden places. In New Mexico it was at the beautiful foot of a mountain (the Sangre de Cristo in the primitive village of El Prado), and also in a mysterious mountain (Kiowa Mountain—the D. H. Lawrence Ranch called Kiowa Ranch, over San Cristobal, New Mexico, near Taos). And in Europe—Zurich, Rome—I worked in back-street *pensions*.

Yet more and more, as I get more worldly and have the security of having survived, I feel that it is not necessary to be *that* far removed from the workings of daily life and the daily lives of people. Indeed, the older I get and the more I write, the more I feel it important to be a part of daily life . . . to know that it surrounds me as I work. I presently live in a large apartment on the West Side of New York City. One of those rooms is mine, and it's an absolute hideaway, yet all around me in the other rooms the life of a family goes on, and I like to know that. I also like to know that twelve flights down I can step onto the street in the midst of a lot of human beings and feel a part of those. Whereas, in the old days, in New Mexico, I was brought up—taught—by Frieda Lawrence to see that simple manual endeavor is part of art. I would work in gardens and dig water ditches and walk in mountains and along rivers when I was not writing, and I felt that it was absolutely essential to my work. That's changing for me now. I'm more city-prone. Maybe the world is changing, too. Maybe solitude is best had in the midst of multitudes.

It's amazing how quickly something gets written. Now, when it comes, it can be on a bus, or in a store. I've stopped in Macy's and written on a dry-goods counter and then suddenly had a whole piece of writing for myself that was accomplished, where earlier in my life I felt I had to spend a week in a house somewhere in the country in order to get that. Conditions change.

INTERVIEWER: Some say that poverty is ennobling to the soul. Is economic stability helpful to a writer? On the other hand, do you think wealth can be harmful?

GOYEN: It can be harmful. This depends on the stage in a writer's life, of course. As a young man, for me—I speak now not as a wealthy or an impoverished man, but as a man looking back when he was younger—it was imperative that I live *very* simply and economically. Living in Taos where—who would have believed it then, fifteen or twenty years later a whole migration of young hippies would come to live and meditate in the desert just where I had lived—I was totally solitary. It was imperative for me and my work that I keep everything simple and have practically nothing at all. I lived in just a mud house with a dirt floor on land that Frieda Lawrence gave me out of friendship. I built it with a friend and a couple of Indians. Yet to live in absolute poverty all his life could harm a writer's work. The hardship and worry over money in writers as they get older is a social horror; grants given to writers should be *sufficient,* so that they are able to live with amplitude and, yes, some dignity.

INTERVIEWER: The genesis of it all goes back to that aircraft carrier, doesn't it?

GOYEN: I thought I was going to die in the war. I was on a

terrible ship. It was the *Casablanca,* the first baby flattop. There were always holes in it, and people dying and it was just the worst place for me to be. I really was desperate. I just wanted to jump off. I thought I was going to die anyway, be killed, and I wanted to die because I couldn't endure what looked like an endless way of life with which I had nothing to do—the war, the ship, and the water . . . I have been terrified of water all my life. I would have fits when I got close to it.

Suddenly—it was out on a deck in the cold—I saw the breath that came from me. And I thought that the simplest thing that I know is what I belong to and where I came from and I just called out to my family as I stood there that night, and it just . . . I saw this breath come from me and I thought —in that breath, in that call, is *their* existence, is their reality . . . and I must shape that and I must write about them—*The House of Breath.*

I saw this whole thing. I saw what was going to be four–five years' work. Isn't that amazing? But I knew it was there. Many of my stories happen that way. It's dangerous to tell my students this because then these young people say, "Gee, all I've got to do, if I really want to write, is wait around for some ship in the cold night, and I'll blow out my breath, and I've got my thing."

INTERVIEWER: So this sustained you?

GOYEN: It brought my life back to me. I saw my relationships; it was extraordinary. Lost times come for us in our lives if we're not phony and if we just listen; it hurts, but it's also very joyous and beautiful . . . it's a redemption . . . it's all those things that we try to find and the world seems to be looking for . . . as a matter of fact, that's the *hunger* of the world. So there it was on the ship and it just came to me. I saw so much . . . that I wouldn't have to go home and they wouldn't have to suffocate me; they wouldn't kill me; I'd find other relationships.

INTERVIEWER: So after the war you didn't go home.

GOYEN: When the war was over, I just dipped into Texas and got my stuff and left and headed towards San Francisco. I had come to love San Francisco when it was the home port for my ship, the aircraft carrier, and I thought that it would be a good place to live. But I passed through Taos, New Mexico, in winter, in February, and I was enchanted. It really was like an Arthurian situation . . . I couldn't leave. It was beautiful and remote, like a Himalayan village, untouched, with this adobe color that was ruby-colored and yellow, all the magical colors of mud. It's not all one color. It's like Rome. Rome looks like that. And the sunlight and the snow . . . just about everyone on foot . . . a few cars . . . high, seventy-five hundred feet.

INTERVIEWER: Did the D. H. Lawrence commune in Taos have anything to do with your staying?

GOYEN: I didn't know anything about the Lawrence legend. Had I, I might not have stayed at all. But I did, and right away I thought that I'd better get a little more money for myself before I settled in to work. So I got a job as a waiter at a very fashionable inn called Sagebrush Inn. I worked as a waiter for a few months until I met Frieda, who came in one night and I waited on her. The whole Lawrence world came to dinner there: Dorothy Brett and Mabel Dodge, Spud Johnson, Tennessee Williams: he was living up at the ranch. They all came to my table. And then the owner of the inn had to come out and say, "This young man is just out of the war and he wants to be a writer." The *worst* thing I wanted said about me; it almost paralyzed me. Well, of course, Tennessee thought, Oh, God, who cares about *another* writer. But Frieda said, "You must come and have tea with me." She said it right away. I went and from that moment . . . we just hit it off. It was almost a love affair. It was the whole world.

So it wasn't Lawrence that brought me to her; circumstances brought me to Frieda and I found her a great pal and a luminous figure in my life on her own terms.

I would go to teas with her. She would have high teas. In

Texas we had a coke. But here it was the first time I met someone who baked bread, you know? She made a cake and brought it out . . . it was wonderful. She wore German clothes, like dirndls, and peasant outfits, and an apron. She was a kitchen frau. A few people came . . . Mabel Dodge had given her this great three-hundred-acre ranch in return for the manuscript of *Sons and Lovers*. That was the exchange. Except she never took *Sons and Lovers* away, so that the manuscript and many others, *Women in Love*, all holograph . . . were there in a little cupboard at the ranch. I could read them and look at them in amazement.

INTERVIEWER: What sort of things did you talk about?

GOYEN: We talked about the simplest things . . . well, really about love, about men and women and about sex, about *physical* living. Of course, I didn't know that I was hearing what Lawrence had heard. Because it was Frieda who gave Lawrence this whole thing and it overwhelmed me.

The various people would come up in the summer and spend time with us, all kinds of people. Just simple people; Indians . . . she was close to Indians. I got very close to three Indians who were really like my family and helped me build my house.

INTERVIEWER: And then people like Tennessee Williams came.

GOYEN: Yes, Tennessee stayed up there with his friend, Frank Merlo. Tennessee told us that he heard Lawrence's voice . . . he was a haunted, poor thing, but he did go a little too far. D. H. Lawrence was whispering things to him. Suddenly Tennessee had a terrible stomachache and it turned out that he had a very bad appendix and had to be brought down to Mabel Dodge. Mabel owned the only hospital; built it and owned it. It was like a European town and we were the only Americans, and I went to this hospital to witness Tennessee's dying . . . he was always dying, you know. He was dying in this Catholic hospital screaming four-letter words and all kinds of things with the nuns running around wearing the most enormous habits, most unsanitary for a hospital. Mabel was wringing her hands and saying "He's a genius, he's a genius." The doctor said, "I don't care; he's going to die, he's got gangrene. His appendix has burst. We have to operate at once." Tennessee said, "Not until I make my will." The doctor said, "How long will the will be?" "Well, everything's going to Frankie," so they sat down, with Frank going through an inventory of all Tennessee's possessions. "What about the house in Rome? You left that out." Tennessee was just writhing in pain. So they made a list of all the things. And then they wheeled him off and he indeed had this operation, which to everyone's surprise he managed to recover from. Eventually he got out of there. . . .

INTERVIEWER: All this time you were working on *The House of Breath*. How did it get published?

GOYEN: It got published through Stephen Spender, indirectly. He came to that little village where I was living. I had sent a piece of it to *Accent,* a wonderful early magazine; it caused quite a kind of thing. I began to get letters. Random House wrote me a letter and said that they hoped this was "part of a book." (All editors do that, I later learned.) They'll say that even if it's just a "letter to the editor" they've seen. That's what editors have to do, God bless them, and I'm glad they do. About that time, Spender, a man I scarcely knew, whose *poetry* I scarcely knew, arrived in Taos on a reading tour. A wealthy lady named Helene Wurlitzer, of the family who made the organs, lived there and brought people into that strange territory to read, and give chamber concerts and so on. I never went to those things because . . . well, I didn't have any shoes; I really was living on mud floors in an adobe house that I had built, utterly primitive, which I loved. I was isolated and terrified with all those things going on in me . . . but I was writing that book. Well, Spender heard that I was there . . . he heard through Frieda, who went to the reading, and so then he asked me if he could come to see me; he treated me as though I were an important writer. He had just read that piece in *Accent* and he asked if there was more that he could read. I showed him some other pieces and he sent those around. They were published and then somebody at Random House sent me a contract right away of two hundred fifty dollars advance for the book, and then promptly was fired. But Spender was very moved by the way I was living there; he wrote a well-known essay called "The Isolation of the American Writer" about my situation there. Nothing would do until Mr. Spender would have me come to London because he thought I was too isolated, too Texan, too hicky. . . . He really took it upon himself to make that kind of decision for me. It was a wonderful thing that he did. The stipulation was that I would bring a girl who had come into my life with me (this blessed girl has passed on among the leaves of autumn), and she was very much a part of my life there in London, and together we were real vagabonds, embarrassing everybody—people like Stephen, and Cyril Connolly, and Elizabeth Bowen, Rose Macaulay, I mean, all of them. . . .

INTERVIEWER: You stayed in Spender's house?

GOYEN: I had a room at the top and Dorothy had a room in the basement, with the stairs between us, creaking stairs. It was an elegant house, an eighteenth-century house in St. John's Wood. At four o'clock teatime in the winter it was dark, and they pulled Florentine brocaded curtains and turned on lights; it was a time of austerity still, but people came to tea. Veronica Wedgewood would arrive. Dorothy wouldn't come up from the basement. She really hated this kind of thing. She vanished. She just wouldn't participate. So I was really quite alone with this. I guess I must have kept her under wraps. I must have been very bad to her. I don't know. I have to think about that some time. But here they would come: Natasha, Stephen's wife who was a gifted pianist and wanted to be a concert pianist, and so musicians came, and painters. Cyril Connolly was often there because he and Stephen were working together. Dame Edith Sitwell came. We went to her house and she read one night; she sat behind a screen because she wouldn't read facing anyone or a group . . . behind a marvelous Chinese screen and you would hear this voice coming through the screen . . . all those people . . . that was a world that Spender gave me and was a great influence in my life and on my work.

INTERVIEWER: What an extraordinary change.

GOYEN: I was thrown into this elegant surround which was precisely the opposite of what I had been doing. It was right for me because my character, Folner, yearned for elegance. Suddenly my country people were singing out their despair in those great elegant houses. I saw cathedrals for the first time . . . I'd not really seen cathedrals . . . I was able to get to Paris and all around there. All this went into *The House of Breath*. I saw the Sistine Chapel—well, that's the first page of *The House of Breath*, "on the dome of my skull, paradises and infernos and annunciations" and so forth. Europe just put it all right—everything that started in a little town in Texas, you see. It saved the book, I think. Because it made that cry, you know . . . it was an *elegant* cry . . . there's nothing better than an elegant cry of despair. . . .

INTERVIEWER: Did people worry what this tremendous change in venue—from Taos to Europe—would do to *The House of Breath*?

GOYEN: Some people worried about it. James Laughlin of New Directions, when I had published a bit, wrote me, "You are ruining your work fast; the influences you are coming into are coming too soon, and you're allowing your personality to overwhelm your talent. Obviously people find your *Texas* personality . . ." (and he could be a snide guy too) ". . . charming and you might be of interest to them for a little while. But you are writing a very serious book and this will be permanently damaging to your work." He really wanted me to get out of there.

INTERVIEWER: Were there other Cassandras about *The House of Breath*?

GOYEN: Well, Auden had kind of looked down his nose at

me. He said it's the kind of writing where the next page is more beautiful than the one just read. "One is just breathless for fear that you're not going to be able to do it," he said, "and that makes me too nervous. I prefer James."

Christopher Isherwood said, "You know, my dear boy, you'll never make it. That is what one feels when one reads you. You'll never survive with this kind of sensibility unless you change, get some armor on yourself." As a matter of fact, he wrote me and warned me again . . . he put it all down in a letter. And that *did* scare me. I was young and I was scared. But I knew that I had no choice. Then that feeling of doom *really* came on me . . . because I had no choice. I knew that I couldn't write any other way.

INTERVIEWER: When you began writing *The House of Breath*, did you expect it to be published? Were you writing for publication?

GOYEN: I was most surely not "writing for publication." But I don't think there is any piece of the novel except one that was not published in magazines before the book itself was published.

INTERVIEWER: You said earlier your father was upset by the book when it was published. Had you been concerned about the family and home-town reaction?

GOYEN: Concerned, yes. I fell out of favor with many people in the town, let's put it that way, and just about disinherited by my own family. I had nasty letters, bad letters from home and heartbroken letters from my mother and my father. Generally the attitude was one of hurt and shock. It was not until fifteen years later that I was able to go back to the town! And even then rather snide remarks were made to me by the funeral director and by the head of the bank. We met on the street.

INTERVIEWER: So when you apply for a loan, you won't do it in that town?

GOYEN: No, and I won't die there, either.

INTERVIEWER: How long did you and the girl stay as Spender's guests in England?

GOYEN: I settled in for the whole year of 1949 . . . and I finished the book in that house at St. John's Wood, in Stephen's house. The girl was there until it got very bad; we had problems, and so she moved to Paris; that made me have to go to Paris to see her there and we had this kind of thing that was going on. When I came back, bringing my manuscript on the *Queen Mary,* she came with me to New York. But then we had one visit with Bob Linscott, my editor, who said to her, "My dear, do you like to eat? Do you like a roof over your head? You'll never have it; he's an artist. I feed him and Random House has kept him alive and probably will have to from now on. Don't marry him, don't even fall in love" . . . and he broke her heart. He really did. Poor Dorothy. He was right; I wasn't about to be saddled down. And so it broke away, and that's okay. Many years later I found a woman exactly like her. Her name was Doris, and so often I say to Doris, "Dorothy," and I'm in trouble.

INTERVIEWER: That was quite a step for an editor to take. What do you think their particular function should be?

GOYEN: Well, really caring for authors . . . not meddling with what they did but loving them so much and letting them know that he cares. Generally at that point, when you're starting, you feel that nobody does. Linscott looked after you and if you had no money, he gave you money. Once Truman Capote met me at the Oak Room of the Plaza. "I'm embarrassed to sit with you," he said when I sat down, "your suit is terrible." I hadn't really thought about what I was wearing. He said, "I'm not going to have you wear that suit anymore. But," he said, "I've ordered drinks for us and if you'll just wait, I'm going to call Bob and tell him that he must buy you a suit that costs at least two hundred and fifty dollars." And he did. Bob gave me money and he told me, "Well I guess he's right." He was lovable, Truman. He did sweet lovely things then.

INTERVIEWER: Carson McCullers was one of Linscott's authors, wasn't she?

GOYEN: I had first known her in this nest that Linscott had up there for these little birdlings of writers. Carson had great vitality and she was quite beautiful in that already decaying way. She was like a fairy. She had the most delicate kind of tinkling, dazzling little way about her . . . like a little star. Like a Christmas, she was like an ornament of a kind. She had no mind and she could make no philosophical statements about anything; she didn't need to. She said far out, wonderfully mad things that were totally disarming, and for a while people would say, "I'll go wherever you go." She'd knock them straight out the window.

INTERVIEWER: What sort of people interested her?

GOYEN: She had a devastating crush on Elizabeth Bowen. She actually got to Bowen's Court: she shambled over there to England and spent a fortnight. I heard from Elizabeth that Carson appeared at dinner the first night in her shorts, tennis shorts; that poor body, you know, in tennis shorts and she came down the stairs; that was her debut. It didn't last long. But that was Carson.

INTERVIEWER: What was distinctive about her stories—as, say, compared to the other Southern "magnolia" writers?

GOYEN: She would try to make her stories scary and the word "haunted" was used, of course, by the literary critics, "the haunted domain." I think that was the French title for Truman's first novel . . . *Other Voices, Other Rooms. Les Domaines Hantés.* But Carson was . . . she was a really truly lost, haunted wonder-creature. It's hard to be that and grow old, because of course you either go mad out of what you see, or I guess you try to imitate that kind of purity. She was a bad imitator. So it was just a bore.

INTERVIEWER: She was not a person to have as an enemy.

GOYEN: She was . . . not tough but she had a nasty . . . well, she had a way of absolutely devastating you; the kind that hurt, that little kind of peeping "drop dead" sort of thing. She had an eye for human frailty and would go right to that; that's why people fled her. They thought, Who needs this? Why be around her?

Then, of course, she was terribly affected by not being able to write. It was a murderous thing, a death blow, that block. She said she just didn't have anything to write. And really, it was as though she had never written. This happens to writers when there are dead spells. We die sometimes. And it's as though we're in a tomb; it's a death. That's what we all fear, and that's why so many of us become alcoholics or suicides or insane—or just no-good philanderers. It's amazing that we survive, though I think survival in some cases is kind of mis-given and it's a bore. It was written recently about Saul Bellow that one of the best things about him is that he survived, he didn't become an alcoholic, he didn't go mad and so forth. And that the true heroism of him lies simply in his endurance. That's the way we look at artists in America. People said to me when I was sixty, "My God, you're one of the ones, how are you. But you look *wonderful.* We didn't know where you were." They thought I was dead, or in an institution or something.

INTERVIEWER: Could her editor, Linscott, help McCullers at all?

GOYEN: Poor Linscott couldn't get any more out of her and then he died before he could help her. I doubt whether he could have; no one could have. She was hopeless. She was just kind of a little expendable thing, you know? She would stay with me days at a time. I put her to bed; she had a little nightgown. I was playing sort of dolly; I was playing house. I sat with her while her Ex-Lax worked. Two or three chocolate Ex-Laxes and three wine glasses, and about three Seconal. And I would sit by her bed and see that it all worked, or at least it all got going in her. And then she was off to sleep.

She had some awful cancer of the nerve ends. This caused

the strokes and she had a stroke finally on the other side until she was very badly paralyzed and then she had just a massive killing stroke. She was absolute skin and bones. They took her down there to Georgia, not far from where Flannery O'Connor lived, where they buried her.

INTERVIEWER: Could she have written an autobiography?

GOYEN: She did not have "a hold of herself," as a person would say, enough to look back and see herself in situations. She never could have written her autobiography; it would be impossible for her . . . she had disguised herself so much . . . And what a past, you know? Her mother . . . the Mother of *all* these people . . . thank God mine seems to be quite okay —I'd be raving mad at this point. Carson's mother was an aggressive lady, all over the place, and she came here once and worked at *Mademoiselle.* She had a notorious time as a fiction editor there. She did the oddest things . . . rejecting stories in her own Georgian way, generally in terms of cooking. I think she wrote to a writer once, "The crust of this story holds its contents well . . ." (she was off on a pie) "but my dear, by the time we get to the custard, it runs." The pie image went on and on. "This pie won't do," she said, ". . . came out of the oven too soon." She was a self-educated lady from the South who very early on had read Katherine Mansfield, for instance, and had told Carson about Mansfield, which was the worst thing she could have done. Once I went with her to meet Carson's plane. When she saw her daughter step out of the plane, she turned to me and said, "I seen the little lamp." I thought, "That's some allusion I'm going to have to find out about." When Carson reached us, she said, "Carson, you know what I told Bill when you appeared?" (She was the kind of lady who would repeat a thing she'd said.) "I told him that I seen the little lamp." Carson burst into tears. I said, "Please tell me what this is that hurts you so." She said, "Well, it's that beautiful story called 'The Doll's House' by Katherine Mansfield. It's the last line of the story. A poor little girl peeks in a garden at a doll's house owned by a snobbish family, and she sees this glowing little lamp inside. Later when the little girl's sister asks why there is a curious glow in her eye, she says, 'I seen the little lamp.' "

INTERVIEWER: What about your own mother?

GOYEN: As a literary person I truly am the offspring of my mother and women like my mother. There's no woman like a Texas woman in her eighties. It's not Southern. She wouldn't have a clue as to what a "Southern lady" was. Hers was a singing way of expressing things, and this I heard so very early that it became my own speech; that's the way I write. I love spending money to talk to her on the phone in Texas an hour at a time because it's just as though the curtain that came down on an opera last night goes right up when I call her tonight. The aria goes right on; it's just wonderful.

INTERVIEWER: What do you talk about?

GOYEN: About how Houston has grown, and how she wants to go back to the little town she left fifty years ago. I write her expressions down; I have to do that to understand what they really mean; it's almost another language. But she keeps breeding it. I mean, she's writing all the time. I may not be writing, but she is. She's alive. . . .

INTERVIEWER: Do you carry a notebook with you to put these things in? Or keep a diary?

GOYEN: Oh yes, I always carry paper with me . . . something to write on, always. And I keep not so much a formal diary any longer, but, well, it's a notebook, and in it I keep most things.

INTERVIEWER: What do you do with those ideas that strike you in the middle of Macy's, say, and you can't record them fully or easily? Are they often unrelated to what you currently are writing?

GOYEN: It's rarely unrelated. When one's really engaged deeply in a piece of work, truly writing it, it takes over almost everything else and you find you're thinking about it constantly and it's a part of everything that happens. Even the clerk in

Macy's suddenly speaks out of the novel that you are writing, it seems, or is a character in it. All the people in the world are suddenly characters in the novel you are writing. Everything contributes. The created piece of work has suddenly replaced what is called real life . . . life as it really is, whatever *that* means . . . so that it's not surprising to have it come at one from all angles.

Therefore, I know that if I've been writing all morning and I've got to buy groceries at noon, I better take paper with me, because I'm going to *keep* writing as I go down the street; you can write on the sack that your groceries come in, and I have!

INTERVIEWER: What about the six years you were an editor at McGraw-Hill? Were you able to write, or did this interfere with your work?

GOYEN: The whole McGraw-Hill period is one that I want to write about. I have been writing about it in my *Memoirs* (my next book). The writer in the world of publishing, and particularly *me* in the world of publishing, who had been so disillusioned and embittered by publishers. . . .

INTERVIEWER: You were disillusioned with your own publishers?

GOYEN: Not my own per se. Just publishing in general—the making of books and the life of the making of books. All these things seemed so dead-end to me, without meaning. In this great place, this huge publishing house, I was a special person, in that I was a special editor. I was brought there to concern myself with serious writers and with new writers and what would be called Good Books, "quality writing." I was so concerned with the writing of my own authors that I considered their books my own and I treated them as such. I entered into their creative process. Nevertheless, I was caught in the competitive crush and thrust of commercial publishing. There was no question of my own writing. I was relieved not to have to worry about my own writing. I scarcely grieved it, or mourned it. It had brought me so little—no more than itself.

I suddenly was not a man who I had known. I was on the phone . . . I hate phones, I really can't manage phones well. I won't answer it generally and if I do I can't talk very long; I just can't do it. But here I was having to live and negotiate on the phone. Editors live that way. With agents and all that. . . . Here I was doing this for the first two or three years. I was drawing up contracts and I never knew what a contract was; I didn't know what they were about.

But I began to fail after the fourth year. I got very disturbed for all kinds of reasons . . . publishing, that's a corrupt thing sometimes. I had my way for a while, but then pretty soon night must fall and I was back with the old budgets and best-selling books and a lot of crap.

INTERVIEWER: I take it your interest in your own writing increased during those six years?

GOYEN: Yes, that was bound to happen. As years passed, I began to be hungry and I wasn't quite sure what that hunger was. Well, of course, it was that I was not writing, and the more I exhausted myself with other writers, the more hungry I became to do my own work. This is an exhausting thing, being an editor, and I had no time left for my own work, no matter how much I wanted it. The demands made on me were almost unbearable. And that was when I left McGraw-Hill—or was asked to do so by Albert Leventhal.

INTERVIEWER: That was in the sixties. In the fifties you were teaching at the New School. Did you find teaching just as demanding? Or was this a more satisfactory way to earn an income while doing your own writing?

GOYEN: Teaching writing is draining too, of course. Especially the way I do it. You see, I believe that everybody can write. And in believing and teaching this, what happens, of course, is enormous productivity on the part of many students. One's students produce so much that he is followed down the street by the mass of stuff he's encouraged! I mean, he's overtaken by it. And there's that much more work to do and more conferences to hold, and it's a depleting and exhausting thing. Just as exhausting as editing.

INTERVIEWER: Is there an ideal occupation for the writer, then? Other than teaching?

GOYEN: Probably teaching is ideal. Because there's a community of writers there, and because the writer is respected and understood as a writer in colleges now. He's brought there as a writer, so it's understood why he's behaving the way he does and what he's doing when he's not around; he's *expected* to write. It's well paid, now, too—universities are paying writers well. It's probably the best. It takes a lot of discipline for a writer to teach writing, though. But in the end, leading writing seminars and workshops is refreshing and exhilarating and creative and in touch with life. I consider teaching one of my callings.

INTERVIEWER: What do you think of your students?

GOYEN: The young people I've been involved with in my classes seem to have no sense of place. It bewildered me at first and then it caused me no little alarm. We've talked about it and what they tell me is often what I've presumed . . . that there isn't much of a place where they come from. I mean, every place looks like every other place. Even suburban places —around here or in Ohio or wherever—all look alike . . . a shopping center, a McDonalds, the bank with the frosted globes on the facade, you know, that's a given building. The repertory theatres all look alike. So that they really don't have a sense of place except through literature. But when they begin to write they can't write about Flaubert's place. So what they're writing about right now is the Princeton campus, and I've told them I don't want to hear about that. I ask them, But didn't you live somewhere before? Wasn't there a room somewhere, a house? A street? A tree? Can't you remember?

There was always a sense of belonging to a place in my childhood. The place. We called the house "the place." "Let's go back to the place," we'd say. I loved that. There was such a strong sense of family and generation and ancestors in it. It was like a monument . . . that's what my impression was and I wrote about it as that. It was a Parthenon to me . . . with that enduring monumentality to it. But these students . . . they've had terrible family problems—they are dissociated . . . they're so disoriented . . . divorce, my God, divorce is a way of life in these generations. I ask them, Don't you have a grandmother? Do you ever go to your grandmother's? Where does she live? Oh, they say, she lives with us; or she lives in an apartment; she lives in the condominium. These elegant old ladies, they don't live in places anymore, either.

INTERVIEWER: To get back to your own work, do you feel that music is reflected in your writings?

GOYEN: It's an absolute, basic part of my work, there's no question, and I think of my writing as music, often; and of my stories as little songs.

INTERVIEWER: "Little songs," of course, is the literal meaning of the word "sonnet." The Albondocani Press has just published an edition of your early poems, poems written before your first novel. What made you abandon poetry for fiction? Faulkner said that all short-story writers are failed poets. Do you feel this is so?

GOYEN: I think an awful lot of them are. I'm not a failed poet, I'm just a poet who made another choice, at a certain point, very early. Actually, I'm so taken by the dramatic form I'm really a playwright manqué! I still consider myself, after having written and seen produced four plays in the professional theatre, manqué in the theatre. And yet I continue to love the form, and fear it more than love it.

INTERVIEWER: Do you think your playwriting has been beneficial to your fiction writing?

GOYEN: I think it has. I think it's made me care more about writing fiction, for one thing.

INTERVIEWER: Do you feel a compromise in the collaborations between director and producer and writer?

GOYEN: No, no, that's welcome to me, all that. I need all the help I can get! I never accept playwriting as a solitary thing. Once you do, you're ruined: because from the beginning it's a collaborative affair, and the sooner you can get it on to a stage, the better. The more you write at the table on a play, alone, the farther away you're going to get from the play. So far as the theatre is concerned, it becomes a *literary* work the more you work on it. But writing for the theatre has made me understand plot. It's helped me with plot in fiction writing.

INTERVIEWER: What European authors and what American authors have meant the most to you?

GOYEN: As for American authors, Hawthorne and Melville have meant a great deal. And Henry James. And two poets— Ezra Pound and T. S. Eliot—have influenced me.

INTERVIEWER: In what ways? They seem odd choices for a Southwestern fiction writer. . . .

GOYEN: I still read, I still study, the *Cantos* of Pound. I found Pound in Texas when I was eighteen or nineteen through a young friend named William Hart. Hart was one of those prodigies, enfants terribles, that materialize in small towns, young men bearing a sense of art and poetry and life as naturally as others bore the instinct to compete and to copulate. He had a great deal to do with my early enlightenment and spiritual salvation in a lower-middle-class environment in an isolated (then) Texas town, where a boy's father considered him a sissy if he played the piano, as I've said, and questioned the sexual orientation of any youth who read poetry.

William Hart was a true pioneer; he brought me Pound, Eliot, and Auden. He was self-taught, finding things for himself out of hunger. He had a high-school education, barely, but afterwards he came and sat in my classes at Rice and listened. He knew more than the professors did sometimes—he really did . . . about Elizabethan drama, and medieval romances. He knew these things. He was a delicate boy, obviously, but not effete. He was French Cajun, from a poor family, and he was on the streets, and could have been in trouble a lot. But he ended up in the library. They felt they had a revolutionary in there. In the Houston Public Library at nineteen he would get up and speak about literature, and Archibald MacLeish, of all people. And oh, how this man Hart spoke. The whole library would turn and listen. He became that kind of town creature, one of those who go down in cities, unheralded . . . they go down into beds of ashes. Well, he brought me Pound.

Pound's *Cantos* hold for me madness and beauty, darkness and mystery, pain, heartbreak, nostalgia. Some of the most beautiful and most haunting were written as a prisoner. He made, above all, *songs,* and he told his stories lyrically, as I have felt driven to tell mine. By ordinary speech, ordinary people. I mean that it seems to me that Pound sometimes speaks from a sort of subtone in his poems like a con man, a back-street hustler, using pieces of several languages, bits of myth, literary quotations and mixed dialects and plain beguiling nonsense. There is a stream, flowing and broken, of *voices* in Pound, echoes, town speech, songs, that deeply brought to me my own predicament, in the home of my parents and in the town where I lived. He helped show me a way to sing about it—it was, as most influences have been for me, as much a *tone,* a sound, a quality, as anything else.

The same for T. S. Eliot. He seemed then so much more American than Pound—but then Pound has the Chinese calligraphy and the heavy Greek and Latin. Eliot's wan songs broken suddenly by a crude word or a street phrase directly influenced me as a way to tell *The House of Breath*; and doom cut through by caprice shocked me and helped me survive in my own place until I could escape; showed me a way of managing the powerful life that I felt tearing through me, and trying to kill me. I saw a way: "Cry, what shall I cry?"—the dark Biblical overtone of the great poem; "the voice of one calling Stetson!" Oh, Eliot got hold of me at that early age and helped me speak for my own place.

The story-telling method of Eliot and Pound—darting, ellip-
tical, circular, repetitive, lyric, self-revealing, simple speech
within grand cadence and hyperbole, educated me and showed
me a way to be taken out of my place, away from my obsessing
relations: saved me from locality, from "regionalism." I knew
then that it was "style" that would save me. I saw Pound as
the most elegant of poets and the most elemental. Both. His
madness partakes of both (elegance and elementalness) and is
a quality of his poetry: "Hast 'ou seen the rose in the steel
dust / (or swansdown ever?) / so light is the urging, so ordered
the dark / petals of iron / we who have passed over Lethe."
That's Canto 74, from the *Pisan Cantos*.

INTERVIEWER: What of the Europeans?

GOYEN: Balzac above all, if just for the sheer fullness of story
in him, for the life-giving detail in his novels. The daily *stuff*
and the *fact* of his writing helped me struggle against a tendency toward the ornate and fantastical and abstract. Then
come Flaubert, Proust. Of the English, Milton—a curious
choice, right? The minor poems of Milton, but *Paradise Lost*
above all. Milton's richness and grandness—his *scope*. I had an
epic sense of my story, my material, and he helped me see it.
Then Dante—the *Inferno*. Heine's poems—their sweet-sad-
ness. The beautiful lyric poems of Goethe. Thomas Mann's
stories, especially "Disorder and Early Sorrow," and *Budden-
brooks*. And some of the lyrical poems of Wordsworth. Poetry
has been a strong influence on me, you see. I read it as often
as fiction.

INTERVIEWER: You weren't influenced by Faulkner in any
way?

GOYEN: No, not at all. His work is monumental, and extremely important to me, but not in any way an influence. It
goes along beside me—*Light in August, Absalom, Absalom*—
but not through me. I can't say why, but I know that that's
true. Maybe he's too *Southern*. If that is a tradition . . . I'm
not part of that. Thank God for my southwestern-ness . . . that
Texan thing. My father, I'm afraid, is a Southerner, a Missis-

sippian, but my mother and her family for generations were native Texas people . . . so that was a strong influence. I knew a lot of my father's family; they're the people I've really written about in *The House of Breath*. But something kept me away from those sicknesses and terrors that come from that Deep South.

INTERVIEWER: *The House of Breath* came out at the same time as other celebrated works—Styron's, Capote's, Mailer's. Did you feel part of a writing generation?

GOYEN: I felt immensely apart. And most certainly did not belong to any "writing generation." I remember, indeed, saying, in an interview with Harvey Breit in 1950 in the *New York Times*, that I felt excited about joining the company of those writers, but that I had not before that time been aware of any of them! I stayed off to myself. I read nothing of "the literary world" when writing *The House of Breath*.

INTERVIEWER: Subsequently, did you ever do any reviews of your contemporaries?

GOYEN: I reviewed *Breakfast at Tiffany's* for the *New York Times Book Review*. Actually it was a fair review . . . but it was critical . . . I called Capote a valentine maker and said I thought he was the last of the valentine makers. Well, this just seemed to shake his life for the longest time.

INTERVIEWER: Do your contemporaries interest you now?

GOYEN: They really don't interest me very much. I still feel apart and, well, I *am* apart from my contemporaries. And they don't know what to *do* about me, or they ignore me. I am led to believe they ignore me.

INTERVIEWER: Hasn't that perhaps something to do with your books having been out of print for a decade or more, until recently?

GOYEN: No, I don't think so. How could it? My books have been in libraries, on reading lists in universities. Somebody was always writing a thesis or a paper on my work and writing to me for my help.

But: if I am so full of the books of all these people—Doris

Lessing and John Updike and X and Y and Z—how will I have a clear head for anything of my *own*? I'm really not very interested in contemporary fiction, anyway. I consider my fiction absolutely separate and apart from and unrelated to "contemporary American fiction."

INTERVIEWER: You feel closer to the European literary tradition?

GOYEN: I do.

INTERVIEWER: Your books continued to remain in print in European editions long after they were unavailable here. Do you have any notion why that is?

GOYEN: No, unless it was because my books were translated by such eminent translators—Ernst Robert Curtius and Elizabeth Schnack in Germany, Maurice Edgar Coindreau in France.

INTERVIEWER: All your novels have a rather unique form: they do not follow a linear line, for one thing. Did *The House of Breath* ever take form as a straightforward narrative and then later get broken down into monologues?

GOYEN: No, no, no. The form of that novel is the way it was written. It was slow, although it poured from me and a whole lot of it was simply *given* to me, absolutely put into my mouth. There were great stretches when nothing came. Then it poured out . . . in pieces, if that's possible. So I thought of it as fragments . . . that was what established its form. I once called it *Cries Down a Well,* and then I called it *Six Elegies.* Later it was *Six American Portraits.* So it came in pieces, but I knew that they were linked.

INTERVIEWER: What do you have against the linear novel?

GOYEN: I always *intend* to write a linear novel when I begin. It's my greatest ambition to write a straightforward novel, and I always feel that I am, you know. I get very close. I thought *Come, the Restorer* was very close to being a linear novel. Then people laughed at me when I finished and said that's not true at all.

INTERVIEWER: What people?

GOYEN: Friends or interviewers, I suppose. What I end up writing each time, you see, is a kind of opera. It's a series of arias and the form is musical, despite myself, and it is lyrical. The outcry is lyrical despite myself. These novels have come to me at their height, passages have come to me in exaltation. So that the gaps between have been my problem and the—I was going to say—*quieter* . . . spaces and moments . . . but I don't mean that, because there are *many* quiet spaces in these books. But the less *intense* spaces seem to be hard for me to manage, somehow. What seems meant for me to do is always to begin what's called the linear novel, and try and try and try . . .

INTERVIEWER: Going back to form: Do you think of the novel as a lot of short stories, or as one big story? Or does it depend upon the novel?

GOYEN: It might. But it seems to me that the unified novel, the organic entity that we call a novel, is a series of parts. How could it not be? I generally make the parts the way you make those individual medallions that go into quilts. All separate and as perfect as I can make them, but knowing that my quilt becomes a whole when I have finished the parts. It is the *design* that's the hardest. Sometimes it takes me a long time to see, or discover, what the parts are to form or make.

INTERVIEWER: Does the completion of one "medallion" lead to another?

GOYEN: No, the completion of one medallion does not usually lead to another. They seem to generate, or materialize, out of themselves and are self-sufficient, not coupled to, or, often, even related to, any other piece. That seems to be what my writing job is: to discover this relationship of parts. Madness, of course, comes from not being able to discover any connection, any relationship at all! And the most disastrous thing that can happen is to *make up*, to *fake*, connections. In a beautiful quilt it looks like the medallions really grow out of one another, organic, the way petals and leaves grow. The problem, then, is to graft the living pieces to one another so that they finally become a living whole. That is the way I've had to work, whatever it means.

INTERVIEWER: Have you made medallions that did not fit into the final quilt?

GOYEN: There's rarely been anything left over, that is, medallions that didn't fit into the final quilt. If the pieces didn't all come together, the whole failed. It's really as though all the pieces were around, hidden, waiting to be discovered, and there were just enough for the design on hand. If, in rare cases, something was left over, one tried to use it as some sort of preamble or "postlude"—that sort of fussy thing. It never worked, even when one felt it was such "fine" writing that it should be kept in. It's this kind of exhibitionism of bad taste that's harmed some good work by good writers.

INTERVIEWER: So you started writing under a quilt and you came out producing quilts.

GOYEN: Producing them is right.

INTERVIEWER: How else would you describe your own writing, or your style?

GOYEN: As a kind of singing. I don't say this because others have said it. But we've spoken of my work as song, earlier, the musicality of my writing and its form. It's impossible for me not to write that way. I write in cadence—that could be very bad. Just as in the theatre, when an actor in rehearsal discovers that lines in a speech rhyme, he or the director is horrified. Someone in the back of the theatre will scream out, "Couplet! Couplet!," meaning, "It rhymes! It rhymes!"

Now, when I speak of writing in cadence, I obviously don't mean "Couplet! Couplet!" Nor am I concerned with alliteration or any kind of fancy language. But I am concerned with the *flow* of language (the influence of Proust). I think of my writing as having to do with singing people: people singing of their lives, generally, arias. The song is the human experience that attracts me and moves me to write.

INTERVIEWER: Are you concentrating now on short stories or novels?

GOYEN: I have less an urge to write the short story, and more of a concern with writing The Book. It has nothing to do with anything but my own lack of a need for the very short form and a deep love for the book itself, for a longer piece of writing.

INTERVIEWER: Some may say you achieved both in *Ghost and Flesh*—a book of short stories which, on rereading, seems a total book rather than a collection of pieces. Was it conceived as a book, or was it a true gathering?

GOYEN: No, it was conceived as a book, it truly was. A sort of song cycle, really, that made up a single, unified work, a thematic unity like Schubert's *Die Winterreise* (which influenced *The House of Breath*—an early Marian Anderson recording. Frieda Lawrence first made it known to me, that is, the poem on which the songs were based).

Ghost and Flesh . . . you can see in those stories . . . wow . . . quite surreal and I loved those, and when that was finished and published, I kind of went off the beam. I think the book made me quite mad, writing it, the obsession of that book; but, on the other hand, *The House of Breath* did not. And that's an obsessed book, you see. It's hard to say these things but something always pulled me through. Of course my critics might say, He *should* have gone mad.

INTERVIEWER: What sort of madness was it?

GOYEN: While I wasn't that sane, I knew that madness—that's the word I use but I don't know if it's quite right—that dangerous thing . . . that terror, and I knew that. I guess I knew when to let it alone.

It comes in a loss of reality. If we say madness that sounds funny. But let's say an other-worldness. It has to do with identity. I go through phases of not knowing my own history. It's amnesiac, almost. I've known this all my life; as a child I've known that. The loss of the sense of the world around me, of the reality. It means that I just have to isolate myself and then I'm okay.

Also, I found a very strong wife. So my choices must have been blessed. God knows, when I brought her home to Texas, people gathered to meet her and congratulate us and one woman came over to me who had known me all my life and said, "My God, I can't tell you how relieved we all are. We thought you were going to bring home some *poetess!*"

INTERVIEWER: Is writing a work of nonfiction markedly different for you from writing fiction? Did you derive equal satisfaction from reconstructing the life of Jesus (in *A Book of Jesus*) as you do composing a novel?

GOYEN: Oh, yes. The excitement was tremendous in writing that book. There was no difference in feeling between that and what I felt when I had written fiction. It was as though I were creating a character in this man. A marvelous experience. Astonishing. A very real man began to live with me, of flesh and blood. He did the same work on me that He did on the people of the New Testament that He walked among: He won me over, enchanted and captured me, finally possessed me. I went rather crazy with the love from Him that I felt. I carried a little New Testament around with me in my pocket and would flip it open and read what He said, at cocktail parties or at dinner tables. A surprising reaction from my listeners generally followed: they were struck by the simplicity, wit, and beauty of what the man said to others, particularly to the wonderful woman at the well.

INTERVIEWER: How do you react to the charges of being a regional writer?

GOYEN: For me, environment is all. Place—as I was saying about my students—is absolutely essential. I know the vogue for the non-place, the placeless place, à la Beckett, is very much an influence on writing these days. It has been said that places don't exist anymore. That everything looks alike. There is the same Howard Johnson on your turnpike in Kansas as there is in Miami and in the state of Washington. And the same kind of architecture dominates the new office buildings and the skyscraper. What is a writer to do? Free the "reality" of his environment? To lament loss of place, to search for it in memory? Because within place is culture, style. We speak of a lost way of life. In many of my books and stories, I've felt the need to re-create, to restore lost ways, lost places, lost styles of living.

INTERVIEWER: Isn't this what Marietta did in *In a Farther Country*? And what was expected of Mr. De Persia, in *Come, the Restorer*?

GOYEN: Exactly. So to this extent, then, I *am* a regional writer. In that my writing begins by being of a region, of a real place. It begins with real people talking like people from that place, and looking like them. Very often regional reality ends there and these people become other people, and this place becomes another place. The tiny town of Charity, in *The House of Breath*, is really Trinity, Texas, truly, accurately described. Once described, however, it ceases to be Charity or Trinity and becomes . . . well, London or Rome. The pasture in front of the house in Charity where a cow named Roma grazed becomes the Elysian Fields, and Orpheus and Eurydice flee across it. The house itself becomes a kind of Parthenon, with friezes of ancient kin.

I think there are moments when I exceed myself as a human being, and become Ulysses, perhaps, or Zeus. It is the point of time at which the human exceeds himself, is transformed beyond himself, that I most care about writing about. This is the lyrical, the apocalyptic, the visionary, the fantastic, the symbolic, the metaphorical, the transfiguratory, transfigurational— all those terms which have been applied to my work.

Now, by "exceeding myself as a human being" I mean in *life*—epiphany moments in life—not in *writing*. I mean those moments when human beings experience an epiphany, a transfiguration (that's the word) are the moments that most excite me. I've seen it in supreme artists who sang or danced or acted, in people who've told me they loved me, in those whose souls have suddenly been reborn before my eyes. These are moments and people I most care about writing about, no matter how small the moment, how humble the person. "I seen the little lamp," the transfigured child said at the end of the Katherine Mansfield story.

INTERVIEWER: Are your closest friends writers? Is talking to other writers helpful or harmful to your work?

GOYEN: My closest friends are theatre people. Painters were once closest to me. For some years I lived among painters. But that changed. Now it's either performers or directors. I love theatre people, they give me a great deal. I don't particularly like writers, and I am not prone to talk about writing. Since they're solitary workers, writers tend to *act out* in public, I believe. They seem to carry more hostility maybe because they are responsible to more people (their characters), to a whole world—like God—than painters or actors. Maybe it's because writers are caught in the English language, which sometimes seems like a sticky web you can't pull your antennae out of, like insects I've watched in webs, and are, in public and when they're with other people, still thrashing about in an invisible web. It is *enraging* to work in words, sometimes; no wonder writers are often nervous and crazy: paint seems to be a more benevolent, a more soothing and serene-making medium.

Musicians always want to play for you, which is wonderful and wordless; painters seem to want to talk only about sex or point out to you the hidden genital configurations in their canvas! Since the writer is truly a seminal person (he spits out his own web, as Yeats said, and then, as I just said, gets caught in it), the truly creative writer, I mean, he's full of the fear and the pride that a maker of *new* things feels. So it's seemed to me.

INTERVIEWER: After one of your books is done, do you divorce yourself from the characters, or do you seem somehow to maintain a contact with them?

GOYEN: Oh, the characters in my first novel haunt me to this day! Actually *haunt* me. And characters like Oil King (from *Come, the Restorer*) who's been in my life a long, long time. I've lived with him and loved him and written about him for many, many years. They stay with me, yes indeed they do. They stay. They not only enter my life, but I begin to see them in life, here, there. I see Marietta McGee quite frequently, in several cities. I had not dreamt she was down in Enseñada, Mexico, until recently when I was there. They seem absolutely to exist in life, when I've seen some of them transferred to the stage: like Oil King in *The Diamond Rattler*—it's as though they read for the part and got it—read for their own role. And Swimma Starnes crops up a lot.

INTERVIEWER: How much of a plan do you have before you begin a novel or a play?

GOYEN: I plan quite a bit. But I'm not too aware of it. That is, I've not got it all down, but I've got a good deal of it thought through or *felt* through, before I begin writing. So that the whole world of it is very much alive and urgent for me. I'm surrounded by it—almost like a saturating scent. I feel it like a heat. The world that I'm going to write has already been created, somehow, in physical sensation before I go about writing it, shaping it, organizing it. My writing begins physically, in *flesh* ways. The writing process, for me, is the business of taking it *from* the flesh state into the spiritual, the letter, the Word.

INTERVIEWER: Do you see, from *The House of Breath* to your latest novel, a progression? Do you see any new directions forthcoming?

GOYEN: There *is* a progression. I'm much freer. And I see a liberation of certain obsessive concerns in my work, a liberation towards joy! I feel that I'm much freer to talk about certain aspects of human relationships than I once was. . . . What was the other question?

INTERVIEWER: Do you see any new directions in your subjects or forms?

GOYEN: That's very hard to say. I'd find that only as I write on. I *do* want very much to write a heavily plotted novel, a melodramatic novel.

INTERVIEWER: Finally, a last question: Why do you write?

GOYEN: And the easiest to answer! I can't imagine *not* writing. Writing simply is a way of life for me. The older I get, the more a way of life it is. At the beginning, it was totally a way of life excluding everything else. Now it's gathered to it marriage and children and other responsibilities. But still, it is simply a way of life before all other ways, a way to observe the world and to move through life, among human beings, and to record it all above all and to shape it, to give it sense, and to express something of myself in it. Writing is something I cannot imagine living without, nor scarcely would want to. Not to live daily as a writing person is inconceivable to me.

ROBERT PHILLIPS
Summer 1975

7. Kurt Vonnegut, Jr.

Recognized as one of America's most widely read authors, Kurt Vonnegut, Jr., remained virtually unknown from 1950, when he first devoted himself exclusively to writing, until 1963, when he published *Cat's Cradle.* Originally described as "science fiction," Vonnegut's work soon expanded beyond and defied the technological, futuristic parameters of the genre.

Born in November, 1922, Vonnegut attended Cornell University from 1940 to 1942 as a chemistry major, and later studied mechanical engineering. While enrolled at the University of Chicago for his master's degree, he worked as a police reporter for the Chicago City News Bureau, a position which was to have much bearing in his writing.

From 1942 to 1945, Vonnegut served in the U.S. Army in Europe. Captured by the Germans in late 1944, he was imprisoned in Dresden and witnessed that city's destruction by the Allied bombing fleets in 1945. Encouraged by a Guggenheim Fellowship, Vonnegut fictionalized that experience in his novel *Slaughterhouse Five,* which appeared in 1969.

Other novels include *Player Piano* (1952), *The Sirens of Titan* (1959), *God Bless You, Mr. Rosewater* (1965), *Breakfast of Champions* (1973), *Jailbird* (1979), and *Deadeye Dick* (1981). He has written two collections of short stories, *Canary in a Cathouse* (1961) and *Welcome to the Monkey House* (1968). A collection of critical essays, *Palm Sunday,* was published in 1981. Vonnegut has written a number of plays, the best known of which is *Happy Birthday, Wanda June.*

A member of the Authors League of America, Vonnegut was elected vice-president of PEN American Center in 1974. Divorced from his first wife in 1979, he is now married to Jill Krementz, the photographer. He lives alternately in New York City and Sagaponack, Long Island.

SPIT AND IMAGE

<u>I N T R O D U C T I O N</u>

It was the childishness of my father, finally, that spoiled Heaven for me. We could be any age we wished back there, provided we had actually attained that age in life on Earth. I myself elected to be thirty-three most of the time, which would have been a comfortable way to spend Eternity -- if only Father hadn't tagged after me everywhere in the shape of a runty, unhappy nine-year-old.

"Father," I would say to him in Heaven, "for the love of God grow up!"

But he would not grow up.

So, just to get away from him, I volunteered to return here to Earth as a doppelganger, a spook whose business it is to let certain people know that they are about to die.

I make myself into a near-double of a doomed person, and then show myself to him very briefly. He **invariably** gets my message: That he is about to die.

****

Yes, and about once every six months I turn into a poltergeist, which is simply a spook who throws a tantrum. Suddenly I can't stand the Universe and my place in it, and the way it's being run. So I will become invisible, and go into somebody's house or apartment, and dump tables and chairs and breakfronts and so on, and throw books and bric-a-brac around.

Manuscript page from *Spit and Image,* a novel by Kurt Vonnegut, Jr.

© Jill Krementz

Kurt Vonnegut, Jr.

This interview with Kurt Vonnegut was originally a composite of four interviews done with the author over the past decade. The composite has gone through an extensive working over by the subject himself, who looks upon his own spoken words on the page with considerable misgivings . . . indeed, what follows can be considered an interview conducted with himself, by himself.

The introduction to the first of the incorporated interviews (done in West Barnstable, Massachusetts, when Vonnegut was forty-four) reads: "He is a veteran and a family man, large-boned, loose-jointed, at ease. He camps in an armchair in a shaggy tweed jacket, Cambridge gray flannels, a blue Brooks Brothers shirt, slouched down, his hands stuffed into his pockets. He shells the interview with explosive coughs and sneezes, windages of an autumn cold and a lifetime of heavy cigarette smoking. His voice is a resonant baritone, Midwestern, wry in its inflections. From time to time he issues the open, alert smile of a man who has seen and reserved within himself almost everything: depression, war, the possibility of violent death, the inanities of corporate public relations, six children, an irregular income, long-delayed recognition."

The last of the interviews which made up the composite was conducted during the summer of 1976, years after the first. The description of him at this time reads: ". . . he moves with the low-keyed amiability of an old family dog. In general, his appearance is tousled: the long curly hair, moustache, and sympathetic smile suggest a man at once amused and saddened by the world around him. He has rented the Gerald Murphy house for the summer. He works in the little bedroom at the end of a hall where Murphy, artist, bon vivant, and friend to the artistic great, died in 1964. From his desk Vonnegut can look out onto the front lawn through a small window; behind him is a large, white canopy bed. On the desk next to the typewriter is a copy of Andy Warhol's Interview, *Clancy Sigal's* Zone of the Interior, *and several discarded cigarette packs.*

"Vonnegut has chain-smoked Pall Malls since 1936 and during the course of the interview he smokes the better part of one pack. His voice is low and gravelly, and as he speaks, the incessant procedure of lighting the cigarettes and exhaling smoke is like punctuation in his conversation. Other distractions, such as the jangle of the telephone and the barking of a small, shaggy dog named Pumpkin, do not detract from Vonnegut's good-natured disposition. Indeed, as Dan Wakefield once said of his fellow Shortridge High School alumnus, 'He laughed a lot and was kind to everyone.' "

INTERVIEWER: You are a veteran of the Second World War?

VONNEGUT: Yes. I want a military funeral when I die—the bugler, the flag on the casket, the ceremonial firing squad, the hallowed ground.

INTERVIEWER: Why?

VONNEGUT: It will be a way of achieving what I've always wanted more than anything—something I could have had, if only I'd managed to get myself killed in the war.

INTERVIEWER: Which is—?

VONNEGUT: The unqualified approval of my community.

INTERVIEWER: You don't feel that you have that now?

VONNEGUT: My relatives say that they are glad I'm rich, but that they simply cannot read me.

INTERVIEWER: You were an infantry battalion scout in the war?

VONNEGUT: Yes, but I took my basic training on the 240-millimeter howitzer.

INTERVIEWER: A rather large weapon.

VONNEGUT: The largest mobile field piece in the army at that time. This weapon came in six pieces, each piece dragged wallowingly by a Caterpillar tractor. Whenever we were told to fire it, we had to build it first. We practically had to invent it. We lowered one piece on top of another, using cranes and jacks. The shell itself was about nine and a half inches in diameter and weighed three hundred pounds. We constructed a miniature railway which would allow us to deliver the shell from the ground to the breech, which was about eight feet above grade. The breechblock was like the door on the vault of a savings and loan association in Peru, Indiana, say.

INTERVIEWER: It must have been a thrill to fire such a weapon.

VONNEGUT: Not really. We would put the shell in there, and then we would throw in bags of very slow and patient explosives. They were damp dog biscuits, I think. We would close the breech, and then trip a hammer which hit a fulminate of mercury percussion cap, which spit fire at the damp dog biscuits. The main idea, I think, was to generate steam. After a while, we could hear these cooking sounds. It was a lot like cooking a turkey. In utter safety, I think, we could have opened the breechblock from time to time, and basted the shell. Eventually, though, the howitzer always got restless. And finally it would heave back on its recoil mechanism, and it would have to expectorate the shell. The shell would come floating out like the Goodyear blimp. If we had had a stepladder, we could have painted "Fuck Hitler" on the shell as it left the gun. Helicopters could have taken after it and shot it down.

INTERVIEWER: The ultimate terror weapon.

VONNEGUT: Of the Franco-Prussian War.

INTERVIEWER: But you were ultimately sent overseas not with this instrument but with the 106th Infantry Division—

VONNEGUT: "The Bag Lunch Division." They used to feed us a lot of bag lunches. Salami sandwiches. An orange.

INTERVIEWER: In combat?

VONNEGUT: When we were still in the States.

INTERVIEWER: While they trained you for the infantry?

VONNEGUT: I was never trained for the infantry. Battalion scouts were elite troops, see. There were only six in each battalion, and nobody was very sure about what they were supposed to do. So we would march over to the rec room every morning, and play ping-pong and fill out applications for Officer Candidate School.

INTERVIEWER: During your basic training, though, you must have been familiarized with weapons other than the howitzer.

VONNEGUT: If you study the 240-millimeter howitzer, you don't even have time left over for a venereal disease film.

INTERVIEWER: What happened when you reached the front?

VONNEGUT: I imitated various war movies I'd seen.

INTERVIEWER: Did you shoot anybody in the war?

VONNEGUT: I thought about it. I did fix my bayonet once, fully expecting to charge.

INTERVIEWER: Did you charge?

VONNEGUT: No. If everybody else had charged, I would have charged, too. But we decided not to charge. We couldn't see anybody.

INTERVIEWER: This was during the Battle of the Bulge, wasn't it? It was the largest defeat of American arms in history.

VONNEGUT: Probably. My last mission as a scout was to find our own artillery. Usually, scouts go out and look for enemy stuff. Things got so bad that we were finally looking for our own stuff. If I'd found our own battalion commander, everybody would have thought that was pretty swell.

INTERVIEWER: Do you mind describing your capture by the Germans?

VONNEGUT: Gladly. We were in this gully about as deep as a World War I trench. There was snow all around. Somebody said we were probably in Luxembourg. We were out of food.

INTERVIEWER: Who was "we"?

VONNEGUT: Our battalion scouting unit. All six of us. And about fifty people we'd never met before. The Germans could see us, because they were talking to us through a loudspeaker. They told us our situation was hopeless, and so on. That was when we fixed bayonets. It was nice there for a few minutes.

INTERVIEWER: How so?

VONNEGUT: Being a porcupine with all those steel quills. I pitied anybody who had to come in after us.

INTERVIEWER: But they came in anyway?

VONNEGUT: No. They sent in eighty-eight millimeter shells instead. The shells burst in the treetops right over us. Those were very loud bangs right over our heads. We were showered with splintered steel. Some people got hit. Then the Germans told us again to come out. We didn't yell "Nuts" or anything like that. We said, "Okay," and "Take it easy," and so on. When the Germans finally showed themselves, we saw they were wearing white camouflage suits. We didn't have anything like that. We were olive drab. No matter what season it was, we were olive drab.

INTERVIEWER: What did the Germans say?

VONNEGUT: They said the war was all over for us, that we were lucky, that we could now be sure we would live through the war, which was more than they could be sure of. As a matter of fact, they were probably killed or captured by Patton's Third Army within the next few days. Wheels within wheels.

INTERVIEWER: Did you speak any German?

VONNEGUT: I had heard my parents speak it a lot. They hadn't taught me how to do it, since there had been such bitterness in America against all things German during the First World War. I tried a few words I knew on our captors, and they asked me if I was of German ancestry, and I said, "Yes." They wanted to know why I was making war against my brothers.

INTERVIEWER: And you said—?

VONNEGUT: I honestly found the question ignorant and comical. My parents had separated me so thoroughly from my Germanic past that my captors might as well have been Bolivians or Tibetans, for all they meant to me.

INTERVIEWER: After you were captured, you were shipped to Dresden?

VONNEGUT: In the same boxcars that had brought up the troops that captured us—probably in the same boxcars that had delivered Jews and Gypsies and Jehovah's Witnesses and so on to the extermination camps. Rolling stock is rolling stock. British mosquito bombers attacked us at night a few times. I guess they thought we were strategic materials of some kind. They hit a car containing most of the officers from our battalion. Every time I say I hate officers, which I still do fairly frequently, I have to remind myself that practically none of the officers I served under survived. Christmas was in there somewhere.

INTERVIEWER: And you finally arrived in Dresden.

VONNEGUT: In a huge prison camp south of Dresden first. The privates were separated from the noncoms and officers. Under the articles of the Geneva Convention, which is a very Edwardian document, privates were required to work for their keep. Everybody else got to languish in prison. As a private, I was shipped to Dresden . . .

INTERVIEWER: What were your impressions of the city itself before the bombing?

VONNEGUT: The first fancy city I'd ever seen. A city full of statues and zoos, like Paris. We were living in a slaughterhouse, in a nice new cement-block hog barn. They put bunks and straw mattresses in the barn, and we went to work every morning as contract labor in a malt syrup factory. The syrup was for pregnant women. The damned sirens would go off and we'd hear some other city getting it—*whump a whump a whumpa whump.* We never expected to get it. There were very few air-raid shelters in town and no war industries, just cigarette factories, hospitals, clarinet factories. Then a siren went off— it was February 13, 1945—and we went down two stories under the pavement into a big meat locker. It was cool there, with cadavers hanging all around. When we came up the city was gone.

INTERVIEWER: You didn't suffocate in the meat locker?

VONNEGUT: No. It was quite large, and there weren't very many of us. The attack didn't sound like a hell of a lot either. *Whump.* They went over with high explosives first to loosen things up, and then scattered incendiaries. When the war started, incendiaries were fairly sizeable, about as long as a shoebox. By the time Dresden got it, they were tiny little things. They burnt the whole damn town down.

INTERVIEWER: What happened when you came up?

VONNEGUT: Our guards were noncoms—a sergeant, a corporal, and four privates—and leaderless. Cityless, too, because they were Dresdeners who'd been shot up on the front and sent home for easy duty. They kept us at attention for a couple of hours. They didn't know what else to do. They'd go over and talk to each other. Finally we trekked across the rubble and they quartered us with some South Africans in a suburb. Every day we walked into the city and dug into basements and shelters to get the corpses out, as a sanitary measure. When we went into them, a typical shelter, an ordinary basement usually, looked like a streetcar full of people who'd simultaneously had heart failure. Just people sitting there in their chairs, all dead. A fire storm is an amazing thing. It doesn't occur in nature. It's fed by the tornadoes that occur in the midst of it and there isn't a damned thing to breathe. We brought the dead out. They were loaded on wagons and taken to parks, large, open areas in the city which weren't filled with rubble. The Germans got funeral pyres going, burning the bodies to keep them from stinking and from spreading disease. One hundred thirty thousand corpses were hidden underground. It was a terribly elaborate Easter egg hunt. We went to work through cordons of German soldiers. Civilians didn't get to see what we were up to. After a few days the city began to smell, and a new technique was invented. Necessity is the mother of invention. We would bust into the shelter, gather up valuables from people's laps without attempting identification, and turn the valuables over to guards. Then soldiers would come in with a flame thrower and stand in the door and cremate the people inside. Get the gold and jewelry out and then burn everybody inside.

INTERVIEWER: What an impression on someone thinking of becoming a writer!

VONNEGUT: It was a fancy thing to see, a startling thing. It was a moment of truth, too, because American civilians and ground troops didn't know American bombers were engaged in saturation bombing. It was kept a secret until very close to the end of the war. One reason they burned down Dresden is that they'd already burned down everything else. You know: "What're we going to do tonight?" Here was everybody all set to go, and Germany still fighting, and this machinery for burning down cities was being used. It was a secret, burning down cities—boiling pisspots and flaming prams. There was all this hokum about the Norden bomb-sight. You'd see a newsreel showing a bombardier with an MP on either side of him holding a drawn .45. That sort of nonsense, and hell, all they were doing was just flying over cities, hundreds of airplanes, and dropping everything. When I went to the University of Chicago after the war the guy who interviewed me for admission had bombed Dresden. He got to that part of my life story and he said, "Well, we hated to do it." The comment sticks in my mind.

INTERVIEWER: Another reaction would be, "We were ordered to do it."

VONNEGUT: His was more humane. I think he felt the bombing was necessary, and it may have been. One thing everybody learned is how fast you can rebuild a city. The engineers said it would take five hundred years to rebuild Germany. Actually it took about eighteen weeks.

INTERVIEWER: Did you intend to write about it as soon as you went through the experience?

VONNEGUT: When the city was demolished I had no idea of the scale of the thing. . . . Whether this was what Bremen looked like or Hamburg, Coventry . . . I'd never seen Coventry, so I had no scale except for what I'd seen in movies. When I got home (I was a writer since I had been on the *Cornell Sun*, except that was the extent of my writing) I thought of writing my war story, too. All my friends were home; they'd had wonderful adventures, too. I went down to the newspaper office, the Indianapolis *News*, and looked to find out what they had about Dresden. There was an item about half an inch long, which said our planes had been over Dresden and two had been lost. And so I figured, well, this really was the most minor sort of detail in World War II. Others had so much more to write about. I remember envying Andy Rooney, who jumped into print at that time; I didn't know him, but I think he was the first guy to publish his war story after the war; it was called *Tail Gunner.* Hell, I never had any classy adventure like that. But every so often I would meet a European and we would be talking about the war and I would say I was in Dresden; he'd be astonished that I'd been there, and he'd always want to know more. Then a book by David Irving was published about Dresden, saying it was the largest massacre in European history. I said, By God, I saw something after all! I would try to write my war story, whether it was interesting or not, and try to make something out of it. I describe that process a little in the beginning of *Slaughterhouse Five*; I saw it as starring John Wayne and Frank Sinatra. Finally, a girl called Mary O'Hare, the wife of a friend of mine who'd been there with me, said, "You were just children then. It's not fair to pretend that you were men like Wayne and Sinatra, and it's not fair to future generations, because you're going to make war look good." That was a very important clue to me.

INTERVIEWER: That sort of shifted the whole focus . . .

VONNEGUT: She freed me to write about what infants we really were: seventeen, eighteen, nineteen, twenty, twenty-one. We were baby-faced, and as a prisoner of war I don't think I had to shave very often. I don't recall that that was a problem.

INTERVIEWER: One more war question; do you still think about the fire-bombing of Dresden at all?

VONNEGUT: I wrote a book about it, called *Slaughterhouse Five*. The book is still in print, and I have to do something about it as a businessman now and then. Marcel Ophuls asked me to be in his film, *A Memory of Justice*. He wanted me to talk about Dresden as an atrocity. I told him to talk to my friend Bernard V. O'Hare, Mary's husband, instead, which he did. O'Hare was a fellow battalion scout, and then a fellow prisoner of war. He's a lawyer in Pennsylvania now.

INTERVIEWER: Why didn't you wish to testify?

VONNEGUT: I had a German name. I didn't want to argue with people who thought Dresden should have been bombed to hell. All I ever said in my book was that Dresden, willy-nilly, *was* bombed to hell.

INTERVIEWER: It was the largest massacre in European history?

VONNEGUT: It was the fastest killing of large numbers of people—one hundred and thirty-five thousand people in a matter of hours. There were slower schemes for killing, of course.

INTERVIEWER: The death camps.

VONNEGUT: Yes—in which millions were eventually killed. Many people see the Dresden massacre as correct and quite minimal revenge for what had been done by the camps. Maybe so. As I say, I never argue that point. I do note in passing that the death penalty was applied to absolutely anybody who happened to be in the undefended city—babies, old people, the zoo animals, and thousands upon thousands of rabid Nazis, of course, and, among others, my best friend Bernard V. O'Hare and me. By all rights, O'Hare and I should have been part of the body count. The more bodies, the more correct the revenge.

INTERVIEWER: The Franklin Library is bringing out a deluxe edition of *Slaughterhouse Five,* I believe.

VONNEGUT: Yes. I was required to write a new introduction for it.

INTERVIEWER: Did you have any new thoughts?

VONNEGUT: I said that only one person on the entire planet benefited from the raid, which must have cost tens of millions of dollars. The raid didn't shorten the war by half a second, didn't weaken a German defense or attack anywhere, didn't free a single person from a death camp. Only one person benefited—not two or five or ten. Just one.

INTERVIEWER: And who was that?

VONNEGUT: Me. I got three dollars for each person killed. Imagine that.

INTERVIEWER: How much affinity do you feel toward your contemporaries?

VONNEGUT: My brother and sister writers? Friendly, certainly. It's hard for me to talk to some of them, since we seem to be in very different sorts of businesses. This was a mystery to me for a while, but then Saul Steinberg—

INTERVIEWER: The graphic artist?

VONNEGUT: Indeed. He said that in almost all arts, there were some people who responded strongly to art history, to triumphs and fiascoes and experiments of the past, and others who did not. I fell into the second group, and had to. I couldn't play games with my literary ancestors, since I had never studied them systematically. My education was as a chemist at Cornell and then an anthropologist at the University of Chicago. Christ—I was thirty-five before I went crazy about Blake, forty before I read *Madame Bovary,* forty-five before I'd even heard of Céline. Through dumb luck, I read *Look Homeward, Angel* exactly when I was supposed to.

INTERVIEWER: When?

VONNEGUT: At the age of eighteen.

INTERVIEWER: So you've always been a reader?

VONNEGUT: Yes. I grew up in a house crammed with books. But I never had to read a book for academic credit, never had to write a paper about it, never had to prove I'd understood it in a seminar. I am a hopelessly clumsy discusser of books. My experience is nil.

INTERVIEWER: Which member of your family had the most influence on you as a writer?

VONNEGUT: My mother, I guess. Edith Lieber Vonnegut. After our family lost almost all of its money in the Great Depression, my mother thought she might make a new fortune by writing for the slick magazines. She took short-story courses at night. She studied magazines the way gamblers study racing forms.

INTERVIEWER: She'd been rich at one time?

VONNEGUT: My father, an architect of modest means, married one of the richest girls in town. It was a brewing fortune based on Lieber Lager Beer and then Gold Medal Beer. Lieber Lager became Gold Medal after winning a prize at some Paris exposition.

INTERVIEWER: It must have been a very good beer.

VONNEGUT: Long before my time. I never tasted any. It had a secret ingredient, I know. My grandfather and his brewmaster wouldn't let anybody watch while they put it in.

INTERVIEWER: Do you know what it was?

VONNEGUT: Coffee.

INTERVIEWER: So your mother studied short story writing—

VONNEGUT: And my father painted pictures in a studio he'd set up on the top floor of the house. There wasn't much work for architects during the Great Depression—not much work for anybody. Strangely enough, though, Mother was right: Even mediocre magazine writers were making money hand over fist.

INTERVIEWER: So your mother took a very practical attitude toward writing.

VONNEGUT: Not to say crass. She was a highly intelligent, cultivated woman, by the way. She went to the same high school I did, and was one of the few people who got nothing but A-plusses while she was there. She went east to a finishing school after that, and then traveled all over Europe. She was fluent in German and French. I still have her high school report cards somewhere. "A-plus, A-plus, A-plus . . ." She was a good writer, it turned out, but she had no talent for the vulgarity the slick magazines required. Fortunately, I was loaded with vulgarity, so, when I grew up, I was able to make her dream come true. Writing for *Collier's* and *The Saturday Evening Post* and *Cosmopolitan* and *Ladies' Home Journal* and so on was as easy as falling off a log for me. I only wish she'd lived to see it. I only wish she'd lived to see all her grandchildren. She has ten. She didn't even get to see the first one. I made another one of her dreams come true: I lived on Cape Cod for many years. She always wanted to live on Cape Cod. It's probably very common for sons to try to make their mothers' impossible dreams come true. I adopted my sister's sons after she died, and it's spooky to watch them try to make her impossible dreams come true.

INTERVIEWER: What were your sister's dreams like?

VONNEGUT: She wanted to live like a member of *The Swiss Family Robinson*, with impossibly friendly animals in impossibly congenial isolation. Her oldest son, Jim, has been a goat farmer on a mountain top in Jamaica for the past eight years. No telephone. No electricity.

INTERVIEWER: The Indianapolis High School you and your mother attended—

VONNEGUT: And my father. Shortridge High.

INTERVIEWER: It had a daily paper, I believe.

VONNEGUT: Yes. *The Shortridge Daily Echo.* There was a print shop right in the school. Students wrote the paper. Students set the type. After school.

INTERVIEWER: You just laughed about something.

VONNEGUT: It was something dumb I remembered about high school. It doesn't have anything to do with writing.

INTERVIEWER: You care to share it with us anyway?

VONNEGUT: Oh—I just remembered something that happened in a high school course on civics, on how our government worked. The teacher asked each of us to stand up in turn and tell what we did after school. I was sitting in the back of the room, sitting next to a guy named J. T. Alburger. He later became an insurance man in Los Angeles. He died fairly recently. Anyway—he kept nudging me, urging me, daring me to tell the truth about what I did after school. He offered me five dollars to tell the truth. He wanted me to stand up and say, "I make model airplanes and jerk off."

INTERVIEWER: I see.

VONNEGUT: I also worked on *The Shortridge Daily Echo.*

INTERVIEWER: Was that fun?

VONNEGUT: Fun and easy. I've always found it easy to write. Also, I learned to write for peers rather than for teachers. Most beginning writers don't get to write for peers—to catch hell from peers.

INTERVIEWER: So every afternoon you would go to the *Echo* office—

VONNEGUT: Yeah. And one time, while I was writing, I happened to sniff my armpits absent-mindedly. Several people saw me do it, and thought it was funny—and ever after that I was given the name "Snarf." In the annual for my graduating class, the class of 1940, I'm listed as "Kurt Snarfield Vonnegut, Jr." Technically, I wasn't really a snarf. A snarf was a person who went around sniffing girls' bicycle saddles. I didn't do that. "Twerp" also had a very specific meaning, which few people know now. Through careless usage, "twerp" is a pretty formless insult now.

INTERVIEWER: What is a twerp in the strictest sense, in the original sense?

VONNEGUT: It's a person who inserts a set of false teeth between the cheeks of his ass.

INTERVIEWER: I see.

VONNEGUT: I beg your pardon; between the cheeks of his or *her* ass. I'm always offending feminists that way.

INTERVIEWER: I don't quite understand why someone would do that with false teeth.

VONNEGUT: In order to bite the buttons off the back seats of taxicabs. That's the only reason twerps do it. It's all that turns them on.

INTERVIEWER: You went to Cornell University after Shortridge?

VONNEGUT: I imagine.

INTERVIEWER: You imagine?

VONNEGUT: I had a friend who was a heavy drinker. If somebody asked him if he'd been drunk the night before, he would always answer off-handedly, "Oh, I imagine." I've always liked that answer. It acknowledges life as a dream. Cornell was a boozy dream, partly because of booze itself, and partly because I was enrolled exclusively in courses I had no talent for. My father and brother agreed that I should study chemistry, since my brother had done so well with chemicals at M.I.T. He's eight years older than I am. Funnier, too. His most famous discovery is that silver iodide will sometimes make it rain or snow.

INTERVIEWER: Was your sister funny, too?

VONNEGUT: Oh, yes. There was an odd cruel streak to her sense of humor, though, which didn't fit in with the rest of her character somehow. She thought it was terribly funny whenever anybody fell down. One time she saw a woman come out of a streetcar horizontally, and she laughed for weeks after that.

INTERVIEWER: Horizontally?

VONNEGUT: Yes. This woman must have caught her heels somehow. Anyway, the streetcar door opened, and my sister happened to be watching from the sidewalk, and then she saw this woman come out horizontally—as straight as a board, face down, and about two feet off the ground.

INTERVIEWER: Slapstick?

VONNEGUT: Sure. We loved Laurel and Hardy. You know what one of the funniest things is that can happen in a film?

INTERVIEWER: No.

VONNEGUT: To have somebody walk through what looks like a shallow little puddle, but which is actually six feet deep. I remember a movie where Cary Grant was loping across lawns at night. He came to a low hedge, which he cleared ever so gracefully, only there was a twenty-foot drop on the other side. But the thing my sister and I loved best was when somebody in a movie would tell everybody off, and then make a grand exit into the coat closet. He had to come out again, of course, all tangled in coat hangers and scarves.

INTERVIEWER: Did you take a degree in chemistry at Cornell?

VONNEGUT: I was flunking everything by the middle of my junior year. I was delighted to join the army and go to war. After the war, I went to the University of Chicago, where I was pleased to study anthropology, a science that was mostly poetry, that involved almost no math at all. I was married by then, and soon had one kid, who was Mark. He would later go crazy, of course, and write a fine book about it—*The Eden Express*. He has just fathered a kid himself, my first grandchild, a boy named Zachary. Mark is finishing his second year in Harvard Medical School, and will be about the only member of his class not to be in debt when he graduates—because of the book. That's a pretty decent recovery from a crackup, I'd say.

INTERVIEWER: Did the study of anthropology later color your writings?

VONNEGUT: It confirmed my atheism, which was the faith of my fathers anyway. Religions were exhibited and studied as the Rube Goldberg inventions I'd always thought they were. We weren't allowed to find one culture superior to any other. We caught hell if we mentioned races much. It was highly idealistic.

INTERVIEWER: Almost a religion?

VONNEGUT: Exactly. And the only one for me. So far.

INTERVIEWER: What was your dissertation?

VONNEGUT: *Cat's Cradle.*

INTERVIEWER: But you wrote that years after you left Chicago, didn't you?

VONNEGUT: I left Chicago without writing a dissertation— and without a degree. All my ideas for dissertations had been rejected, and I was broke, so I took a job as a P.R. man for General Electric in Schenectady. Twenty years later, I got a letter from a new dean at Chicago, who had been looking through my dossier. Under the rules of the university, he said, a published work of high quality could be substituted for a dissertation, so I was entitled to an M.A. He had shown *Cat's Cradle* to the anthropology department, and they had said it was half-way decent anthropology, so they were mailing me my degree. I'm class of 1972 or so.

INTERVIEWER: Congratulations.

VONNEGUT: It was nothing, really. A piece of cake.

INTERVIEWER: Some of the characters in *Cat's Cradle* were based on people you knew at G.E., isn't that so?

VONNEGUT: Dr. Felix Hoenikker, the absent-minded scientist, was a caricature of Dr. Irving Langmuir, the star of the

G.E. research laboratory. I knew him some. My brother worked with him. Langmuir was wonderfully absent-minded. He wondered out loud one time whether, when turtles pulled in their heads, their spines buckled or contracted. I put that in the book. One time he left a tip under his plate after his wife served him breakfast at home. I put that in. His most important contribution, though, was the idea for what I called "Ice-9," a form of frozen water that was stable at room temperature. He didn't tell it directly to me. It was a legend around the laboratory—about the time H. G. Wells came to Schenectady. That was long before my time. I was just a little boy when it happened—listening to the radio, building model airplanes.

INTERVIEWER: Yes?

VONNEGUT: Anyway—Wells came to Schenectady, and Langmuir was told to be his host. Langmuir thought he might entertain Wells with an idea for a science-fiction story —about a form of ice that was stable at room temperature. Wells was uninterested, or at least never used the idea. And then Wells died, and then, finally, Langmuir died. I thought to myself: "Finders, keepers—the idea is mine." Langmuir, incidentally, was the first scientist in private industry to win a Nobel Prize.

INTERVIEWER: How do you feel about Bellow's winning the Nobel Prize for Literature?

VONNEGUT: It was the best possible way to honor our entire literature.

INTERVIEWER: Do you find it easy to talk to him?

VONNEGUT: Yes. I've had about three opportunities. I was his host one time at the University of Iowa, where I was teaching and he was lecturing. It went very well. We had one thing in common, anyway—

INTERVIEWER: Which was—?

VONNEGUT: We were both products of the anthropology department of the University of Chicago. So far as I know, he never went on any anthropological expeditions, and neither did

I. We invented preindustrial peoples instead—I in *Cat's Cradle* and he in *Henderson the Rain King.*

INTERVIEWER: So he is a fellow scientist.

VONNEGUT: I'm no scientist at all. I'm glad, though, now that I was pressured into becoming a scientist by my father and my brother. I understand how scientific reasoning and playfulness work, even though I have no talent for joining in. I enjoy the company of scientists, am easily excited and entertained when they tell me what they're doing. I've spent a lot more time with scientists than with literary people, my brother's friends, mostly. I enjoy plumbers and carpenters and automobile mechanics, too. I didn't get to know any literary people until the last ten years, starting with two years of teaching at Iowa. There at Iowa, I was suddenly friends with Nelson Algren and José Donoso and Vance Bourjaily and Donald Justice and George Starbuck and Marvin Bell, and so on. I was amazed. Now, judging from the reviews my latest book, *Slapstick*, has received, people would like to bounce me out of the literary establishment—send me back where I came from.

INTERVIEWER: There were some bad reviews?

VONNEGUT: Only in *The New York Times, Time, Newsweek, The New York Review of Books,* the *Village Voice,* and *Rolling Stone.* They loved me in Medicine Hat.

INTERVIEWER: To what do you attribute this rancor?

VONNEGUT: *Slapstick* may be a very bad book. I am perfectly willing to believe that. Everybody else writes lousy books, so why shouldn't I? What was unusual about the reviews was that they wanted people to admit now that I had never been any good. The reviewer for the Sunday *Times* actually asked critics who had praised me in the past to now admit in public how wrong they'd been. My publisher, Sam Lawrence, tried to comfort me by saying that authors were invariably attacked when they became fabulously well-to-do.

INTERVIEWER: You needed comforting?

VONNEGUT: I never felt worse in my life. I felt as though I were sleeping standing up on a boxcar in Germany again.

INTERVIEWER: That bad?

VONNEGUT: No. But bad enough. All of a sudden, critics wanted me squashed like a bug. And it wasn't just that I had money all of a sudden, either. The hidden complaint was that I was barbarous, that I wrote without having made a systematic study of great literature, that I was no gentleman, since I had done hack writing so cheerfully for vulgar magazines—that I had not paid my academic dues.

INTERVIEWER: You had not suffered?

VONNEGUT: I had suffered, all right—but as a badly educated person in vulgar company and in a vulgar trade. It was dishonorable enough that I perverted art for money. I then topped that felony by becoming, as I say, fabulously well-to-do. Well, that's just too damn bad for me and for everybody. I'm completely in print, so we're all stuck with me and stuck with my books.

INTERVIEWER: Do you mean to fight back?

VONNEGUT: In a way. I'm on the New York State Council for the Arts now, and every so often some other member talks about sending notices to college English departments about some literary opportunity, and I say, "Send them to the chemistry departments, send them to the zoology departments, send them to the anthropology departments and the astronomy departments and physics departments, and all the medical and law schools. That's where the writers are most likely to be."

INTERVIEWER: You believe that?

VONNEGUT: I think it can be tremendously refreshing if a creator of literature has something on his mind other than the history of literature so far. Literature should not disappear up its own asshole, so to speak.

INTERVIEWER: Let's talk about the women in your books.

VONNEGUT: There aren't any. No real women, no love.

INTERVIEWER: Is this worth expounding upon?

VONNEGUT: It's a mechanical problem. So much of what happens in storytelling is mechanical, has to do with the technical problems of how to make a story work. Cowboy stories and policeman stories end in shoot-outs, for example, because shoot-outs are the most reliable mechanisms for making such stories end. There is nothing like death to say what is always such an artificial thing to say: "The end." I try to keep deep love out of my stories because, once that particular subject comes up, it is almost impossible to talk about anything else. Readers don't want to hear about anything else. They go gaga about love. If a lover in a story wins his true love, that's the end of the tale, even if World War III is about to begin, and the sky is black with flying saucers.

INTERVIEWER: So you keep love out.

VONNEGUT: I have other things I want to talk about. Ralph Ellison did the same thing in *Invisible Man.* If the hero in that magnificent book had found somebody worth loving, somebody who was crazy about him, that would have been the end of the story. Céline did the same thing in *Journey to the End of Night:* he excluded the possibility of true and final love— so that the story could go on and on and on.

INTERVIEWER: Not many writers talk about the mechanics of stories.

VONNEGUT: I am such a barbarous technocrat that I believe they can be tinkered with like Model T Fords.

INTERVIEWER: To what end?

VONNEGUT: To give the reader pleasure.

INTERVIEWER: Will you ever write a love story, do you think?

VONNEGUT: Maybe. I lead a loving life. I really do. Even when I'm leading that loving life, though, and it's going so well, I sometimes find myself thinking, "My goodness, couldn't we talk about something else for just a little while?" You know what's really funny?

INTERVIEWER: No.

VONNEGUT: My books are being thrown out of school libraries all over the country—because they're supposedly obscene. I've seen letters to small-town newspapers that put *Slaughterhouse Five* in the same class with *Deep Throat* and *Hustler* magazine. How could anybody masturbate to *Slaughterhouse Five*?

INTERVIEWER: It takes all kinds.

VONNEGUT: Well, that kind doesn't exist. It's my religion the censors hate. They find me disrespectful towards their idea of God Almighty. They think it's the proper business of government to protect the reputation of God. All I can say is, "Good luck to them, and good luck to the government, and good luck to God." You know what H. L. Mencken said one time about religious people? He said he'd been greatly misunderstood. He said he didn't hate them. He simply found them comical.

INTERVIEWER: When I asked you a while back which member of your family had influenced you most as a writer, you said your mother. I had expected you to say your sister, since you talked so much about her in *Slapstick*.

VONNEGUT: I said in *Slapstick* that she was the person I wrote for—that every successful creative person creates with an audience of one in mind. That's the secret of artistic unity. Anybody can achieve it, if he or she will make something with only one person in mind. I didn't realize that she was the person I wrote for until after she died.

INTERVIEWER: She loved literature?

VONNEGUT: She wrote wonderfully well. She didn't read much—but then again, neither in later years did Henry David Thoreau. My father was the same way: he didn't read much, but he could write like a dream. Such letters my father and sister wrote! When I compare their prose with mine, I am ashamed.

INTERVIEWER: Did your sister try to write for money, too?

VONNEGUT: No. She could have been a remarkable sculptor, too. I bawled her out one time for not doing more with the talents she had. She replied that having talent doesn't carry with it the obligation that something has to be done with it. This was startling news to me. I thought people were supposed to grab their talents and run as far and fast as they could.

INTERVIEWER: What do you think now?

VONNEGUT: Well—what my sister said now seems a peculiarly feminine sort of wisdom. I have two daughters who are as talented as she was, and both of them are damned if they are going to lose their poise and senses of humor by snatching up their talents and desperately running as far and as fast as they can. They saw me run as far and as fast as I could—and it must have looked like quite a crazy performance to them. And this is the worst possible metaphor, for what they actually saw was a man sitting still for decades.

INTERVIEWER: At a typewriter.

VONNEGUT: Yes, and smoking his fool head off.

INTERVIEWER: Have you ever stopped smoking?

VONNEGUT: Twice. Once I did it cold turkey, and turned into Santa Claus. I became roly-poly. I was approaching two hundred and fifty pounds. I stopped for almost a year, and then the University of Hawaii brought me to Oahu to speak. I was drinking out of a coconut on the roof of the Ili Kai one night, and all I had to do to complete the ring of my happiness was to smoke a cigarette. Which I did.

INTERVIEWER: The second time?

VONNEGUT: Very recently—last year. I paid Smokenders a hundred and fifty dollars to help me quit, over a period of six weeks. It was exactly as they had promised—easy and instructive. I won my graduation certificate and recognition pin. The only trouble was that I had also gone insane. I was supremely happy and proud, but those around me found me unbearably opinionated and abrupt and boisterous. Also: I had stopped writing. I didn't even write letters any more. I had made a bad trade, evidently. So I started smoking again. As the National Association of Manufacturers used to say, "There's no such thing as a free lunch."

INTERVIEWER: Do you really think creative writing can be taught?

VONNEGUT: About the same way golf can be taught. A pro can point out obvious flaws in your swing. I did that well, I think, at the University of Iowa for two years. Gail Godwin and John Irving and Jonathan Penner and Bruce Dobler and John Casey and Jane Casey were all students of mine out there. They've all published wonderful stuff since then. I taught creative writing badly at Harvard—because my marriage was breaking up, and because I was commuting every week to Cambridge from New York. I taught even worse at City College a couple of years ago. I had too many other projects going on at the same time. I don't have the will to teach any more. I only know the theory.

INTERVIEWER: Could you put the theory into a few words?

VONNEGUT: It was stated by Paul Engle—the founder of the Writers Workshop at Iowa. He told me that, if the workshop ever got a building of its own, these words should be inscribed over the entrance: "Don't take it all so seriously."

INTERVIEWER: And how would that be helpful?

VONNEGUT: It would remind the students that they were learning to play practical jokes.

INTERVIEWER: Practical jokes?

VONNEGUT: If you make people laugh or cry about little black marks on sheets of white paper, what is that but a practical joke? All the great story lines are great practical jokes that people fall for over and over again.

INTERVIEWER: Can you give an example?

VONNEGUT: The Gothic novel. Dozens of the things are published every year, and they all sell. My friend Borden Deal recently wrote a Gothic novel for the fun of it, and I asked him what the plot was, and he said, "A young woman takes a job in an old house and gets the pants scared off her."

INTERVIEWER: Some more examples?

VONNEGUT: The others aren't that much fun to describe:

somebody gets into trouble, and then gets out again; somebody loses something and gets it back; somebody is wronged and gets revenge; Cinderella; somebody hits the skids and just goes down, down, down; people fall in love with each other, and a lot of other people get in the way; a virtuous person is falsely accused of sin; a sinful person is believed to be virtuous; a person faces a challenge bravely, and succeeds or fails; a person lies, a person steals, a person kills, a person commits fornication.

INTERVIEWER: If you will pardon my saying so, these are very old-fashioned plots.

VONNEGUT: I guarantee you that no modern story scheme, even plotlessness, will give a reader genuine satisfaction, unless one of those old-fashioned plots is smuggled in somewhere. I don't praise plots as accurate representations of life, but as ways to keep readers reading. When I used to teach creative writing, I would tell the students to make their characters want something right away—even if it's only a glass of water. Characters paralyzed by the meaninglessness of modern life still have to drink water from time to time. One of my students wrote a story about a nun who got a piece of dental floss stuck between her lower left molars, and who couldn't get it out all day long. I thought that was wonderful. The story dealt with issues a lot more important than dental floss, but what kept readers going was anxiety about when the dental floss would finally be removed. Nobody could read that story without fishing around in his mouth with a finger. Now, there's an admirable practical joke for you. When you exclude plot, when you exclude anyone's wanting anything, you exclude the reader, which is a mean-spirited thing to do. You can also exclude the reader by not telling him immediately where the story is taking place, and who the people are—

INTERVIEWER: And what they want.

VONNEGUT: Yes. And you can put him to sleep by never having characters confront each other. Students like to say that they stage no confrontations because people avoid confrontations in modern life. "Modern life is so lonely," they say. This is laziness. It's the writer's job to stage confrontations, so the characters will say surprising and revealing things, and educate and entertain us all. If a writer can't or won't do that, he should withdraw from the trade.

INTERVIEWER: Trade?

VONNEGUT: Trade. Carpenters build houses. Storytellers use a reader's leisure time in such a way that the reader will not feel that his time has been wasted. Mechanics fix automobiles.

INTERVIEWER: Surely talent is required?

VONNEGUT: In all those fields. I was a Saab dealer on Cape Cod for a while, and I enrolled in their mechanic's school, and they threw me out of their mechanic's school. No talent.

INTERVIEWER: How common is storytelling talent?

VONNEGUT: In a creative writing class of twenty people anywhere in this country, six students will be startlingly talented. Two of those might actually publish something by and by.

INTERVIEWER: What distinguishes those two from the rest?

VONNEGUT: They will have something other than literature itself on their minds. They will probably be hustlers, too. I mean that they won't want to wait passively for somebody to discover them. They will insist on being read.

INTERVIEWER: You have been a public relations man and an advertising man—

VONNEGUT: Oh, I imagine.

INTERVIEWER: Was this painful? I mean—did you feel your talent was being wasted, being crippled?

VONNEGUT: No. That's romance—that work of that sort damages a writer's soul. At Iowa, Dick Yates and I used to give a lecture each year on the writer and the free enterprise system. The students hated it. We would talk about all the hack jobs writers could take in case they found themselves starving to death, or in case they wanted to accumulate enough capital to finance the writing of a book. Since publishers aren't putting money into first novels any more, and since the magazines have died, and since television isn't buying from young freelancers any more, and since the foundations give grants only to old poops like me, young writers are going to have to support themselves as shameless hacks. Otherwise, we are soon going to find ourselves without a contemporary literature. There is only one genuinely ghastly thing hack jobs do to writers, and that is to waste their precious time.

INTERVIEWER: No joke.

VONNEGUT: A tragedy. I just keep trying to think of ways, even horrible ways, for young writers to somehow hang on.

INTERVIEWER: Should young writers be subsidized?

VONNEGUT: Something's got to be done, now that free enterprise has made it impossible for them to support themselves through free enterprise. I was a sensational businessman in the beginning—for the simple reason that there was so much business to be done. When I was working for General Electric, I wrote a story, "Report on the Barnhouse Effect," the first story I ever wrote. I mailed it off to *Collier's*. Knox Burger was fiction editor there. Knox told me what was wrong with it and how to fix it. I did what he said, and he bought the story for seven hundred and fifty dollars, six weeks' pay at G.E. I wrote another, and he paid me nine hundred and fifty dollars, and suggested that it was perhaps time for me to quit G.E. Which I did. I moved to Provincetown. Eventually, my price for a short story got up to twenty-nine hundred dollars a crack. Think of that. And Knox got me a couple of agents who were as shrewd about storytelling as he was—Kenneth Littauer, who had been his predecessor at *Collier's*, and Max Wilkinson, who had been a story editor for MGM. And let it be put on the record here that Knox Burger, who is about my age, discovered and encouraged more good young writers than any other editor of his time. I don't think that's ever been written down anywhere. It's a fact known only to writers, and one that could easily vanish, if it isn't somewhere written down.

INTERVIEWER: Where is Knox Burger now?

VONNEGUT: He's a literary agent. He represents my son Mark, in fact.

INTERVIEWER: And Littauer and Wilkinson?

VONNEGUT: Littauer died ten years ago or so. He was a colonel in the Lafayette Escadrille, by the way, at the age of twenty-three—and the first man to strafe a trench. He was my mentor. Max Wilkinson has retired to Florida. It always embarrassed him to be an agent. If some stranger asked him what he did for a living, he always said he was a cotton planter.

INTERVIEWER: Do you have a new mentor now?

VONNEGUT: No. I guess I'm too old to find one. Whatever I write now is set in type without comment by my publisher, who is younger than I am, by editors, by anyone. I don't have my sister to write for any more. Suddenly, there are all these unfilled jobs in my life.

INTERVIEWER: Do you feel as though you're up there without a net under you?

VONNEGUT: And without a balancing pole, either. It gives me the heebie-jeebies sometimes.

INTERVIEWER: Is there anything else you'd like to add?

VONNEGUT: You know the panic bars they have on the main doors of schools and theaters? If you get slammed into the door, the door will fly open?

INTERVIEWER: Yes.

VONNEGUT: The brand name on most of them is "Vonduprin." The "Von" is for Vonnegut. A relative of mine was caught in the Iroquois Theater Fire in Chicago a long time ago, and he invented the panic bar along with two other guys. "Prin" was Prinz. I forget who "Du" was.

INTERVIEWER: O.K.

VONNEGUT: And I want to say, too, that humorists are very commonly the youngest children in their families. When I was the littlest kid at our supper table, there was only one way I could get anybody's attention, and that was to be funny. I had to specialize. I used to listen to radio comedians very intently, so I could learn how to make jokes. And that's what my books are, now that I'm a grownup—mosaics of jokes.

INTERVIEWER: Do you have any favorite jokes?

VONNEGUT: My sister and I used to argue about what the funniest joke in the world was—next to a guy storming into a coat closet, of course. When the two of us worked together, incidentally, we could be almost as funny as Laurel and Hardy. That's basically what *Slapstick* was about.

INTERVIEWER: Did you finally agree on the world's champion joke?

VONNEGUT: We finally settled on two. It's sort of hard to tell either one just flat-footed like this.

INTERVIEWER: Do it anyway.

VONNEGUT: Well—you won't laugh. Nobody ever laughs. But one is an old "Two Black Crows" joke. The "Two Black Crows" were white guys in blackface—named Moran and Mack. They made phonograph records of their routines, two supposedly black guys talking lazily to each other. Anyway, one of them says, "Last night I dreamed I was eating flannel cakes." The other one says, "Is that so?" And the first one says, "And when I woke up, the blanket was gone."

INTERVIEWER: Um.

VONNEGUT: I told you you wouldn't laugh. The other champion joke requires your cooperation. I will ask you a question, and you will have to say "No."

INTERVIEWER: O.K.

VONNEGUT: Do you know why cream is so much more expensive than milk?

INTERVIEWER: No.

VONNEGUT: Because the cows hate to squat on those little bottles. See, you didn't laugh again, but I give you my sacred word of honor that those are splendid jokes. Exquisite craftsmanship.

INTERVIEWER: You seem to prefer Laurel and Hardy over Chaplin. Is that so?

VONNEGUT: I'm crazy about Chaplin, but there's too much

distance between him and his audience. He is too obviously a genius. In his own way, he's as brilliant as Picasso, and this is intimidating to me.

INTERVIEWER: Will you ever write another short story?

VONNEGUT: Maybe. I wrote what I thought would be my last one about eight years ago. Harlan Ellison asked me to contribute to a collection he was making. The story's called "The Big Space Fuck." I think I am the first writer to use "fuck" in a title. It was about firing a space ship with a warhead full of jizzum at Andromeda. Which reminds me of my good Indianapolis friend, about the only Indianapolis friend I've got left—William Failey. When we got into the Second World War, and everybody was supposed to give blood, he wondered if he couldn't give a pint of jizzum instead.

INTERVIEWER: If your parents hadn't lost all their money, what would you be doing now?

VONNEGUT: I'd be an Indianapolis architect—like my father and grandfather. And very happy, too. I still wish that had happened. One thing, anyway: One of the best young architects out there lives in a house my father built for our family the year I was born—1922. My initials, and my sister's initials, and my brother's initials are all written in leaded glass in the three little windows by the front door.

INTERVIEWER: So you have good old days you hanker for.

VONNEGUT: Yes. Whenever I go to Indianapolis, the same question asks itself over and over again in my head: "Where's my bed, where's my bed?" And if my father's and grandfather's ghosts haunt that town, they must be wondering where all their buildings have gone to. The center of the city, where most of their buildings were, has been turned into parking lots. They must be wondering where all their relatives went, too. They grew up in a huge extended family which is no more. I got the slightest taste of that—the big family thing. And when I went to the University of Chicago, and I heard the head of the Department of Anthropology, Robert Redfield, lecture on the folk society, which was essentially a stable, isolated extended family, he did not have to tell me how nice that could be.

INTERVIEWER: Anything else?

VONNEGUT: Well—I just discovered a prayer for writers. I'd heard of prayers for sailors and kings and soldiers and so on— but never of a prayer for writers. Could I put that in here?

INTERVIEWER: Certainly.

VONNEGUT: It was written by Samuel Johnson on April 3, 1753, the day on which he signed a contract which required him to write the first complete dictionary of the English language. He was praying for himself. Perhaps April third should be celebrated as "Writers' Day." Anyway, this is the prayer: "O God, who hast hitherto supported me, enable me to proceed in this labor, and in the whole task of my present state; that when I shall render up, at the last day, an account of the talent committed to me, I may receive pardon, for the sake of Jesus Christ. Amen."

INTERVIEWER: That seems to be a wish to carry his talent as far and as fast as he can.

VONNEGUT: Yes. He was a notorious hack.

INTERVIEWER: And you consider yourself a hack?

VONNEGUT: Of a sort.

INTERVIEWER: What sort?

VONNEGUT: A child of the Great Depression. And perhaps we should say something at this point how this interview itself was done—unless candor would somehow spoil everything.

INTERVIEWER: Let the chips fall where they may.

VONNEGUT: Four different interviews with me were submitted to *The Paris Review.* These were patched together to form a single interview, which was shown to me. This scheme worked only fairly well, so I called in yet another interviewer to make it all of a piece. I was that person. With utmost tenderness, I interviewed myself.

INTERVIEWER: I see. Our last question. If you were Commissar of Publishing in the United States, what would you do to alleviate the present deplorable situation?

VONNEGUT: There is no shortage of wonderful writers. What we lack is a dependable mass of readers.

INTERVIEWER: So—?

VONNEGUT: I propose that every person out of work be required to submit a book report before he or she gets his or her welfare check.

INTERVIEWER: Thank you.

VONNEGUT: Thank *you*.

DAVID HAYMAN
DAVID MICHAELIS
GEORGE PLIMPTON
RICHARD L. RHODES
Summer 1977

8. Nadine Gordimer

Nadine Gordimer was born in Springs, the Transvaal, a small town near Johannesburg, South Africa, in 1923. Her father was a Jewish watchmaker who had immigrated from Lithuania at the age of thirteen; her mother was an Englishwoman. Raised "on the soft side" of South Africa's color bar, her concern with South Africa's apartheid system plays a large role in her novels.

Gordimer began writing at the age of nine; six years later she published her first story in *Forum*, a Johannesburg weekly. Though her formal education was interrupted by illness and she was taught primarily by a private tutor, Gordimer did study for one year at the University of Witwatersrand in 1945. Her first collection of short stories, *Face to Face* (1949), was followed by *The Soft Voice of the Serpent*, which was published in the United States in 1952. Her first novel, *The Lying Days*, appeared in 1953, and she won worldwide acclaim for *Burger's Daughter* in 1980. Her eighth novel, *July's People* (1981), appeared shortly after her seventh collection of short stories, *A Soldier's Embrace* (1980).

Honored internationally for her work, she has received, among other awards, the W. H. Smith Literary Award, the James Tait Black Memorial Prize, and the Booker Prize. France honored her with its Grand Aigle d'Or in 1975, and the University of Leuven in Belgium awarded her a doctorate of literature in 1980. She is an honorary member of the American Academy of Arts & Letters and serves as vice-president of PEN International.

you͞ve escaped altogether. Because without the Kafka will-

power you can(t reach out ~~or be caught (the same thing, here)~~

from ~~in~~ nothing and nowhere. I was going to call it a desert,

and of ~~from old habit~~, but where's the sand, where's the camels,

where's the air?— I'm still <u>mensch</u> enough to c rack a joke—

you see? Oh ~~but~~ I forgot—you didn't like my jokes, my

                        unfortunately you had no life in you,
fooling around with kids. My poor boy,∧in all those books

and diaries and letters (the ones you posted, to strangers,
                                    it   before you put the words
to women) you said a hundred times ~~youxwerexxunfitxforxxifxt~~

~~kikaughxyouxpukxthexwords~~ in my mouth, in your literary w ay,

How   ~~youxhadxnoxiifexinxyouxx~~
in ~~thatxletterxix~~ ~~(imaginary~~ letter: you were 'unfit for life',
                                        clawed on it
~~Came Dun~~
~~and so~~ death ~~was always~~, how would you s ay, naturally to you.
                        of vigour
        naturally
It doesn't come ~~so easily~~ to a man like ~~me~~ I was, I can tell

you, and so here I am writing, talking— I don't know if there
                    who   I'vs've
is a word for t his is Anyway, it's Hermann Kafka; I outlived
                ∧   Here The Pajar B
you~~xxandxitxwasxxryxxaennexxafxthexwordx~~ ~~you, there~~, the same as∧

here.

    That is what you really accuse me of, you know, ~~in~~
                        Notice
sixty or so pages~~xtthe~~ length of that letter varies a ~~bit~~ bit

~~littla~~ from language to language, of course it's been translated
                        from
into everything ~~known~~— I don't know what, Hottentot and Iceland-
        to
ic ~~to~~ Chinese, though you wrote it 'for me' in German.)

I outlived you, not for seven years, as an old sick man, after

you died, but while you were young and alive. ~~It's as~~ Clear

as daylight, from the examples you give of being afraid of

me, from the time you were a little boy. You were not

afraid, you were envious. At first, when I took you swimming

and you say you felt yourself a ~~nothing~~, puny and weak,

beside my big, strong naked body in the change-house, all
                    old
right, you say you were proud of such a father, a father

with a fine physique... And may I remind you that father

It's not Cifa
flew

A page from a Nadine Gordimer short story.

Nadine Gordimer

This interview with Nadine Gordimer took place in two parts—in the fall of 1979, when she was in America on a publicity tour for her most recent novel, Burger's Daughter, *and in the spring of 1980, when she was here to see her son graduate from college.*

Our first meeting was in a room set aside for us by her publisher, The Viking Press—one of those conference rooms made cozy by lots of books and claustrophobic by its lack of windows. The hotel room where our second meeting took place was slightly more conducive to amiable conversation. But Gordimer does not waste words in conversation any more than she does in her prose. On both occasions she was ready to begin our interview the moment I walked in the door and ready to end it the moment the hour she had suggested for our meeting was up. Her clarity and mental focus allow her to express a great deal in a short amount of time.

A petite, birdlike, soft-spoken woman, Gordimer manages to combine a fluidity and gentleness with the seemingly restrained and highly structured workings of her mind. It was as if the thirty-five-odd years that she had devoted to writing at the time we met had trained her to distill passion—and as a South African writer she is necessarily aware of being surrounded by passion on all sides—into form, whether of the written or spoken word. At the same time, she conveyed a sense of profound caring about the subject matter of her writing; those subjects natural to any writer concerned with the human condition, but set, in her case, in the heightened context of South African life. Her manner seemed to say, "Yes, these are important subjects we're discussing. Now let's get through talking about them so I can get back to the business of writing about them."

INTERVIEWER: Do you have seasons in South Africa, or is it hot all year round?

GORDIMER: Oh no, we have seasons. Near the equator, there's very little difference in the seasons. But right down where we are, at the end of the continent, and also high up where I live in Johannesburg—6,000 feet up—you have very different seasons. We have a sharp, cold winter. No snow—it's rather like your late fall or early spring—sunny, fresh, cold at night. We have a very definite rainy season. But you don't see rain for about half the year. You forget that rain exists. So it's a wonderful feeling when you wake up one day, and you smell the rain in the air. Many of the old houses, like ours, have galvanized iron or tin roofs. It's very noisy when there's a heavy rain—it just gallops down on the roof. The house that I was brought up in had a tin roof, so it's one of my earliest memories, lying in bed and listening to the rain . . . and hail, which, of course, on a tin roof is deafening.

INTERVIEWER: When was your first trip out of South Africa?

GORDIMER: My first trip out was to what was then called Rhodesia—Zimbabwe. That might seem very much the same thing as South Africa to you, but it isn't. Zimbabwe is Central Africa, subtropical, shading into tropical. But my first real trip out was much later. I had already published two books—I was thirty years old. I went to Egypt, on my way to England, and America. Perhaps it was a good transition. In London I felt at home, but in an unreal way—I realized when I got there that my picture of London came entirely from books. Particularly Dickens and Virginia Woolf. The writers who, I'd thought, had impressed me with the features of English life, like Orwell, did not have this evocation when I was actually in the place; they were not writers with a strong sense of place. Woolf and Dickens obviously were. So that when I walked around in Chelsea I felt that this was definitively Mrs. Dalloway's country. I remember I stayed in a hotel near Victoria Station. And at night, these dark, sooty buildings, the dampness when one leant against a wall—absolutely decayed buildings . . .

INTERVIEWER: Were you as unprepared for this first trip off the African continent, and as awed by it, as Rebecca in your novel, *Guest of Honour?*

GORDIMER: No, my mother, who hadn't been back to England for about twenty years, prepared me. She provided me with woolly underwear and whatnot, which I threw away after I arrived. But Rebecca's trip to Switzerland . . . I think descriptions of impressions from the air are something that writers nowadays have to be careful of. Like train journeys in mid-nineteenth century literature . . . they made such a change in people's lives. They produced a . . . leap in consciousness, especially so far as time was concerned. I can imagine what it must have been, the thought of taking a train that was to go rushing through the countryside. There were so many descriptions of trains in the literature of the day. But I think writers must be careful now not to overdo the use of travel as a metaphor for tremendous internal changes. "The journey" now is by air, and think of how many writers use this—in my own books it appears in *The Conservationist* and in *Guest of*

Honour. And indeed, in *Burger's Daughter,* Rosa Burger takes her first trip out of South Africa; I had to resist the temptation to talk about the journey—I describe only the landing, because that particular piece of the landscape could be useful later on.

INTERVIEWER: Was this trip to England a sort of "back to the roots" expedition?

GORDIMER: No. But it brought an understanding of what I was, and helped me to shed the last vestiges of colonialism. I didn't know I was a colonial, but then I had to realize that I was. Even though my mother was only six when she came to South Africa from England, she still would talk about people "going home." But after my first trip out, I realized that "home" was certainly and exclusively—Africa. It could never be anywhere else.

INTERVIEWER: What brought your parents to South Africa?

GORDIMER: The same thing brought them both. They were part of the whole colonial expansion. My maternal grandfather came out in the 1890s with a couple of brothers. South Africa was regarded as a land of opportunity for Europeans. And indeed, he went prospecting for diamonds in Kimberley. I don't think he found very much—maybe some small stones. After that, his entire life was the stock exchange. He was what we call a "tickey-snatcher." A tickey was a tiny coin like a dime —alas, we don't have it anymore. It was equal to three English pence. "Tickey" is a lovely word, don't you think? Well, my grandfather was a tickey-snatcher on the stock exchange, which meant that he sat there all day, and that he bought and sold stocks—making a quick buck.

My father's story is really not such a happy one. He was born in Lithuania, and he went through the whole Jewish pogrom syndrome, you know. He had hardly any schooling. There wasn't any high school for Jewish kids in his village. His father was a shipping clerk and there were twelve children. I'm sure they must have been very poor. Their mother was a seamstress. As soon as my father was twelve or thirteen the idea was that he would just go—*somewhere*, either to America or wherever —it was the time of the great expansion, you know, the early 1900s. So his was the classic Ellis Island story—thirteen years old, not speaking a word of English, traveling in the hold of a ship, but all the way to Africa instead of America—it must have been extraordinary. He was a very unadventurous man; he didn't have a strong personality—he was timid. He still is a mystery to me. I wonder if he didn't burn himself out in this tremendous initial adventure, whether it wasn't really too much for him, and once having found a niche for himself somewhere, he just didn't have the guts to become much of a personality. There was something *arrested* about my father.

INTERVIEWER: What did he do once he got to Africa?

GORDIMER: Like many poor Jews—one either became a shoe-maker, a tailor, or a watchmaker. He had learned watchmaking. All he had was a little bag with his watchmaking tools. He went to the Transvaal, to the goldfields. He took his little suitcase and went around the mines and asked the miners if anybody wanted a watch fixed. And he would take the watches away to a little room he had somewhere: he would just sit there and mend watches. Then he bought a bicycle and he'd go back round the mines. But by the time I came on the scene he had a little jeweler's shop and he was no longer a watchmaker—he employed one. Indeed, he imported his brother-in-law from Russia to do it. By now my father was the tycoon of the family. He brought *nine* sisters out of Lithuania—the poor man— saving up to bring one after the other. I found out later that he hated them all—we didn't ever have family gatherings. I don't know why he hated them so much.

INTERVIEWER: Where exactly was this jeweler's shop?

GORDIMER: In a little town called Springs, which was thirty miles from Johannesburg. I grew up in a small, gold-mining town of about 20,000 people.

INTERVIEWER: What were the schools like there?

GORDIMER: Well, I've had little formal education, really. I

had a very curious childhood. There were two of us—I have an elder sister—and I was the baby, the spoiled one, the darling. I was awful—brash, a show-off, a dreadful child. But maybe that had something to do with having a lot of energy that didn't find any outlet. I wanted to be a dancer—this was my passion, from the age of about four to ten. I absolutely adored dancing. And I can still remember the pleasure, the release, of using the body in this way. There was no question but that I was to be a dancer, and I suppose maybe I would have been. But at the age of ten, I suddenly went into a dead faint one day, having been a very skinny but very healthy child. Nobody took much notice. But then it happened again. So I was taken to the family doctor, and it was discovered that I had an incredibly rapid heartbeat. Nobody had noticed this; it was, I suppose, part of my excitability and liveliness. It was discovered that I had an enlarged thyroid gland, which causes a fast heartbeat and makes one hyperactive. Well, I've since discovered that this isn't a serious malady at all. It happens to hundreds of people—usually at puberty. But my mother got very alarmed. This rapid pulse should have been ignored. But my mother was quite sure that it meant that I had a "bad heart." So she went immediately to the convent where I attended school and told the nuns, "This child mustn't have any physical training, she mustn't play tennis, she mustn't even swim." At ten, you know, you don't argue with your mother—she tells you you're sick, you believe her. When I would be about to climb stairs, she would say, "Now, take it slowly, *remember your heart.*" And then of course the tragedy was that I was told I musn't dance anymore. So the dancing stopped like that, which was a terrible deprivation for me.

It's really only in the last decade of my life that I've been able to face all this. When I realized what my mother had done to me, I went through, at the age of twenty, such resentment —this happens to many of us, but I *really* had reason. When I was thirty, I began to understand why she did it, and thus to pity her. By the time she died in '76 we were reconciled. But it was an extraordinary story.

In brief, my mother was unhappily married. It was a dreadful marriage. I suspect she was sometimes in love with other men; but my mother would never have dreamt of having an affair. Because her marriage was unhappy, she concentrated on her children. The chief person she was attracted to was our family doctor. There's no question. I'm sure it was *quite* unconscious, but the fact that she had this "delicate" daughter, about whom she could be constantly calling the doctor—in those days doctors made house calls, and there would be tea and cookies and long chats—made her keep my "illness" going in this way. Probably I was being wrongly treated anyway, so that what medication should have cleared up, it didn't, and symptoms persisted. Of course, I began to feel terribly important. By that time I was reading all sorts of books that led me to believe my affliction made me very interesting. I was growing up with this legend that I was very delicate, that I had something wrong with my heart.

When I was eleven—I don't know how my mother did this —she took me out of school completely. For a year I had no education at all. But I read tremendously. And I retreated into myself, I became very introspective. She changed my whole character. Then she arranged for me to go to a tutor for three hours a day. She took me there at ten in the morning and picked me up at one. It was such incredible loneliness—it's a terrible thing to do to a child. There I was, all on my own, doing my work; a glass of milk was brought to me by this woman—she was very nice, but I had no contact with other children. I spent my whole life, from eleven to sixteen, with older people, with people of my mother's generation. She carted me around to tea parties—I simply lived her life. When she and my father went out at night to dinner she took me along . . . I got to the stage where I could really hardly talk to other children. I was a little old woman.

INTERVIEWER: What about your sister's relationship to you during this time?

GORDIMER: My sister is four years older than I am. She went away to university; she wasn't really a companion to me. I stopped going to the tutor when I was fifteen or sixteen. So that was the extent of my formal education.

When I was twenty-one or twenty-two, already a published writer, I wanted to go to university to get a little more formal education. But since I hadn't matriculated, I could only do occasional courses at the University of the Witwatersrand— that's Afrikaans for "ridge of white waters." There was something called "general studies"—this was just after the war, and there were lots of veterans who had interrupted their education, and so it was very nice for me—there were people my own age mixed up with the others. A few years ago I gave a graduation address at that same university.

INTERVIEWER: Are you one of these writers to whom they're always trying to give honorary degrees?

GORDIMER: I don't accept them in South Africa. I've taken one—in Belgium in 1981, from the University of Leuven. It turned out to be quite extraordinary, because the man who got an honorary degree with me, Monsignor Oscar Romero, was assassinated two weeks later in El Salvador. In Belgium he had given the most marvelous address. He was such a striking man. He received a standing ovation for about eight minutes from the students. And two weeks later he was lying on the floor of a church, dead.

INTERVIEWER: How long did you go to university?

GORDIMER: One year. This was the first time in my life I'd mixed with blacks, and was more or less the beginning of my political consciousness. Perhaps the good thing about being carted around with my parents was that they would sit playing gin rummy or something while I wandered around the host's house seeing what I could find to read. I discovered everybody from Henry Miller to Upton Sinclair. It was Sinclair's *The*

Jungle that really started me thinking about politics: I thought, good God, these people who are exploited in a meat-packing factory—they're just like blacks here. And the whole idea that people came to America, not knowing the language, having to struggle in sweat shops . . . I didn't relate this to my own father, because my father was bourgeois by then . . . but I related it to the blacks. Again, what a paradox that South Africa was the blacks' *own country,* but they were recruited just as if they had been migrant workers for the mines. So I saw the analogy. And that was the beginning of my thinking about my position vis-à-vis blacks. But though I didn't know anything—I was twelve or thirteen, and leading the odd kind of life I did, living in books—I began to think about these things before, perhaps, I was ready for them. When I got to university, it was through mixing with other people who were writing or painting that I got to know black people as equals. In a general and inclusive, nonracial way, I met people who lived in the world of ideas, in the world that interested me passionately.

In the town where I lived, there was no mental food of this kind at all. I'm often amazed to think how they live, those people, and what an oppressed life it must be, because human beings *must* live in the world of ideas. This dimension in the human psyche is very important. It was there, but they didn't know how to express it. Conversation consisted of trivialities. For women, household matters, problems with children. The men would talk about golf or business or horseracing or whatever their practical interests were. Nobody ever talked about, or even around, the big things—life and death. The whole existential aspect of life was never discussed. I, of course, approached it through books. Thought about it on my own. It was as secret as it would have been to discuss my parents' sex life. It was something so private, because I felt that there was nobody with whom I could talk about these things, just *nobody.* But then, of course, when I was moving around at university, my life changed. From Europe—it was just after the war—

came Existentialism, and at home in South Africa there was great interest in movements of the Left, and black national movements. At that time, the Communist party and various other leftist movements were not banned. So there were all sorts of Marxist discussion groups. This was an area of thought and conviction I simply never had heard mentioned before. I'd only read about it. And there, of course, were people who were mixing with blacks. So it was through people who were writing, painting, or acting that I started mixing with blacks.

INTERVIEWER: What did you do after that year at university? Did you begin any political activity?

GORDIMER: No, you see I was writing then—a lot. I was concentrating tremendously on writing. I wasn't really interested in politics. My approach to living as a white supremacist, perforce, among blacks, was, I see now, the humanist approach, the individualistic approach. I felt that all I needed, in my own behavior, was to ignore and defy the color bar. In other words, my own attitude toward blacks seemed to be sufficient action. I didn't see that it was pretty meaningless until much later.

INTERVIEWER: Were you living on your own then?

GORDIMER: No, I wasn't. In that way I was extremely backward. But you have to look at the kind of dependency that had been induced in me at the crucial age of ten. When other kids were going off to the equivalent of what's known as "summer camp"—"Nadine can't go camping, she's got a *bad heart!* If people go on a hike, she can't go. She's got to stay with mama." A child like that becomes very corrupt, a kind of jester, an entertainer for grown-ups. Especially at the age of fifteen and sixteen. Adults find you charming. You flirt with other people's husbands instead of with boys your own age. It's a very corrupting thing. I was rather a good mimic. Perhaps it was the beginning of having an ear for dialogue? So I would take off people. Grown-ups would sit around at drink parties, getting a little tight, and there was Nadine prancing around, rather cruelly imitating people whom they knew. It didn't occur to them that the moment their backs were turned I was doing it to them as well.

At any rate, I was still living at home when I went to university, and I used to commute by train into Johannesburg. Then my sister got married and lived in Johannesburg, so that when I didn't want to go home I would go to her, which was very nice for me, to have a base there. But I still didn't have the guts, I don't know why, to move out of home, the mining town of Springs. And you see, I wasn't earning enough by my writing, heaven knows, to live on. I was doing something that no kid does nowadays—I was living off my father. On the other hand, my needs were so modest. It never occurred to me that one would want a car—now every kid has a jalopy—this was just not the kind of thing that I would have dreamt of. All I wanted was to buy books. I earned enough with my writing here and there to do this, and of course I also used the library tremendously, which, again, people don't seem to do so much anymore. When I talk to young writers, and I say, "Have you read this or that?"—"Well, no, but books are so expensive . . ."—I say, "Well for God's sake! The central library is a wonderful library. For heaven's sake, use it! You're never going to be able to write if you don't read!"

INTERVIEWER: Perhaps the isolation of your childhood helped you to become a writer—because of all the time it left you for reading—lonely though it must have been.

GORDIMER: Yes . . . perhaps I would have become a writer anyway. I was doing a bit of writing before I got "ill." I wanted to be a journalist as well as a dancer. You know what made me want to become a journalist? Reading Evelyn Waugh's *Scoop* when I was about eleven. Enough to make anybody want to be a journalist! I absolutely adored it. I was already reading a lot, obviously, but of course I was reading without any discrimination. I would go to the library and wander around, and one book led to another. But I think that's the best way. An Oxford student who is doing a thesis on my writing came to visit me in Johannesburg the other day. I did something I've not done before. I told him, "Right, here are boxes of my papers, just do what you like." I liked him so much—he was so very intelligent and lively. I would meet him at lunch. He would emerge, and so would I, from our separate labors. Suddenly he brought out a kid's exercise book—a list, that I'd kept for about six months when I was twelve, of books that I'd read, and I'd written little book reviews. There was a review of *Gone With the Wind*. Do you know what was underneath it? My "review" of Pepys's *Diary*. And I was still reading kid's books at the time, devouring those, and I didn't see that there was any difference between these and *Gone With the Wind* or Pepys's *Diary*.

INTERVIEWER: Were you publishing stories in the *New Yorker* before you published your first book?

GORDIMER: No. I published a book of stories in South Africa, in 1949. I must have started publishing stories in the *New Yorker* when I was twenty-six. I had one story in the *New Yorker*, and several in journals like *Virginia Quarterly Review*, the *Yale Review*—the traditional places where young writers in the fifties submitted their work. Then my first book was published abroad—a book of short stories.

INTERVIEWER: You sent your manuscripts around to these magazines?

GORDIMER: No, no, by that time I had an agent. It came about that I had an agent in New York. I never sent anything on impulse to those magazines, because I wasn't familiar at all with American publications. The publications I was familiar with were the English ones. Of course, publishers in those days usually watched magazines. And my first publisher, Simon and Schuster, became interested in me through reading that first story of mine in the *New Yorker*. Katharine White became my editor and friend at the *New Yorker*. She told me, years after, that all those other stories which were in my first book had already been submitted to the *New Yorker* via my agent. But they had been read by the slush-pile people. She had never seen them, and she regretted very much that she hadn't. But of course these things happen. And I don't quite know how that *one* story surfaced.

INTERVIEWER: Who was your agent?

GORDIMER: My agent was an extraordinary man called Sidney Satenstein. He was an extremely rich man who loved writers. He had no children, and I think writers were his children. He had very few writers really, because he wasn't principally an agent. I came to him through somebody who knew him and knew my work and said, "It's ridiculous—you should have an agent abroad." He was such an incredible man—a sort of John O'Hara character, or even coarser, really. He spent half his time flying to Las Vegas to gamble, or to Florida to play golf. He was a kind of caricature rich American. He always had a cigar in his mouth. He was big, and wore the most ghastly clothes—checked trousers and things like that. He was an absolute darling. Of course he gave me a completely false idea of what an agent was. When I met him I was exactly thirty—though he had taken me on in my mid-twenties—and he was in his mid-sixties. He established a sort of fatherly relationship with me, very fond. Strangely enough, he really liked my writing, which surprised me. One wouldn't have thought that my writing—especially my stories—would have interested *him.* But they did. He was incredible. He knew the circumstances of my life. I was newly divorced, I had a small child—a baby, indeed, eighteen months old—and I had no money. And he really fought for me. If somebody bought something of mine —and after all, I was totally unknown—he insisted that I was a hot property. He got sufficient money for me to live on. When Simon and Schuster bought my first book of stories, they wanted to know if I was writing a novel, and indeed I was. And again he pushed them to give me what would now be considered a *teeny* advance, the amount someone would get to write a line today, but then publishers were not so generous, nor writers so demanding. But at least they gave me a modest sum that I could live on. And once the book was well along, and they saw part of it, Satenstein said to them, you've just *got* to give her more, she's got nothing. So they gave me another advance—all due to him. He used to send me enormous bottles of French perfume. The times I came here— twice—while he was alive, he threw parties for me at the 21 Club, with caviar and sturgeon . . . he had a big heart, and style.

Unfortunately, he died—of a heart attack—just when I began to get known and make a success. He deserved better, because it would have been terribly exciting for him. At least he was able to be thrilled with the response to my first novel. Though not a best seller—I've never been that—it was a big critical success here . . . a completely unknown writer with a front page review in *The New York Times*.

INTERVIEWER: What role do you feel politics and the constant conflict it evokes in South Africa have played in your development as a writer?

GORDIMER: Well, it has turned out to have played a very important role. I would have been a writer anyway; I was writing before politics impinged itself upon my consciousness. In my writing, politics comes through in a didactic fashion very rarely. The kind of conversations and polemical arguments you get in *Burger's Daughter*, and in some of my other books— these really play a very minor part. For various reasons to do with the story, they had to be there. But the real influence of politics on my writing is the influence of politics on people. Their lives, and I believe their very personalities, are changed by the extreme political circumstances one lives under in South Africa. I am dealing with people; here are people who are shaped and changed by politics. In that way my material is profoundly influenced by politics.

INTERVIEWER: Do you see that as an advantage for a writer?

GORDIMER: Not really. Life is so apparently amorphous. But as soon as you burrow down this way or that . . . you know Goethe's maxim? "Thrust your hand deep into life, and whatever you bring up in it, that is you, that is your subject." I think that's what writers do.

INTERVIEWER: If you had grown up in a country that was not politically oppressed, might you have become a more abstract writer?

GORDIMER: Maybe. Take a writer whom I admire tremendously, the greatest American short-story writer ever, Eudora Welty. In a strange way, if she had lived where I've lived, she might have turned these incredible gifts of hers more outward —she might have written more, she might have tackled wider subjects. I hesitate to say this, because what she's done she's done wonderfully. But the fact is that she hasn't written very much; I don't think she ever developed fully her gifts as a novelist. She was not forced by circumstance to come to grips with something different. And I don't believe it's just a matter of temperament, because my early writing had qualities similar to hers. I got to hate that word about my work—"sensitive." I was constantly being compared to Katherine Mansfield. I am *not* by nature a political creature, and even now there is so much I don't like in politics, and in political people—though I admire tremendously people who are politically active— there's so much lying to oneself, self-deception, there has to be —you don't make a good political fighter unless you can pretend the warts aren't there.

INTERVIEWER: Do you have the same complaint about Virginia Woolf's novels as you do with Eudora Welty's?

GORDIMER: No, because Virginia Woolf extended herself the other way. I mean she really concentrated totally on that transparent envelope that she'd find for herself. There are two ways to knit experience, which is what writing is about. Writing is making sense of life. You work your whole life and perhaps you've made sense of one small area. Virginia Woolf did this incomparably. And the complexity of her human relationships, the economy with which she managed to portray them . . . staggering. But you can't write a novel like *Burger's Daughter* with the sensibility of a Virginia Woolf. You have to find some other way. You're always trying to find some other way. I'm interested in both ways of writing. I started off by being interested in that transparent envelope.

INTERVIEWER: Was Woolf a big influence when you began writing?

GORDIMER: Midway, I think—after I'd been writing for about five years. She can be a very dangerous influence on a young writer. It's easy to fall into the cadence. But the content isn't there. The same could be said for a completely different kind of writer like Dos Passos, or Hemingway. You've got to be very careful, or you do if you are a writer like me, starting out with an acute sensibility and a poor narrative gift. My narrative gift was weak in my early novels—they tend to fall into beautiful set pieces. It was only with *The Late Bourgeois World*, which was published in 1966, that I began to develop narrative muscle. From then on, my struggle has been not to lose the acute sensitivity—I mean the acuteness of catching nuance in behavior (not in description, because as you get more mature that falls into place) and to marry it successfully to a narrative gift. Because the kind of subjects that are around me, that draw me, that I see motivating me, require a strong narrative ability.

INTERVIEWER: Do you feel that your political situation—the political situation in South Africa—gave you a particular incentive as a writer?

GORDIMER: No. For instance, in *Burger's Daughter*, you could say on the face of it that it's a book about white Communists in South Africa. But to me, it's something else. It's a book about commitment. Commitment is not merely a political thing. It's part of the whole ontological problem in life. It's part of my feeling that what a writer does is to try to make sense of life. I think that's what writing is, I think that's what painting is. It's seeking that thread of order and logic in the disorder, and the incredible waste and marvelous profligate character of life. What all artists are trying to do is to make sense of life. So you see, I would have found my themes had I been an American or an English writer. They are there if one knows where to look . . . if one is pushed from within.

INTERVIEWER: How do you feel that fiction from relatively nonoppressed countries compares with that produced in countries where the political situation necessitates a certain amount of political consciousness?

GORDIMER: To me, it's all a matter of the quality of the writing. To me, that is everything. I can appreciate a tremendously subjective and apolitical piece of writing. If you're a writer, you can make the death of a canary stand for the whole mystery of death. That's the challenge. But, of course, in a sense you are "lucky" if you have great themes. One could say that about the Russians in the nineteenth century. Would they have been the wonderful writers they are if they hadn't had that challenge? They also had the restrictions that we chafe against in South Africa—censorship, and so on. And yet it seems on the face of it to have had only a good effect on writing. Then I think it depends. It can have a deleterious effect. In South Africa, among young blacks who are writing —it's difficult for them to admit it, but they know this—they have to submit to an absolute orthodoxy within black consciousness. The poem or the story or the novel must follow a certain line—it's a kind of party line even though what is in question is not a political party, but it *is*, in the true sense of the word, a party line. For example, nobleness of character in blacks must be shown. It's pretty much frowned upon if there's a white character who is human. It's easy enough to understand this and it's important as a form of consciousness-raising for young blacks to *feel* their own identity, to recite poems which simply exalt blackness and decry everything else, and often to exalt it in crude terms, in crude images, clichés. That's fine as a weapon of propaganda in the struggle, which is what such writing is, primarily. But the *real* writers are victims of this, because as soon as they stray from one or two clearly defined story lines, they're regarded as . . .

INTERVIEWER: Traitors. Are there many blacks writing and publishing in South Africa?

GORDIMER: There are a lot, and there's a fairly good relationship between black and white writers. Literature is one of the few areas left where black and white feel some identity of purpose; we all struggle under censorship, and most white writers feel a strong sense of responsibility to promote, defend, and help black writers where possible.

INTERVIEWER: *Burger's Daughter* was banned three weeks after it was published, wasn't it?

GORDIMER: Yes, and it remained banned for several months. Then it was unbanned. I was pleased, as you can imagine. Not only for myself, but because it established something of a precedent for other writers, since there are in that book blatant contraventions of certain Acts. In that book I published a document that was a real document, distributed by the students in the 1976 riots in Soweto, and banned by the government. It's in the book with all the misspellings and grammatical mistakes . . . everything exactly as it was; and indeed that's important because, as Rosa points out, these kids rioted because they felt their education wasn't good enough. And when you read the text of that pathetic little pamphlet you can see what the young blacks meant, because that's as well as they could write at the age of sixteen or seventeen, when they were ready to matriculate. So here is one example where, indeed, I flagrantly crossed the line to illegality. Now that the book has been unbanned, it's going to be a difficult thing for the censors to ban other books on evidence of such transgressions.

INTERVIEWER: Why was the book unbanned?

GORDIMER: If I hadn't been a writer who's known abroad and if this hadn't been a book that happened to receive serious attention at a high level abroad—it obviously made the censors feel rather foolish—the book would not have been released. So there we are.

INTERVIEWER: Is it common for a book to be unbanned?

GORDIMER: Well, not so quickly. Of my two previous books, one, *A World of Strangers,* was banned for twelve years, and the other, entitled *The Late Bourgeois World,* for ten; after that length of time most books are pretty well dead.

INTERVIEWER: How does a book get banned?

GORDIMER: First of all, if the book is imported, the authorities embargo it. In other words, it's just like any other cargo arriving at the docks. It is embargoed at Customs and the customs officer sends the book off to the Censorship Board. He's got a list of suspects. For instance, a South African writer like myself would be on it, you see, because they know the kind of subjects I've chosen, and, in any case, I've had three books banned previously. So would somebody like James Baldwin; several of his books were banned. Then there's another way that books get embargoed with the possible outcome of a ban. After normal distribution, somebody, some Mother Grundy, old busybody, reads a book that's already in the bookshops, objects to it, and sends it off to the Censorship Board with a complaint. On the recommendation of just one person, a committee will read the book to see if it's "objectionable." But while it's being read by the censors, it's under embargo, which means that although there are copies in the bookshops the bookseller can't sell them; he's got to put them away, take them off the shelves. Sometimes the book is then released. It happened to my novel, *A Guest of Honour*; it happened to *The Conservationist. The Conservationist,* I think, was held by the censors for ten weeks, which is iniquitous because the first ten weeks in a book's life are crucial from the point of view of sales. Then it was released by the director of the board. The members of the censor's committee—there are a number of those, usually with three people comprising a committee—read the book, each writes an independent report, and if these concur that the book should be banned or released, right, it's done. If they don't concur, then a fourth person has to be brought in. If they concur that the book is undesirable, then it is banned. The author isn't told. The decision is published in the government gazette, which is published once a week. And that's the end of the book.

INTERVIEWER: What happens then? Is it like what happened with *Ulysses*? Do people scrounge around frantically trying to get hold of it and hide it when policemen walk by?

GORDIMER: People do, people do. Books are usually banned only for sale and distribution but not for *possession*, so that if you've already bought the book you may keep it; but you may not lend it to me or the person across the road, and you may not sell it.

INTERVIEWER: You can't lend it?

GORDIMER: No. This, of course, is perfectly ridiculous. Everybody lends banned books all the time. But people are very nervous, for instance, about buying them abroad or having them sent. They're rather too timid about that. They don't like to have to smuggle them in.

INTERVIEWER: So there isn't much smuggling going on?

GORDIMER: Some people don't, some do. But with some of us, it's a point of honor always to do this.

INTERVIEWER: To smuggle?

GORDIMER: Yes, of course. It's a legitimate form of protest. But unfortunately, when a book is banned, very few copies get around.

INTERVIEWER: Getting back to the idea that oppressed societies produce better writers . . .

GORDIMER: Well, I don't know. I think in the case of Latin American countries, they seem to have experienced so many forms of oppression and for so long that it's become a normal state. But notice that they all write about the same thing . . . the themes are as obsessive as the African ones. *The* theme among the remarkable Latin American writers is the corrupt dictator. Nevertheless, despite the sameness of theme, I regard this as the most exciting fiction in the world being written today.

INTERVIEWER: Which Latin American novelists?

GORDIMER: García Márquez, of course. Hardly necessary even to name Borges. Borges is the only living successor to Franz Kafka. Alejo Carpentier was absolutely wonderful. *The Kingdom of the Earth* is an exquisite little novel—it's brilliant. Then there's Carlos Fuentes, a magnificent writer. Mario Vargas Llosa. And Manuel Puig. These just roll off my tongue quickly; there are others. But always there's this obsessive theme—the corrupt dictator. They all write about it; they're obsessed by it.

INTERVIEWER: I suppose that an oppressed culture such as South Africa's creates the possibility for heroes to exist, and that this is why some of your novels, such as *A Guest of Honour* and *Burger's Daughter,* have heroes as their motivating force.

GORDIMER: Well, you know, it amazes me . . . I come to America, I go to England, I go to France . . . nobody's at risk. They're afraid of getting cancer, losing a lover, losing their jobs, being insecure. It's either something that you have no control over, like death—the atom bomb—or it's something with which you'd be able to cope anyway, and that is not the end of the world; you'll get another job or you'll go on state relief or something of this nature. It's only in my own country that I find people who voluntarily choose to put everything at risk —in their personal life. I mean to most of us, the whole business of falling in love is so totally absorbing, nothing else matters. It's happened to me. There have been times in my life when I have put the person I was in love with far ahead of my work. I would lose interest, I wouldn't even care if the book was coming out. I'd forget when it was being published and I wouldn't worry about the reception it got because I was in such a state of anguish over some man. And yet the people I know who are committed to a *political* cause never allow themselves to be deflected by this sort of personal consideration or ambition.

INTERVIEWER: How do you think romantic love manifests itself in families such as Rosa's, where people's passions lie in politics?

GORDIMER: This is what interested me so much, and this is what I partly tried to explore in the relationship between that girl and her family, who loved her, exploited her, but at the same time felt that they were doing this not for each other or to each other, but because the *cause* demanded it.

INTERVIEWER: We get only very brief glimpses of the love affair between Burger and his wife. In fact, the reader hardly gets any picture either of their relationship or of Rosa's mother at all.

GORDIMER: That was one of the points that's fascinated me about such people: you could know them very well, and yet even in their intimate relations with one another they remained intensely secretive; it's part of the discipline that you have to have. I have a very, very close friend—no character in the book is modeled on her, I might add—but much that I know or have discovered intuitively about such people started with my fascination with her. She has been my closest friend for many years—she's a political exile now—and we've talked nights and days. She's one of the few people for whom I suppose I'd put myself physically at risk if there were to be cause. There are so many things I don't know about her that normally would come out in confidences between people who are as close as we are, and it's because of her political commitment that I can't ask her and she won't tell me. I think that this could extend even to family relationships. It's part of the discipline that the more you know, the more dangerous you are to the people around you. If you and I are working together in an underground movement, the less I know about you the better.

INTERVIEWER: We've talked about the South American writers you admire. What about other writers?

GORDIMER: Lots of novelists say they don't read other novelists, contemporary ones. If this is true, it's a great pity. Imagine, if you had lived in the nineteenth century and not read the writers that we now turn back to so lovingly, or even if you had lived in the twentieth century and hadn't read Lawrence or Hemingway, Virginia Woolf and so on. At different times in my life I've—liked is not the word—I've been psychologically *dependent* upon different writers. Some have remained influential in my life and some haven't, and some I suppose I've forgotten and do them an injustice by not mentioning. When I first began to write, I wrote short stories, and of course I still do; I've written a great many. It's a form that I love to write and to read. I was very influenced by American, Southern, short-story writers. Eudora Welty was a great influence on me. Years later, when I met Eudora, visited her in Jackson, there were such parallels between the way she was living, even then, and my life: a black man was mowing the lawn! There was a kind of understanding. Of course, this really had nothing to do with the fact that I thought she was a superb short-story writer. Katherine Anne Porter was an influence on me. Faulkner. Yes. But, again, you see, one lies, because I'm sure that when we were doing the five-finger exercises of short-story writing, Hemingway must have influenced *everybody* who began to write in the late forties, as I did. Proust has been an influence on me, all my life—an influence so deep it frightens me . . . not only in my writing, but in my attitudes to life. Then later came Camus, who was quite a strong influence, and Thomas Mann, whom I've come to admire more and more. E. M. Forster, when I was a young girl; when I was in my twenties—he was very important to me. And I still think *Passage to India* is an absolutely wonderful book that cannot be killed by being taught in the universities.

INTERVIEWER: In what way did Hemingway influence you?

GORDIMER: Oh, through his short stories. The reduction, you know, and also the use of dialogue. Now I think a great failure in Hemingway's short stories is the omnipresence of Hemingway's voice. People do not speak for themselves, in their own thought patterns; they speak as Hemingway does. The "he said," "she said" of Hemingway's work. I've cut these attributions out of my novels, long ago. Some people complain that this makes my novels difficult to read. But I don't care. I simply cannot stand he-said/she-said any more. And if I can't make readers *know* who's speaking from the tone of voice, the turns of phrase, well, then I've failed. And there's nothing anyone can do about it.

INTERVIEWER: It certainly enforces concentration when one is reading your novels.

GORDIMER: Yes.

INTERVIEWER: The dashes are very effective.

GORDIMER: Oh, that's very old. It started with Sterne's *Tristram Shandy.*

INTERVIEWER: What technique did you use that was the same?

GORDIMER: A kind of interior monologue that jumps about from different points of view. In *The Conservationist,* sometimes it's Mehring speaking from inside himself, observing, and sometimes it's a totally dispassionate view from outside.

INTERVIEWER: It's a much more standard narrative technique than that of *Burger's Daughter.*

GORDIMER: Well, no, it isn't you know. In *The Conservationist* you've got interior monologue and you have a real narrator. It's not always Mehring speaking. But the line between when he is and when he isn't is very vague, my theory being that the central personality is there, whether it's being observed from outside or whether from inside—it's the same entity.

INTERVIEWER: You mentioned that the way in which you came up with the structure of *Burger's Daughter,* in which Rosa is always speaking to somebody, was from the idea that when one is writing one always has a listener in mind.

GORDIMER: Oh, no, not in your writing, in your *life.* I believe that in your life, in your thoughts when you are alone, you are always addressing yourself to somebody.

INTERVIEWER: And you are not doing this when you write?

GORDIMER: No, because you're no longer yourself when you're writing; you're projecting into other people. But I think in your life, and sometimes even in the conduct of your life, you're imagining that some particular person is seeing your actions. And you're turning away, sometimes, from others.

INTERVIEWER: How has Faulkner influenced you? Do you see any similarities in the structure of *Burger's Daughter* and, say, *As I Lay Dying*?

GORDIMER: No, none at all, and I don't think there could be any influence there. I think the big time when people influence you is when you're very young and you start to write; after that you slough off what you don't need and you painfully hammer out your own style.

INTERVIEWER: There's a similarity between the way your method of narration in *Burger's Daughter* and some of Faulkner's books address themselves to the relative nature of "truth."

GORDIMER: Yes. Well, of course it is a method that points out the relativity of truth. The point I'm trying to make is about the relationship between style and point of view; in a sense, style is the point of view, or the point of view is the style.

INTERVIEWER: Right, and that's why you choose to structure your narratives in the way that you do.

GORDIMER: And then it was Proust who said that style is the moment of identification between the writer and his situation. Ideally that is what it should be—one allows the situation to dictate the style.

INTERVIEWER: So that you are expressing a point of view, with the style that you choose, about the way life is in South Africa.

GORDIMER: Yes. I'm expressing a point of view of the way life is for that particular person and the people around her (in the case of *Burger's Daughter*), and, by extension, a view of life itself.

INTERVIEWER: In Conor Cruise O'Brien's review of *Burger's Daughter*, which appeared in *The New York Review of Books*, he says that your novel is constructed with a "properly deceptive art." He talks about how the construction makes the book seem as if it were a book in which nothing happens, and then several cataclysmic things do, in fact, happen. I was wondering if you have any response.

GORDIMER: For me again, so little of the construction is objectively conceived. It's organic and instinctive and subconscious. I can't tell you how I arrive at it. Though, with each book, I go through a long time when I know what I want to do and I'm held back and puzzled and appalled because I don't know before I begin to write how I'm going to do it, and I always fear that I can't do it. You see, in *Guest of Honour*, I wrote a political book, a book that needed certain objective entities relating to and acting upon the character's life in particular. And I wrote that book as a conventional narrative so that at the point where there was indeed a big party congress there was no difficulty then in presenting it almost like a play. Then I wrote *The Conservationist*, where I chose to ignore that one had to explain anything at all. I decided that if the reader didn't make the leap in his mind, if the allusions were puzzling to him—too bad. But the narrative would have to carry the book in the sense of what is going on in the characters' minds and going on in their bodies; the way they believed things that they did *really were*. Either the reader would make the leap or not, and if the reader was puzzled now and then—too bad. In other words, the novel was full of private references between the characters. Of course, you take a tremendous risk with such a narrative style, and when you do succeed, I think it's the ideal. When you don't, of course, you irritate the reader or you leave him puzzled. Personally, as a reader, I don't mind being puzzled. Perhaps the writer doesn't know the consequences implied in his/her books, because there's a choice of explanations; and, as a reader, I enjoy that. To me, it's an important part of the exciting business of reading a book, of being stirred, and of having a mind of your own. And so, as a writer, I take the liberty of doing this.

INTERVIEWER: You don't consciously create a complete structure before you begin writing a novel?

GORDIMER: No. For *Burger's Daughter,* perhaps four or five pages of very scrappy notes for the whole book. But, for me, those half sentences or little snatches of dialogue are tremendously important; they are the core of something. And I've only got to look at them, and know that that's the next stage in the book that I'm coming to.

INTERVIEWER: Is this the way you usually write your novels?

GORDIMER: Yes. With me it's really a very natural process once I get started. An organic process.

INTERVIEWER: How long do you prepare before you get started?

GORDIMER: It's so difficult for me to say because, looking back at *Burger's Daughter,* for example, I know that I've been fascinated by the kind of person Rosa is for many years. It's as if the secret of a life is there, and slowly I'm circling, coming closer and closer to it. Perhaps there are other themes that present themselves but finally spin off instead of drawing me to them. I suppose one's ready for different things at different times in one's life. And also, in a country where so much is changing, the quality of life around one is changing; so that perhaps I wouldn't be attracted now to write the book that I wrote ten years ago, and vice versa.

INTERVIEWER: So you feel that the way your books are written is more an inevitable phenomenon than a conscious choice.

GORDIMER: I don't think any writer can say why he chooses this or that or how a theme impinges itself. It may have been around for a long time and then a stage comes in your life when your imagination is ready for it and you can deal with it.

INTERVIEWER: I wanted to ask you about *The Conservationist,* in which death is almost an obsessive theme. There are certain sections where it is continually brought up in ritualized ways: the man hopping up from his grave in different people's minds throughout the book, and the ritual of killing the goat to get back at Solomon's injury . . .

GORDIMER: In *The Conservationist* there's a resurrection theme, and that is also a political theme. At the end of the book there's a disguised message. The slogan of the biggest banned liberation movement, a kind of battle cry widely adopted, is the African word, "mayibuye." This means, "Africa, come back." You can see the whole idea of resurrection is there. And if you look at the end of *The Conservationist* you'll see that this thought is reworded, but it is actually what is said when the unknown man is reburied: that although he is nameless and childless, he has all the children of other people around him; in other words, the future. He has people around him who are not his blood brothers and sisters but who stand for them. And that he has now been put with proper ceremony into his own earth. He has taken possession of it. There's a suggestion of something that has been planted, that is going to grow again.

INTERVIEWER: This theme is repeated in one of your short stories—"Six Feet of the Country."

GORDIMER: Yes. But the repetition is in reverse: "Six Feet" was written years before *The Conservationist.* Oddly enough, that early story is based on a true incident.

INTERVIEWER: Do you have a fascination with death?

GORDIMER: Not consciously, but then . . . how can any thinking person not have? Death is really the mystery of life, isn't it? If you ask, "What happens when we die? Why do we die?" you are asking, "Why do we live?" Unless one has a religion . . . Without a religious explanation, one has only the Mount Everest argument: "I climb it because it's there. I live because there is the gift of life." It's not an answer, really, it's an evasion. Or, "I think my purpose on this earth is to make life better." Progress is the business of making life more safe and more enjoyable . . . fuller, generally. But that justification, it stops short of death, doesn't it? The only transcendent principle is that you are then seeking to improve the human lot for future generations. But we still don't get past the fact that it's a turnabout business; it's your turn and then it's mine, and life is taken up by somebody else. Human beings are never reconciled to this. In my own life I am made puzzled and uneasy by my attitude and that of others to death. If somebody dies young it's so terrible, it's such a tragedy, and the sense of waste is so strong; you think of all the promise that was there. And then if people live into old age, there's the horror of decay, especially—it's awful to say—but especially with exceptional people; when you see their minds going and their bodies falling to pieces, and they want to die and you want them to die, then that's equally terrible. So it's the mere fact of death that we can't accept? We say it's terrible if people die young, and we say it's terrible if they go on living too long.

INTERVIEWER: Are you a religious or mystical person?

GORDIMER: I'm an atheist. I wouldn't even call myself an agnostic. I am an atheist. But I think I have a basically religious temperament, perhaps even a profoundly religious one. I went through a stage in my life when I was about thirty-two or thirty-three years old—when I was very fascinated by the writings of Simone Weil. In the end, her religious philosophy left me where I was. But I felt that there was something there that answered to a need that I felt, *my* "need for roots" that she wrote about so marvelously. I couldn't find the same solution.

INTERVIEWER: How do you feel about Conor Cruise O'Brien's idea about there being Christian overtones in *Burger's Daughter*?

GORDIMER: Well, I'm thinking of that. I'm sure that many of my friends, people who know me well, laughed because they know that, as I say, I'm an atheist. But he hit on something that is there in me, a certain inclination—more than that—a pull. Perhaps, brought up differently in a different milieu, in a different way, I might have been a religious person.

INTERVIEWER: Then there is the resurrection of the black man in *The Conservationist.*

GORIMER: But of course the idea of resurrection comes from the Greeks, from the Egyptians. You can begin to believe in a collective unconscious without having religious beliefs.

INTERVIEWER: I've noticed that sensual elements play a key role in your writing: smells, textures, sexuality, bodily functions. You don't write about the so-called "beautiful people," the leisured class of South Africa, and the beautiful environment in which they must live. In fact, I noticed that almost all of the white women in your *Selected Stories* are physically and mentally both highly unattractive and middle-class. Does this reflect the way in which you view white colonialists in your country?

GORDIMER: I don't make such judgments about people. After all, I'm a white colonial woman myself, of colonial descent. Perhaps I know us too well through myself. But if somebody is partly frivolous or superficial, has moments of cruelty or self-doubt, I don't write them off, because I think that absolutely everybody has what are known as human failings. My black characters are not angels either. All this role-playing that is done in a society like ours—it's done in many societies, but it's more noticeable in ours—sometimes the role is forced upon you. You fall into it. It's a kind of song-and-dance routine, and you find yourself, and my characters find themselves, acting out these preconceived, ready-made roles. But, of course, there are a large number of white women of a certain kind in the kind of society that I come from who . . . well, the best one can say of them is that one can excuse them because of their ignorance of what they have allowed themselves to become. I see the same kind of women here in the U.S. You go into one of the big stores here and you can see these extremely well-dressed, often rather dissatisfied-looking, even sad-looking middle-aged women, rich, sitting trying on a dozen pairs of shoes; and you can see they're sitting there for the morning. And it's a terribly agonizing decision, but maybe the heel should be a little higher or maybe . . . should I get two pairs? And a few blocks away it's appalling to see in what poverty and misery other people are living in this city, New York. Why is it that one doesn't criticize that American woman the same way one does her counterpart in South Africa? For me, the difference is that the rich American represents class difference and injustice, while in South Africa the injustice is based on both class *and* race prejudice.

INTERVIEWER: What about the "beautiful people" of South Africa?

GORDIMER: They're featured very prominently in an early book of mine called *A World of Strangers* but very rarely since then, until the character of Mehring in *The Conservationist.* They are not the most interesting people in South Africa, believe me . . . although they may regard themselves as such.

INTERVIEWER: Is it intentional that so often the physical details of characters are not brought home strongly in your work? One gets a very strong sense of the mind's workings in major characters, but often a very limited sense of what they actually look like.

GORDIMER: I think that physical descriptions of people should be minimal. There are exceptions—take Isaac Bashevis Singer. He very often starts off a story by giving you a full physical description. If you look very closely at the description, of course it's extremely good. He stamps character on a twist of the nose or a tuft of red beard. My own preference is for physical description to come piecemeal at times when it furthers other elements in the text. For instance, you might describe a character's eyes when another character is looking straight into them so it would be natural . . . a feature of that particular moment in the narrative. There might be another scene later, where the character whose eyes you've described is under tension, and is showing it by tapping her foot or picking at a hangnail—so if there was something particular about her hands, that would be the time to talk about them. I'm telling you this as if it were something to be planned. It isn't. It comes at the appropriate moment.

INTERVIEWER: In the introduction to your *Selected Stories*, you say that: "My femininity has never constituted any special kind of solitude, for me. In fact, my only genuine connection with the social life of the town (when I was growing up) was through my femaleness. As an adolescent, at least, I felt and followed sexual attraction in common with others; that was a form of communion I could share. Rapunzel's hair is the right metaphor for this femininity: by means of it I was able to let myself out and live in the body, with others, as well as—alone —in the mind." You go on to say you "question the existence of the specific solitude of woman-as-intellectual when that woman is a writer, because when it comes to their essential faculty as writers, all writers are androgynous beings."

What about the process of becoming a writer, of becoming an androgynous being? Isn't that a struggle for women?

GORDIMER: I hesitate to generalize from my own experience. I would consider it an arrogance to state my own experience as true for all women. I really haven't suffered at all from being a woman. It's inconceivable, for example, that I could ever have become interested in a man who regarded women as nonbeings. It's never happened. There would be a kind of war between us. I just take it for granted, and it has always happened, that the men in my life have been people who treated me as an equal. There was never any question of fighting for this. I'm somebody who has lived a life as a woman. In other words, I've been twice married, I've brought up children, I've done all the things that women do. I haven't avoided or escaped this, supposing that I should have wished to, and I don't wish to and never wished to. But, as I say, I don't generalize, because I see all around me women who are gifted and intelligent who *do* have these struggles and who indeed *infuriate* me by allowing themselves to be used by men. It's the mental abuse that I think of, really, women who give up their development as human beings because they're willing to subordinate this to some man. As for my attitude to feminism . . . I always have become indignant over the fact that women in professions don't have the same working conditions or salaries as men. In my own country—I don't know how it is here—as soon as a woman is married, if she's a schoolteacher, for example, she's paid less because she's regarded as a poor risk: she's probably going to have a baby and interrupt her career. And if she comes back to teaching when she's older, she is still paid on a lower grade because she's married. This I think is disgusting. I see it as part of the whole question of human rights and disaffected groups in various societies.

INTERVIEWER: Certainly it must appear even more clearly in that light from the perspective of someone living in South Africa.

GORDIMER: Black women have so many terrible disabilities that they share in common with men—the oppression of racism—that the whole feminist movement means something quite different there. Unless feminism is seen as merely part of the general struggle for black liberation, and the struggle of all, white and black, against racial oppression, it has no validity in South Africa, in any view. So as far as writing is concerned, I cannot help generalizing from my own experience that, in writing, sex doesn't matter; it's the writing that matters. I can't see why any publisher should care whether you're a man or a woman if you've written a good book. Or if you've written a bad book that he thinks he can make a commercial success of . . . there are plenty of those.

INTERVIEWER: You also say in the introduction to *Selected Stories,* "I know that writers need solitude and seek alienation of a kind every day of their lives." How do you gain your own solitude, and maintain it within your family? Where do you write?

GORDIMER: Of course, now my family's grown up and it's

easier. But I did manage to maintain it when my children were young, I suppose, by being rather ruthless. I think writers, artists, are very ruthless, and they have to be. It's unpleasant for other people, but I don't know how else we can manage. Because the world will never make a place for you. My own family came to understand and respect this. Really, when my children were quite small they knew that in my working hours they must leave me alone; if they came home from school and my door was closed, they left and they didn't turn on the radio full blast. I was criticized for this by other people. But my own children don't hold it against me. I still had time that I spent with them. What I have also sacrificed, and it hasn't been a sacrifice for me, is a social life; and as I've got older, I'm less and less interested in that. When I was young I did go through some years when I enjoyed party-going very much and stayed out all night. But in the end, the loss next day, the fact that I had a hangover and that I couldn't work, quickly outweighed the pleasure; and, as time has gone by, I've kept more and more to myself. Because a writer doesn't only need the time when he's actually writing—he or she has got to have time to think and time just to let things work out. Nothing is worse for this than society. Nothing is worse for this than the abrasive, if enjoyable, effect of other people.

INTERVIEWER: What conditions do you find to be most conducive to writing?

GORDIMER: Well, nowhere very special, no great, splendid desk and cork-lined room. There have been times in my life, my God, when I was a young divorced woman with a small child living in a small apartment with thin walls when other people's radios would drive me absolutely mad. And that's still the thing that bothers me tremendously—*that* kind of noise. I don't mind people's voices. But Muzak or the constant clack-clack of a radio or television coming through the door . . . well, I live in a suburban house where I have a small room where I work. I have a door with direct access to the garden—a great luxury for me—so that I can get in and out without anybody bothering me or knowing where I am. Before I begin to work I pull out the phone and it stays out until I'm ready to plug it in again. If people really want you, they'll find you some other time. And it's as simple as that, really.

INTERVIEWER: How long do you usually work every day? Or do you work every day?

GORDIMER: When I'm working on a book I work every day. I work about four hours nonstop, and then I'll be very tired and nothing comes anymore, and then I will do other things. I can't understand writers who feel they shouldn't have to do any of the ordinary things of life, because I think that this is necessary; one has got to keep in touch with that. The solitude of writing is also quite frightening. It's quite close sometimes to madness, one just disappears for a day and loses touch. The ordinary action of taking a dress down to the dry cleaner's or spraying some plants infected with greenfly is a very sane and good thing to do. It brings one back, so to speak. It also brings the world back. I have formed the habit, over the last two books I've written, of spending half an hour or so reading over what I'd written during the day just before I go to bed at night. Then, of course, you get tempted to fix it up, fuss with it, at night. But I find that's good. But if I've been with friends or gone out somewhere, then I won't do that. The fact is that I lead a rather solitary life when I'm writing.

INTERVIEWER: Is there a time of day that's best?

GORDIMER: I work in the morning. That's best for me.

INTERVIEWER: How long does it usually take you to write a book?

GORDIMER: It depends. The shortest has been about eighteen months. *Burger's Daughter* took me four years.

INTERVIEWER: Four years of steady writing?

GORDIMER: I wrote one or two other things, small things. Sometimes when I'm writing I get a block, and so I stop and write a short story, and that seems to set me going. Sometimes when I'm writing a book I get ideas for stories, and they're just tucked away. But alas, as I get older, I get fewer ideas for short stories. I used to be teeming with them. And I'm sorry about that because I like short stories.

INTERVIEWER: What about writer's block? Is that a problem for you?

GORDIMER: No. And I say so, as you see, with hesitation and fear and trembling because you always feel that that demon is waiting behind the back of your brain.

INTERVIEWER: You have the short story to loosen you up?

GORDIMER: Yes, and occasionally I do some nonfiction piece, usually something involving travel. For me, this is a kind of relaxation. During the time I was writing *Burger's Daughter* I did two such pieces.

INTERVIEWER: You don't even have minor fits of procrastination, endless cups of tea or things like that?

GORDIMER: No, no. Though I do have, not blocks but . . . problems moving on from one stage to the next; particularly when I've got something done with and it's worked well. For instance, I finished that chapter with Brandt Vermeulen, you know, the nationalist in *Burger's Daughter*, which went unexpectedly well. I simply wrote it just like that and it all came right. I had been dreading it. I had been dreading getting the tone of voice and everything right. And then, knowing where I was going on from there, there was suddenly an inability to get out of that mood and into another; and so there were perhaps a few awful days; because when that happens, I don't stop and do something else. I sit in front of that paper for the normal time that I would be writing. And then, well, I break through.

INTERVIEWER: There's no specific routine that gets you from the bedroom or the living room into the writing room, bridging that terrifying gap between not writing and writing?

GORDIMER: No—that's the advantage if you're free to choose the time you're going to write. That's the advantage of writing in the morning. Because then one gets up and in one's sub-conscious mind one knows: I am going to write. Whatever small thing you have to do, such as talking to other people at breakfast, it's only done with one part of you, so to speak; just done on the surface. The person with whom I live, my husband, understands this and has for a very long time. And he knows that to say to me at breakfast, "What shall we do about so-and-so?" or, "Would you read this letter?"—he knows that isn't the time to ask. I get irritable, and irritated, I don't want to be asked to do things then. And I don't want to phone an order to the grocer at that time. I just want to be left alone to eat my breakfast. Ideally, I like to walk around a bit outside, which you can do, of course, with a garden. But I often think that even that becomes a kind of procrastination because it's so easy then to see a weed that one has to stop and pull up and then one sees some ants and wonders, where are they going? So the best thing to do is to go into the room and close the door and sit down.

INTERVIEWER: Do you go through much revision of your work?

GORDIMER: As time goes by, less and less. I used to. When I was young, I used to write three times as much as the work one finally reads. If I wrote a story, it would be three times the final length of that story. But that was in the very early times of my writing. Short stories are a wonderful discipline against overwriting. You get so used to cutting out what is extraneous.

INTERVIEWER: Do you ever find critics useful?

GORDIMER: Yes, but you must remember they're always after the event, aren't they? Because then the work's already done. And the time you find you agree with them is when they come to the same conclusions you do. In other words, if a critic objects to something that I know by my lights is right, that I did the best I could and that it's well done, I'm not affected by the fact that somebody didn't like it. But if I have doubts about a character or something that I've done, and these doubts are confirmed by a critic, then I feel my doubts confirmed and I'm glad to respect that critic's objections.

INTERVIEWER: Frequently writers say they don't read reviews because even one bad review among ten shining ones can be devastating.

GORDIMER: Of course, it depends very much on the reviewer. There are people who are not reviewers, one or two, to whom I give my books to read, perhaps even in manuscript. I am sick with apprehension while they are reading them. And certainly there are certain reviewers I would be very wounded by if they were to say, "Well, this one's rotten."

INTERVIEWER: But this hasn't happened yet.

GORDIMER: Not yet. With *Burger's Daughter* I've had, out of perhaps fifty or sixty reviews, two bad ones.

INTERVIEWER: You say that writers are androgynous. Do you recognize any difference between masculine and feminine writing, such as say, Woolf's versus Hemingway's writing?

GORDIMER: Hemingway is such an extreme example, and his writing is really an instance of machismo, isn't it? Henry James could have been a woman. E. M. Forster could have been. George Eliot could have been a man. I used to be too insistent on this point that there's no sex in the brain; I'm less insistent now—perhaps I'm being influenced by the changing attitude of women toward themselves in general? I don't think there's anything that women writers don't know. But it may be that there are certain aspects of life that they can deal with a shade better, just as I wonder whether any woman writer, however great, could have written the marvelous war scenes in *War and Peace*. By and large, I don't think it matters a damn what sex a writer is, so long as the work is that of a real *writer*. I think there *is* such a thing as "ladies' writing," for instance, feminine writing; there are "authoresses" and "poetesses." And there are men, like Hemingway, whose excessive "manliness" is a concomitant part of their writing. But with so many of the male writers whom I admire, it doesn't matter too much. There doesn't seem to be anything *they* don't know, either. After all, look at Molly Bloom's soliloquy. To me, that's the ultimate proof of the ability of either sex to understand and convey the inner workings of the other. No woman was ever "written" better by a woman writer. How did Joyce know? God knows how, and it doesn't matter. When I was a young woman, a young girl, I wrote a story about a man who had lost his leg. He couldn't accept this, the reality of it, until he was sitting recuperating in the garden and saw a locust that had its leg off; he saw the locust struggling because it felt its leg was still there. I don't know how I wrote that story, somehow I just imagined myself into it. A psychiatrist once told me it was a perfect example of penis envy.

INTERVIEWER: Is there anything, new or otherwise, that you hope to do with your writing in the future?

GORDIMER: I would always hope to find the one right way to tackle whatever subject I'm dealing with. To me, that's the real problem, and the challenge of writing. There's no such feeling as a general achievement. You cannot say that because I have managed to say what I wanted to say in one book, that it is now inside me for the next, because the next one is going to have a different demand. And until I find out how to write it, I can't tackle it.

INTERVIEWER: In other words, you don't know the question until you have the answer?

GORDIMER: Yes. I would like to say something about how I feel in general about what a novel, or any story, ought to be. It's a quotation from Kafka. He said, "A book ought to be an icepick to break up the frozen sea within us."

JANNIKA HURWITT
Fall 1979/Spring 1980

9. James Merrill

James Merrill has been described as "one of our indispensable poets." Since his *First Poems* of 1951, he has published eleven collections of poetry, and his work has appeared in, among other periodicals, the *New Yorker* and the *Atlantic*. Awarded the Bollingen Prize for Poetry in 1973, he won the Pulitzer Prize in 1977 for *Divine Comedies*. He has been honored with two National Book Awards: the first in 1967 for *Nights and Days*, and the second in 1979 for *Mirabell*, which one critic called "as central to our generation as *The Waste Land* to the one before us." He has also written two novels, *The (Diblos) Notebook* and *The Seraglio*, and two plays, *The Immortal Husband* and *The Bait*. In 1971 he was elected to the National Institute of Arts and Letters. Of his own work, James Merrill has said, "What I think I try to do for the world is to be fresh and true towards my language and in my responses. To try to match the intensity of experience that life has given me with the intensity and complexity of language." His most recent collections are *From the First Nine: Poems 1947–1976* and *The Changing Light at Sandover*.

Born in New York City in 1926, Merrill graduated summa cum laude from Amherst in 1947. In 1982 he received an honorary doctorate from Yale University. He divides his time between homes in Stonington, Connecticut, and his friend David Jackson's house in Key West, Florida.

BETTER MATHEMATICS OF COURSE BUT DULLER. WHO WANTS 2 UNHAPPY
FACT THAT AFE S 1-16 R IN FORMING YEARS 20- TO 50, PRODUCTIVE
50 TO ?- DECLINING. HOROSCOPE TRIES TO ACCOMODATE 2 REALFMAT
HEMATIC OF LIFE WITH 2 DREAM OF IMMORTALITY. YET 2 STARS
R ULE US. (you must promote - you cannot escape!) INDEED & SO OUR SCHEME 2 LIFT UFE UP.
& make the world. Yes. KEEPING EARTH AS AN ANCHOR POORLY IN 2 TROUBLED
DEEPWATER S/O F UNIVERSAL POWER. AS AN ANCHOR STARS. (figure ?) & BIOLOGY OR
EARTH SNAPPED A WAY UNDER US IN OBEDIENCE 2 STARS. 2 DEAD MOON IS A TEST
AS STARS BIOL. VE BLIEVE E RULES SUPREME. 2 DEAD MOON IS A TEST
AMENT. TO OUR FAILURE. IT SPRUN OFF TAKEN INTO P UFF BALL
OF DUST THE DEBRIS OF OUR WORLD. (now was closer?) VE MADE IT AS A OF DUST
(more was chilli) THE ROTATION OF EARTH GATHERED UP OUR DEBRIS INTO
A TIDY REAINDER (is the last two r) YES & THAT FROM ROTATION.
(You had constructed this phase of that matter?) MADE AN EXTRA LAYER AROUND earth -
A SLOOSER SKIN US MATERIALS MADE NONGRAVITATED BY ATOM. ENERGY
2 4 POINTS OF CONTACT WE SPOKE OF HELD OUR SKIN W PLACE
THEY STRAWED & BROKE OUR VAST SKEIN SHIVERED BROKE INTO
FLAME ME WE FELL. [MM. Rain's weary] THAT ME SENFANTS
IS OUR 15TH CONTACT, their tears, OUR SYMPATHY.] & 2 CLOUDS
CAME 2 COOL, 2 DUST GATHERED 2 ATMOSPEIR & CLEARE D &
GOD MERCIFULLY TOOK US IN. WE STARED OUT AT 2 ROUND DEAD
BALL AS AT A N EMPTY THOUGHT.

For a time, one of James Merrill's methods of inspiration was derived from
the use of a Ouija board. The above Ouija transcription page is from the
summer of 1976 and is reworked in *Mirabell* 2.2.

James Merrill

My first glimpse of James Merrill, a dozen years ago, was in black and white. It was a photograph of him, in the Brinnin and Read anthology called The Modern Poets. *He had just turned toward the camera—his mouth slightly open, as if not expecting an observer—from a piano on which was propped a mazy score. He had on an open white dress shirt, which had the effect of elongating his neck, of giving his seated figure a slim, tense elegance. There was a pack of Chesterfields on a table in the foreground, and the edge of a potted fern.*

When I visited him during July 1981, it was as if that old photograph had been retouched—by time, and in color. The piano is on the top floor of the poet's house in Stonington, Connecticut, and he was playing it when I walked in. He turned, as if surprised. This time he was wearing a royal blue T-shirt and white slacks. His face was older, but the lines draw out a puckish quality in his features. He remains slim, his brown hair silvered, and now he smokes Camels. He had been practicing the Adagio of Haydn's "Sonata in A," the one with the plucked arpeggio accompaniment—and the source, Merrill supposes, of Granados's "The Lady and the Nightingale," itself the source (he grins) of "Besame mucho."

We are in a big room, airy, sunny, nearly all windows, with a chessboard linoleum floor. Merrill and David Jackson, with whom he has lived for nearly thirty years, added this rooftop room to the building on Water Street they bought in 1956. There are shops on the ground floor, rented apartments on the second; the top two stories are theirs. (For years the outside was a dull aubergine, but it had just been repainted a shade of leg makeup.) Soon after, they had enclosed the roof and added a planked deck that overlooks the village and a dazzling swatch of Long Island Sound; in the cellar of nearby Connecticut College's museum they found a marble bust of the Roman emperor Otho. It was sold to them for a song. Blackface removed, it was set up outside, and presides over the deck.

Inside, near where the poet had been practicing at the baby Steinway, is a circle: three eccentric chairs and a Victorian sofa in one of Fortuny's magic-formula stamped cottons, low cases of novels and Gallimard paperbacks (one case hides a futon), and a freestanding garlic-head fireplace that from one end of the room faces a huge Larry Rivers landscape at the other.

Merrill has a reputation for being one of the best readers of poetry before the public. One hears why. His light baritone, with its urbane accent, has an expressive range of inflections. He laughs easily, and has a quick, enharmonic wit. On second thought, it is like his poetic voice. There is a self-possession to it that guards an abiding seriousness difficult to draw out—and thereby the more convincing.

INTERVIEWER: You've left your house in Athens for good now, right?

MERRILL: It looks that way.

INTERVIEWER: And your original decision to settle there—was that just an accumulation of accidents?

MERRILL: Oh, there's no accident. I went first to Greece to visit Kimon Friar in 1950. Between then and 1959, when I went back with David, we'd gone to a great number of other places too—to the Orient and, either together or separately, all over Europe, except Greece. And suddenly here was a place—I can't tell you how much we liked it. We liked Stonington, too, but didn't want to stay there all year round. It had slowly dawned on us, as it continues to dawn on young people in Stonington, that it's a community of older people by and large. Nearly all our friends were five to *fifty* years older than we were. And in Greece we began seeing, for a change, people our own age, or younger.

INTERVIEWER: I presume you came to Stonington to get away from New York. If, by analogy, you went to Athens to get away from things in America, what was it you found there?

MERRILL: Things that have mostly disappeared, I'm afraid. The dazzling air, the drowsy waterfronts. Our own ignorance, even: a language we didn't understand two words of at first. That *was* a holiday! You could imagine that others were saying extraordinarily fascinating things—the point was to invent, if not what they were saying, at least its implications, its over tones. Also, in those days foreign tourists were both rare and welcome, and the delighted surprise with which the Greeks acknowledged our ability to put two words together, you know, was irresistible.

INTERVIEWER: What sort of people did you find yourselves falling in with? Other Americans?

MERRILL: No, certainly not. In fact, even Greeks who spoke English or French had to be extremely charming for us to want to see them more than once. We wanted to learn Greek and we also wanted to learn *Greece*, and the turn of mind that made a Greek.

INTERVIEWER: It can't be accidental, then, that your leaving Greece coincides with the completion of your trilogy—

MERRILL: Probably not. A coincidence over which I had no control was that, within a year of my finishing the trilogy, David had come to see that Athens was no longer a livable place. We'd both seen this day coming, I'm afraid, but for one reason or another neither of us wanted to believe his eyes. If he'd stayed on, I'd still be going back and forth. Maria might have been another reason for staying. Even after her death—or especially after her death, as her role in the poem grew clearer—I couldn't have faced, right away, cutting ourselves off from the friends we'd had in common, friends also in their own right, who made all the difference.

INTERVIEWER: That's Maria Mitsotáki? Was she really—

MERRILL: Everything I say she was in the trilogy? Oh yes, and more. Her father had indeed been prime minister, three times, I think—but under which king? Constantine I or George II, or both? I'm vague about things like that. I'm vague too about her husband, who died long before our time. They'd lived in South Africa, in London . . . Maria went home for a visit and was stranded in Athens during the whole German occupation. Horrible stories—and wonderful ones: dashing young cousins in the underground, hidden for weeks in bedroom closets. Literary men fell in love with her, quite understandably—aside from being an enchantment to look at, she *never missed a thing you said.*

INTERVIEWER: Your trilogy attests to a warm, intimate relationship with Maria Mitsotáki and W. H. Auden. Did working on the poem *change* your feelings about them?

MERRILL: In a way, yes. The friendships, which had been merely "real" on earth—subject to interruption, mutual convenience, states of health, like events that have to be scheduled "weather permitting"—became ideal. Nothing was hazed over by reticence or put off by a cold snap. Whenever we needed them, there they were; and a large part of *that* wonder was to feel how deeply they needed *us.* I can't pretend to have known Wystan terribly well in *this* world. He liked me, I think, and approved of my work; and liked the reassurance of David's and my being in Athens to stand by Chester Kallman [Auden's friend and collaborator] when emergencies arose. But he was twenty years older and had been famous while I was still in boarding school, and—well, it took the poem, and the almost jubilant youthfulness he recovers after death, to get me over my shyness. With Maria it was different. In the years we knew her she saw very few people, but we were part of that happy few. Many of her old friends whom she no longer saw couldn't imagine what had come over her—"she's given us up for those *Americans!*" We simply adored her. It seemed like the perfection of intimacy, light, airy, without confessions or possessiveness—yet one would have to be Jung or Dante to foresee her role in the poem.

INTERVIEWER: You hadn't even an inkling of that role when you began the poem?

MERRILL: Oh, no. It's true, I began "Ephraim" within days of hearing that she'd died—and felt, I suppose, enough of a coincidence to list her among the characters. There's only one mention of her in the whole "Book of Ephraim," yet I kept her in, and look what happened! The cassia shrub on the terrace —how could the poem have ended without it? I couldn't bring *it* home to America, though I did the next best thing and sneaked some seedpods through customs. They've given rise to that rather promising affair out there on the deck.

INTERVIEWER: Panning the Ouija board transcripts for poetic gold—*that* must have been a daunting project. How did you go about it?

MERRILL: The problem changed from volume to volume. With "Ephraim," many of the transcripts I had made from Ouija board sessions had vanished, or hadn't been saved. So I mainly used whatever came to hand, except for the high points which I'd copied out over the years into a special notebook. Those years—time itself—did my winnowing for me. With *Mirabell* it was, to put it mildly, harder. The transcript was

enormous. What you see in the poem might be half, or two-
fifths, of the original. Most of the cuts were repetitions: things
said a second or third time, in new ways often, to make sure
we'd understood. Or further, unnecessary illustrations of a
point. I haven't looked at them for several years now, and can
only hope that nothing too vital got left out. Getting it onto
the page seemed really beyond me at first, perhaps because I'd
begun imagining a poem the same length as "Ephraim." By
the time the fourteen-syllable line occurred to me (that exchange with Wystan is largely contrived) I'd also decided
where to divide it into books, so it all got under way at last.

With *Scripts*, there was no shaping to be done. Except for
the minutest changes, and deciding about line breaks and so
forth, the Lessons you see on the page appear just as we took
them down. The doggerel at the fêtes, everything. In between
the Lessons—our chats with Wystan or Robert [Morse] or Uni
[the trilogy's resident unicorn]—I still felt free to pick and
choose; but even there, the design of the book just swept me
along.

INTERVIEWER: You don't feel that too much was sacrificed
for the sake of shapeliness?

MERRILL: If so, perhaps no accident? I came upon the pages
of one of our very earliest evenings with Ephraim. He's giving
us a lecture about the senses: POLISH THE WINDOWS OF
YOUR EYES, etc., each sense in turn. That obviously prefig-
ures, by over twenty years, one of the themes crucial to Volume
3—but isn't it nicer and less daunting somehow to have it
emerge casually, without pedantry?

Then there were things outside the transcript—things in
"life" which kept staring me in the face, only I couldn't see
them, as if I'd been hypnotized, until the danger was past.
Only this year I was in my study, playing the perhaps ten
thousandth game of Patience since beginning "Ephraim." I'm
using my old, nearly effaced Greek cards with their strange
neoclassical royalties; and I do a little superstitious trick when
I'm through. I reassemble the deck so that the Queen of Hearts

is at the bottom, facing up. Now on those old-style Greek cards the queens are all marked K, for Kyria—Lady. It's what George calls Mother Nature, and I'd simply never made the connection. Furthermore, the kings are all marked B, for Basileus. God B of Hearts? "You're nothing but a pack of cards!" You can be sure I'd have dragged all that in if I'd thought of it in time. Plus another clever but expendable allusion to the graveyard scene of the *Rake*, where Tom calls upon the Queen of Hearts and is saved. Driven out of his wits, but saved.

Other things, that in retrospect seem indispensable, came to hand just when they were needed, as if by magic. Stephen Yenser explaining the Golden Section when I was halfway through "Ephraim." Marilyn Lavin telling me about the X-rayed Giorgione—I'd already written V and W—and hunting up the relevant article. Stephen Orgel's book on the masque, which he sent me not a moment too soon. A friend of my nephew's, Michael Beard, writing me a letter on the metaphysical implications of Arabic calligraphy. A month or so later I would simply need to versify some of his phrases in order to make that little lyric about the Bismillah formula. Then Alfred Corn's joke about E—Ephraim—equalling any emcee squared. I felt like a perfect magpie.

INTERVIEWER: What do the Ouija transcripts look like?

MERRILL: Like first-grade compositions. Drunken lines of capitals lurching across the page, gibberish until they're divided into words and sentences. It depends on the pace. Sometimes the powers take pity on us and slow down.

INTERVIEWER: The Ouija board, now. I gather you use a homemade one, but that doesn't exactly help me to imagine it or its workings. An overturned teacup is your pointer?

MERRILL: Yes. The commercial boards come with a funny see-through planchette on legs. I find them too cramped. Besides, it's so easy to make your own—just write out the alphabet, and the numbers, and your YES and NO (punctuation marks too, if you're going all out) on a big sheet of cardboard. Or use brown paper—it travels better. On our Grand Tour, whenever we felt lonely in the hotel room, David and I could just unfold our instant company. He puts his right hand lightly on the cup, I put my left, leaving the right free to transcribe, and away we go. We get, oh, five hundred to six hundred words an hour. Better than gasoline.

INTERVIEWER: What *is* your fuel, would you say? With all the other disciplines available to a poet, why this one?

MERRILL: Well, don't you think there comes a time when everyone, not just a poet, wants to get beyond the Self? To reach, if you like, the "god" within you? The board, in however clumsy or absurd a way, allows for precisely that. Or if it's still *yourself* that you're drawing upon, then that self is much stranger and freer and more far-seeing than the one you thought you knew. Of course there are disciplines with grander pedigrees and similar goals. The board happens to be ours. I've stopped, by the way, recommending it to inquisitive friends.

INTERVIEWER: When did you start using a Ouija board?

MERRILL: Frederick Buechner gave me one as a birthday present in 1953. As I recall, we sat down then and there to try it, and got a touching little story from a fairly simple soul—that engineer "dead of cholera in Cairo," who'd met Goethe. I used it in the first thing I ever wrote about the Ouija board (a poem called "Voices from the Other World"), although by that time the *experiences* behind this poem were mine and David's. We started in the summer of 1955. But the spirit we contacted— Ephraim—was anything but simple. So much so that for a long time I felt that the material he dictated really couldn't be used —then or perhaps ever. I felt it would be like cheating, or plagiarizing from some unidentifiable source. Oh, I put a few snippets of it into *The Seraglio*, but that was just a novel, and didn't count. Twenty years later, though, I was yet again trying to tell the whole story as fiction, through a set of characters bearing little resemblance to David or me. I'd got about fifty pages done, hating every bit of it. I'm not a novelist, and never was. No accident, then, that I simply "forgot" the manuscript in a taxi in Atlanta, and never recovered it—well, all that's described in "The Book of Ephraim." But I went on, I didn't take the hint. I put together all the drafts and notes for those lost pages, and proceeded to forget *these* in a hotel room in Frankfurt! By now I was down to just two pages of an opening draft. As I sat glaring at them, the prose began to dissolve into verse. I marked the line-breaks with a pencil, fiddled a bit, typed it up, and showed the two versions to a friend who said quite firmly, "You must never write prose again." At that point "The Book of Ephraim" crystallized, and got written without any particular trouble.

INTERVIEWER: Throughout the trilogy you have many "voices"—Wallace Stevens, Gertrude Stein, Pythagoras, Nefertiti . . . How does this work? Do they simply break in, or do you ask specifically for them?

MERRILL: Either way. Most of the time, we never knew what to expect. Last summer, for instance, we were about to sit down at the board—no, I was already in my chair—when David called from the kitchen. He can never keep abreast of the rising postal rates, and wanted to know which stamp to put on his letter. I called back, "Put on an Edna St. Vincent Millay"— I'd bought a sheet of her commemoratives just that week. And when we started at the board, there she was. Very embarrassing on both sides, as it dawned on the poor creature that we hadn't meant to talk to *her* at all.

INTERVIEWER: Does what Auden tells you via the Ouija board remind you of him . . . I mean, are there distinctive phrases or sentiments that could only be his?

MERRILL: Some of his best-known sentiments get revised— his Christian views, for instance—but the turns of phrase sound very like him, to my ears. Remember, though, that we never knew each other well, not in *this* world.

INTERVIEWER: Would the Ouija board be your instrument— like a keyboard on which a musician composes or improvises?

MERRILL: Not a bit! If anything, the keyboard was us. And

our one obligation, at any given session, was to be as "well tempered" as possible.

INTERVIEWER: So the Ouija board is by no means a mnemonic device—it is not something to get you going . . .

MERRILL: No. At least, not something to start me *writing*. In other ways, evidently, it did start us "going"—thinking, puzzling, resisting, testing the messages against everything we knew or thought possible.

INTERVIEWER: What is David's function when you use the Ouija board?

MERRILL: That's a good question. According to Mirabell, David is the subconscious shaper of the message itself, the "Hand," as they call him. Of the two of us, he's the spokesman for human nature, while I'm the "Scribe," the one in whose words and images the message gets expressed. This would be a fairly rough distinction, but enough to show that the transcripts as they stand could never have come into being without him. I wonder if the trilogy shouldn't have been signed with both our names—or simply "by DJ, as told to JM"?

INTERVIEWER: Could not the "they" who move the teacup around the board be considered the authors of the poems?

MERRILL: Well, yes and no. As "they" keep saying throughout, language is the human medium. It doesn't exist—except perhaps as vast mathematical or chemical formulas—in that realm of, oh, cosmic forces, elemental processes, whom *we* then personify, or tame if you like, through the imagination. So, in a sense, all these figures are our creation, or mankind's. The powers they represent are real—as, say, gravity is "real" —but they'd be invisible, inconceivable, if they'd never passed through our heads and clothed themselves out of the costume box they found there. *How* they appear depends on us, on the imaginer, and would have to vary wildly from culture to culture, or even temperament to temperament. A process that Einstein could entertain as a formula might be described by an African witch doctor as a crocodile. What's tiresome is when people exclusively insist on the forms they've imagined. Those powers don't need churches in order to be sacred. What they do need are fresh ways of being seen.

INTERVIEWER: Does the idea of the Ouija board ever embarrass you—I mean that you have this curious collaborator?

MERRILL: From what I've just said, you see how pompous I can get. The mechanics of the board—this absurd, flimsy contraption, creaking along—serves wonderfully as a hedge against inflation. I think it does embarrass the sort of reader who can't bear to face the random or trivial elements that coalesce, among others, to produce an "elevated" thought. That doesn't bother me *at all*.

INTERVIEWER: Does the Ouija board ever manifest maniacal tendencies? Do you ever feel yourself lost in its grip?

MERRILL: Thanks perhaps to a certain ongoing resistance, we seem to have held our own. We kept it as a parlor game for the first twenty years. Those early voices in *Mirabell* gave us, I admit, a nasty turn. Looking back, though, I've the sense that we *agreed* to let them take us over, for the sake of the poem. Poems can do that, even when you think you're writing them all by yourself. Oh, we've been scared at times. A friend who sat with us at the board just once went on to have a pretty awful experience with some people out in Detroit. She was told to go west, and to sail on a certain freighter on a certain day, and the name of the island where she'd meet her great-grandmother reincarnated as a Polynesian teenager who would guide her to a mountain cave where in turn an old man . . . and so forth. Luckily she collapsed before she ever made it to California. I don't believe she was being manipulated by the other people. The experience sounds genuine. But she didn't have the strength to use it properly—whatever I mean by that! It would seem that David and I *have* that strength; or else, that we've been handled with kid gloves. A number of friends have been scared *for* us over the years. One of them took me to a Trappist monastery, to talk to one of the more literary priests. It was a lovely couple of hours. I read from some of the transcripts, filling in as much as I could of the background. After-

wards, the priest admitted that they'd all been warned in semi-
nary against these devilish devices, but that, frankly, I'd read
nothing to him that he didn't believe himself. I suspect a lot
of people use the board to guide them through life—"What's
next week's winning lottery number?"—and get the answers
they deserve. Our voices are often very illuminating when we
bring up a dilemma or a symptom, but they never *tell* us what
to do. At most they suggest the possibilities, the various consequences. Now that I think of it, our friend might have misread
a hint for a command, or a metaphorical itinerary of self-
discovery for a real trip to Hawaii.

INTERVIEWER: What about more conventional aids to inspiration—drugs? Drink?

MERRILL: Liquor, in my parents' world, was always your
reward at the end of a hard day—or an easy day, for that matter
—and I like to observe that old family tradition. But I've never
drunk for inspiration. Quite the contrary—it's like the wet
sponge on the blackboard. I do now and then take a puff of
grass, or a crumb of Alice Toklas fudge, when I've reached the
last drafts of a poem. That's when you need X-ray eyes to see
what you've done, and the grass helps. Some nice touches can
fall into place.

INTERVIEWER: In hindsight, do you have any general feelings
about the occult, about the *use* of the occult in poetry?

MERRILL: I've never much liked hearing about it. Usually the
people who write about it have such dreadful style. Yeats is
almost the only exception I can think of. The first thing to do
is to get rid of that awful vocabulary. It's almost acceptable
once it's purged of all those fancy words—"auras" and "astral
bodies."

INTERVIEWER: Has it been a kind of displaced religion for
you? I take it you *have* a religious streak somewhere in you.

MERRILL: Oh, that's a very good phrase for it—"displaced religion." I never felt at home with the "pastoral" Episcopalian-
ism I was handed. Unctuous mouthings of scripture, a system
that like the courtier-shepherds and milkmaids at the Petit Tria-

non seemed almost willfully deluded, given the state of the world and the fears and fantasies already raging in my little head. Mademoiselle's Catholicism corresponded more to these. She taught me the Ave Maria—without which the Lord's Prayer calls up the image of dry bread in a motherless reformatory. Even her Jesus, next to the Protestant one, was all blood and magic—the face on Veronica's napkin, the ghastly little Sacred Heart hanging above her bed, like something out of a boy's book about Aztec sacrifice, or something the gardener pulled out of the earth. These images *connected.* I mean, we used napkins the size of Veronica's at every meal. As Shaw reminds us, Christ wasn't out to proselytize. He said that God was in each of us, a spark of pure potential. He held no special brief for the Family. All very sensible, but I'm afraid I've long since thrown out the baby with the churchly bathwater. The need, as you say, remained. I never cared for the pose of the atheist—though the Angels came round to that, you know, in their way, insisting on man as master of his own destiny.

INTERVIEWER: You don't describe yourself as having been a very good student, and still seem a bit self-conscious as an "intellectual."

MERRILL: Ummmh . . .

INTERVIEWER: No accident, then, that the trilogy's caps are all unrelieved meaning? A case of the return of the repressed?

MERRILL: You're probably exactly right there, at least where the "Grand Design" is concerned. Also in passages—like Mirabell on Culture or Technology—where the proliferation of crisp ideas sounds almost like a Shaw preface. Not at all the kind of page I could turn out by myself. On the other hand, a lot of what we're loosely calling "meaning" turns out, on inspection, to be metaphor, which leads one back towards language: wordplay, etymology, the "wholly human instrument" (as Wystan says) I'd used and trusted—like every poet, wouldn't you say?—to ground the lightning of ideas. We could say that the uppercase represented a *range* of metaphor, a depth of meaning, that hadn't been available to me in earlier poems.

Victor Hugo described his voices as his own conscious powers multiplied by five, and *he* was probably exactly right there, too.

INTERVIEWER: Though your trilogy takes up the ultimate question of origins and destiny, you are not a poet—like Yeats or Auden or Lowell—who has taken on political issues in your work. Or is that very avoidance itself a kind of "stand"?

MERRILL: The lobbies? The candidates' rhetoric—our "commitments abroad"? The Shah as Helen of Troy launching a thousand missile carriers? One whiff of all that, and I turn purple and start kicking my cradle. I like the idea of nations, actually, and even more those pockets of genuine strangeness within nations. Yet those are being emptied, turned inside out, made to conform—in the interest of what? The friendly American smile we're told to wear in our passport photos? Oh, it's not just in America. You can go to an outdoor concert in Athens—in that brown, poisonous air the government isn't strong enough to do anything about—and there are the president and the prime minister in their natty suits, surrounded by flashbulbs, hugging and patting each other as if they hadn't met for months. God have mercy on whoever's meant to be impressed by that. Of course I can't conceive of anyone *choosing* public life, unless from some unspeakable hidden motive.

INTERVIEWER: What newspapers do you read?

MERRILL: In Europe the Paris *Herald*—I get very American over there, and it's so concise. Here, I never learned how to read a paper. My first year away at school, I watched my classmates, some of them littler than I was, frowning over the war news or the financial page. They already knew how! I realized then and there I couldn't hope to catch up. I told this to Marianne Moore before introducing her at her Amherst reading in 1956. She looked rather taken aback, as I did myself, a half hour later, when in the middle of a poem she was reading —a poem I thought I knew—I heard my name. "Now Mr. Merrill," she was saying, "tells me he doesn't read a newspaper. That's hard for me to understand. The things one would miss! Why, only last week I read that our U.S. Customs Bureau was collecting all the egret and bird-of-paradise feathers we'd confiscated during the twenties and thirties—collecting them and sending them off to Nepal, where they're *needed. . . .*" And then she went right on with her poem.

INTERVIEWER: I'll have to interrupt. Why were those feathers needed in Nepal?

MERRILL: Oh, headdresses, regalia . . . *you* must remember —the papers were full of it!

But let's be serious for a moment. If our Angels are right, every leader—president or terrorist—is responsible for keeping his ranks thinned out. Good politics would therefore encourage death in one form or another—if not actual, organized bloodshed, then the legalization of abortion or, heaven forbid, the various chemical or technological atrocities. Only this last strikes me as truly immoral, perhaps because it's a threat that hadn't existed before my own lifetime. I take it personally. That bit in "The Broken Home"—"Father Time and Mother Earth, / A marriage on the rocks"—isn't meant as a joke. History in our time *has* cut loose, *has* broken faith with Nature. But poems, even those of the most savage incandescence, can't deal frontally with such huge, urgent subjects without sounding grumpy or dated when they should still be in their prime. So my parents' divorce dramatized on a human scale a subject that couldn't have been handled otherwise. Which is what a "poetic" turn of mind allows for. You don't see eternity *except* in the grain of sand, or history except at the family dinner table.

By the time I returned, three months later, to resume our conversation, the cassia had been potted with a seaweed mulch, moved to an exposed spot indoors (but chaperoned by a matronly Norfolk pine), bloomed, and shed a buttercup dandruff all over the bookcase and stairwell. Down those stairs to the right is Merrill's study. To the left, where we turn, are the living and dining rooms, and the rest of the house. These rooms have best been described in Merrill's own poems. Section B of "The

Book of Ephraim" sketches the dining room, scene of so many séances: the "walls of ready-mixed matte 'flame' " with their collage of pictures and icons; the "turn of the century dome / Expressing white tin wreaths and fleur-de lys / In palpable relief to candlelight"; under it, the milk-glass tabletop, no Ouija board on it today. (With his trilogy completed, the poet tells me, he never "uses" the board to spring a poem; in fact, he and DJ rarely consult it—"perhaps a courtesy call when the moon's full, or to see that a recently dead friend gets in with the right crowd. They say it's time we weaned ourselves from all this—do admit they have a point.")

But we sit in the living room, whose rug, wallpaper, and immense Victorian mirror dominate the opening pages of Mirabell. A card table has been set up in the middle of the room, where the poet has been opening and answering his mail. There is a great deal of clutter, which adds to the impression of a boutique fantasque. What is not in this room? There are two chairs, a horsehair divan where we sit, and an Eames chair. A watercolor by a friend in Atlanta had just arrived and the only place for it is the Eames; so there he sits, a whimsical hussar with a fennel shako, whose greatcoat's fur collar turns into a caterpillar. There are piles of new books here and there, a heap of magazines in a swan-clip (I can see Time, Scientific American, The New York Review of Books*). There is a Maxfield Parrish that belonged to his father, a Madeleine Lemaire (not roses, but violets), and half a dozen other pictures. On cabinets and tables against the walls are cacti and shells, a glass bowl filled with glass globes, a tanagra, an Instamatic, a snapshot of his goddaughter, medallions and boxes, a wooden nickel, a pair of miniature cloisonné deer, a Javanese puppet head on a pin, a Venetian mask, an upheld hand of the Buddha . . .*

The poet pours out two cups of Hu Kwa.

INTERVIEWER: You had a very privileged childhood, in the normal sense of "privileged"—wealth, advantages. But the privilege also of being able to turn the pain of that childhood into art. How do you look back on it now?

MERRILL: Perhaps turning it into art came naturally . . . I mean, it's hard to speak of a child having a sense of reality or unreality, because after all, what are his criteria? It strikes me now maybe that during much of my childhood I found it difficult to *believe* in the way my parents lived. They seemed so utterly taken up with engagements, obligations, ceremonies —every child must feel that, to some extent, about the grown-ups in his life. The excitement, the emotional quickening *I* felt in those years came usually through animals or nature, or through the servants in the house—Colette knew all about that —whose lives seemed by contrast to make such perfect *sense*. The gardeners had their hands in the earth. The cook was dredging things with flour, making pies. My father was merely making money, while my mother wrote names on place-cards, planned menus, and did her needlepoint. Her masterpiece— not the imaginary fire screen I describe in the poem—depicted the façade of the Southampton house. I could see how stylized it was. The designer had put these peculiar flowers all over the front lawn, and a stereotyped old black servant on either side. Once in a while my mother would let me complete a stitch. It fascinated me. It had nothing really to do with the world, yet somehow . . . Was it the world becoming art?

INTERVIEWER: The picture your poems paint of yourself as a child is of someone who's bored. Were you?

MERRILL: We shouldn't exaggerate. There were things I enjoyed enormously, like fishing—something responding and resisting from deep, deep down. It's true, sometimes I must have been extremely bored, though never inactive. My mother remembers asking me, when I was five or six, what I wanted to do when I was grown up. Didn't I want, she asked, to go downtown and work in Daddy's office? "Oh no," I said, "I'll be too tired by then." Because, you see, everything was ar-ranged: to so-and-so's house to play, the beach for lunch, a tennis lesson. As we know, the life of leisure doesn't give us a moment's rest. I didn't care for the games or the playmates. I don't recall there being anyone I really liked, my own age, until I went away to school.

INTERVIEWER: There may be links between that boredom and an impulse to write, to make up a life of your own. I suppose you were a great reader as a child?

MERRILL: Was I? I loved stories, but can't remember being very curious about the books in the library. Once, all by myself, I opened a copy of Barrie's *Dear Brutus* to the following unforgettable bit of dialogue: "Where is your husband, Alice?" "In the library, sampling the port." Now I knew what port was: it was where ships went. And I knew what a sample was because even *I* had been consulted as to new wallpaper and upholstery. Suddenly a surrealist bit of language! But generally I read what I was told to read, not always liking it. My mother gave me *Mrs. Wiggs and the Cabbage Patch* and I remember throwing it out the window. By then I was . . . eight? A couple of years later I read *Gone With the Wind.* No one told me there were any other novels, *grown-up* novels. I must have read it six or seven times in succession; I thought it was one of a kind. As for *good* literature—one got a bit of it at school, but not at home.

INTERVIEWER: You began' writing at that age too?

MERRILL: I had written at least one poem when I was seven or eight. It was a poem about going with the Irish setter into my mother's room—an episode that ended up in "The Broken Home." The Irish setter *was* named Michael and I think the poem began: "One day while she lay sleeping, / Michael and I went peeping." My first publication was in the *St. Nicholas* magazine, a quatrain: "Pushing slowly every day / Autumn finally makes its way. / Now when the days are cool, / We children go to school." They wanted a drawing to illustrate your verses. And that gave me my first *severe* aesthetic lesson, because when the poem and sketch were printed—the sketch showed a little boy on the crest of a hill heading for a school-house far below—I saw to my consternation that, although I'd drawn the windows of the schoolhouse very carefully with a ruler, the editors had made them crooked, as befitted a child's drawing. Of course they were right. But the lesson sank in: one must act one's age and give people what they expect.

INTERVIEWER: A ballroom, empty of all but ghostly presences, is an image, or *scene* of instruction, that recurs in key poems during your career. I'm thinking of "A Tenancy" in *Water Street,* "The Broken Home" in *Nights and Days,* the Epilogue to the trilogy. It is a haunting image, and seems a haunted one as well. What associations and significance does that room have for you?

MERRILL: The original, the primal ballroom—in Southampton—would have made even a grown-up gasp. My brother once heard a Mrs. Jaeckel say, "Stanford White put his *heart* into this room." Four families could have lived in it. Two pianos *did,* and an organ, with pipes that covered the whole upper half of a wall, and a huge spiral column of gilded wood in each corner. And a monster stone fireplace with a buffalo head above it. At night it was often dark; people drank before dinner in the library. So that, after being sent to bed, I'd have to make my way through the ballroom in order to get upstairs. Once I didn't—I sat clutching my knees on one of the window seats, hidden by the twenty-foot-high red damask curtain, for hours it seemed, listening to my name being called throughout the house. Once I was allowed to stay up, before a party, long enough to see the chandeliers lit—hundreds of candles. It must have answered beautifully to my father's Gatsby side. It's a room I remember *him* in, not my mother. He took me aside there, one evening, to warn me—with tears in his eyes—against the drink in his hand. We didn't *call* it the ballroom —it was the music room. Some afternoons my grandmother played the organ, rather shyly. One morning a house guest, a woman who later gave me piano lessons in New York, played through the whole score of *Pagliacci* for me, singing and explaining. That was my first "opera." Looking back, even going back to visit while my father still had that house, I could see how much grander the room was than any of the uses we'd put it to, so maybe the ghostly presences appeared in order to make up for a thousand unrealized possibilities. That same sense probably accounts for my "redecoration" in the Epilogue—making the room conform to an ideal much sunnier, much more silvery, that I began to trust only as an adult, while keeping carefully out of my mind (until that passage had been written) the story of how Zeus cuts off the scrotum, or "ballroom," of his father Cronus and throws it into the sea, where it begins to foam and shine, and the goddess of Love and Beauty is born.

INTERVIEWER: As a young poet starting out in the fifties, what did you look forward to? What did you imagine yourself writing in, say, 1975?

MERRILL: I was a perhaps fairly typical mixture of aspiration and diffidence. Certainly I could never see beyond the poem I was at work on. And since weeks or months could go by between poems, I tried to make each one "last" as long as possible, to let its meanings ever so slowly rise to the surface I peered into—enchanted and a touch bored. I looked forward, not without apprehension, to a lifetime of this.

INTERVIEWER: How would you now characterize the author of *The Black Swan*?

MERRILL: This will contradict my last answer about "starting out in the fifties." By then I'd come to see what hard work it was, writing a poem. But *The Black Swan*—those poems written in 1945 and 1946 had simply bubbled up. Each took an afternoon, a day or two at most. Their author had been recently dazzled by all kinds of things whose existence he'd never suspected, poets he'd never read before, like Stevens or Crane; techniques and forms that could be recovered or reinvented from the past without their having to sound old-fashioned, thanks to any number of stylish "modern" touches like slant rhyme or surrealist imagery or some tentative approach to the conversational ("Love, keep your eye peeled"). There were effects in Stevens, in the *Notes*, which I read before anything else—his great ease in combining abstract words with gaudy visual or sound effects . . . "That alien, point-blank, green and actual Guatemala," or those "angular anonymids" in their blue and yellow stream. You didn't have to be exclusively decorative *or* in deadly earnest. You could be grand *and* playful. The astringent abstract word was always there to bring your little impressionist picture to its senses.

INTERVIEWER: But he—that is, the author of *The Black Swan*—is someone you now see as a kind of happy emulation of literary models?

MERRILL: No, not a bit. It seems to me, reading those poems over—and I've begun to rework a number of them—that the only limitation imposed upon them was my own youth and limited skill; whereas looking back on the poems in *The Country of a Thousand Years of Peace,* it seems to me that each of at least the shorter ones bites off much less than those early lyrics did. They seem the product of a more competent, but in a way smaller, spirit. Returning to those early poems *now*, obviously in the light of the completed trilogy, I've had to marvel a bit at the resemblances. It's as though after a long lapse or, as you put it, displacement of faith, I'd finally, with the trilogy, reentered the church of those original themes. The colors, the elements, the magical emblems: they were the first subjects I'd found again at last.

INTERVIEWER: About the progress of a poem, a typical poem —one, say, you've never written—is it a *problem* that you feel nagging you and try to solve by writing? Are you led on by a subject, or by chance phrases?

MERRILL: Often it's some chance phrases, usually attached but not always—not even always attached to a subject, though if the poem is to go anywhere it has somehow to develop a subject fairly quickly, even if that subject is a blank shape. A poem like "About the Phoenix"—I don't know where any of it came from, but it kept drawing particles of phrases and images to itself.

INTERVIEWER: But by "subject" you mean essentially an event, a person . . .

MERRILL: . . . a scene . . .

INTERVIEWER: . . . a landscape?

MERRILL: A kind of action . . .

INTERVIEWER: . . . that has not necessarily happened to you?

MERRILL: Hmmm. And then I think one problem that has presented itself over and over, usually in the case of a poem of a certain length, is that you've got to end up saying the right thing. A poem like "Scenes of Childhood" made for a terrible impasse because at the point where my "I" is waking up the next morning, after a bad night, I had him say that *dawn was worse.* It took me a couple of weeks to realize that this was something that couldn't be said under nearly any circumstances without being dishonest. Dawn is not worse, the sacred sun rises and things look up. Once I reversed myself, the poem ended easily enough. I had the same problem with "An Urban Convalescence," before writing those concluding quatrains. It broke off at the lowest point: "The heavy volume of the world / Closes again." But then something affirmative had to be made out of it.

INTERVIEWER: You're so self-conscious about *not* striking attitudes that the word "affirmative" makes me wonder . . .

MERRILL: No, think of music. I mean, you don't *end* pieces with a dissonance.

INTERVIEWER: When you write a poem, do you imagine an immediate audience for it?

MERRILL: Oh, over the years I've collected a little anthology of ideal readers.

INTERVIEWER: Living and dead?

MERRILL: Now, now . . . But *yes,* why not? Living, dead,

imaginary. Is this diction crisp enough for Herbert? Is this stanza's tessitura too high for Maggie Teyte? The danger with your close friends is that they're apt to take on faith what you *meant* to do in a poem, not what you've done. But who else has their patience? Three or four friends read the trilogy as it came out, a few pages at a time. I don't see how I could have kept going without their often very detailed responses.

INTERVIEWER: Are these reactions ever of any practical help? Would they lead you to change a line?

MERRILL: That's the point! Ideally you'd think of everything yourself, but in practice . . . There were two lines in "Ephraim," about a stream reflecting aspen. The word "aspen" ended one sentence, and "Boulders" began the next. Madison Morrison, out in Oklahoma, sent me this little note on that section: "Aspen. Boulders . . . Colorado Springs?" I'd never have seen that by myself. Nine times out of ten, of course, I use those misgivings to confirm what I've done. So-and-so thinks a passage is obscure? *Good*—it stays obscure: that'll teach him! No wonder that the most loyal reader gets lost along the way—feels disappointed by a turn you've taken, and simply gives up.

INTERVIEWER: Yet one of your strengths as a poet is so to disarm your reader, often by including his possible objections.

MERRILL: That might even be the placating gesture of a child who is inevitably going to disappoint his parents before he fulfills the expectations they haven't yet learned to have. I was always very good at seeming to accede to what my father or mother wanted of me—and then going ahead to do as I pleased.

We move into Merrill's small study. As a rule, he works here every day from early morning until noon. One wall is books, with a built-in daybed on which is laid out a balked game of Patience. On his desk are dictionaries. Next to it a blue Selectric sprouting

*a draft. Friends look on, from photographs thumbtacked to the
wall behind. One is of Proust.*

INTERVIEWER: You say in "The Book of Ephraim" that
you've read Proust for the last time. Is that true?

MERRILL: I thought so when I said it, but in fact—just before
starting to write the party scene which ends the Epilogue—I
took a quick look at *Le Temps retrouvé*.

INTERVIEWER: In a sense, Proust has been the greatest influence on your career, wouldn't you agree?

MERRILL: I would.

INTERVIEWER: Odd for a poet to have a novelist over his
shoulder.

MERRILL: Why? I certainly didn't feel his influence when I
was writing novels. My attention span when writing or "observing" is so much shorter than his, that it's only in a poem—in
miniature as it were—that something of his flavor might be
felt.

INTERVIEWER: Speaking of influences, one could mention
Stevens, Auden, Bishop, a few others. What have you sought
to learn from other poets, and how in general have you adapted
their example to your practice?

MERRILL: Oh, I suppose I've learned things about writing,
technical things, from each of them. Auden's penultimate
rhyming, Elizabeth's way of contradicting something she's just
said, Stevens's odd glamorizing of philosophical terms. Aside
from all that, what I think I *really* wanted was some evidence
that one didn't have to lead a "literary" life—belong to a
ghetto of "creativity." That one could live as one pleased, and
not be shamefaced in the glare of renown (if it ever came) at
being an insurance man or a woman who'd moved to Brazil and
played samba records instead of discussing X's latest volume.
It was heartening that the *best* poets had this freedom. Auden
did lead a life that looked literary from a distance, though
actually I thought it was more a re-creation of school and

university days: much instruction, much giggling, much untidiness. Perhaps because my own school years were unhappy for extracurricular reasons I didn't feel completely at ease with all that. So much was routine—and often wildly entertaining of course: once, a long lunchtime discussion with Chester Kallman about whether three nineteen- or twenty-year-old guests who were expected for dinner should be offered *real drinks* culminated that evening in Wystan's removing three tiny, tiny glasses from the big hearts-and-flowers cupboard and asking *me* to "make vodka and tonics for our young friends." (I gave them straight vodka, of course.) The point's not that Wystan was stingy—or if he was, who cares?—but that his conflicting principles (Don't Waste Good Liquor on the Young versus *Gastrecht,* or the Sacred Duty of a Host) arrived at a solution that would have made Da Ponte smile. Soon everyone was having a good time. One of the young Englishmen proposed—this was late in the sixties—that poems should appear in common, everyday places: on books of matches, beer cans, toilet paper. "I sense the need," said Chester rolling his eyes, "for applied criticism."

It was du côté de chez Elizabeth, though, that I saw the daily life that took my fancy even more, with its kind of random, Chekhovian surface, open to trivia and funny surprises, or even painful ones, today a fit of weeping, tomorrow a picnic. I could see how close that life was to her poems, how much the life and the poems gave to one another. I don't mean I've "achieved" anything of the sort in *my* life or poems, only that Elizabeth had more of a talent for life—and for poetry—than anyone else I've known, and this has served me as an ideal.

INTERVIEWER: When you read someone else's poem, what do you read *for?* What kind of pleasure do you take? What kind of hesitations do you have?

MERRILL: Well, I'm always open to what another poet might do with *the line,* or with a stanza. I don't know what particular turn of phrase I look for, but it's always very important, the phrasing of the lines—Elizabeth's elegy for Lowell struck me as such a masterpiece because you read the poem a couple of times and felt you knew it by heart. Every line fell in the most wonderful way, which is perhaps something she learned from Herbert. You find it *there.* I think you find it very often in French poetry.

INTERVIEWER: You're drawn, then, primarily to technical matters?

MERRILL: To the extent that the phrasing leads to the content. I don't really know how to separate those. The poems I most love are so perfectly phrased that they seem to say something extraordinary, whether they do or not.

INTERVIEWER: Increasingly, your work has exhibited a striking range in what would once have been called its poetic diction. Conversational stops and starts alternate with stanza-long sentences bristling with subordinate clauses. Scientific jargon lies down with slang. What guides these choices?

MERRILL: Taste, instinct, temperament . . . Too much poetry sounds like side after side of modern music, the same serial twitterings, the same barnyard grunts. Just as I love multiple meanings, I try for contrasts and disruptions of tone. Am I wrong—in the old days didn't the various meters imply different modes or situations, like madness, love, war? It's too late, in any event, to rely very much on meter—look at those gorgeous but imbecile antistrophes and semichoruses in Swinburne or Shelley or whoever. I'm talking from a reader's point of view, you understand. Poets will rediscover as many techniques as they need in order to help them write better. But for a reader who can hardly be trusted to hear the iambics when he opens *The Rape of the Lock,* if anything can fill the void left by these obsolete resources, I'd imagine it would have to be diction or "voice." Voice in its fullest tonal range—not just bel canto or passionate speech. From my own point of view, this range would be utterly unattainable without meter and rhyme and those forms we are talking about.

Of course, they breed echoes. There's always a lurking air of pastiche which, consciously or unconsciously, gets into your diction. That doesn't much bother me, does it you? No voice is as individual as the poet would like to think. In the long run I'd rather have what I write remind people of Pope or Yeats or Byron than of the other students in that year's workshop.

INTERVIEWER: The hallmark of your poetry is its *tone*, the way its concerns are observed and presented. And much of its effect depends on your fondness for paradox. Is that a cultivated habit of mind with you? A deliberate way into, and out of, the world and the poem?

MERRILL: It's hard to know. "Cultivated" certainly in the gardening sense of the word—which doesn't explain the mystery of the seed. I suppose that early on I began to understand the relativity, even the reversibility, of truths. At the same time as I was being given a good education I could feel, not so much from my parents, but from the world they moved in, that kind of easygoing contempt rich people have for art and scholarship —"these things are all right *in their place,* and their place is to ornament a life rather than to nourish or to shape it." Or when it came to sex, I had to face it that the worst iniquity my parents (and many of my friends) could imagine was for me a blessed source of pleasure and security—as well as suffering, to be sure. There was truth on both sides. And maybe having arrived at *that* explained my delight in setting down a phrase like, oh, "the pillow's dense white dark" or "Au fond each summit is a cul-de-sac," but the explanation as such neither delights nor convinces me. I believe the secret lies primarily in the nature of poetry—and of science too, for that matter—and that the ability to see both ways at once isn't merely an idiosyncrasy but corresponds to how the world needs to be seen: cheerful *and* awful, opaque *and* transparent. The plus and minus signs of a vast, evolving formula.

INTERVIEWER: I want to come back to a phrase you just used —"pleasure and security." Would those twinned feelings also

account for your affectionate and bracing reliance on traditional forms?

MERRILL: Yes, why not? Now and then one enjoys a little
moonwalk, some little departure from tradition. And the forms
themselves seem to invite this, in our age of "breakthroughs."
Take the villanelle, which didn't really change from "Your
eyen two wol slay me sodenly" until, say, 1950. With Empson's
famous ones rigor mortis had set in, for any purposes beyond
those of vers de société. Still, there were tiny signs. People
began repunctuating the key lines so that each time they re-
curred, the meaning would be slightly different. Was that just
an extension of certain cute effects in Austin Dobson? In any
case, "sodenly" Elizabeth's ravishing "One Art" came along,
where the key lines seem merely to approximate themselves,
and the form, awakened by a kiss, simply toddles off to a new
stage in its life, under the proud eye of Mother, or the Muse.
One doesn't, I mean, have to be just a stolid "formalist." The
forms, the meters and rhyme-sounds, are far too liberating for
that.

INTERVIEWER: Liberating?

MERRILL: From one's own smudged images and anxiety
about "having something to say." *Into* the dynamics of—well,
the craft itself.

INTERVIEWER: Few words can make contemporary poets
cringe more than "great"—I mean, when applied to poems or
poets. That's something that certainly doesn't hold for other
arts, say, painting. Why do you suppose this is so? Is the whole
category outdated?

MERRILL: I hope not. Just because "great" is now a talk-show
word meaning competent or agreeable, it doesn't follow that
we have to take this lying down. It's really the bombast, the
sunless pedantry—waste products of ideas—that make us
cringe. They form on a text like mildew. Straining for exaltation, coasting off into complacency . . . Words keep going
bankrupt and ringing false, and as you say, this wouldn't be true

in painting. A "new" Revlon color doesn't invalidate a Matisse that used it fifty years earlier. Subjects date more quickly; you don't see many weeping Magdalens or meadows full of cows in the galleries nowadays, and I can't think of much celestial machinery in poetry between *The Rape of the Lock* and "Ephraim." But painters still go to museums, don't they? They've *seen* great paintings and even survived the shock. Now surely *some* of our hundred thousand living American poets have read the great poems of the Western world, and kept their minds open to the possibilities.

INTERVIEWER: Is "heroism" or "high tone" the word I want to pinpoint what's been missing from American literature these past decades? Or do those terms mean anything to you?

MERRILL: Oh, heroism's possible, all right, and the high tone hasn't deserted some of us. Trouble is, our heroes more and more turn up as artists or invalids or both—the sort that won't be accepted as heroic except by fellow artists (or fellow sufferers). Sir Edmund Hillary will "do" of course, but I don't gasp at his achievement the way I do at Proust's. Must this leave the healthy, uncreative reader at a loss, not being sick or special enough to identify? Does he need to, after all? It's not as though only people in superb physical shape were thrilled by the conquest of Everest. And Proust is subtle enough to persuade us that the real feat has been one not of style but of memory, therefore within even the common man's power to duplicate. It's not the prevailing low tone so much as the imaginative laziness. We don't see life as an adventure. We know that our lives are in our hands; and far from freeing us, this knowledge has become a paralyzing weight.

INTERVIEWER: An adventure without obvious dragons and princesses, composed merely of the flat circumstances of a given life—that's not always apparent to the naked eye.

MERRILL: No. Yet your life, and that means people and places and history along with *la vie intérieure*, does keep growing and blossoming, and is always *there* as potential subject matter; but the blossom needs to be fertilized—you don't just versify your engagement book—and when that bee comes can't ever be predicted or willed.

INTERVIEWER: You'd disagree, then, with Auden, who said he was a poet *only* when actually writing a poem.

MERRILL: Lucky him. What was he the rest of the time?

INTERVIEWER: A citizen, I believe he said.

MERRILL: Oh. Well, that citizen must have heard a lot of funny sounds from the poet pigeonhole next door. I certainly do. Whether you're at your desk or not when a poem's under way, isn't there that constant eddy in your mind? If it's strong enough all sorts of random flotsam gets drawn into it, how selectively it's hopeless to decide at the time. I try to break off, get away from the page, into the kitchen for a spell of mixing and marinating which gives the words a chance to sort themselves out behind my back. But there's really no escape, except perhaps the third drink. On "ordinary" days, days when you've nothing on the burner, it might be safe to say that you're not a poet at all: more like a doctor at a dinner party, just another guest until his hostess slumps to the floor or his little beeper goes off. Most of those signals are false alarms—only they're not. Language *is* your medium. You can be talking or writing a letter, and out comes an observation, a "sentence-sound" you rather like. It needn't be your own. And it's not going to make a poem, or even fit into one. But the *twinge* it gives you—and it's this, I daresay, that distinguishes you from the "citizen"— reminds you've got to be careful, that you've a condition that needs watching . . .

INTERVIEWER: Sounds like that doctor's turning into a patient.

MERRILL: Doesn't it! How about lunch?

J. D. MCCLATCHY
Summer/Fall 1981

10. Gabriel García Márquez

Gabriel García Márquez was born in 1928 in the small Colombian town of Aracataca. Surrounded by banana plantations, its neighboring village is called Macondo, which would later become the setting for *One Hundred Years of Solitude.* Márquez, who provided the. His first published writings were nonetheless reportorial—appearing in the Colombian newspaper *El Espectador,* where he was a reporter and film critic; for a few years in the mid-1950s he worked as a foreign correspondent based in Rome and Paris.

García Márquez's first short stories were written at night after the other journalists had left the office, but it took a few years and the prodding of a few close friends before they were published. Today his fiction has been translated into more than twenty languages and includes *Leaf Storm* (1955), *No One Writes to the Colonel* (1961), and *The Evil Hour* (1962). It was not until 1967, however, when *One Hundred Years of Solitude,* a book he had been struggling to write for many years, was published that he achieved international recognition. Immediately hailed as a masterpiece, the novel won the best foreign book prize in 1969 from the Académie Française. In 1975, *The Autumn of the Patriarch*—a continuation of his fictional investigation of solitude and its relationship to power —was greeted with equivalently high praise. His most recent work is *Chronicle of a Death Foretold.*

Since 1961 he has made his home in Mexico City. He has been married for more than twenty years to his childhood sweetheart, Mercedes, and they have two sons, Rodrigo, a student at Harvard, and Gonsalvo, a flutist studying in Paris.

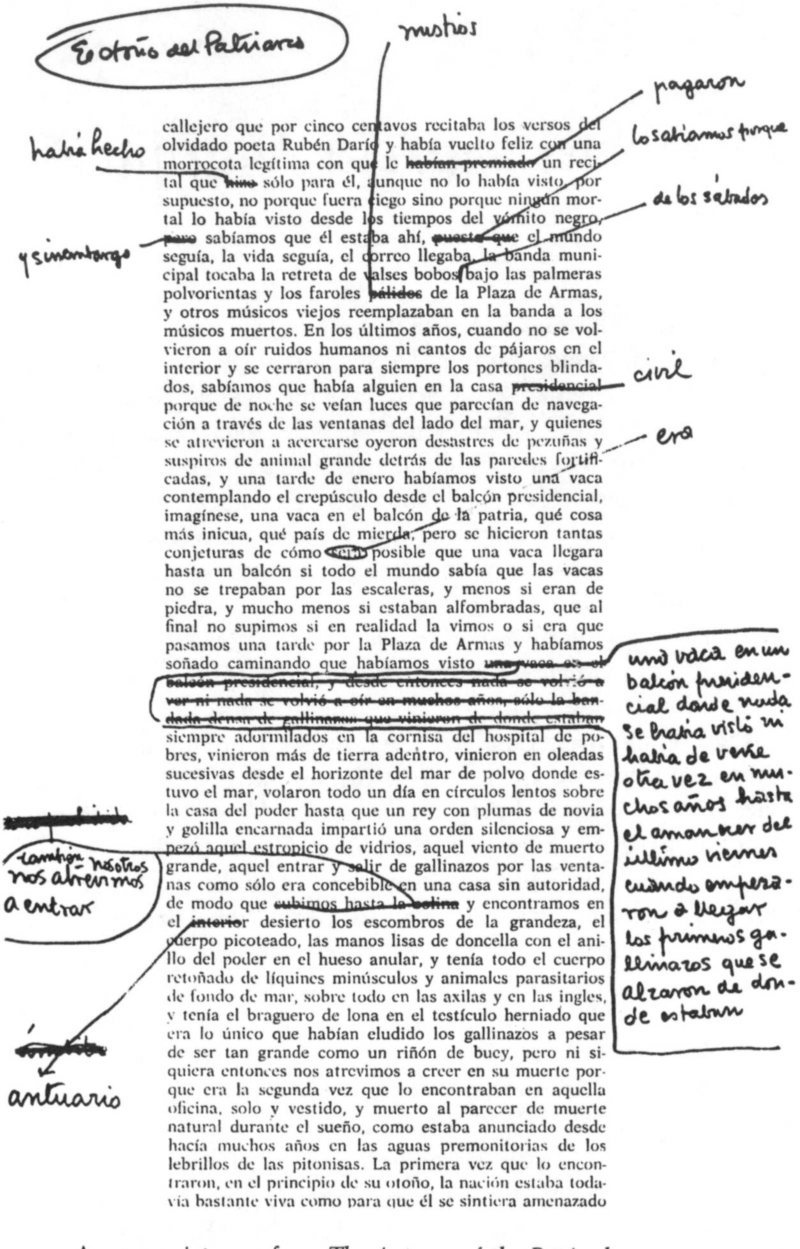

callejero que por cinco centavos recitaba los versos del olvidado poeta Rubén Darío y había vuelto feliz con una morrocota legítima con que le habían premiado un recital que hizo sólo para él, aunque no lo había visto, por supuesto, no porque fuera ciego sino porque ningún mortal lo había visto desde los tiempos del vómito negro, pero sabíamos que él estaba ahí, puesto que el mundo seguía, la vida seguía, el correo llegaba, la banda municipal tocaba la retreta de valses bobos bajo las palmeras polvorientas y los faroles pálidos de la Plaza de Armas, y otros músicos viejos reemplazaban en la banda a los músicos muertos. En los últimos años, cuando no se volvieron a oír ruidos humanos ni cantos de pájaros en el interior y se cerraron para siempre los portones blindados, sabíamos que había alguien en la casa presidencial porque de noche se veían luces que parecían de navegación a través de las ventanas del lado del mar, y quienes se atrevieron a acercarse oyeron desastres de pezuñas y suspiros de animal grande detrás de las paredes fortificadas, y una tarde de enero habíamos visto una vaca contemplando el crepúsculo desde el balcón presidencial, imagínese, una vaca en el balcón de la patria, qué cosa más inicua, qué país de mierda, pero se hicieron tantas conjeturas de cómo sería posible que una vaca llegara hasta un balcón si todo el mundo sabía que las vacas no se trepaban por las escaleras, y menos si eran de piedra, y mucho menos si estaban alfombradas, que al final no supimos si en realidad la vimos o si era que pasamos una tarde por la Plaza de Armas y habíamos soñado caminando que habíamos visto una vaca en el balcón presidencial, y desde entonces nada se volvió a ver ni nada se volvió a oír en muchos años, sólo la bandada densa de gallinazos que vinieron de donde estaban siempre adormilados en la cornisa del hospital de pobres, vinieron más de tierra adentro, vinieron en oleadas sucesivas desde el horizonte del mar de polvo donde estuvo el mar, volaron todo un día en círculos lentos sobre la casa del poder hasta que un rey con plumas de novia y golilla encarnada impartió una orden silenciosa y empezó aquel estropicio de vidrios, aquel viento de muerto grande, aquel entrar y salir de gallinazos por las ventanas como sólo era concebible en una casa sin autoridad, de modo que subimos hasta la colina y encontramos en el interior desierto los escombros de la grandeza, el cuerpo picoteado, las manos lisas de doncella con el anillo del poder en el hueso anular, y tenía todo el cuerpo retoñado de líquines minúsculos y animales parasitarios de fondo de mar, sobre todo en las axilas y en las ingles, y tenía el braguero de lona en el testículo herniado que era lo único que habían eludido los gallinazos a pesar de ser tan grande como un riñón de buey, pero ni siquiera entonces nos atrevimos a creer en su muerte porque era la segunda vez que lo encontraban en aquella oficina, solo y vestido, y muerto al parecer de muerte natural durante el sueño, como estaba anunciado desde hacía muchos años en las aguas premonitorias de los lebrillos de las pitonisas. La primera vez que lo encontraron, en el principio de su otoño, la nación estaba todavía bastante viva como para que él se sintiera amenazado

El otoño del Patriarca
mustios
pagaron
los sabíamos porque
de los sábados
había hecho
y sin embargo
civil
era
una vaca en un balcón presidencial donde nada se había visto ni había de verse otra vez en muchos años hasta el amanecer del último viernes cuando empezaron a llegar los primeros gallinazos que se alzaron de donde estaban
también nosotros nos atrevimos a entrar
antuario

A manuscript page from *The Autumn of the Patriarch*.

Gabriel García Márquez

Gabriel García Márquez was interviewed in his studio/office located just behind his house in San Ángel Inn, an old and lovely section, full of the spectacularly colorful flowers of Mexico City. The studio is a short walk from the main house. A low elongated building, it appears to have been originally designed as a guest house. Within, at one end, are a couch, two easy chairs, and a makeshift bar—a small white refrigerator with a supply of acqua minerale *on top.*

The most striking feature of the room is a large blown-up photograph above the sofa of García Márquez alone, wearing a stylish cape and standing on some windswept vista looking somewhat like Anthony Quinn.

García Márquez was sitting at his desk at the far end of the studio. He came to greet me, walking briskly with a light step. He is a solidly built man, only about five feet eight or nine in height, who looks like a good middleweight fighter—broad-chested, but perhaps a bit thin in the legs. He was dressed casually in corduroy slacks with a light turtleneck sweater and black leather boots. His hair is dark and curly brown and he wears a full moustache.

The interview took place over the course of three late afternoon meetings of roughly two hours each. Although his English is quite good, García Márquez spoke mostly in Spanish and his two sons shared the translating. When García Márquez speaks, his body often rocks back and forth. His hands too are often in motion making small but decisive gestures to emphasize a point, or to indicate a shift of direction in his thinking. He alternates between leaning forward towards his listener, and sitting far back with his legs crossed when speaking reflectively.

INTERVIEWER: How do you feel about using the tape recorder?

GARCIA MARQUEZ: The problem is that the moment you know the interview is being taped, your attitude changes. In my case I immediately take a defensive attitude. As a journalist, I feel that we still haven't learned how to use a tape recorder to do an interview. The best way, I feel, is to have a long conversation without the journalist taking any notes. Then afterward he should reminisce about the conversation and write it down as an impression of what he felt, not necessarily using the exact words expressed. Another useful method is to take notes and then interpret them with a certain loyalty to the person interviewed. What ticks you off about the tape recording everything is that it is not loyal to the person who is being interviewed, because it even records and remembers when you make an ass of yourself. That's why when there is a tape recorder, I am conscious that I'm being interviewed; when there isn't a tape recorder, I talk in an unconscious and completely natural way.

INTERVIEWER: Well, you make me feel a little guilty using

it, but I think for this kind of an interview we probably need it.

GARCIA MARQUEZ: Anyway, the whole purpose of what I just said was to put you on the defensive.

INTERVIEWER: So you have never used a tape recorder yourself for an interview?

GARCIA MARQUEZ: As a journalist, I never use it. I have a very good tape recorder, but I just use it to listen to music. But then as a journalist I've never done an interview. I've done reports, but never an interview with questions and answers.

INTERVIEWER: I heard about one famous interview with a sailor who had been shipwrecked.

GARCIA MARQUEZ: It wasn't questions and answers. The sailor would just tell me his adventures and I would rewrite them trying to use his own words and in the first person, as if he were the one who was writing. When the work was published as a serial in a newspaper, one part each day for two weeks, it was signed by the sailor, not by me. It wasn't until twenty years later that it was published and people found out I had written it. No editor realized that it was good until after I had written *One Hundred Years of Solitude*.

INTERVIEWER: Since we've started talking about journalism, how does it feel being a journalist again, after having written novels for so long? Do you do it with a different feel or a different eye?

GARCIA MARQUEZ: I've always been convinced that my true profession is that of a journalist. What I didn't like about journalism before were the working conditions. Besides, I had to condition my thoughts and ideas to the interests of the newspaper. Now, after having worked as a novelist, and having achieved financial independence as a novelist, I can really choose the themes that interest me and correspond to my ideas. In any case, I always very much enjoy the chance of doing a great piece of journalism.

INTERVIEWER: What is a great piece of journalism for you?

GARCIA MARQUEZ: *Hiroshima* by John Hersey was an exceptional piece.

INTERVIEWER: Is there a story today that you would especially like to do?

GARCIA MARQUEZ: There are many, and several I have in fact written. I have written about Portugal, Cuba, Angola, and Vietnam. I would very much like to write on Poland. I think if I could describe exactly what is now going on, it would be a very important story. But it's too cold now in Poland; I'm a journalist who likes his comforts.

INTERVIEWER: Do you think the novel can do certain things that journalism can't?

GARCIA MARQUEZ: Nothing. I don't think there is any difference. The sources are the same, the material is the same, the resources and the language are the same. *The Journal of the Plague Year* by Daniel Defoe is a great novel and *Hiroshima* is a great work of journalism.

INTERVIEWER: Do the journalist and the novelist have different responsibilities in balancing truth versus the imagination?

GARCIA MARQUEZ: In journalism just one fact that is false prejudices the entire work. In contrast, in fiction one single fact that is true gives legitimacy to the entire work. That's the only difference, and it lies in the commitment of the writer. A novelist can do anything he wants so long as he makes people believe in it.

INTERVIEWER: In interviews a few years ago, you seemed to look back on being a journalist with awe at how much faster you were then.

GARCIA MARQUEZ: I do find it harder to write now than before, both novels and journalism. When I worked for newspapers, I wasn't very conscious of every word I wrote, whereas now I am. When I was working for *El Espectador* in Bogotá, I used to do at least three stories a week, two or three editorial notes every day, and I did movie reviews. Then at night, after everyone had gone home, I would stay behind writing my novels. I liked the noise of the Linotype machines, which sounded like rain. If they stopped, and I was left in silence, I wouldn't be able to work. Now, the output is comparatively small. On a good working day, working from nine o'clock in the morning to two or three in the afternoon, the most I can write is a short paragraph of four or five lines, which I usually tear up the next day.

INTERVIEWER: Does this change come from your works being so highly praised or from some kind of political commitment?

GARCIA MARQUEZ: It's from both. I think that the idea that I'm writing for many more people than I ever imagined has created a certain general responsibility that is literary and political. There's even pride involved, in not wanting to fall short of what I did before.

INTERVIEWER: How did you start writing?

GARCIA MARQUEZ: By drawing. By drawing cartoons. Before I could read or write I used to draw comics at school and at home. The funny thing is that I now realize that when I was in high school I had the reputation of being a writer, though I never in fact wrote anything. If there was a pamphlet to be written or a letter of petition, I was the one to do it because I was supposedly the writer. When I entered college I happened to have a very good literary background in general, considerably above the average of my friends. At the university in Bogotá, I started making new friends and acquaintances, who introduced me to contemporary writers. One night a friend lent me a book of short stories by Franz Kafka. I went back to the pension where I was staying and began to read *The Metamorphosis*. The first line almost knocked me off the bed. I was so surprised. The first line reads, "As Gregor Samsa awoke that morning from uneasy dreams, he found himself transformed in his bed into a gigantic insect. . . ." When I read the line I thought to myself that I didn't know anyone was allowed to write things like that. If I had known, I would have started writing a long time ago. So I immediately started writing short stories. They are totally intellectual short stories because I was writing them on the basis of my literary experience and had not yet found the link between literature and life. The stories were published in the literary supplement of the newspaper *El Espectador* in Bogotá and they did have a certain success at the time—probably because nobody in Colombia was writing intellectual short stories. What was being written then was mostly about life in the countryside and social life. When I wrote my first short stories I was told they had Joycean influences.

INTERVIEWER: Had you read Joyce at that time?

GARCIA MARQUEZ: I had never read Joyce, so I started reading *Ulysses.* I read it in the only Spanish edition available. Since then, after having read *Ulysses* in English as well as a very good French translation, I can see that the original Spanish translation was very bad. But I did learn something that was to be very useful to me in my future writing—the technique of the interior monologue. I later found this in Virginia Woolf, and I like the way she uses it better than Joyce. Although I later realized that the person who invented this interior monologue was the anonymous writer of the *Lazarillo de Tormes.*

INTERVIEWER: Can you name some of your early influences?

GARCIA MARQUEZ: The people who really helped me to get rid of my intellectual attitude towards the short story were the writers of the American Lost Generation. I realized that their literature had a relationship with life that my short stories didn't. And then an event took place which was very important with respect to this attitude. It was the Bogotazo, on the ninth of April, 1948, when a political leader, Gaitan, was shot and the people of Bogotá went raving mad in the streets. I was in my pension ready to have lunch when I heard the news. I ran towards the place, but Gaitan had just been put into a taxi and was being taken to a hospital. On my way back to the pension, the people had already taken to the streets and they were demonstrating, looting stores and burning buildings. I joined them. That afternoon and evening, I became aware of the kind of country I was living in, and how little my short stories had to do with any of that. When I was later forced to go back to Barranquilla on the Caribbean, where I had spent my childhood, I realized that that was the type of life I had lived, knew, and wanted to write about.

Around 1950 or '51 another event happened that influenced my literary tendencies. My mother asked me to accompany her to Aracataca, where I was born, and to sell the house where I spent my first years. When I got there it was at first quite shocking because I was now twenty-two and hadn't been there since the age of eight. Nothing had really changed, but I felt that I wasn't really looking at the village, but I was *experiencing* it as if I were reading it. It was as if everything I saw had already been written, and all I had to do was to sit down and copy what was already there and what I was just reading. For all practical purposes everything had evolved into literature: the houses, the people, and the memories. I'm not sure whether I had already read Faulkner or not, but I know now that only a technique like Faulkner's could have enabled me to write down what I was seeing. The atmosphere, the decadence, the heat in the village were roughly the same as what I had felt in Faulkner. It was a banana plantation region inhabited by a lot of Americans from the fruit companies which gave it the same sort of atmosphere I had found in the writers of the Deep South. Critics have spoken of the literary influence of Faulkner, but I see it as a coincidence: I had simply found material that had to be dealt with in the same way that Faulkner had treated similar material.

From that trip to the village I came back to write *Leaf Storm*, my first novel. What really happened to me in that trip to Aracataca was that I realized that everything that had occurred in my childhood had a literary value that I was only now appreciating. From the moment I wrote *Leaf Storm* I realized I wanted to be a writer and that nobody could stop me and that the only thing left for me to do was to try to be the best writer in the world. That was in 1953, but it wasn't until 1967 that I got my first royalties after having written five of my eight books.

INTERVIEWER: Do you think that it's common for young writers to deny the worth of their own childhoods and experiences and to intellectualize as you did initially?

GARCIA MARQUEZ: No, the process usually takes place the other way around, but if I had to give a young writer some advice I would say to write about something that has happened to him; it's always easy to tell whether a writer is writing about something that has happened to him or something he has read or been told. Pablo Neruda has a line in a poem that says "God help me from inventing when I sing." It always amuses me that the biggest praise for my work comes for the imagination, while the truth is that there's not a single line in all my work that does not have a basis in reality. The problem is that Caribbean reality resembles the wildest imagination.

INTERVIEWER: Whom were you writing for at this point? Who was your audience?

GARCIA MARQUEZ: *Leaf Storm* was written for my friends who were helping me and lending me their books and were very enthusiastic about my work. In general I think you usually do write for someone. When I'm writing I'm always aware that this friend is going to like this, or that another friend is going to like that paragraph or chapter, always thinking of specific people. In the end all books are written for your friends. The problem after writing *One Hundred Years of Solitude* was that now I no longer know whom of the millions of readers I am writing for; this upsets and inhibits me. It's like a million eyes are looking at you and you don't really know what they think.

INTERVIEWER: What about the influence of journalism on your fiction?

GARCIA MARQUEZ: I think the influence is reciprocal. Fiction has helped my journalism because it has given it literary value.

Journalism has helped my fiction because it has kept me in a close relationship with reality.

INTERVIEWER: How would you describe the search for a style that you went through after *Leaf Storm* and before you were able to write *One Hundred Years of Solitude*?

GARCIA MARQUEZ: After having written *Leaf Storm*, I decided that writing about the village and my childhood was really an escape from having to face and write about the political reality of the country. I had the false impression that I was hiding myself behind this kind of nostalgia instead of confronting the political things that were going on. This was the time when the relationship between literature and politics was very much discussed. I kept trying to close the gap between the two. My influence had been Faulkner; now it was Hemingway. I wrote *No One Writes to the Colonel, The Evil Hour,* and *The Funeral of Mama Grand,* which were all written at more or less the same time and have many things in common. These stories take place in a different village from the one in which *Leaf Storm* and *One Hundred Years of Solitude* occur. It is a village in which there is no magic. It is a journalistic literature. But when I finished *The Evil Hour,* I saw that all my views were wrong again. I came to see that in fact my writings about my childhood were *more* political and had more to do with the reality of my country than I had thought. After *The Evil Hour* I did not write anything for five years. I had an idea of what I always wanted to do, but there was something missing and I was not sure what it was until one day I discovered the right tone—the tone that I eventually used in *One Hundred Years of Solitude*. It was based on the way my grandmother used to tell her stories. She told things that sounded supernatural and fantastic, but she told them with complete naturalness. When I finally discovered the tone I had to use, I sat down for eighteen months and worked every day.

INTERVIEWER: How did she express the "fantastic" so naturally?

GARCIA MARQUEZ: What was most important was the expression she had on her face. She did not change her expression at all when telling her stories, and everyone was surprised. In previous attempts to write *One Hundred Years of Solitude,* I tried to tell the story without believing in it. I discovered that what I had to do was believe in them myself and write them with the same expression with which my grandmother told them: with a brick face.

INTERVIEWER: There also seems to be a journalistic quality to that technique or tone. You describe seemingly fantastic events in such minute detail that it gives them their own reality. Is this something you have picked up from journalism?

GARCIA MARQUEZ: That's a journalistic trick which you can also apply to literature. For example, if you say that there are elephants flying in the sky, people are not going to believe you. But if you say that there are four hundred and twenty-five elephants in the sky, people will probably believe you. *One Hundred Years of Solitude* is full of that sort of thing. That's exactly the technique my grandmother used. I remember particularly the story about the character who is surrounded by yellow butterflies. When I was very small there was an electrician who came to the house. I became very curious because he carried a belt with which he used to suspend himself from the electrical posts. My grandmother used to say that every time this man came around, he would leave the house full of butterflies. But when I was writing this, I discovered that if I didn't say the butterflies were yellow, people would not believe it. When I was writing the episode of Remedios the Beauty going to heaven, it took me a long time to make it credible. One day I went out to the garden and saw a woman who used to come to the house to do the wash and she was putting out the sheets to dry and there was a lot of wind. She was arguing with the wind not to blow the sheets away. I discovered that if I used the sheets for Remedios the Beauty, she would ascend. That's how I did it, to make it credible. The problem for every writer is credibility. Anybody can write anything so long as it's believed.

INTERVIEWER: What was the origin of the insomnia plague in *One Hundred Years of Solitude*?

GARCIA MARQUEZ: Beginning with Oedipus, I've always been interested in plagues. I have studied a lot about medieval plagues. One of my favorite books is *The Journal of the Plague Year* by Daniel Defoe, among other reasons because Defoe is a journalist who sounds like what he is saying is pure fantasy. For many years I thought Defoe had written about the London plague as he observed it. But then I discovered it was a novel, because Defoe was less than seven years old when the plague occurred in London. Plagues have always been one of my recurrent themes—and in different forms. In *The Evil Hour*, the pamphlets are plagues. For many years I thought that the political violence in Colombia had the same metaphysics as the plague. Before *One Hundred Years of Solitude*, I had used a plague to kill all the birds in a story called *The Day After Saturday*. In *One Hundred Years of Solitude* I used the insomnia plague as something of a literary trick, since it's the opposite of the sleeping plague. Ultimately, literature is nothing but carpentry.

INTERVIEWER: Can you explain that analogy a little more?

GARCIA MARQUEZ: Both are very hard work. Writing something is almost as hard as making a table. With both you are working with reality, a material just as hard as wood. Both are full of tricks and techniques. Basically very little magic and a lot of hard work are involved. And as Proust, I think, said, it takes ten percent inspiration and ninety percent perspiration. I never have done any carpentry but it's the job I admire most, especially because you can never find anyone to do it for you.

INTERVIEWER: What about the banana fever in *One Hundred Years of Solitude*? How much of that is based on what the United Fruit Company did?

GARCIA MARQUEZ: The banana fever is modeled closely on

reality. Of course, I've used literary tricks on things which have not been proved historically. For example, the massacre in the square is completely true, but while I wrote it on the basis of testimony and documents, it was never known exactly how many people were killed. I used the figure three thousand, which is obviously an exaggeration. But one of my childhood memories was watching a very, very long train leave the plantation supposedly full of bananas. There could have been three thousand dead on it, eventually to be dumped in the sea. What's really surprising is that now they speak very naturally in the Congress and the newspapers about the "three thousand dead." I suspect that half of all our history is made in this fashion. In *The Autumn of the Patriarch*, the dictator says it doesn't matter if it's not true now, because sometime in the future it will be true. Sooner or later people believe writers rather than the government.

INTERVIEWER: That makes the writer pretty powerful, doesn't it?

GARCIA MARQUEZ: Yes, and I can feel it too. It gives me a great sense of responsibility. What I would really like to do is a piece of journalism which is completely true and real, but which sounds as fantastic as *One Hundred Years of Solitude*. The more I live and remember things from the past, the more I think that literature and journalism are closely related.

INTERVIEWER: What about a country giving up its sea for its foreign debt, as in *The Autumn of the Patriarch*?

GARCIA MARQUEZ: Yes, but that actually happened. It's happened and will happen many times more. *The Autumn of the Patriarch* is a completely historical book. To find probabilities out of real facts is the work of the journalist and the novelist, and it is also the work of the prophet. The trouble is that many people believe that I'm a writer of fantastic fiction, when actually I'm a very realistic person and write what I believe is the true socialist realism.

INTERVIEWER: Is it utopian?

GARCIA MARQUEZ: I'm not sure if the word utopian means the real or the ideal. But I think it's the real.

INTERVIEWER: Are the characters in *The Autumn of the Patriarch*, the dictators, for example, modeled after real people? There seem to be similarities with Franco, Perón, and Trujillo.

GARCIA MARQUEZ: In every novel, the character is a collage: a collage of different characters that you've known, or heard about or read about. I read everything that I could find about Latin American dictators of the last century, and the beginning of this one. I also talked to a lot of people who had lived under dictatorships. I did that for at least ten years. And when I had a clear idea of what the character was going to be like, I made an effort to forget everything I had read and heard, so that I could invent, without using any situation that had occurred in real life. I realized at one point that I myself had not lived for any period of time under a dictatorship, so I thought if I wrote the book in Spain, I could see what the atmosphere was like living in an established dictatorship. But I found that the atmosphere was very different in Spain under Franco from that of a Caribbean dictatorship. So the book was kind of blocked for about a year. There was something missing and I wasn't sure what it was. Then overnight, I decided that the best thing was that we come back to the Caribbean. So we all moved back to Barranquilla in Colombia. I made a statement to the journalists which they thought was a joke. I said that I was coming back because I had forgotten what a guava smelled like. In truth, it was what I really needed to finish my book. I took a trip through the Caribbean. As I went from island to island, I found the elements which were the ones that had been lacking from my novel.

INTERVIEWER: You often use the theme of the solitude of power.

GARCIA MARQUEZ: The more power you have, the harder it is to know who is lying to you and who is not. When you reach absolute power, there is no contact with reality, and that's the worst kind of solitude there can be. A very powerful person, a dictator, is surrounded by interests and people whose final aim is to isolate him from reality; everything is in concert to isolate him.

INTERVIEWER: What about the solitude of the writer? Is this different?

GARCIA MARQUEZ: It has a lot to do with the solitude of power. The writer's very attempt to portray reality often leads him to a distorted view of it. In trying to transpose reality he can end up losing contact with it, in an ivory tower, as they say. Journalism is a very good guard against that. That's why I have always tried to keep on doing journalism, because it keeps me in contact with the real world, particularly political journalism and politics. The solitude that threatened me after *One Hundred Years of Solitude* wasn't the solitude of the writer; it was the solitude of fame, which resembles the solitude of power much more. My friends defended me from that one, my friends who are always there.

INTERVIEWER: How?

GARCIA MARQUEZ: Because I have managed to keep the same friends all my life. I mean I don't break or cut myself off from my old friends, and they're the ones who bring me back to earth; they always keep their feet on the ground and they're not famous.

INTERVIEWER: How do things start? One of the recurring images in *The Autumn of the Patriarch* is the cows in the palace. Was this one of the original images?

GARCIA MARQUEZ: I've got a photography book that I'm going to show you. I've said on various occasions that in the genesis of all my books there's always an image. The first image I had of *The Autumn of the Patriarch* was a very old man in a very luxurious palace into which cows come and eat the curtains. But that image didn't concretize until I saw the photograph. In Rome I went into a bookshop where I started looking at photography books, which I like to collect. I saw this photograph, and it was just perfect. I just saw that was how it was going to be. Since I'm not a big intellectual, I can find my antecedents in everyday things, in life, and not in the great masterpieces.

INTERVIEWER: Do your novels ever take unexpected twists?

GARCIA MARQUEZ: That used to happen to me in the beginning. In the first stories I wrote I had a general idea of the mood, but I would let myself be taken by chance. The best advice I was given early on was that it was all right to work that way when I was young because I had a torrent of inspiration. But I was told that if I didn't learn technique, I would be in trouble later on when the inspiration had gone and the technique was needed to compensate. If I hadn't learned that in time, I would not now be able to outline a structure in advance. Structure is a purely technical problem and if you don't learn it early on you'll never learn it.

INTERVIEWER: Discipline then is quite important to you?

GARCIA MARQUEZ: I don't think you can write a book that's worth anything without extraordinary discipline.

INTERVIEWER: What about artificial stimulants?

GARCIA MARQUEZ: One thing that Hemingway wrote that greatly impressed me was that writing for him was like boxing. He took care of his health and his well-being. Faulkner had a reputation of being a drunkard, but in every interview that he gave he said that it was impossible to write one line when drunk. Hemingway said this too. Bad readers have asked me if I was drugged when I wrote some of my works. But that illustrates that they don't know anything about literature or drugs. To be a good writer you have to be absolutely lucid at every moment of writing, and in good health. I'm very much against the romantic concept of writing which maintains that the act of writing is a sacrifice, and that the worse the economic conditions or the emotional state, the better the writing. I think you have to be in a very good emotional and physical state. Literary creation for me requires good health, and the Lost Generation understood this. They were people who loved life.

INTERVIEWER: Blaise Cendrars said that writing is a privilege compared to most work, and that writers exaggerate their suffering. What do you think?

GARCIA MARQUEZ: I think that writing is very difficult, but so is any job carefully executed. What is a privilege, however, is to do a job to your own satisfaction. I think that I'm excessively demanding of myself and others because I cannot tolerate errors; I think that it is a privilege to do anything to a perfect degree. It is true though that writers are often megalomaniacs and they consider themselves to be the center of the universe and society's conscience. But what I most admire is something well done. I'm always very happy when I'm traveling to know that the pilots are better pilots than I am a writer.

INTERVIEWER: When do you work best now? Do you have a work schedule?

GARCIA MARQUEZ: When I became a professional writer the biggest problem I had was my schedule. Being a journalist meant working at night. When I started writing full-time I was forty years old, my schedule was basically from nine o'clock in the morning until two in the afternoon when my sons came back from school. Since I was so used to hard work, I felt guilty that I was only working in the morning; so I tried to work in the afternoons, but I discovered that what I did in the afternoon had to be done over again the next morning. So I decided that I would just work from nine until two-thirty and not do anything else. In the afternoons I have appointments and interviews and anything else that might come up. I have another problem in that I can only work in surroundings that are familiar and have already been warmed up with my work. I cannot write in hotels or borrowed rooms or on borrowed typewriters. This creates problems because when I travel I can't work. Of course, you're always trying to find a pretext to work less. That's why the conditions you impose on yourself are more difficult all the time. You hope for inspiration whatever the circumstances. That's a word the romantics exploited a lot. My Marxist comrades have a lot of difficulty accepting the word, but whatever you call it, I'm convinced that there is a special state of mind in which you can write with great ease and things just flow. All the pretexts—such as the one where you can only write at home—disappear. That moment and that state of mind seem to come when you have found the right theme and the right ways of treating it. And it has to be something you really like, too, because there is no worse job than doing something you don't like.

One of the most difficult things is the first paragraph. I have spent many months on a first paragraph, and once I get it, the rest just comes out very easily. In the first paragraph you solve most of the problems with your book. The theme is defined, the style, the tone. At least in my case, the first paragraph is a kind of sample of what the rest of the book is going to be. That's why writing a book of short stories is much more difficult than writing a novel. Every time you write a short story, you have to begin all over again.

INTERVIEWER: Are dreams ever important as a source of inspiration?

GARCIA MARQUEZ: In the very beginning I paid a good deal of attention to them. But then I realized that life itself is the greatest source of inspiration and that dreams are only a very small part of that torrent that is life. What is very true about my writing is that I'm quite interested in different concepts of dreams and interpretations of them. I see dreams as part of life in general, but reality is much richer. But maybe I just have very poor dreams.

INTERVIEWER: Can you distinguish between inspiration and intuition?

GARCIA MARQUEZ: Inspiration is when you find the right

theme, one which you really like; that makes the work much easier. Intuition, which is also fundamental to writing fiction, is a special quality which helps you to decipher what is real without needing scientific knowledge, or any other special kind of learning. The laws of gravity can be figured out much more easily with intuition than anything else. It's a way of having experience without having to struggle through it. For a novelist, intuition is essential. Basically it's contrary to intellectualism, which is probably the thing that I detest most in the world —in the sense that the real world is turned into a kind of immovable theory. Intuition has the advantage that either it is, or it isn't. You don't struggle to try to put a round peg into a square hole.

INTERVIEWER: Is it the theorists that you dislike?

GARCIA MARQUEZ: Exactly. Chiefly because I cannot really understand them. That's mainly why I have to explain most things through anecdotes, because I don't have any capacity for abstractions. That's why many critics say that I'm not a cultured person. I don't quote enough.

INTERVIEWER: Do you think that critics type you or categorize you too neatly?

GARCIA MARQUEZ: Critics for me are the biggest example of what intellectualism is. First of all, they have a theory of what a writer should be. They try to get the writer to fit their model, and if he doesn't fit, they still try to get him in by force. I'm only answering this because you've asked. I really have no interest in what critics think of me; nor have I read critics in many years. They have claimed for themselves the task of being intermediaries between the author and the reader. I've always tried to be a very clear and precise writer, trying to reach the reader directly without having to go through the critic.

INTERVIEWER: How do you regard translators?

GARCIA MARQUEZ: I have great admiration for translators except for the ones who use footnotes. They are always trying to explain to the reader something which the author probably did not mean; since it's there, the reader has to put up with it. Translating is a very difficult job, not at all rewarding, and very badly paid. A good translation is always a re-creation in another language. That's why I have such great admiration for Gregory Rabassa. My books have been translated into twenty-one languages and Rabassa is the only translator who has never asked for something to be clarified so he can put a footnote in. I think that my work has been completely re-created in English. There are parts of the book which are very difficult to follow literally. The impression one gets is that the translator read the book and then rewrote it from his recollections. That's why I have such admiration for translators. They are intuitive rather than intellectual. Not only is what publishers pay them completely miserable, but they don't see their work as literary creation. There are some books I would have liked to translate into Spanish, but they would have involved as much work as writing my own books and I wouldn't have made enough money to eat.

INTERVIEWER: What would you have liked to translate?

GARCIA MARQUEZ: All Malraux. I would have liked to translate Conrad, and Saint Exupéry. When I'm reading I sometimes get the feeling that I would like to translate this book. Excluding the great masterpieces, I prefer reading a mediocre translation of a book than trying to get through it in the original language. I never feel comfortable reading in another language, because the only language I really feel inside is Spanish. However, I speak Italian and French, and I know English well enough to have poisoned myself with *Time* magazine every week for twenty years.

INTERVIEWER: Does Mexico seem like home to you now? Do you feel part of any larger community of writers?

GARCIA MARQUEZ: In general, I'm not a friend of writers or artists just because they are writers or artists. I have many friends of different professions, amongst them writers and artists. In general terms, I feel that I'm a native of any country in Latin America but not elsewhere. Latin Americans feel that Spain is the only country in which we are treated well, but I personally don't feel as though I'm from there. In Latin America I don't have a sense of frontiers or borders. I'm conscious of the differences that exist from one country to another, but in my mind and heart it is all the same. Where I really feel at home is the Caribbean, whether it is the French, Dutch, or English Caribbean. I was always impressed that when I got on a plane in Barranquilla, a black lady with a blue dress would stamp my passport, and when I got off the plane in Jamaica, a black lady with a blue dress would stamp my passport, but in English. I don't believe that the language makes all that much difference. But anywhere else in the world, I feel like a foreigner, a feeling that robs me of a sense of security. It's a personal feeling, but I always have it when I travel. I have a minority conscience.

INTERVIEWER: Do you think that it's an important thing for Latin American writers to live in Europe for awhile?

GARCIA MARQUEZ: Perhaps to have a real perspective from outside. The book of short stories I'm thinking of writing is about Latin Americans going to Europe. I've been thinking about it for twenty years. If you could draw a final conclusion out of these short stories, it would be that Latin Americans hardly ever get to Europe, especially Mexicans, and certainly not to stay. All the Mexicans I've ever met in Europe always leave the following Wednesday.

INTERVIEWER: What effects do you think the Cuban Revolution has had on Latin American literature?

GARCIA MARQUEZ: Up until now it has been negative. Many writers who think of themselves as being politically committed feel obligated to write stories not about what they want, but about what they think they should want. That makes for a certain type of calculated literature that doesn't have anything to do with experience or intuition. The main reason for this is that the cultural influence of Cuba on Latin America has been very much fought against. In Cuba itself, the process hasn't developed to the point where a new type of literature or art has been created. That is something that needs time. The great cultural importance of Cuba in Latin America has been to serve as a kind of bridge to transmit a type of literature which had existed in Latin America for many years. In a sense, the boom in Latin American literature in the United States has been caused by the Cuban Revolution. Every Latin American writer of that generation had been writing for twenty years, but the European and American publishers had very little interest in them. When the Cuban Revolution started there was suddenly a great interest about Cuba and Latin America. The revolution turned into an article of consumption. Latin America came into fashion. It was discovered that Latin American novels existed which were good enough to be translated and considered with all other world literature. What was really sad is that cultural colonialism is so bad in Latin America that it was impossible to convince the Latin Americans themselves that their own novels were good until people outside *told* them they were.

INTERVIEWER: Are there some lesser-known Latin American writers you especially admire?

GARCIA MARQUEZ: I doubt there are any now. One of the best side effects of the boom in Latin American writing is that publishers are always on the lookout to make sure that they're not going to miss the new Cortázar. Unfortunately many young writers are more concerned with fame than with their own work. There's a French professor at the University of Toulouse who writes about Latin American literature; many young authors wrote to him telling him not to write so much about me because I didn't need it anymore and other people did. But what they forget is that when I was their age the critics weren't writing about me, but rather about Miguel Angel Asturias. The point I'm trying to make is that these young writers are wasting their time writing to critics rather than working on their own writing. It's much more important to write than to be written about. One thing that I think was very important about my literary career was that until I was forty years old, I never got one cent of author's royalties, though I'd had five books published.

INTERVIEWER: Do you think that fame or success coming too early in a writer's career is bad?

GARCIA MARQUEZ: At any age it's bad. I would have liked for my books to have been recognized posthumously, at least in capitalist countries, where you turn into a kind of merchandise.

INTERVIEWER: Aside from your favorites, what do you read today?

GARCIA MARQUEZ: I read the weirdest things. I was reading Muhammad Ali's memoirs the other day. Bram Stoker's *Dracula* is a great book, and one I probably would not have read many years ago because I would have thought it was a waste of time. But I never really get involved with a book unless it's recommended by somebody I trust. I don't read any more fiction. I read many memoirs and documents, even if they are forged documents. And I reread my favorites. The advantage of rereading is that you can open at any page and read the part that you really like. I've lost this sacred notion of reading only "literature." I will read anything. I try to keep up to date. I read almost all the really important magazines from all over the world every week. I've always been on the lookout for news since the habit of reading the teletype machines. But after I've read all the serious and important newspapers from all over, my wife always comes around and tells me of news I hadn't heard. When I ask her where she read it, she will say that she read it in a magazine at the beauty parlor. So I read fashion magazines and all kinds of magazines for women and gossip magazines. And I learn many things that I could only learn from reading them. That keeps me very busy.

INTERVIEWER: Why do you think fame is so destructive for a writer?

GARCIA MARQUEZ: Primarily because it invades your private life. It takes away from the time that you spend with friends, and the time that you can work. It tends to isolate you from the real world. A famous writer who wants to continue writing has to be constantly defending himself against fame. I don't really like to say this because it never sounds sincere, but I would really have liked for my books to have been published after my death, so I wouldn't have to go through all this business of fame and being a great writer. In my case, the only advantage in fame is that I have been able to give it a political use. Otherwise, it is quite uncomfortable. The problem is that you're famous for twenty-four hours a day and you can't say, "Okay, I won't be famous until tomorrow," or press a button and say, "I won't be famous here or now."

INTERVIEWER: Did you anticipate the extraordinary success of *One Hundred Years of Solitude*?

GARCIA MARQUEZ: I knew that it would be a book that would please my friends more than my others had. But when my Spanish publisher told me he was going to print eight thousand copies I was stunned, because my other books had never sold more than seven hundred. I asked him why not start slowly, but he said he was convinced that it was a good book and that all eight thousand copies would be sold between May and December. Actually they were all sold within one week in Buenos Aires.

INTERVIEWER: Why do you think *One Hundred Years of Solitude* clicked so?

GARCIA MARQUEZ: I don't have the faintest idea, because I'm a very bad critic of my own works. One of the most frequent explanations that I've heard is that it is a book about the private lives of the people of Latin America, a book that was written from the inside. That explanation surprises me because in my first attempt to write it the title of the book was going to be *The House*. I wanted the whole development of the novel to take place inside the house, and anything external would be just in terms of its impact on the house. I later abandoned the title *The House*, but once the book goes into the town of Macondo it never goes any further. Another explanation I've heard is that every reader can make of the characters in the book what he wants and make them his own. I don't want it to become a film, since the film viewer sees a face that he may not have imagined.

INTERVIEWER: Was there any interest in making it into a film?

GARCIA MARQUEZ: Yes, my agent put it up for one million dollars to discourage offers and as they approximated that offer she raised it to around three million. But I have no interest in a film, and as long as I can prevent it from happening, it won't. I prefer that it remain a private relationship between the reader and the book.

INTERVIEWER: Do you think any books can be translated into films successfully?

GARCIA MARQUEZ: I can't think of any one film that improved on a good novel, but I can think of many good films that came from very bad novels.

INTERVIEWER: Have you ever thought of making films yourself?

GARCIA MARQUEZ: There was a time when I wanted to be a film director. I studied directing in Rome. I felt that cinema was a medium which had no limitations and in which everything was possible. I came to Mexico because I wanted to work in film, not as a director but as a screenplay writer. But there's a big limitation in cinema in that it's an industrial art, a whole industry. It's very difficult to express in cinema what you really want to say. I still think of it, but it now seems like a luxury which I would like to do with friends but without any hope of really expressing myself. So I've moved farther and farther away from the cinema. My relation with it is like that of a couple who can't live separated, but who can't live together either. Between having a film company or a journal, though, I'd choose a journal.

INTERVIEWER: How would you describe the book on Cuba that you're working on now?

GARCIA MARQUEZ: Actually, the book is like a long newspaper article about what life in Cuban homes is like, how they have managed to survive the shortages. What has struck me during the many trips that I've made to Cuba in the last two years is that the blockade has created in Cuba a kind of "culture of necessity," a social situation in which people have to get along without certain things. The aspect that really interests me is how the blockade has contributed to changing the mentality of the people. We have a clash between an anticonsumer society and the most consumption-oriented society in the world. The book is now at a stage where after thinking that it would be just an easy, fairly short piece of journalism, it is now turning into a very long and complicated book. But that doesn't really matter, because all of my books have been like that. And besides, the book will prove with historical facts that the real world in the Caribbean is just as fantastic as in the stories of *One Hundred Years of Solitude*.

INTERVIEWER: Do you have any long-range ambitions or regrets as a writer?

GARCIA MARQUEZ: I think my answer is the same as the one I gave you about fame. I was asked the other day if I would be interested in the Nobel Prize, but I think that for me it would be an absolute catastrophe. I would certainly be interested in deserving it, but to receive it would be terrible. It would just complicate even more the problems of fame. The only thing I really regret in life is not having a daughter.

INTERVIEWER: Are there any projects now underway you can discuss?

GARCIA MARQUEZ: I'm absolutely convinced that I'm going to write the greatest book of my life, but I don't know which one it will be or when. When I feel something like this—which I have been feeling now for awhile—I stay very quiet, so that if it passes by I can capture it.

PETER H. STONE
Winter 1981

11. Carlos Fuentes

Described as "a chameleon among his Latin American contemporaries," Carlos Fuentes—essayist, dramatist, novelist, and political pamphleteer—in fact stands out among the distinguished Latin American writers of international renown. Born on November 11, 1928, in Mexico City, Mexico, he travelled extensively from a very young age as his father changed diplomatic posts. The international appeal of his work is obvious: his books have been widely translated and his plays have been produced in a range of cities, including Barcelona, Vienna, Paris, and Brussels.

Educated at the Colegio Frances Morelos (L.L.B., 1948), he followed a course of graduate study first at the National University of Mexico and then at the Institut des Hautes Etudes Internationales in Geneva, which led to his career in international affairs. A secretary of the Mexican delegation to the International Labor Organization, he eventually became cultural attaché to the Mexican Embassy in Geneva (1950–52) and press secretary to the United Nations Information Center, Mexico City (1954). He served as the Mexican ambassador to France from 1975 to 1977.

Eight novels by Fuentes have been published in the United States, including *Where the Air Is Clear* (1960), *The Good Conscience* (1961), *The Death of Artemio Cruz* (1964), *Aura* (1965), *A Change of Skin* (1968), *Terra Nostra* (1976), *The Hydra Head* (1979), and *Distant Relations* (1981). He has also published a collection of short stories, *Burnt Water* (1981).

Fuentes has held various teaching posts, at Cambridge University, Barnard College, Columbia University, the University of Pennsylvania, and Princeton University. He is currently on the faculty of Harvard University.

CAPÍTULO

a saber. Diez años después del cuento de las naranjas, peras e higos
los Four Jodiditos están tocando rockazteck en la disco flotante de
Ada Ching frente a la Califurnace Beach en Old Acapulkey y mis padres
aprovechan la circuncisión, como quien dice, para pedirle al tío Homero
que los invite a pasar navidad y año nuevo en su casa amurallada de
Peachy Tongue Beach,

—Cómo se llamaba cuando tú eras niño, pregunta mi madre y mi
padre ríe, oye si no fue hace tanto, recuerdas, insiste ella, sí, se
llamaba Pichilingue pero todo se ha modernizado insensiblemente, y el
tío Homero siempre ha sabido acomodarse al cambio sin sacrificar lo
permanente, así dice él y si no fuera tan inmensamente gordo que todo
diminutivo le es extraño y su persona acabaría por agigantarse, lo
llamaríamos el Tío Jarrito donde todo cabe sabiéndolo acomodar, pero
ahora en México todo es corrupción verbal hasta Jarrito de Harry como
en Jarrito Homovero, el Trigésimo Tercer Presidente de los USA (Errare
Trumanum Est) y el propio tío Homero, para mantener con el mundo editorial
anglo las excelentes relaciones que debe mantener en su calidad de Presidente de la Academia Mexicana de la Lengua correspondiente de la Real
Academia de Madrid, admite el kimonó, Chabela de los Angeles, de que
su dirección privada sea Mel O'Field Road aunque el prócer liberal
don Melchor Ocampo dé de tumbos en su michoacana tumba y que su oficina
esté en la Frank Wood Avenue por más que le pese a don Panchito Madero
en la suya y además, quién se acuerda ya de ellos?, están muertos, dice
mi mami tubi, verdaderamente muertos, angel, porque ya nadie los recuerda,
eso es estar muerto, nada más eso, tú no crees?

Cuando escucha estas cosas el tío don Homero Fagoaga finge un sollozo

---

A manuscript page from Carlos Fuentes's novel *Cristóbal Nonato*.

Carlos Fuentes

Carlos Fuentes was interviewed on a snowy December day at his home in Princeton, New Jersey—a large Victorian house in the old residential section. He is a tall, heavyset man, dressed on that winter's day in a turtleneck sweater and jacket. The Fuenteses' house was lightly heated in the European manner, and felt chilly. A Christmas tree stood in the drawing room. His two young children were out ice skating with Mrs. Fuentes. A considerable art collection was on display in the room—Oriental bronzes, pre-Columbian ceramics, and Spanish colonial Santos —reflecting Fuentes's cultural background and his various diplomatic assignments. On the walls were paintings and prints by Picabia, Miró, Matta, Vasarely, among others—most of them gifts given him by artist friends.

The interview was conducted in the library in front of a blazing fire with a hot pot of coffee available. The walls were

*lined with books. It is at a simple desk in this room that Carlos
Fuentes does his work—in front of a window that on this December day looked out on ice-laden shrubbery and trees barely
visible in the snow flurries.*

In 1958, he startled Mexico with Where the Air Is Clear,
a caustic analysis of Mexico after the 1910–20 revolution; The
Good Conscience *(1959), a* bildungsroman *that describes the
education of Jaime Ceballos and his ultimate absorption into
the Mexican establishment;* The Death of Artemio Cruz
(1962), inspired in part by Orson Welles's Citizen Kane; Holy
Place *(1967) and* A Change of Skin *(1968), both of which deal
with Mexico, albeit from totally different perspectives:* Holy
Place *traces the Oedipal meanderings of a young man in-
fatuated with his mother;* A Change of Skin *studies Mexico in
relation to the "outside world" of the sixties by examining the
relationships between foreigners and Mexicans.*

Terra Nostra *(1976) strikes out in a different direction. There
Fuentes investigates the Mediterranean roots of Hispanic culture in order to discover where that culture "went wrong." He
finds its fatal sin in Philip II's maniacal search for purity and
orthodoxy, his ruthless extirpation of the heterodox (Jewish and
Arabian) elements in Spanish culture.* Terra Nostra, *along with
Fuentes's recent essays on Cervantes, marks a new epoch in
pan-Hispanic studies, a new way to find unity in the fragmented
Hispanic world.*

The Hydra Head *(1979) returns to contemporary Mexico
so that Fuentes can study the nature of power, symbolized
by Mexico's oil deposits. In 1981, Fuentes published (in
Spanish)* Distant Relations, *an examination of the writer's
need to know all and tell all, and (in English)* Burnt Water,
*a collection of short stories from various periods in the author's
career.*

*During the years he spent as Mexican ambassador to France,
Fuentes found it impossible to write, and the interview began*

with his description of his return to writing after he had left his government post.

FUENTES: I left my post as ambassador to France on the first of April, 1977, and immediately rented a house on the outskirts of Paris, where I could begin to write again. I had not written a word for two years, being a conscientious diplomat. The house I rented, as it turned out, had belonged to Gustave Doré and it brought back all my yearnings for form and terror. Doré's illustrations for "Little Red Riding Hood," for example: they're so incredibly erotic! The little girl in bed with the wolf! Those were the signs under which my latest novel, *Distant Relations,* was born.

INTERVIEWER: Why did you find it impossible to write while you were ambassador?

FUENTES: Diplomacy in a sense is the opposite of writing. You have to disperse yourself so much: the lady who comes in crying because she's had a fight with the secretary; exports and imports; students in trouble; thumbtacks for the embassy. Writing requires the concentration of the writer, demands that nothing else be done except that. So I have all this pent-up energy which is flowing out right now. I'm writing a great deal these days. Besides, I have learned how to write. I didn't know how to write before, and I guess I learned by being a bureaucrat. You have so much mental time on your hands when you are a bureaucrat: you have time to think and to learn how to write in your head. When I was a young man I suffered a great deal because I faced the challenge of Mallarmé's blank page every day without knowing exactly what I was going to say. I fought the page, and paid for it with ulcers. I made up for it with sheer vigor, because you have vigor when you are writing in your twenties and thirties. Then later on you have to use your energy wisely. When I look back on it, I think perhaps it was the fact that I was behind an official desk for two years that left my mind free to write within itself, to prepare what

I was going to write once I left that post. So now I can write before I sit down to write, I can use the blank page in a way I couldn't before.

INTERVIEWER: Tell us how the process of writing takes place within you.

FUENTES: I am a morning writer; I am writing at eight-thirty in longhand and I keep at it until twelve-thirty, when I go for a swim. Then I come back, have lunch, and read in the afternoon until I take my walk for the next day's writing. I must write the book out in my head now, before I sit down. I always follow a triangular pattern on my walks here in Princeton: I go to Einstein's house on Mercer Street, then down to Thomas Mann's house on Stockton Street, then over to Herman Broch's house on Evelyn Place. After visiting those three places, I return home, and by that time I have mentally written tomorrow's six or seven pages.

INTERVIEWER: You write in longhand?

FUENTES: First I write it out in longhand, and then when I feel I "have" it, I let it rest. Then I correct the manuscript and type it out myself, correcting it until the last moment.

INTERVIEWER: Is the rewriting extensive or is most of the rewriting taken into account during the mental writing?

FUENTES: By the time I get it on paper, it is practically finished: there are no missed sections or scenes. I know basically how things are going and I have it more or less fixed, but at the same time I am sacrificing the element of surprise in myself. Everyone who writes a novel knows he is involved in the Proustian problem of in some way knowing what he is going to write and at the same time being amazed at what is actually coming out. Proust only wrote when he had lived what he was going to write, and yet he had to write as though he knew nothing about it—which is extraordinary. In a way we are all involved in the same adventure: to know what you are going to say, to have control over your material, and at the same time to have that margin of freedom which is discovery, amazement, and a precondition of the freedom of the reader.

INTERVIEWER: It's possible in England and the United States to write a history of editors and their influence on literature. Would such a history be possible in the Hispanic world?

FUENTES: Impossible, because the dignity of Spanish hidalgos would never allow a menial laborer to come and tell us what to do with our own work. It comes from the fact that we are caught in a terrible kind of schizophrenia made up of extreme pride, and extreme individualism which we inherited from Spain. The hidalgo expects everyone else to respect him, just as he kowtows to superior power. If you were to try to edit anyone's text in Latin America, even a hack, he would resign immediately, accusing you of censoring or insulting him.

INTERVIEWER: You would say then that your relationship to your society is rather different from that of an American writer? That, for example, the hidalgo image suggests the greater dignity of writing in your culture?

FUENTES: My situation as a Mexican writer is like that of writers from Eastern Europe. We have the privilege of speech in societies where it is rare to have that privilege. We speak for others, which is very important in Latin America, as it is in Central Europe. Of course you have to pay for that power: either you serve the community or you fall flat on your face.

INTERVIEWER: Does that mean that you see yourself as the official representative of your culture?

FUENTES: No, I hope not. Because I always remember that remark by the French Surrealist Jacques Vaché, "Nothing kills a man as much as having to represent his country." So I hope it isn't true.

INTERVIEWER: Do you see a difference between the social roles of American and Latin American writers?

FUENTES: We have to do more things in our culture than American writers do in theirs. They can have more time for themselves and for their writing, whereas we have social demands. Pablo Neruda used to say that every Latin American writer goes around dragging a heavy body, the body of his people, of his past, of his national history. We have to assimilate the enormous weight of our past so we will not forget what gives us life. If you forget your past, you die. You fulfill certain functions for the collectivity because they are obligations you have as a citizen, not as a writer. Despite that, you reserve your esthetic freedom and your esthetic privileges. This creates a tension, but I think it is better to have the tension than to have no tension at all, as sometimes happens in the United States.

INTERVIEWER: In your earlier works you focus on the life of Mexico after the 1910–1920 Revolution. That is your Mexico, and I can see you in those works as a Mexican writer. But after you became so popular internationally, say, with *The Death of Artemio Cruz*, I wonder if your concept of your role changed?

FUENTES: No. I think all writers live off of obsessions. Some of these come from history, others are purely individual, and still others belong to the realm of the purely obsessive, which is the most universal thing a writer has in his soul. My obsessions are in all my books: they have to do with fear. All of my books are about fear—the universal sensation of fear about who might be coming through the door, about who desires me, whom do I desire and how can I achieve my desire. Is the object of my desire the subject of my desire in the mirror I am watching? These obsessions are in all my works, along with the more general, historical context I deal with, but both in history and individuality, my theme is being incomplete because we fear the world and ourselves.

INTERVIEWER: You spoke of writing in your head while you were ambassador and continuing to do so now that you are writing again. I wonder if at some point—especially since you are away from your country and speaking a different language —writing first in your head and editing mentally has changed the nature of your writing.

FUENTES: You must understand that I am a peculiar case in Mexican literature because I grew up far from Mexico, because Mexico is an imaginary space for me, and has never ceased to be so, I might add. My Mexico and my Mexican history take place in my mind. Its history is something I have dreamed, imagined, and is not the actual history of the country. When as a young man I finally went to live in Mexico, of course I had to compare my dreams, my fears of that country with reality. This created a profound tension, the result of which was *Where the Air Is Clear,* a book nobody else could have written in Mexico. Nobody had written a novel about the postrevolutionary era as it was reflected in the city, in the social structure, in the survival of so many ancient strands of our imaginary and historical life. This came, I say, out of my discovering Mexico with a sense of fear and enchantment when I was fifteen years old. Being outside of Mexico has always helped me enormously.

INTERVIEWER: Are you saying that seeing Mexico from both a physical and a mental distance enables you to see it more clearly than you could if you were there?

FUENTES: Yes, I have a perspective on Mexico which is renewed, you see, by surprise. Quevedo, the great Spanish baroque poet, expresses this when he says, "Nothing astonishes me because the world has bewitched me." I am still bewitched by Mexico. As you say, I live using a different language, but this helps me enormously with the Spanish language. I grew up with American English and yet I was able to maintain my Spanish. Spanish became something I had to maintain and re-create. When I am outside of Mexico, the same sensation of being alone with the language and wrestling with it becomes extremely powerful, whereas when I am in Mexico, it is immediately debased into asking for coffee, answering the phone, and whatnot. For me Spanish becomes an extraordinary experience when I am outside of Mexico. I feel I have to maintain it for myself. It becomes a very demanding fact of my life.

INTERVIEWER: Have you ever been tempted to write in English?

FUENTES: No, I very soon came to realize that the English language did not need one more writer. That the English language has an unbroken tradition of excellence and when it goes to sleep there is always an Irishman who appears and wakes it up.

INTERVIEWER: Knowing so many languages, which language do you dream in?

FUENTES: I dream in Spanish; I also make love in Spanish—this has created tremendous confusion at times, but I can only do it in Spanish. Insults in other languages don't mean a damn thing to me, but an insult in Spanish really sets me hopping. Let me tell you about a curious experience I had this summer. I was writing a novella about the adventures of Ambrose Bierce in Mexico. Bierce went to Mexico during the Revolution, in 1914, to join up with Pancho Villa's army. I had the problem that the voice had to be Bierce's, and it was extremely difficult to render in Spanish. I had to make Bierce speak with his voice, which is available to me in his stories, so I wrote the novella in English. It was an absolutely terrifying experience. I would be writing along in English when suddenly from under the table Mr. Faulkner would appear and say aah, aah, can't do that, and from behind the door Mr. Melville would appear and say, can't do it, can't do it. All these ghosts appeared; the narrative tradition in English asserted itself so forcefully that it hamstrung me. I felt very sorry for my North American colleagues who have to write with all these people hanging from the chandeliers and rattling the dishes. You see, in Spanish we have to fill in the great void that exists between the seventeenth and the twentieth centuries. Writing is more of an adventure, more of a challenge. There is only a great desert between Cervantes and ourselves, if you except two nineteenth-century novelists, Clarin and Galdos.

INTERVIEWER: Is this one of the reasons for the epic surge in Latin American novels, this effort to encompass more social and historical perspectives in each work?

FUENTES: Well, I remember ten years ago I was talking to an American writer, Donald Barthelme, and he said, "How do you do it in Latin America? How do you manage to write these immense novels? Come up with all these subjects, these very, very long novels? Is there no paper shortage in Latin America? How do you do these things? We find we have great difficulty in the United States as American writers to find subjects. We write slim books, slimmer and slimmer books." But what I answered on that occasion is that our problem is that we feel we have everything to write about. That we have to fill four centuries of silence. That we have to give voice to all that has been silenced by history.

INTERVIEWER: You do feel that Latin American writers are trying to create a cultural identity for themselves?

FUENTES: Yes, and here I think we have a very strong link with the writers of Central and Eastern Europe. If you had asked me today where the novel is alive and kicking, I would say it's basically in Latin America and in so-called Eastern Europe, which the Czechoslovaks insist on calling Central Europe. They think of Eastern Europe as Russia. In any case, there you have two cultural zones where people feel that things have to be said, and if the writer does not say them, nobody will say them. This creates a tremendous responsibility; it puts a tremendous weight on the writer, and also creates a certain confusion, because one could say, Oh, the mission is important, the theme is important, therefore the book has to be good, and that is not always the case. How many novels have you read in Latin America that are full of good intentions—denouncing the plight of the Bolivian miner, of the Ecuadorian banana picker—and turn out to be terrible novels which do nothing for the Bolivian tin miner or the Ecuadorian banana picker, or anything for literature either . . . failing on all fronts because they have nothing but good intentions.

But still, we had a whole past to talk about. A past that was silent, that was dead, and that you had to bring alive through language. And so for me writing was basically this need to establish an identity, to establish a link to my country and to a language which I—along with many other writers of my generation—felt we in some way had to slap around, and wake up, as if we were playing the game of Sleeping Beauty.

INTERVIEWER: Can it be said, though, that you are speaking for several generations of Spanish and Latin American writers who have a double culture, who have one foot in their local culture and the other in an external, Western culture?

FUENTES: One of the basic cultural factors of Latin America is that it is an eccentric branch of the culture of the West. It is Western and it is not Western. So we feel that we have to know the culture of the West even better than a Frenchman or an Englishman, and at the same time we have to know our own culture. This sometimes means going back to the Indian cultures, whereas the Europeans feel they don't have to know our cultures at all. We have to know Quetzalcoatl *and* Descartes. They think Descartes is enough. So Latin America is a constant reminder to Europe of the duties of its universality. Therefore, a writer like Borges is a typically Latin American writer. The fact that he is so European only indicates that he is Argentinian. No European would feel obliged to go to the extremes Borges does to create a reality, not to mirror a reality but to create a new reality to fill in the cultural voids of his own tradition.

INTERVIEWER: Which writers are missing from the evolution of fiction in Spanish? You mentioned Faulkner and Melville, and I could easily imagine Balzac and Dickens.

FUENTES: They are all present because we have appropriated them. Your question is important because it emphasizes the fact that Latin American writers have to appropriate the writers of other traditions in order to fill a void. Sometimes, to our astonishment, we discover an extraordinary sense of coincidence. A lot of fuss has been made about the great influence of Joyce and Faulkner on the Latin American novel. Well, two things have to be said: first, the poets of the Spanish language in the earlier part of this century coincide with the great poets of the English language. Neruda is writing at the same time as

Eliot, but Neruda is writing in a rain-drenched town in southern Chile where there are no libraries. Nevertheless, he is on the same wavelength as Eliot. It is the poets who have maintained the language for us novelists: without the poets, without Neruda, Vallejo, Paz, Huidobro, or Gabriela Mistral, there would be no Latin American novel. Second, the great modern novelists of Europe and the United States have revolutionized the sense of time in the Western novel as it had been conceived since the eighteenth century, since Defoe, Richardson, and Smollett. This breaking up of time, this refusal to accept the singular concept of linear time which the West had been imposing economically and politically, coincides profoundly with our sense of circular time, which comes from the Indian religions. Our idea of time as a spiral, our basic historical vision, is derived both from Vico and from our everyday experience of times that coexist. You have the Iron Age in the mountains and the twentieth century in our cities. This recognition that time is not linear is particularly strong in Faulkner because he is a baroque writer and because he shares the baroque with Latin America. He is probably the only Western novelist in the twentieth century who has the same sense of defeat and loss that we have.

INTERVIEWER: But Faulkner is also re-creating a post-agrarian culture.

FUENTES: The passage from an agrarian culture to a post-agrarian culture is our own situation, but more than anything, Faulkner is a writer of defeat. He is the one American writer who says "We are not only a success story; we are also the history of defeats," and this he shares with us. Latin America is made up of historically and politically failed societies, and this failure has created a subterranean language—since the Conquest. The baroque in Latin America was the response of the New World to the Old World: it took a form of European culture, the baroque, and transformed it into a hiding place for Indian culture, for black culture, for the great syncretism which is the culture of Spanish and Portuguese America. We insert ourselves into that tradition when we write today.

INTERVIEWER: This burden of the past we mentioned earlier is extremely important, isn't it? It creates a heavy load that every Latin American writer has to bear. It also deforms language because every word resounds into the past as well as into the future.

FUENTES: I think it was Allen Tate who disparagingly referred to Faulkner as a Dixie Gongorist, which I think is really the highest praise because it links Faulkner to this culture of the incomplete, of the voracious, of the intertextual which is the baroque. There is a culture of the Caribbean, I would say, that includes Faulkner, Carpentier, García Márquez, Derek Walcott, and Aimé Césaire, a trilingual culture in and around the whirlpool of the baroque which is the Caribbean, the Gulf of Mexico. Think of Jean Rhys's *Wide Sargasso Sea*.

INTERVIEWER: Did you get this sense of cultural perspective as you were growing up or as you were writing?

FUENTES: As I was growing up. Let me explain: a few years ago, a friend of mine, Tito Gerassi, got permission from Jean-Paul Sartre to write his biography. He said, "I have a great idea; I'm going to ask Sartre to write down the books he read as a child, and from there I'll see what his intellectual formation was." Later Gerassi came back to me and said, "What are these books, I've never heard of them?" The books Sartre had read as a child were the books we read in the Latin world, which I read as a child: Emilio Salgari, without whom there would be no Italian, French, Spanish, or Latin American literature. Also Michel Zévaco. These authors are part of our tradition but are not part of the Anglo-Saxon tradition. I was lucky because I had both: I read Salgari and Zévaco as well as Mark Twain and Robert Louis Stevenson. Ed Doctorow told me that he became a writer because he read Sabatini, the author of *Captain Blood*. You're invited into such a marvelous world in those books! You are sailing towards that island on a wonderful Spanish galleon!

I never want to get off; I want to spend the rest of my life looking for Treasure Island.

INTERVIEWER: But I was wondering if as you grew up you had a sense of somehow representing your culture to other cultures.

FUENTES: I did. Let me tell you another anecdote. I was a Mexican child growing up in Washington in the thirties. I went to public school, I was popular, as you must be to be happy in an American school, until the Mexican government expropriated foreign-owned oil holdings on March 18, 1938. I became a leper in my school, nobody would talk to me, everyone turned their backs on me because there were screaming headlines every day talking about Mexican Communists stealing "our" oil wells. So I became a terrible Mexican chauvinist as a reaction. I remember going to see a Richard Dix film at the Keith Theater in Washington in 1939, a film in which Dix played Sam Houston. When the Alamo came around, I jumped up in my seat shouting "Death to the gringos! ¡Viva México!" When the war started, Franklin Roosevelt organized a meeting in December of 1939 of children from all over the world to speak for peace. I was chosen to represent Mexico and I was dressed as a little Mexican *charro* with a big sombrero and I went and made my speech for peace in the name of Mexico.

INTERVIEWER: I asked you about it because you have an objective vision of what Mexico is, and at the same time you seem to feel that Mexico is within you.

FUENTES: I am grateful for my sense of detachment because I can say things about my country other people don't say. I offer Mexicans a mirror in which they can see how they look, how they talk, how they act, in a country which is a masked country. Of course, I realize that my writings are my masks as well, verbal masks I offer my country as mirrors. Mexico is defined in the legend of Quetzalcoatl, the Plumed Serpent, the god who creates man and is destroyed by a demon who offers him a mirror. The demon shows him he has a face when he thought he had no face. This is the essence of Mexico: to discover you have a face when you thought you only had a mask.

INTERVIEWER: Is Stendhal's image of the novel as a mirror moving along a highway ironic for you?

FUENTES: It poses a problem because I don't think literature can content itself with being either a mask or a mirror of reality. I think literature creates reality or it is not literature at all. You have to write "La marquise sortit à cinq heures," to copy the banal details of life, but this is not enough. The mirror is also a way to augment reality; it augments reality or it does nothing.

INTERVIEWER: We seem to have interpolated Alice's mirror here. There is the mirror in which we see ourselves, the mirror we present to others, and the mirror we pass through. But as you grow up this third mirror is frightening.

FUENTES: It is a neurotic mirror. It's related to desire and to holes. The baroque poet Quevedo is very close to me in my conception of literature as a mirror. For Quevedo the purity of the mirror and the impurity of the asshole are invariably linked. After all, in Spanish, mirror is *espejo*, a *speculum* which contains the word *culo*—asshole. It's the center of the world for Quevedo, the pleasure hole through which you receive and expel desire. So Quevedo can sing of the purity of the reflection in the mirror. I always have him with me in a painting by Cuevas in which he is holding up a mirror saying, "Look at yourself in this mirror." It's as though the mirror were the mind and the mouth and the eyes which will finally expel reality through the *culo*, the *speculum*. I've always thought this way when thinking about the mirror: the mirror and the latrine are inseparable.

INTERVIEWER: How does the germ of the text take root in your imagination? Where does the subject matter of your work begin?

FUENTES: I think my books are derived from city images, and

the city of my dreams or nightmares is Mexico City. Paris or New York just do not stimulate my writing. Many of my stories are based on things I have seen there. The story "The Doll Queen" in *Burnt Water*, for example, is something I saw every afternoon when I was in my teens. There was an apartment house: on the first floor you could see through the windows, and everything was normal. Then at night it was transformed into an extraordinary place full of dolls and flowers, dead flowers and a doll or a girl lying on a bier. I am a city writer and I cannot understand literature outside the city. For me it is Mexico City and its masks and mirrors, the twitchy little images I see when I look at the base of this totem-city, in the mud of the city— the city a space where people move, meet, and change.

INTERVIEWER: I don't mean to ask you a reductive question, but what hooks you, what makes you start writing?

FUENTES: That wonderful thing Hamlet says about "a fiction, a dream of passion." My fiction is a dream of passion, born of a cry that says "I am incomplete. I want to be complete, to be enclosed. I want to add something." So *Artemio Cruz*, for example, is a novel of voices. I think literature is born from a voice: you discover a voice and you want to give it a body of paper, but it is the voice that will be the reality of the novel.

INTERVIEWER: You heard Artemio Cruz's voice?

FUENTES: Yes, it was his voice that said, "I am dying in this present. I am a body and I am losing my existence. It is draining out of me." He had a past and was going to die and his memory was going to die. And another voice, the collective voice said, "We will outlive this individual and we will project a world of words with language and memory which will go on." But it was simply a question of many voices meeting in a literary space and demanding their incarnation.

INTERVIEWER: *Aura*, published in the same year, seems so different from *Artemio Cruz*, so experimental.

FUENTES: *Aura* is written in the second person singular, the voice poets have always used and that novelists also have a right to use. It's a voice that admits it doesn't know everything, and after all you are a novelist because you don't know everything. Unlike the epic poet who does know everything. Homer knows exactly how doors close and, as Auerbach says, closing a door in Homer takes four verses and the death of Hector takes four verses because they are equally important. But this poetic voice says that we are not alone, that something else accompanies us. In writing *Aura*, I was consciously using a particular tradition and without tradition there can be no creation. *Aura* came to me from a great Japanese film, *Ugetsu*. In it, a man goes to war just after he marries a young courtesan, who becomes the purest of wives. When he comes back, he finds she has committed suicide. The town had been taken by some soldiers and in order to avoid rape she killed herself. He goes to her grave and finds her beautiful body perfectly preserved. The only way he can recover her is through an old crone who captures the girl's voice and speaks to him. This is an extraordinary tradition: the old woman with magic powers. Here I insert myself into a tradition that goes back to Faulkner, to Henry James, to Miss Havisham in Dickens, to the countess in Pushkin's *Queen of Spades*, and back to the White Goddess. I'm very much in agreement with Virginia Woolf when she says that when you sit down to write, you must feel the whole of your tradition in your bones, all the way back to Homer.

INTERVIEWER: You also gave voice in *Aura* to a subject not often discussed, Napoleon III's intervention in Mexico, Maximilian and Carlota.

FUENTES: I am obsessed with Carlota: she is one of my ghosts. But my country is a land where the life of death is very important, as is the death of life. It is curious that I wrote *Artemio Cruz* and *Aura* at the same time. They complement each other in that *Artemio Cruz* is about the death of life and *Aura* is about the life of death.

INTERVIEWER: The witch in *Aura* is a specific type of woman. What other female images appear in your work?

FUENTES: I've been attacked for depicting very impure women, but this is because of the negative vision my culture has had of women. A culture that combines Arabs, Spaniards, and Aztecs is not very healthy for feminism. Among the Aztecs, for example, the male gods all represent a single thing: wind, water, war, while the goddesses are ambivalent, representing purity and filth, day and night, love and hate. They constantly move from one extreme to another, from one passion to another, and this is their sin in the Aztec world. There is a pattern of female ambiguity in my novels.

INTERVIEWER: In this idea of an image of woman created by men, you automatically conjure up movie actresses, and this reminds me of Claudia Nervo in *Holy Place.*

FUENTES: Oh, of course. She would be the supreme example. But last summer I wrote a play about two women, two great symbols of the face in Mexico, María Félix and Dolores del Río. It is called *Orchids in the Moonlight,* from the camp tango in the old Hollywood musical *Flying Down to Rio.* The two women think they are María Félix and Dolores del Río and behave as such, and you might well assume that they are the actresses in exile in Venice until you discover that it is Venice, California, that the women are two *chicanas,* and that nothing is what it seems. But the real faces of the actresses are there, projected on the stage, those incredible faces never aging, because as Diego Rivera once said to them, "Skulls as beautiful as yours never grow old."

INTERVIEWER: In *Holy Place* you deal with the impact of the female on the male: the protagonist, Mito, seems to lose his identity in the presence of his mother. Like Carlota or the witch, she seems to be an extreme feminine type.

FUENTES: No, because I don't think Claudia Nervo is an extreme. On the contrary, it is Mexican men who make an extreme of her. She is only defending herself. She is a central figure and the men won't allow women to be central figures; they are banished to the extremes because Mexico is a country where women are condemned to be whores or nuns. A woman is either la Malinche, the Indian who helped Cortés and betrayed her race, or Sor Juana Inés de la Cruz, the nun who divests herself of her voice and her personality, under pressure from religious and political authority. Nowadays in Mexico women are saying they are neither whores nor nuns but many things. They are usurping a role that men have reserved for themselves. Things are changing.

INTERVIEWER: You have seen Mexico undergo a tremendous change, from the Mexico that nationalized the oil fields in 1938 to Mexico today. I assume the society has crumbled the way it has here, that the entire value structure has been transformed. I was wondering how that historical reality enters your very mythical vision of the culture?

FUENTES: In Mexico all these changing realities only point up the fact that there is a tradition, that myths are a tradition, that myths breathe, and that they nourish the epics, the tragedies, and even the melodramas of our contemporary life. Because the society is crumbling, we are in a terrible situation of stock-taking. Mexico, all of Latin America in fact, has been fooled by the illusion of progress. If only we could imitate the United States, France, and Great Britain we could become rich, prosperous, and stable. This has not happened. Suddenly we are in 1980 and we know that in your world too, progress has become an illusion, so now we must look back on our tradition, which is all we really have. Our political life is fragmented, our history shot through with failure, but our cultural tradition is rich, and I think the time is coming when we will have to look at our own faces, our own past—look into this mirror we have been talking about.

INTERVIEWER: Has Mexican culture fallen the way it has in New York, where money is the only index of worth? Has materialism leveled Mexican society?

FUENTES: No. Your culture has no past; it lives only in the present. Mexico is a culture with many coexisting times. We have a horrible bourgeoisie in Mexico, much worse than yours, a know-nothing bourgeoisie proud of being ignorant. But we also have the majority of the people who have the spiritual value of religion. Ah yes, now it appears that religion, which we have attacked so much in the past, is a cultural value that exists in the depths of Mexico. I mean the sense of the sacred, not Catholic values, the sense that the rabbit can be sacred, that everything can be sacred. If you go to the land of the Tarahumaras you see they don't care a hoot about material things. They care about reenacting the origins, being present at the origins all over again. They find their health in the past, not in the future.

INTERVIEWER: But as you have already shown in your spy novel *The Hydra Head*, Mexico with its vast oil reserves is going to be thrown into the center of things.

FUENTES: Yes. Oil is going to affect the society. I am writing a novel, *Cristóbal Nonato*, that takes place on October 12, 1992, the five-hundredth anniversary of the discovery of the New World. I'm wondering what Mexico City and the country will be like then, when we take stock of having been discovered by Europeans five centuries ago.

INTERVIEWER: What is your projection? Don't tell all your secrets, just give us an idea.

FUENTES: Oh, it's a gloomy projection. This is not a science fiction novel: there are no gadgets. The story is told by an unborn child and it is what he hears that creates his impression of the world into which he is going to be thrown. The life of Mexico City will almost have been destroyed because you can't have a city of thirty million people with all its physical problems—being high up in the sky, cold, surrounded by mountains that keep the smog down, with water having to be brought from far away, and sewage having to be pumped out. The city will drown in shit; that's what will happen to Mexico.

INTERVIEWER: I can't help thinking of *Terra Nostra*: that novel also takes place in the future, between June and December of 1999. Of course, in that novel your primary concern is the past and your scope is vast.

FUENTES: This is a much more comical novel. Its scope is much more concentrated. The very fact that the narrator is inside his mother's womb limits its possibilities drastically. The information he receives is limited—what he hears and what his genes tell him. I am not trying to do anything like *Terra Nostra*, which is an excursion into Mediterranean culture, into all the worlds we come from, and into the creation of power in our society.

INTERVIEWER: Now that you have given us a glimpse of *Cristóbal Nonato* I wonder if you would mind talking about a text I know of only by hearsay, a book you wrote as a boy in Chile after you left Washington in 1941. Do you remember that book?

FUENTES: I remember it very well. I have always been trapped in a way by English because of living in Washington, so when we moved to Chile I found myself recovering Spanish. That was when I was eleven. Chile at that moment was the country of the great poets—Gabriela Mistral and Pablo Neruda, in particular. It was also the most politicized country in Latin America. I ended up, of course, in a British school because the British schools in Chile and Argentina were the best. I was promptly dressed up in a blazer, a school tie, and a little grey cap. We did calisthenics at seven a.m. alongside the Andes, got caned, and celebrated Allied victories: every time Montgomery won a battle, we had to throw our caps in the air and shout hip, hip, hurrah. There were many budding writers in the school, The Grange, it was called: Luis Alberto Heyremans, a playwright now deceased, and both José Donoso and Jorge Edwards, novelists. One of my best friends, who has now become a great Kant scholar, was Roberto Torretti: he and I wrote that novel together. We had many problems because there we were, a Mexican and a Chilean writing a novel that started in Marseilles. Novels had to start in Marseilles because that was where the Count of Monte Cristo made his appearance. Where else could a ship set sail from if not Marseilles with the Château d'If out ahead. The problem, which Dumas did not have, was how to make the people talk: would it be in Mexican or Chilean? We compromised and made them speak like Andalusians. From Marseilles, the novel moved on to Haiti: we had read *Jane Eyre* and were very impressed by mad women in attics. We included a gloomy castle on top of a mountain, Sans Souci—all of this before Alejo Carpentier had written his novel about Haiti, *The Kingdom of this World.* The novel took place there in those gloomy surroundings with mad women chained to their beds and young masters making love to mulatto girls. It went on for about four hundred pages.

INTERVIEWER: Did anyone ever read this Gothic tome?

FUENTES: Not exactly. I read it out loud to David Alfaro Siqueiros, the muralist. He was my victim. He had to flee Mexico because he was involved in an assassination attempt on the life of Trotsky. He went to Chile and was painting a bombastic mural in a small town, Chillán, to which Mexico had donated a school after an earthquake had destroyed the local school. My father was chargé d'affaires, and since Siqueiros was not making much money, and depended somewhat on the embassy, we invited him over quite often. He was a charming man, so after dinner I told him to sit down and listen to my novel. He had no way out. He dozed off, of course, and had a good siesta.

INTERVIEWER: So you combined the English Gothic novel, Dumas, and Salgari?

FUENTES: Yes. It was very dramatic, not at all picturesque. We thought it very gloomy and Brontë-like. We were greatly influenced by Charlotte and Emily Brontë, as was everyone in our group in Chile. Branwell Brontë was the height of decadence for us. You had to be like the Brontës to be good artists.

INTERVIEWER: Those puritans were the height of decadence?

FUENTES: Well, we thought so—the Moors, the hints of

incest. Imagine how the Brontës are seen by thirteen-year-olds in Chile in 1942.

INTERVIEWER: Did you write a great deal before publishing?

FUENTES: Yes. When I moved back to Mexico City I was put into a Catholic school—for the first time in my life. We had left Chile and moved to Buenos Aires, but I couldn't stand the schools there—it was the beginning of the Perón period and the fascist influence on education was intolerable. So I demanded to go to Mexico. Alas, when I got there I was put in a Catholic school. The school made me into a writer because it taught me about sin, that everything you did was sinful. So many things could be sins and therefore became so pleasurable that they set me to writing. If things were forbidden, one had to write them, and things are pleasurable if they are forbidden.

INTERVIEWER: Has the idea of sin as a stimulus to writing stayed with you?

FUENTES: Yes. I suppose I started to write *Terra Nostra* in that Catholic school in Mexico City. St. John Chrysostom says that purely spiritual love between a man and a woman should be condemned because their appetites grow so much and lust accumulates. This is an essential point in *Terra Nostra,* where people can never meet in the flesh and have others do the actual fornication for them. I learned a lot in Catholic school.

INTERVIEWER: What brand of Catholicism did you have in Mexico City?

FUENTES: It was a very political Catholicism totally allied to the conservative interpretation of Mexican history. There was a teacher there who would arrive with a calla lily at the beginning of each school year. He would say, "This is a pure Catholic youth before he goes to a dance." Then he would throw the lily on the floor and trample it. After, he would pick up the rag of a lily and say, "This is a Catholic after he goes to a dance and kisses a girl." Then he would throw the flower into the waste basket. They rewrote Mexican history in favor of Maximilian, in favor of Porfirio Díaz, the dictator who precipitated the Revolution, and all images of law and order. I was thrown out of school for a month because I dared to celebrate the birthday of Benito Juárez, the Indian who became president of Mexico, an image of liberalism in our country.

INTERVIEWER: We see how you began to write: how did you decide *what* to write at the beginning of your professional career?

FUENTES: I decided I had to write the novel of the Mexico I was living. The Mexican novel was locked into certain genres: there were Indian novels, novels of the Revolution, and proletarian novels. For me those were like medieval walls constraining the possibilities of Mexican fiction. The Mexico City I was living in belied those restraints because it was like a medieval city that had suddenly lost its walls and drawbridges and sprawled outside itself in a kind of carnival. You had European nobility stranded in Mexico because of the war, an up-and-coming bourgeoisie, unbelievable bordellos lit up in neon near the fish markets where the smell of the women and the smell of the fish mingled. The writer Salvador Elizondo would go there and slit the prostitutes' armpits while he made love to them so he could make love in a gush of blood. Then mariachi music all night long. Mexico City found in the late forties and fifties its baroque essence, a breaking down of barriers, an overflow. I remember dancing the mambo in astounding cabarets and that was the origin of *Where the Air Is Clear*: Mexico City as the protagonist of postrevolutionary life in Mexico. I felt that nothing had been said about that in a novel.

INTERVIEWER: Were there any other writers or artists in your family?

FUENTES: Not particularly: my father was a diplomat, my mother a housewife. My father's brother was an interesting poet, but he died of typhoid at twenty. My great-aunt was a sort of Grandma Moses for poetry in Vera Cruz. She wrote about the tropics, the lakes, and the sea, and was quite well known.

INTERVIEWER: Were there any myths about either your uncle or your great-aunt that might have created a literary prototype for you?

FUENTES: The only myth was a great-grandmother, Clotilde Vélez de Fuentes. She had her fingers cut off by bandits when she was on the stagecoach between Vera Cruz and Mexico City. She wouldn't take off her rings so they chopped off her fingers. She's the only myth I can remember.

INTERVIEWER: How did your family react to your becoming a writer, to your earning a living by writing?

FUENTES: Well, my parents told me to study law because they said I would die of hunger if I tried to live off my writing in Mexico. I also visited the great poet and humanist Alfonso Reyes and he reminded me that Mexico is a very formalistic country and that if I had no title people wouldn't know how to deal with me. "You'll be like a teacup without a handle," he said. I wasn't unhappy about studying law once I began. First, I went to Geneva, my first trip to Europe, where I learned discipline. Back in Mexico I was able to study with great teachers who had fled Spain during the Spanish Civil War. The former dean of the University of Seville, Manuel Pedroso, told me that if I wanted to understand criminal law I should read *Crime and Punishment* and that if I wanted to understand mercantile law I should read Balzac, and forget the dreary statutes. He was right, so I immediately found a conjuncture between the social and narrative dimensions of my life. I might have become a corporate lawyer, but I wrote *Where the Air Is Clear* instead. What energy I had then: I wrote that novel in four years while finishing law school, working at the University of Mexico, getting drunk every night, and dancing the mambo. Fantastic. No more. You lose energy and you gain technique.

INTERVIEWER: Your second novel quickly followed the first.

FUENTES: My second was actually my first. I was already writing *The Good Conscience*, a more traditional book, when it was washed away in the flood of *Where the Air Is Clear*. That novel was more than a book for me: it was my life. It made a big splash: it was praised to heaven and damned to hell. One critic said it was only fit to be flushed down the toilet. Now I find to my chagrin that it is required reading for fifteen-year-old girls in the Convent of the Sacred Heart in Mexico City.

INTERVIEWER: So we have the creation of a world which takes on its own shape, a kind of Faulknerian or Balzacian world. Is it still alive?

FUENTES: I've never left it. In the preface I wrote for *Burnt Water*, I mention an imaginary apartment house in Mexico City: Artemio Cruz lives in splendor in the penthouse and Aura the witch lives in the basement. Somewhere in between I have all my other characters. I think I have always been caught in the tension of illusory realism because the realism of these novels is illusory. I hope I am a decent reader of Cervantes, and he, after all, inaugurated realism by casting doubt on reality. This illusory realism is one pole of my writing and the other pole is the fantastic dimension, which is extremely real because it takes place in the mind. People think of Balzac merely as a realistic social writer, they forget his fantastic novels. So the lesson of Balzac is deeper for me than appearances would suggest.

INTERVIEWER: You are very much aware of the continuity of your writing.

FUENTES: In a sense my novels are one book with many chapters: *Where the Air Is Clear* is the biography of Mexico City; *The Death of Artemio Cruz* deals with an individual in that city; *A Change of Skin* is that city, that society, facing the world, coming to grips with the fact that it is part of civilization and that there is a world outside that intrudes into Mexico. There is a collective psyche in these books which is negated and individualized. But no character speaks alone because there is the sense, I hope, that there is a ghost on every page, with every character. All of this culminates in *Distant Rela-*

tions, a ghost story about the ghost of literature, about this world as a creation of fiction, a dangerous fiction you are afraid to hand over to the reader. *Distant Relations* is the novel I care most for. It says the most about me as a writer and my interests in literature. It is about writing, the only novel I have ever written about writing. It is a story told by one character to another who in turn tells it to me, Fuentes. I will not be satisfied until the story is completely told. I must know the whole story, but once I have it I must pass it on to you readers like a gift from the devil. As the title suggests, it is a story about distant relations, about a family in the New World and the Old World whose whole story cannot be told because no text could contain the whole story. It also deals with the influence of France on the Caribbean nations, the ghosts of French writers who came from Latin America, like Lautréamont or Heredia. The novel deals with the origins of fiction, how no story can ever be fully told, how no text can ever be fully exhausted.

INTERVIEWER: Both *Terra Nostra* and *Distant Relations* deal with origins: the first maps out the Mediterranean and Spanish sources of Spanish American culture and the second describes the origin of the literary text, your vain attempt to absorb and express a total history. This desire we see in both novels for a totality of one kind or another reflects one of the common concerns of the novelists of the so-called boom of the Latin American novel during the sixties. How do you understand this "boom"?

FUENTES: I would say with García Márquez that we are writing one novel in Latin America, with a Colombian chapter written by García Márquez, a Cuban chapter written by Carpentier, an Argentine chapter by Julio Cortázar and so on. We live in a continent where the novel is a recent development, where many things have been left unsaid. It is difficult to speak of individuals because a fusion has taken place: characters from *Artemio Cruz* appear in *One Hundred Years of Solitude*, while in *Terra Nostra* there are characters from *One Hundred Years of Solitude,* from Carpentier's *Explosion in a Cathedral,* Cabrera Infante's *Three Sad Tigers,* and Cortázar's *Hopscotch.* There is a constant intertextuality which is indicative of the nature of writing in Latin America.

INTERVIEWER: So you never felt isolated as a Mexican writer, or that your work was for Mexicans only?

FUENTES: I think I was conscious from the very beginning of my career that it was ridiculous to speak of Mexican literature or Peruvian literature or Chilean literature, that if we were to have any meaning, any universality it would have to be within the wider range of this tattered, mendicant language we call Spanish.

INTERVIEWER: Some Spanish-American writers have suggested that it was only during the sixties that they could imagine a readership that extended from Mexico City to Buenos Aires.

FUENTES: This was not the case for me. I founded and directed a lively magazine in the fifties called *Revista Mexicana de Literatura,* and in 1955 we were publishing Julio Cortázar's early short stories, Cuban poets like Cintio Vitier and José Lezama Lima, even a short story coauthored by Jorge Luis Borges and Adolfo Bioy Casares. By the mid-fifties I felt the traditional barriers had been broken down. The readership was developing at the same time so that there was an intellectual and even a material underpinning for the boom when it appeared. There were publishing houses, distributors, and the authors' knowledge that we belonged to the same linguistic community.

INTERVIEWER: Why were the sixties so favorable to a communal spirit among the writers?

FUENTES: The Cuban Revolution certainly provided a meeting place. Such fervor and hope were raised by the Cuban Revolution! Havana became a focal point until the Cubans developed their tropical socialist realism and began to excommunicate people. Ultimately they destroyed the possibility of a community, but the Cuban Revolution played a fundamental role in creating a sense of unity. I was there when Castro came into Havana. That was a galvanizing moment in our lives, and retrospectively it still is. An extraordinary thing happened then in the history of Spanish-American literature: everybody prominent in the boom was a friend of everybody else. Now this has sadly ended. Now that we enter middle age the friendship has broken, and people have become enemies for personal or political reasons. We look back with nostalgia.

INTERVIEWER: Your personal vision of the boom reminds me of the paucity of biographical and autobiographical materials in the Hispanic world. Only now are we beginning to see writers describing their relation to historical events in Latin America. There are texts like José Donoso's *Personal History of the Boom,* but there is no tradition of memoirs or autobiographies.

FUENTES: I'll tell you why: there is a fear of what is written because it compromises you. I remember arriving at the Mexican embassy in Paris and asking for some information left, I thought, by one of my predecessors. I was interested in his ideas about French politics: it turned out that he never wrote anything because some day it might be used against him.

INTERVIEWER: You have mentioned the influence of *Citizen Kane* on *Artemio Cruz.* Have films been important to your writing?

FUENTES: I'm a great moviegoer. The greatest day in my life as a child was when my father took me to New York City to see the World's Fair and *Citizen Kane,* when I was ten years old. And that struck me in the middle of my imagination and never left me. Since that moment, I've always lived with the ghost of *Citizen Kane.* There are few other great movies which I am conscious of when I write. Buñuel's work would be another. Von Stroheim would be another one, especially the great version of *The Merry Widow* he did as a silent film, without the waltzes. Great scenes of love between John Gilbert and

Mae Murray, in beds of black sheets, and beautiful women playing the flute and tambourine around them with their eyes blindfolded. And finally when the love comes to a climax, they pull the curtains of the little bed, so they are totally isolated from sight; we are there seeing the absence of sight—a series of reflections unseen and imagined, which I found very powerful. But beyond that I don't view it as an influence.

I think the comedians have influenced everybody, the Marx Brothers are among the greatest artists of the twentieth century. The greatest anarchists and revolutionaries, and destroyers of property. The people who make the world shriek and explode with laughter and absurdity. I think they have influenced practically everybody. Keaton and Chaplin. But then literature is another thing. It's a verbal process which is very different from the film, very, very different.

INTERVIEWER: Then you don't feel that film will usurp the novel?

FUENTES: I was talking a few months ago in Mexico with one of the great film makers of our time, Luis Buñuel. He was eighty years old, and I was asking how he looked back on his career and on the destiny of the film. He said, "I think films are perishable, because they depend too much on technology, which advances too quickly and the films become old-fashioned, antiques. What I hope for is that technology advances to the point that films in the future will depend on a little pill which you take; then you sit in the dark, and from your eyes you project the film you want to see on a blank wall."

INTERVIEWER: Somebody would come along and close your eyes.

FUENTES: Yes, there will be censors. But the film would be projected inside your head, then. They'd have to kill you. It would be the final proof of artistic freedom.

INTERVIEWER: What do you do to promote your own work? Do you submit to talk shows?

FUENTES: Perhaps each nation has the Siberia it deserves. In

the Soviet Union a writer who is critical, as we know, is taken
to a lunatic asylum. In the United States, he's taken to a talk
show. There they have to deal with the KGB, here they have
to deal with Johnny Carson, which is much more withering, I
suspect. Phillip Roth has said, in comparing his situation to
that of Milan Kundera, the Czech writer, that in the United
States, everything goes and nothing is important. In Czecho-
slovakia, nothing goes and everything is important. So this
gives the writer an added dimension he doesn't have here.

I was in Paris last year. A book of mine was being launched
and they said that I had to go on television. I didn't want to.
They said no, no, it sells a lot of books—the program, called
Apostrophes, is very popular; it's seen by about thirty million
people in France. I said, "Okay, let's go and see what happens." It was a terrifying experience because there was a petu-
lant Frenchman who kept cutting me, so I couldn't express my
ideas. He wanted things to go very quickly, and I couldn't say
anything. I was very unhappy at what had happened and with
what I had said. I went back with Sylvia, my wife, to the
apartment. The concierge was waiting up for us and she said,
"Ah, I just turned off the television. How wonderful. It was
magnificent, marvelous." I said, "No, it was terrible. It was
awful. I didn't like the things I said." And she said, "But Mr.
Fuentes, I didn't hear anything you said. I saw you. *I saw you.* "
People who are glued to the television are really in the deepest
recess of their soul, hoping to see themselves, because this will
be the apotheosis of their identity. Walter Benjamin says a very
good thing about the real revolution of the nineteenth century
being the invention of photography. All throughout history,
people had been faceless, and suddenly people had a face. The
first photographs were kept in jewel boxes lined with velvet
because they were precious. They were your identity. Now
suddenly you have this possibility of being seen by thirty, forty,
fifty million people. You have an identity. You exist. You are
someone. No matter how fleetingly, no matter how briefly.

Talk about the end of feudalism. There it is. The end of feudalism happens in front of your TV.

INTERVIEWER: Have you ever contemplated writing your memoirs?

FUENTES: Oh, yes. I want to do that very much when the time comes and I keep lots of interesting notes. I think that in Mexico and Latin America it is a good idea to start thinking of the genre of the memoir, of leaving something, of creating in that genre. My generation has done a great deal to create a narrative tradition and we probably have time to create a memoir tradition. After all, it has existed in the past, in Cortés's letters and in Bernal Díaz del Castillo's personal history of the conquest of Mexico. And now I see this promise in Guillermo Cabrera Infante's book of boyhood in Havana.

INTERVIEWER: Do you think you will continue to write at the same rate you have been?

FUENTES: Well, it has become physically easier for me to write. Time passes and the past becomes the present. What you were living and thought you had lost forever is ancillary to your work. Then suddenly it acquires a shape, it exists in an order of time all its own and this order of time demands a literary form. So then these presences of the past are there in the center of your life today. You thought they were unimportant or that they had died, but they have just been looking for their chance. If you try to force a theme when you are twenty-five and have lived less, you find you can't do a thing with it. Suddenly it offers itself gratuitously. At fifty I find there is a long line of characters and shapes demanding words just outside my window. I wish I could capture all of them, but I won't have enough time. The process of selection is terrifying because in selecting you necessarily kill something.

INTERVIEWER: This is a fantastic image, a double apprenticeship: an initial phase of writing being itself a gestation period followed now by a period of painful plenitude.

FUENTES: When your life is half over, I think you have to

see the face of death in order to start writing seriously. There are people who see the end quickly, like Rimbaud. When you start seeing it, you feel you have to rescue these things. Death is the great Maecenas, Death is the great angel of writing. You must write because you are not going to live any more.

ALFRED MACADAM
CHARLES RUAS
Winter 1981

12. John Gardner

When he died in a motorcycle accident in September 1982, John Gardner left behind a prodigious legacy—approximately thirty books of fiction, translation, and criticism which he had produced over a twenty-year span. A University of Iowa Ph.D., Gardner took his first academic teaching post at Oberlin College in 1958. A professor of medieval and Renaissance English literature, he devoted much of his time to the compilation of Old English works, among them three books on Chaucer, as well as *The Complete Works of the Gawain-Poet* (1965) and a collection of Middle English poetry. Among the many grants he was awarded were the Danforth Fellowship (1970–73) and a Guggenheim Fellowship (1973–75).

Gardner was a superb teller of medieval fireside stories, and his juvenile works include *Dragon, Dragon and Other Tales* (1975) and *Gudgekin, the Thistle Girl* (1976). Of his adult fiction, *Grendel* (1971) received high critical praise, and in 1976, *October Light* won the National Book Critics' Circle Award for fiction.

Other novels of his include *The Sunlight Dialogues* (1972), *Nickel Mountain* (1973), and *Mickelsson's Ghosts* (1982). In his controversial work *On Moral Fiction* (1978), Gardner examines the relation of "morality" to literature, and laments the absence of honesty in modern works of fiction. He saw the fiction writer as "a center of energy for people," and he sought to fulfill this role himself by making the academic circuit of literature and creative writing departments. Some of his teaching posts included those at Northwestern University, Bennington College, and the State University of New York at Binghamton, where he taught until his death. In 1983, *On Becoming a Novelist* was published posthumously.

Days passed, and weeks, and Vlemk became so changed that often not even the
regulars at the tavern seemed to know him as he groped his way past them on his
way to the bathroom or out to the alley. He forgot about the Princess, or remembered
her only as one remembers certain moments from one's childhood. Sometimes if
someone spoke of her, and if it was early in the evening, when Vlemk was still relatively
sober, Vlemk would smile like a man who knows more than he's telling about something,
and it would cross people's minds, especially the barmaid's, that Vlemk and the
princess were closer than one might think. But since he was a mute and declined
to write notes, no one pressed him. Anyway, no one wanted to get close to him; he
smell like an old sick bear.

Things went from bad to worse for Vlemk the box-painter. He no longer spoke
of life as "boxing him in," not only because the expression bored him but also, and
mainly, because the box had become such a given of his existence that he no
longer noticed it. bleary-eyed

Then one morning as he was lying in a gutter, squinting up and
exploring a newly broken tooth with his tongue, a carriage of black
leather with golden studs drew up beside him and, at a command from the person
inside, stopped.

"Driver," said voice
that seemed as near as Vlemk's heart, "who is that unfortunate creature in the
gutter?"

Vlemk turned his head and tried to focus his eyes, but it was
useless. The carriage was, like a shadow
on a painted box-lid.

"I'm sorry, Princess," said the driver, "I have no idea."

When he heard it was the Princess, Vlemk thought briefly of raising one
hand to hide his face, but his will remained inactive and he was as he was.

"Throw the poor creature a coin," said the Princess. "I hope he's not
past using it."

After a moment something landed, plop, on Vlemk's belly, and the carriage
drove away. Slowly, Vlemk moved one hand toward the cool place--his shirt had
lost its buttons, and the coin lay flat on his pale, grimy skin--where at last
his, groping fingers found it and dragged it back down to the ground
beside him, where it would be safe while he napt. Hours later
he sat up abruptly and realized what had happened. He looked down at his hand.
There lay the coin, real silver with a picture of the king on it.

"How strange!" thought Vlemk.

When he'd gotten to his feet and moved carefully to the streetcorner,
touching the walls of the buildings with one hand, he found that he had no idea
where he was, much less how he'd gotten there, and no idea which direction to
take to reach his house. When he waved to hurrying passers-by, silently moving
his loose, mute mouth, they ducked their heads, touching their hats, and hurried
around him as they would if he were Death. He on alone, hunting for some
landmark, but it was as if all the streets of the city had been
arranged in new patterns. He shook his head, still moving his mouth,
unaware that he was doing it. In his right hand clenched--so tightly that
the rim of it bit into his flesh--the coin with the picture of the king on it.

Three days later, having carefully thought it from every point of
view, having bathed and trimmed his beard and washed his old black suit
in the sink in the studio, and having dried it on the railing of the balcony,
Vlemk the box-painter started up the toward the
Royal Palace, carrying the box with the talking picture
In his pocket he had a note which he'd lettered, and intended to
hand her as he gave her the box. "Here is the gift I promised you," the note
read, "a picture so real it can speak. I release you, from your promise
to talk with me, since Respectfully, Vlemk the Box-Painter."

He arrived at the palace, as he had planned to do, just at the time when
the Princess would be coming in from walking her dogs. The last of the sunset
was fading from the clouds, and here and there pockets of fog were taking
shape, intruding on the smoothly mown slopes from ponds and woods. To Vlemk's
dismay, the outer gates of iron stood open, the grayhounds saw him, they
would tear him to bits, but then he noticed that all around the front of the
palace carriages, and near the arched front door aristocrats, stood talking
and laughing in their splendid dress. It seemed to him unlikely that they would
let the grayhounds kill him, though he learned enough
to know that in these matters nothing is ever quite certain.
But the dogs, he thought the next instant, were the least of it. How could he
walk in, in the middle of a party of aristocrats, and give the Princess his card
and present? How would he even find her? As he drew nearer, moving more slowly
now, he saw that the clothes were all of material, with clasps
and buckles, buttons, epaulettes, and swordhilts of gold and silver. He looked

A John Gardner manuscript page.

Nancy Crampton

John Gardner

The following interview incorporates three done with John Gardner over the last decade of his life. After interviewing him in 1971, Frank McConnell wrote of the thirty-nine-year-old author as one of the most original and promising younger American novelists. His first four novels—The Resurrection (1966), The Wreck of Agathon (1970), Grendel (1971) and The Sunlight Dialogues (1972)—represented, in the eyes of many critics and reviewers, a new and exhilarating phase in the enterprise of modern writing, a consolidation of the resources of the contemporary novel and a leap forward—or backward—into a reestablished humanism. "One finds in his books elements of the three major strains of current fiction: the elegant narrative gamesmanship of Barth or Pynchon, the hyperrealistic Gothicism of Joyce Carol Oates and Stanley Elkin, and the cultural, intellectual history of Saul Bellow. Like so many characters in current fiction, Gardner's are men on the fringe, men shocked into the consciousness that they are living lives which seem to be determined, not by their own will, but by massive myths, cosmic fictions over which they have no control (e.g., Ebeneezer Cooke in Barth's Sot-Weed Factor, Tyrone Slothrop in Pynchon's Gravity's Rainbow); but Gardner's characters are philosophers on the fringe, heirs, all of them, to the great debates over authenticity and bad faith which characterize our era. In Grendel, for example, the hero-monster is initiated into the Sartrean vision of Nothingness by an ancient, obviously well-read Dragon: a myth speaking of the emptiness of all myths: 'Theory-makers. . . . They'd map out roads through Hell with their crackpot theories, their here-to-the-moon-and-back lists of paltry facts. Insanity—the simplest insanity ever devised!' His heroes—like all men—are philosophers who are going to die; and their characteristic discovery—the central creative energy of Gardner's fiction—is that the death of consciousness finally justifies consciousness itself. The myths, whose artificiality contemporary writers have been at such pains to point out, become in Gardner's work real and life-giving once again, without ever losing their modern character of fictiveness.

"Gardner's work may well represent, then, the new 'conservatism' which some observers have noted in the current scene. But it is a conservatism of high originality, and, at least in Gardner's case, of deep authority in his life. When he guest-taught a course in 'Narrative Forms' at Northwestern University, a number of his students were surprised to find a modern writer—and a hot property—enthusiastic, not only about Homer, Virgil, Appolonius Rhodius, and Dante, but deeply concerned with the critical controversies surrounding those writers, and with mistakes in their English translations. As the interview following makes clear, Gardner's job in and affection for ancient writing and the tradition of metaphysics is, if anything, greater than for the explosions and involutions of modern fiction. He is, in the full sense of the word, a literary man.

" 'It's as if God put me on earth to write,' Gardner observed once. And writing, or thinking about writing, takes up much of his day. He works, he says, usually on three or four books at the same time, allowing the plots to cross-pollinate, shape and qualify each other."

Sara Matthiessen describes Gardner in the spring of 1978 (additional works published by then included October Light; On Moral Fiction was about to be published). Matthiessen arrived with a friend to interview him at the Breadloaf Writer's Colony in Vermont: "After we'd knocked a couple of times, he opened the door looking haggard and just-wakened. Dressed in a purple sateen, bell-sleeved, turtle-neck shirt and jeans, he was an exotic figure: unnaturally white hair to below his shoulders, of medium height, he seemed an incarnation from the medieval era central to his study. 'Come in!' he said, as though there were no two people he'd rather have seen than Sally and me, and he led us into a cold, bright room sparsely equipped with wooden furniture. We were offered extra socks against the chill. John lit his pipe, and we sat down to talk."

INTERVIEWER: You've worked in several different areas: prose, fiction, verse, criticism, book reviews, scholarly books, children's books, radio plays; you wrote the libretto for a recently produced opera. Could you discuss the different genres? Which one have you most enjoyed doing?

GARDNER: The one that feels the most important is the novel. You create a whole world in a novel and you deal with values in a way that you can't possibly in a short story. The trouble is that since novels represent a whole world, you can't write them all the time. After you finish a novel, it takes a couple of years to get in enough life and enough thinking about things to have anything to say, any clear questions to work through. You have to keep busy, so it's fun to do the other things. I do book reviews when I'm hard up for money, which I am all the time. They don't pay much, but they keep you going. Book reviews are interesting because it's necessary to keep an eye on what's good and what's bad in the books of a society worked so heavily by advertising, public relations, and so on. Writing reviews isn't really analytical, it's for the most part quick reactions—joys and rages. I certainly never write a review about a book I don't think worth reviewing, a flat-out bad book, unless it's an enormously fashionable bad book. As for writing children's books, I've done them because when my kids were growing up I would now and then write them a story as a Christmas present, and then after I became sort of successful, people saw the stories and said they should be published. I like them, of course. I wouldn't give junk to my kids. I've also done scholarly books and articles. The reason I've done those is that I've been teaching things like Beowulf and Chaucer for a long time. As you teach a poem year after year, you realize, or anyway convince yourself, that you understand the poem and that most people have got it slightly wrong. That's natural with any poem, but during the years I taught lit courses, it was especially true of medieval and classical poetry. When the general critical view has a major poem or poet *badly* wrong, you feel like you ought to straighten it out. The studies of Chaucer since the fifties are very strange stuff: like the theory that Chaucer is a frosty Oxford-donnish guy shunning carnality and cupidity. Not true. So close analysis is useful. But writing novels—and maybe opera libretti—is the kind of writing that gives me greatest satisfaction; the rest is more like entertainment.

INTERVIEWER: You have been called a "philosophical novelist." What do you think of the label?

GARDNER: I'm not sure that being a philosophical novelist is better than being some other kind, but I guess that there's not much doubt that, in a way at least, that's what I am. A writer's material is what he cares about, and I like philosophy the way some people like politics, or football games, or unidentified flying objects. I read a man like Collingwood, or even Brand

Blanchard or C. D. Broad, and I get excited—even anxious—filled with suspense. I read a man like Swinburn on Time and Space and it becomes a matter of deep concern to me whether the structure of space changes near large masses. It's as if I actually think philosophy will solve life's great questions—which sometimes, come to think of it, it does, at least for me. Probably not often, but I like the illusion. Blanchard's attempt at a logical demonstration that there really *is* a universal human morality, or the recent flurry of theories by various majestical cranks that the universe is stabilizing itself instead of flying apart—those are lovely things to run into. Interesting and arresting, I mean, like talking frogs. I get a good deal more out of the philosophy section of a college bookstore than out of the fiction section, and I more often read philosophical books than I read novels. So sure, I'm "philosophical," though what I write is by no means straight philosophy. I make up stories. Meaning creeps in of necessity, to keep things clear, like paragraph breaks and punctuation. And, I might add, my friends are all artists and critics, not philosophers. Philosophers—except for the few who are my friends—drink beer and watch football games and defeat their wives and children by the fraudulent tyranny of logic.

INTERVIEWER: But insofar as you *are* a "philosophical novelist," what is it that you do?

GARDNER: I write novels, books about people, and what I write is philosophical only in a limited way. The human dramas that interest me—stir me to excitement and, loosely, vision—are always rooted in serious philosophical questions. That is, I'm bored by plots that depend on the psychological or sociological quirks of the main characters—mere melodramas of healthy against sick—stories which, subtly or otherwise, merely preach. Art as the wisdom of Marcus Welby, M.D. Granted, most of fiction's great heroes are at least slightly crazy, from Achilles to Captain Ahab, but the problems that make great heroes act are the problems no sane man could have gotten around either. Achilles, in his nobler, saner moments, lays down the whole moral code of *The Iliad*. But the violence and anger triggered by war, the human passions that overwhelm Achilles' reason and make him the greatest criminal in all fiction—they're just as much a problem for lesser, more ordinary people. The same with Ahab's desire to pierce the Mask, smash through to absolute knowledge. Ahab's crazy, so he actually tries it; but the same Mask leers at all of us. So, when I write a piece of fiction I select my characters and settings and so on because they have a bearing, at least to me, on the old unanswerable philosophical questions. And as I spin out the action, I'm always very concerned with springing discoveries— actual philosophical discoveries. But at the same time I'm concerned—and finally *more* concerned—with what the discoveries do to the character who makes them, and to the people around him. It's that that makes me not really a philosopher, but a novelist.

INTERVIEWER: The novel *Grendel* is a retelling of the Beowulf story from the monster's point of view. Why does an American writer living in the twentieth century abandon the realistic approach and borrow such legendary material as the basis for a novel?

GARDNER: I've never been terribly fond of realism because of certain things that realism seems to commit me to. With realism you have to spend two hundred pages proving that somebody lives in Detroit so that something can happen and be absolutely convincing. But the value systems of the people involved is the important thing, not the fact that they live on Nine Mile Road. In my earlier fiction I went as far as I could from realism because the easy way to get to the heart of what you want to say is to take somebody else's story, particularly a nonrealistic story. When you tell the story of Grendel, or Jason and Medeia, you've got to end it the way the story ends— traditionally, but you can get to do it in your own way. The result is that the writer comes to understand things about the

modern world in light of the history of human consciousness;
he understands it a little more deeply, and has a lot more fun
writing it.

INTERVIEWER: But why specifically *Beowulf*?

GARDNER: Some stories are more interesting than others.
Beowulf is a terribly interesting story. It gives you some really
wonderful visual images, such as the dragon. It's got Swedes
looking over the hills and scaring everybody. It's got mead
halls. It's got Grendel, and Grendel's mother. I really do believe that a novel has to be a feast of the senses, a delightful
thing. One of the better things that has happened to the novel
in recent years is that it has become rich. Think of a book like
Chimera or *The Sot-Weed Factor*—they may not be very good
books, but they are at least rich experiences. For me, writers
like John O'Hara are interesting only in the way that movies
and TV plays are interesting; there is almost nothing in a John
O'Hara novel that couldn't be in the movies just as easily. On
the other hand, there is no way an animator, or anyone else,
can create an image from *Grendel* as exciting as the image in
the reader's mind: Grendel is a monster, and living in the first
person, because we're all in some sense monsters, trapped in
our own language and habits of emotion. Grendel expresses
feelings we all feel—enormous hostility, frustration, disbelief,
and so on, so that the reader, projecting his own monster,
projects a monster which is, for him, the perfect horror show.
There is no way you can do that in television or the movies,
where you are always seeing the kind of realistic novel O'Hara
wrote . . . Gregory Peck walking down the street. It's just the
same old thing to me. There are other things that are interesting in O'Hara, and I don't mean to put him down excessively,
but I go for another kind of fiction: I want the effect that a
radio play gives you or that novels are always giving you at their
best.

INTERVIEWER: You do something very interesting in *Grendel*. You never name Beowulf, and in the concluding scene you

describe him in such a way as to give the impression that Grendel is really confronting, not Beowulf or another human being, but the dragon. That seems a significant change from the poem.

GARDNER: I didn't mean it to be a change. As a medievalist, one knows there are two great dragons in medieval art. There's Christ the dragon, and there's Satan the dragon. There's always a war between those two great dragons. In modern Christian symbolism a sweeter image of Jesus with the sheep in his arms has evolved, but I like the old image of the warring dragon. That's not to say Beowulf really is Christ, but that he's Christ-like. Actually, he is many things. When Grendel first sees Beowulf coming, Grendel thinks of him as a sort of machine, and what comes to the reader's mind is a kind of computer, a spaceman, a complete alien, unknown. The inescapable mechanics of the universe. At other times, Beowulf looks like a fish to Grendel. He comes in the season of Pisces when, among other things, you stab yourself in the back. On other occasions, Grendel sees other things, one after another, and for a brief flash, when he is probably hallucinating—he's fighting, losing blood very badly because he has his arm torn off—Grendel thinks he's fighting the dragon instead of Beowulf. At the end of the story, Grendel doesn't know *who* he's fighting. He's just fighting something big and horrible and sure to kill him, something that he could never have predicted in the universe as he understood it, because from the beginning of the novel, Grendel feels himself hopelessly determined, hopelessly struggling against—in the profoundest sense—the way things are. He feels there's no way out, that there's no hope for living consciousness, particularly *his* consciousness, since, for reasons inexplicable to him, he's on the wrong side, Cain's side instead of mankind's.

INTERVIEWER: It seems to me that determinism is affliction imposed on him by the *scop*.

GARDNER: It's true, but only partly. In the novel, he's undeniably pushed around by the universe, but also not to believe, not to have faith in life. What happens is, in the story, the shaper, the *scop*, the court poet comes to this horrible court that's made itself what it is by killing everybody, beating people, chopping them to death, and the poet looks at this havoc around him and makes up a story about what a wonderful court it is, what noble ideals it has. The courtiers are just dumb enough to believe it, just as Americans have believed the stories about Sam Adams and Ethan Allen and all those half-mythical heroes. George Washington once stood for thirty minutes stuttering in a rage before executing a private for a minor misdeed. Sam Adams was like a well-meaning Marxist agitator. Constantly lied. He told Boston that New York had fallen when it hadn't fallen. Or anyway so one of my characters claims. I no longer remember what the truth is.

INTERVIEWER: But that's an important moment in Grendel's development, isn't it, when he hears this story?

GARDNER: He hears the story and is tempted to believe it. And for certain reasons, partly because he is kicked out of the mead hall, he decides to reject the myth. That's Grendel's hard luck, because when he goes to the mead hall and wants to be a good monster and doesn't want to kill people anymore, Hrothgar's warriors don't know that, and they throw spears at him and hurt him.

INTERVIEWER: You don't see yourself, as a novelist, analogous to the *scop* in the telling of a story?

GARDNER: Oh, sure. Absolutely. I absolutely believe every artist is in the position of the *scop*. As I tried to make plain in *On Moral Fiction*, I think that the difference right now between good art and bad art is that the good artists are the people who are, in one way or another, creating, out of deep and honest concern, a vision of life-in-the-twentieth-century that is worth pursuing. And the bad artists, of whom there are many, are whining or moaning or staring, because it's fashionable, into the dark abyss. If you believe that life is fundamentally a volcano full of baby skulls, you've got two main choices as an artist: You can either stare into the volcano and count the skulls for the thousandth time and tell everybody, "There are the skulls; that's your baby, Mrs. Miller." Or you can try to build walls so that fewer baby skulls go in. It seems to me that the artist ought to hunt for positive ways of surviving, of living. You shouldn't lie. If there aren't any, so far as you can see, you should say so, like the *Merdistes*. But I don't think the *Merdistes* are right—except for Céline himself, by accident, because Céline (as character, not as author) is comic; a villain so outrageous, miserable, and inept that we laugh at him and at all he so earnestly stands for. I think the world is not all merde. I think it's possible to make walls around at least some of the smoking holes.

INTERVIEWER: Won't this have the effect of transforming the modern writer into a didactic writer?

GARDNER: Not didactic. The didactic writer is anything but moral because he is always simplifying the argument, always narrowing away, getting rid of legitimate objections. *Mein Kampf* is a moralistic book—a stupid, ugly one. A truly moral book is one which is radically open to persuasion, but looks hard at a problem, and keeps looking for answers. It gives you an absolutely clear vision, as if the poet, the writer, had nothing to do with it, had just done everything in his power to imagine how things are. It's the situation of Dostoevsky and Nietzsche —an illusion I use in *On Moral Fiction.* Nietzsche sets up this abstract theory of the Superman according to which a person can kill or do anything he wants because there is no basis of law except the herd. God doesn't speak; dead. So the people get together and vote to have a red light on Highway 61 where there's no traffic. It's three o'clock in the morning. You're travelling, and there's a red light, and you decide to jump the light. A car pulls out of the weeds, a policeman and he comes after you. If you're a superman, you politely and gently kill him, put him back in the weeds, and drive on. The theory of the superman is kind of interesting, abstractly. The question is, is it right? Will it work? Can human beings live with it? So Dostoevsky sets up the experiment imaginatively. Obviously he doesn't want to go out and actually kill somebody to see if it works, so he imagines a perfectly convincing St. Petersburg, and a perfectly convincing person who would do this. (What student in all St. Petersburg would commit a murder? What relatives would he have? What friends? What would his pattern be? What would he eat?) Dostoevsky follows the experiment out and finds out what does happen.

I think all great art does this, and you don't have to do it realistically. Obviously Raskolnikov could have been a giant saurian, as long as his character is consistent and convincing, tuned to what we know about actual feeling. The point is realism of imagination, convincingness of imagination. The novelist pursues questions, and pursues them thoroughly. Not only when does it rain and when doesn't it rain, but can we tolerate rain? What can we be made to tolerate? What should we not allow ourselves to be made to tolerate? And so on. So that finally, what's moral in fiction is chiefly its way of looking. The premise of moral art is that life is better than death; art hunts for avenues to life. The book succeeds if we're powerfully persuaded that the focal characters, in their fight for life, have won honestly or, if they lose, are tragic in their loss, not just tiresome or pitiful.

INTERVIEWER: So you have a strong sense of mission, or of a goal, in modern fiction.

GARDNER: Yes, I do. In my own way, anyway. I want to push the novel in a new direction, or back to an old one—Homer's or the Beowulf-Poet's. Of course, a lot of other writers are trying to do something rather different—Barth and Pynchon, I grant them their right—grudgingly. But to paraphrase the Imagists, I want "no ideas but in *energeia*"—Aristotle's made-up word for (excuse the jazz), "the actualization of the potential which exists in character and situation." Philosophy as plot.

I think no novel can please for very long without plot as the center of its argument. We get too many books full of meaning by innuendo—the ingenious symbol, the allegorical overlay, stories in which *events* are of only the most trivial importance, just the thread on which the writer strings hints of his "real" meaning. This has been partly a fault of the way we've been studying and teaching literature, of course. Our talk of levels and all that. For instance, take John Updike's *Couples*. It's a fairly good book, it seems to me, but there's a good reason no one reads it anymore: contrived phrases bear all the burden. Symbolically constructed names; descriptions of a living room which slyly hint at the expansion of the universe; or Updike's whole cunning trick with Christian iconography, circles and straight lines—circles traditionally associated with reason, straight lines with faith. You work the whole symbolic structure out and you're impressed by Updike's intelligence—maybe, in this book, even wisdom—but you have difficulty telling the fornicators apart. Reading *Couples* is like studying science while watching pornographic movies put together from random scraps on the cutting-room floor.

INTERVIEWER: You want novels to be whole entertainments, then.

GARDNER: Sure! Look: it's impossible for us to read Dostoevsky as a writer of thrillers anymore, because of this whole weight of explanation and analysis we've loaded on the books. And yet *The Brothers Karamazov* is obviously, among other things, a thriller novel. (It also contains, to my mind, some pretentious philosophizing.) What I've wanted to do, in *The Sunlight Dialogues*, for example, is write a book—maybe not a novel—that you could read as entertainment. Where there's straight philosophizing, here as in *The Resurrection*, it's present because that's what the character would say (or so I thought at the time), present because that's what makes him behave as he does. No meaning but emotion-charged action and emotional reaction.

INTERVIEWER: The classical forms, like *Grendel,* are not your only models, nor do you always adhere to the superficial nature of the form you've chosen—for instance, there are parts in the *Sunlight Dialogues* that parody Faulkner.

GARDNER: Sure. In fact, the whole conception of the book is in a way parodic of Faulkner, among others—the whole idea of family and locale. A lot of times I've consciously taken a writer on. In the first novel I did, I used the title *The Resurrection* to give the reader a clue as to what's wrong with Tolstoy in his *Resurrection.* I don't think many readers notice, and of course it doesn't matter. In fact, a friend of mine who's a very good critic asked me one time if I were aware that I'd used a title that Tolstoy had used. That's all right. If I sounded too much like Tolstoy, then my novel would be a critical footnote.

INTERVIEWER: How about your contemporaries? Has any of their work influenced your writing?

GARDNER: Of course I'm aware of modern writers . . . and some writers have changed my way of thinking. I don't always like what Bill Gass does—though I do immensely like much of his fiction—but I certainly have changed my writing style because of his emphasis on language, that is, his brilliant use of it in books. It has always seemed to me that the main thing you ought to be doing when you write a story is, as Robert Louis Stevenson said, to set a "dream" going in the reader's mind . . . so that he opens the page, reads about three words, and drops into a sort of trance. He's seeing Russia instead of his living room. Not that he's *passive.* The reader hopes and judges. I used to think that words and style should be transparent, that no word should call attention to itself in any way; that you could say the plainest thing possible to get the dream going. After I read some early Gass—"The Pedersen Kid," I think—I realized that you don't really interfere with the dream by saying things in an interesting way. Performance is an important part of the show. But I don't, like Gass, think language is of value when it's opaque, more decorative than communicative. Gass loves those formalist arguments. He's said, for instance, that it's naïve to think of characters as real—that it's absurd to cry for little Nell. It may be absurd to cry at that particular death, because in that case the writing is lousy. But what happens in real fiction is identical to what happens in a dream—as long as we have the right to wake up screaming from a nightmare, we have the right to worry about a character. Gass has a funny theory. But I have borrowed a great many elements from it—I'm sure I owe more to him than to any other living writer. And I have learned a few things from slightly contemporary writers. About symbols, for instance. If you stop with James Joyce, you may write a slightly goofy kind of symbolic novel. Joyce's fondness for the "mannered" is the least of it. At the time Joyce was writing, people were less attuned than they are now to symbolic writing, so he sometimes let himself get away with bald, obvious symbols. Now, thanks largely to the New Criticism, any smart college freshman can catch every symbol that comes rolling along. The trouble is that if a reader starts watching the play of symbolism and missing what's happening to the characters, he gets an intellectual apprehension of the book, and that's pretty awful. He might as well read philosophy or meditations on the wounds of Christ. But you still need resonance, deep effect. You have to build into the novel the movement from particular to general. The question is, how do you get a symbolic structure without tipping your hand? A number of modern writers have shown ways of doing it. The red herring symbols of Pynchon, the structural distractions of Barth, the machine-gun energy of Gaddis. Above all, Gass's verbal glory.

INTERVIEWER: Do you, like Joyce, play to the reader subliminally through symbolism, or do you make fairly overt statements by demonstrating what certain values can lead to?

GARDNER: I try to be as overt as possible. Plot, character, and action first. I try to say everything with absolute directness so that the reader sees the characters moving around, sees the house they're moving through, the landscape, the weather, and so on. I try to be absolutely direct about moral values and dilemmas. Read it to the charwoman, Richardson said. I say, make it plain to her dog. But when you write fiction such as mine, fantastic or quasi-realistic fiction, it happens inevitably that as you're going over it, thinking about it, you recognize unconscious symbols bubbling up to the surface, and you begin to revise to give them room, sort of nudge them into sight. Though ideally the reader should never catch you shaking a symbol at him. (Intellect is the chief distractor of the mind.) The process of writing becomes more and more mysterious as you go over the draft more and more times; finally everything is symbolic. Even then you keep pushing it, making sure that it's as coherent and self-contained as a grapefruit. Frequently, when you write a novel you start out feeling pretty clear about your position, what side you're on; as you revise, you find your unconscious pushing up associations that modify that position, force you to reconsider.

INTERVIEWER: You began *October Light*, you've said, with the idea that "the traditional New England values are the values we should live by: good workmanship, independence, unswerving honesty—" but these proved oversimple. Is the process of fiction always the process of discovery for you? In other words, do you often find that the idea that prompted the fiction turns out to be too simple, or even wrong?

GARDNER: I always start out with a position I later discover to be too simple. That's the nature of things—what physicists call complementarity. What's interesting is that my ideas prove too simple in ways I could never have anticipated. In everything I've written I've come to the realization that I was missing something, telling myself lies. That's one of the main pleasures of writing. What I do is follow the drama where it goes; the potential of the characters in their given situation. I let them go where they have to go, and analyze as I'm going along what's involved, what the implications are. When I don't like the implications, I think hard about it. Chasing implications to the wall is my one real skill. I think of ways of dramatically setting up contrasts so that my position on a thing is clear to me, and then I hound the thing till it rolls over. I certainly wouldn't ever fake the actions, or the characters, or make people say what they wouldn't say. I never use sleight-of-wits like Stanley Elkin—though no one can fail to admire a really good sophist's skill.

INTERVIEWER: How important is setting?

GARDNER: Setting is one of the most powerful symbols you have, but mainly it serves characterization. The first thing that makes a reader read a book is the characters. Say you're standing in a train station, or an airport, and you're leafing through books; what you're hoping for is a book where you'll like the characters, where the characters are interesting. To establish powerful characters, a writer needs a landscape to help define them; so setting becomes important. Setting is also a powerful vehicle of thematic concerns; in fact, it's one of the most powerful. If you're going to talk about the decline of Western civilization or at least the possibility of that decline, you take an old place that's sort of worn out and run-down. For instance, Batavia, New York, where the Holland Land Office was . . . the beginning of a civilization . . . selling the land in this country. It was, in the beginning, a wonderful, beautiful place with the smartest Indians in America around. Now it's this old, run-down town which has been urban-renewalized just about out of existence. The factories have stopped and the people are poor and sometimes crabby; the elm trees are all dead, and so are the oaks and maples. So it's a good symbol. If you're writing the kind of book I was writing in *Sunlight Dialogues* or *The Resurrection*, both of them books about death, both spiritual death and the death of civilization, you choose a place like that. I couldn't have found, in my experience, a better setting. It's just not a feeling you have in San Francisco. If I was going to write a book about southern Illinois, which in fact I did in

King's Indian, that's another, completely different feeling. There it's as if human beings had never landed; the human beings—the natives, anyway—seem more like gnomes. You choose the setting that suits and illuminates your material.

INTERVIEWER: *The Resurrection, Sunlight Dialogues, Nickel Mountain, October Light,* all take place in your native surroundings, more or less; do you find that you need distance on a place before you can write about it? Would you have been able to get a proper perspective on these places in the East, and the type of people who live there, if you'd not spent a good deal of your time in the West and Midwest?

GARDNER: I don't really think so. It's true that *The Resurrection* and *Sunlight Dialogues* take place in Batavia. I wrote one of them in California, the other partly in California, and partly in southern Illinois. So I was using memories from my childhood. Every once in a while, I'd go back and see my parents and go over and see the Brumsteds and the characters who show up in the story, and I'd look the streets over and think, that'd be funny to put in a novel, or whatever. But *Nickel Mountain* is set in the Catskills, which I'd only passed through once or twice, and when I did *October Light,* which came out of a very direct and immediate experience in the East, I'd just moved back to the East after years away. I'd never been in Vermont, and the landscape and the feeling of the people is not at all like western New York. I had never seen anything like it; I certainly didn't have any distance on it. It may be that ten years from now when I look the book over I'll see that I didn't do it very well, but now it feels just as authentic to me as the other books I've written. So I don't think you necessarily do need distance. It is certainly true though that memory selects well. What you keep in your memory is psychologically symbolic, hence powerful, so that when you write about things that you knew a long time ago, you're going to get a fairly powerful evocation of place. I think one sees that in Bernard Malamud's work. When he writes about his childhood, his early memories of New York, you get a very powerful sense of the place. But I think in *A New Life*, written out of immediate experience, you get a more superficial sense of place.

It's different; nobody could deny that the landscapes in *A New Life* are vivid, it's just that they don't have that *lived* feeling that the earlier cityscapes have. You have to write about what's useful and that's the problem; you can't just write about the place that's the most digested for you. In a really good writer's work you'll see that a writer doesn't have to have been around a place very long at all. John Fowles' novel *Daniel Martin* has got some long sections on Los Angeles which seem to be absolutely incredible. You'd swear he grew up there. Most people writing about Los Angeles can only see the phoniness, the greenery, and the gilt. Fowles sees everything, and he gets in it.

INTERVIEWER: Your *belief* in literature, your affection for it as a living force, goes back pretty far in your childhood. Did you read mostly the classics when you were a boy?

GARDNER: Not mostly—we had a lot of books. My mother was a schoolteacher, and my father was a farmer who loved to read: classics, Shakespeare, and of course, the Bible. They were great reciters of literature, too. I've had visitors—sophisticated people—who've heard my father recite things, and have been amazed at how powerfully he does it. It's an old country tradition, but my father was and is the best. We'd be put to bed with a recital of poetry, things like that. At Grange meetings, for instance, my mother and father would do recitations as part of the evening's entertainment. Or while my father was milking the cows my mother would come out and read something to him—*Lear*, say—leaving out the part of whomever my father felt like being that day, and he'd answer his lines from the cow.

INTERVIEWER: He actually had the whole thing memorized?

GARDNER: Oh, sure. Lots of plays. And he'd write things— lay sermons, stories—while he was driving his tractor: compose them in his head, rather like Ben Hodge in *Sunlight.* Not that Ben Hodge is exactly like my father. My father isn't weak-willed. My father knows hundreds of poems, including some very long ones. Beautiful to listen to. A lot of people that we dismiss as terrible poets, like Longfellow, are changed entirely when you say their poems out loud—as they were intended to be. It's like singing; a song can't be very complex; the tune takes up part of the energy so that the words are kind of silly on the page, but when you sing it, it may be wonderful. The same thing happens with oral poetry—lots of stuff that's thin, even goofy on the page can be recited beautifully. That's one of the reasons I write the way I do. Oral stuff written. I hope that comes through.

INTERVIEWER: Did you do any writing as a child?

GARDNER: I started writing stories when I was five or so—making these books I'd send to relatives every Christmas. And around eight, I was writing longer things . . . I wrote in ledger books given to me by my grandmother the lawyer. I really enjoyed writing on ledger paper: there's something nice about a page with a red line down the middle.

INTERVIEWER: Do you still use them?

GARDNER: No, I own my own typewriter now. Very professional.

INTERVIEWER: Is there an advantage to growing up on a farm?

GARDNER: Farm boys have some advantages; it depends on the family. I learned to love the land at least partly because my parents did—working it, watching things grow. Farm boys spend a lot of time with animals of all kinds. I liked it. Some don't. Also, sometimes on the happiest farms, the hunger comes to get away from all that work, and so they may see New York with more excited eyes than some New Yorkers do; or Chicago, or Los Angeles. I love all those places, even the ones that everybody else hates. I have a little trouble with Cleveland, but parts of it are nice. But except for short stints in San

Francisco, Chicago, and Detroit, my whole life has been spent in the country, working with plants and animals, reading and writing. It's nice to live in the country when you grew up there and worked yourself to death in the old days and now you don't have to; you just have a few horses and you play.

INTERVIEWER: What did you study at college?

GARDNER: The usual things—wanted to major in chemistry for a while. In graduate school I studied creative writing and medieval literature mostly. It was useful. I learned a lot of things about an older kind of literature that I thought would be handy in writing my own works, if only because I wouldn't be doing the same thing as everybody else.

INTERVIEWER: Is your fiction at all autobiographical? Do you write about people you know specifically, do you write about yourself?

GARDNER: Sometimes. My fiction is usually autobiographical, but in a distant, almost unrecognizable way. Once in a while, as in the story "Redemption," I write pretty close to what happened. But I fictionalized that too—which worries me, in fact. When you get to an event that close to real life and you change the characters, you run the risk of your sister, or your mother or father, thinking: "You don't understand me. That wasn't what I was thinking." I *know* that's not what they were thinking, but I need searchlights on a piece, so I have to change characters, make them more appropriate to the fictional idea, the *real* subject, which isn't just history. Usually, though, I'm not interested—as Updike and Malamud are—in celebrating my own life. I use feelings that I have myself—the only feelings I know, directly—and I deal them out to a group of characters, and let the characters fight out the problems that I've been fighting out. Characteristically there's a battle in my fiction between the hunger for roots, stability, law, and another element in my character which is anarchic. I hate to obey speed laws. I hate to park where it says you have to park. I hate to have to be someplace on time. And in fact I often don't do those things I know I should do, which of course fills me with uneasiness and guilt. Every time you break the law you pay, and every time you obey the law you pay. That compulsion not to do what people tell me, to avoid tic repetitions, makes me constantly keep pushing the edges. It makes me change places of living, or change my life in one way or another, which often makes me very unhappy. I wish I could just settle down. I keep promising myself that really soon now I'm going to get this little farm or maybe house and take care of it, never move again. But I'll probably never do it. Anyway, the autobiographical element is more emotional than anything else.

INTERVIEWER: How do you name your characters?

GARDNER: Sometimes I use characters from real life, and sometimes I use their real names—when I do, it's always in celebration of people that I like. Once or twice, as in *October Light*, I've borrowed other people's fictional characters. Naming is only a problem, of course, when you make the character up. It seems to me that every character—every person—is an embodiment of a very complicated, philosophical way of looking at the world, whether conscious or not. Names can be strong clues to the characters system. Names are magic. If you name a kid John, he'll grow up a different kid than if you named him Rudolph. I've used real characters in every single novel, except in *Grendel*, where it's impossible—they didn't have our kinds of names in those days—but even in *Grendel* I used jokes and puns that give you clues to who I'm talking about. For instance, there's a guy named Red Horse, which is really a sorrel, which is really George Sorel. And so on. Sometimes I put real, live characters into books under fictional names—to protect the real person from what the fiction makes of him—and thus I get the pleasure of thinking, for example, what my cousin Bill would do if he were confronted with a particular problem. I get to understand my cousin Bill, whom I love, in a way I never understood him before. I get to see him in a situation perhaps more grave, certainly more compromising, than any he's ever been in. Besides using real people, as I've said, I get great pleasure out of stealing other people's writings. Actually, I do that at least partly because of a peculiar and unfortunate quality of my mind: I remember things. Word for word. I'm not always aware of it. Once in college, I wrote a paragraph of a novel which was word for word out of Joyce's "The Dead," and I wasn't aware of it at all. I absolutely wasn't. My teacher at the time said, Why did you do this? He wasn't accusing me of plagiarism, he was just saying it was a very odd thing to do. I realized then that I had a problem. Of course, it was a big help when I was a teacher, because I could quote long passages of Beowulf and things like that. Once I realized that I also accidentally quote, that I'm constantly alluding to things I'm not consciously aware of, I began to develop this allusive technique—at least when it's fiction—so that nobody could accuse me of plagiarism, since it's so obvious that I'm alluding. In fact, sometimes I have great fun with it. Particularly in *Jason and Medeia*, where I took long sections of writing by Bill Gass, whom I'm enormously fond of, and with whom I completely disagree on almost everything unimportant, and altered a few words to mess up his argument. And in *The Wreck of Agathon* I took long sections out of Jean-Paul Sartre, changed all the images, but kept the rest directly translated. So I use everything.

INTERVIEWER: How do your victims react? Is Sartre aware? Or Gass?

GARDNER: I'm sure Sartre has never heard of me. I hope he'd be amused. As for Gass, he knows why I do it: partly from impishness, partly for a comically noble reason which has to do with Gass's present and future fame.

INTERVIEWER: How do you react to Peter Prescott's insinuation in *Newsweek* that you plagiarized in your *Life and Times of Chaucer*?

GARDNER: With a sigh.

INTERVIEWER: How about the charge that you're, excuse the expression, a male chauvinist?

GARDNER: Consciously, I'm a feminist; but neither the best things we do or the worst are fully conscious. That's why the effect of art is so important. One does not consciously make oneself more bestial by reading pornographic books, and I think only the worst sort of people become consciously "better" people by reading the Bible. When I'm accused of male chauvinism, as I was in one review of *Nickel Mountain,* I'm indignant and hurt; but I watch myself more closely to see if it's true. I've also been accused of being antihomosexual. I'm glad I was accused, because although I wasn't aware of that bigotry, the accusation was just. I don't want to hurt people.

INTERVIEWER: What about the influences of being a teacher?

GARDNER: My academic career has, of course, had considerable influence on my writing of fiction and poetry, though I hope my writing has had no effect on my scholarship and teaching—except to boost my university salary, attract students I might otherwise not meet, and get me invited to visit now and then at other universities. When I first began teaching my main job was in creative writing, and I discovered very quickly that it's fairly easy to transform an eager, intelligent student to a publishing creative writer. Silly as it sounds, that discovery was a shock to my ego and changed my whole approach to writing fiction. (I was twenty-four, twenty-five at the time.) Since I found out that anyone has stories he can tell, and, once you've shown him a little technique, can tell them relatively well, I was determined to set myself apart from the herd (I was reading that devil Nietzsche then) by writing as other people couldn't. I became a mildly fanatic stylist, and experimenter with form, and so on. Also, I quit teaching creative writing, maybe partly from annoyance that my students were as good as I was, but mainly in hopes of learning the things I had to know to become a good writer. I began teaching history of criticism courses, which turned out to be one of the most valuable experiences in my life.

INTERVIEWER: I don't mean to dwell on this, but it's obviously a subject you've thought about a lot. Any more specific effects of your teaching on your writing?

GARDNER: Two more, at least. One is, it's given me material —a lot of it—with which to give a modern story-line resonance. For instance, though I don't mention it in the novel, Chief Fred Clumly in *Sunlight* once read Dante on a ship, though he no longer remembers it. It sank deep into the swamp of his mind and now throws strange light on his modern-seeming problems. The narrator of the novel has obviously read and pondered hard on Malory's *Morte D'Arthur*, which presents a medieval world view totally oppressed to Dante's. I mention this not because I care how readers read the novel but because it shows, more clearly than anything else I can say, the usefulness of my scholarly work in my writing. Nobody but Blake—except possibly Stanley Elkin—can churn up ideas and images with the genius of Blake. But stealing the ideas and images of brilliant men like Dante and Malory (and of course many others), forcing them into confrontation, trying to find some sane resolution to the opposition of such minds and values, a writer can not only get new insights but get, far more important, rich texture and an energy of language beyond the energy of mere conflict in plot. Which is to say, my subject really is (as one critic once mentioned), human history—the conflict of ideas and emotions through the ages.

The other important effect of my teaching on my writing is that, working with intelligent undergraduate and graduate students—and working alongside intelligent teachers—I have a clear idea of my audience, or anyway of a hypothetical audience. I don't think a writer can write well without some such notions. One may claim one writes for oneself, but it's a paltry claim. One more word on all this, I'm obviously convinced that my scholarly career has made me a better writer than I would have been without it, but I'm no longer concerned—as I was in my tempestuous, ego-maddened youth—with proving myself the greatest writer of all time. What I notice now is that all around me there are first-rate writers, and in nearly every case it seems to me that what makes them first-rate is their similar involvement in teaching and scholarship. There are exceptions—maybe William Gaddis, I'm not sure. (A brilliant writer, though I disapprove of him.) Perhaps the most important exception is John Updike, who, unlike John Hawkes, Bill Gass, Stanley Elkin and Saul Bellow and so on, is not a teacher. But the exception means nothing, because, teacher or not, he's the most academic of all.

INTERVIEWER: What about the teaching of creative writing?

GARDNER: When you teach creative writing, you discover a great deal. For instance, if a student's story is really wonderful, but thin, you have to analyze to figure out why it's thin; how you could beef it up. Every discovery of that kind is important. When you're reading only classical and medieval literature, all the bad stuff has been filtered out. There are no bad works in either Greek or Anglo-Saxon. Even the ones that are minor are the very best of the minor, because everything else has been lost or burned or thrown away. When you read this kind of literature, you never really learn how a piece can go wrong, but when you teach creative writing, you see a thousand ways that a piece can go wrong. So it's helpful to me. The other thing that's helpful when you're teaching creative writing is that there are an awful lot of people who at the age of seventeen or eighteen can write as well as you do. That's a frightening discovery. So you ask yourself, What am I doing? Here I've decided that what I'm going to be in life is to be this literary artist, at best; I'm going to stand with Tolstoy, Melville, and all the boys. And there's this kid, nineteen, who's writing just as well. The characters are vividly perceived, the rhythm in the story is wonderful. What have I got that he hasn't got? You begin to think harder and harder about what makes great fiction. That can lead you to straining and overblowing your own fiction, which I've done sometimes, but it's useful to think about.

INTERVIEWER: What are some specific things you can teach in creative writing?

GARDNER: When you teach creative writing, you teach peo-

ple, among other things, how to plot. You explain the principles, how it is that fiction *thinks*. And to give the kids a sense
of how a plot works, you just spin out plot after plot after plot.
In an hour session, you may spin out forty possible plots, one
adhering to the real laws of *energeia*, each one a balance of the
particular and general—and not one of them a story that you'd
really want to write. Then one time, you hit one that *catches*
you for some reason—you hit on the story that expresses your
unrest. When I was teaching creative writing at Chico State,
for instance, one of many plots I spun out was *The Resurrection*.

INTERVIEWER: How does this work?

GARDNER: One plot will just sort of rise above all the others
for reasons that you don't fully understand. All of them are
interesting, all of them have interesting characters, all of them
talk about things that you could talk about; but one of them
catches you like a nightmare. Then you have no choice but to
write it; you can't forget it. It's a weird thing. If it's the kind
of plot you really don't want to do because it involves your
mother too closely, or whatever, you can try to do something
else. But the typewriter keeps hissing at you and shooting
sparks, and the paper keeps wrinkling and the lamp goes off and
nothing else works, so finally you do the one that God said
you've got to do. And once you do it, you're grounded. It's an
amazing thing. For instance, before I wrote the story about the
kid who runs over his younger brother ("Redemption"), always, regularly, every day I used to have four or five flashes of
that accident. I'd be driving down the highway and I couldn't
see what was coming because I'd have a memory flash. I
haven't had it once since I wrote the story. You really do
ground your nightmares, you *name* them. When you write a
story, you have to play that image, no matter how painful, over
and over until you've got all the sharp details so you know
exactly how to put it down on paper. By the time you've run
your mind through it a hundred times, relentlessly worked
every tic of your terror, it's lost its power over you. That's what

bibliotherapy is all about, I guess. You take crazy people and have them write their story, better and better, and soon it's just a story on a page, or, more precisely, everybody's story on a page. It's a wonderful thing. Which isn't to say that I think writing is done for the health of the writer, though it certainly does incidentally have that effect.

INTERVIEWER: Do you feel that literary techniques can really be taught? Some people feel that technique is an artifice or even a hindrance to "true expression."

GARDNER: Certainly it can be taught. But a teacher has to *know* technique to teach it. I've seen a lot of writing teachers because I go around visiting colleges, visiting creative writing classes. A terrible number of awful ones, grotesquely bad. That doesn't mean that one should throw writing out of the curriculum; because when you get a good creative writing class it's magisterial. Most of the writers I know in the world don't know how they do what they do. Most of them *feel* it out. Bernard Malamud and I had a conversation one time in which he said that he doesn't know how he does those magnificent things he sometimes does. He just keeps writing until it comes out right. If that's the way a writer works, then that's the way he had to work, and that's fine. But I like to be in control as much of the time as possible. One of the first things you have to understand when you are writing fiction—or teaching writing—is that there are different ways of doing things, and each one has a slightly different effect. A misunderstanding of this leads you to the Bill Gass position: that fiction can't tell the truth, because every way you say the thing changes it. I don't think that's to the point. I think that what fiction does is sneak up on the truth by telling it six different ways and finally releasing it. That's what Dante said, that you can't really get at the poetic, inexpressible truths, that the way things are leaps up like steam between them. So you have to determine very accurately the potential of a particular writer's style and help that potential develop at the same time, ignoring what you think of his moral stands.

I hate nihilistic, cynical writing. I hate it. It bothers me, and worse yet, bores me. But if I have a student who writes with morbid delight about murder, what I'll have to do (though of course I'll tell him I don't like this kind of writing, that it's immoral, stupid and bad for civilization), is say what is successful about the work and what is not. I have to swallow every bit of my moral feelings to help the writer write his way, his truth. It may be that the most moral writing of all is writing which shows us how a murderer feels, how it happens. It may be it will protect us from murderers someday.

INTERVIEWER: You've recently had essays appear on the subject of what you call "moral fiction" and "moral criticism." Some readers might have trouble with the word "moral." Could you explain what you mean by "moral"? The word, as you've acknowledged, has pejorative implications these days.

GARDNER: I know. It shouldn't. I certainly don't mean fiction that preaches. I'm talking mainly—though not exclusively—about works of fiction that are moral in their process. That is to say, the way they *work* is moral. Good works of fiction study values by testing them in imagined/real situations, testing them hard, being absolutely fair to both sides. The real moral writer is the opposite of the minister, the preacher, the rabbi. Insofar as he can, the preacher tries to keep religion as it always was, outlawing contraceptives or whatever; his job is conservative. The writer's job on the other hand, is to be radically open to persuasion. He should, if possible, not be committed to one side more than to the other—which is simply to say that he wants to affirm life, not sneer at it—but he has to be absolutely fair, understand the moral limits of his partisanship. His affirmation has to be earned. If he favors the cop, he must understand the arguments for life on the side of the robber.

INTERVIEWER: What would be "immoral" literature?

GARDNER: Mainly, fiction goes immoral when it stops being fair, when it stops trusting the laboratory experiment. You lie about characters, you make people do what you want them to do. This is characteristic of most hot-shot writers around now. I would agree with people who get nervous around the word "morality," because usually the people who shout "immoral" are those who want to censor things, or think that all bathroom scenes or bedroom scenes or whatever are wicked. That kind of morality is life-denying, evil. But I *do* think morality is a real thing that's worth talking about. I thought of using some other word so that people wouldn't be mad at me for talking like a minister, but I decided that's the right word. It means what it means, and the fact that it's out of style doesn't matter very much. It's like patriotism, which has got a very bad name because devils keep yelling for it. Ultimately patriotism ought not to mean that you hate all other countries. It ought to mean that you love certain things about your country; you don't want them to change. Unfortunately, when you say "patriotism," everybody goes "aargh." Same thing with morality.

INTERVIEWER: Do you see the risk of dogmatism in your thesis on what fiction and criticism ought to be?

GARDNER: No, only a risk of dogmatism in stubborn or witless misinterpretations of my thesis, of which there have been, alas, many. I'm sure that no matter how carefully I write about true morality, some self-righteous ignoramus will read it too fast and say, "Aha, he's on our side." He will use me to support awful ideas, and I'm sorry about that. I don't think real morality can ever be codified. You can't say "Thou shalt not," and you can't say "Thou shalt." What you *can* say is that this is how people feel and why they feel the way they do. My argument in *Moral Fiction* is this: that immoral fiction is indifferent to the real issues. I'm saying that there's good and evil. And in particular situations, maybe the only healthy situation is universal destruction. I would never set up a morality that's goody-goody. Sometimes morality is awful. Fiction can never pronounce ultimate solutions, but it can lead to understanding. It leads, and that's all. It gives visions of what's possible. If I were going to write a book which told people how to live, I would write an incredibly meticulous book about Indian gurus, Jewish heroes, Christian saints. I would present every right argument and show clearly and logically what the wrong sides are. It would be simple, except that logic is never to be trusted. And everybody who read my book would say, if I did my job brilliantly, that's the way to live. The trouble is they wouldn't read the book because it would be boring, and even if they did read and understand, they wouldn't be moved to action. The book wouldn't be interesting because it wouldn't show people we care about growing toward the truth. If you show characters struggling to know what's right, and in the process of the novel you work out their issues more and more clearly, whether the character heroically wins or tragically loses, *then* you move the reader, having first moved yourself. I think morality has to be persuasive. And you can only be persuasive if you start with imperfect human beings. Of course, if you wind up with *perfect* human beings, that's a bore too. I guess the morality of the fiction is the seriousness of the question and the seriousness of the concern with imaginary people's lives and feelings—a reflection of real people's lives and feelings—not the seriousness or logicality of the answer.

INTERVIEWER: Should the writer examine the morality of a piece before, say, the quality of its prose, its interest and saleability?

GARDNER: Certainly morality should come first—for writers, critics, and everybody else. People who change tires. People in factories. They should always ask, Is this moral? Not, Will it sell? If you're in construction and building houses out of shingles and you realize that you're wiping out ten thousand acres of Canadian pine every year, you should ask yourself, Can I make it cheaper or as cheaply out of clay? Because clay is inexhaustible. Every place there's dirt. A construction owner should say, I don't have to be committed to this particular product: I can go for the one which will make me money, *and* make a better civilization. Occasionally businessmen actually do that. The best will even settle for a profit cut. The same thing is true of writers—ultimately it comes down to, are you making or are you destroying? If you try very hard to create ways of living, create dreams of what is possible, then you win. If you don't, you may make a fortune in ten years, but you're not going to be read in twenty years, and that's that. Why do something cheap? I can't understand people who go for the moment of the book. In the long run, Melville's estate is worth vastly more than the estate of Octave Thanet. Octave Thanet was, I think, the best-selling novelist of the nineteenth century. Melville told the truth, Thanet told high-minded lies. All liars are soon dead, forgotten. Dickens' novels didn't sell half as well as a novel of Octave Thanet's called *A Slave to Duty*. But you haven't heard of her, right? I know of her only because I know obscure facts.

INTERVIEWER: And that is why certain works of fiction have lasted, and others have disappeared?

GARDNER: Of course. So I believe. The ones that last are the ones that are true. You look at Faulkner and John O'Hara. John O'Hara outsold Faulkner, he circled Faulkner at the time they were writing. Ten years after his death, O'Hara's books are out of print. We all read Faulkner, nobody reads O'Hara. Dreiser in some ways, some of the time, is one of the worst writers who ever lived. *An American Tragedy*, for instance, is an endless book with terrible sentences like "He found her extremely intellectually interesting." But by the time you finish the book, you've sopped your vest. He's a great writer, though he wrote badly. But what he does morally, that is to say, what he does in terms of analysis of character and honest statement about the way the world is, is very good. Of course, some writers last a long time because of their brilliance, their style; Fitzgerald is a good example—a fine stylist. But he never quite got to the heart of things. *That's* what should concern the critics. If a critic is concerned with only how well the sentences go, or how neat the symbolic structure is, or how new the devices are, he's going to exaggerate the importance of mediocre books. Samuel Beckett—surely one of the great writers of our time, despite my objections—is loved by critics, but except for John Fowles, I hear no one pointing out that the tendency of all he says is wrong. He says it powerfully, with comi-tragic brilliance, and he believes it, but what he says is not quite sound. Every night Samuel Beckett goes home to his wife, whom he's lived with all these years; he lies down in bed with her, puts his arms around her, and says, "No meaning again today . . ." Critics can say, and do say, Well, it doesn't matter what he says, it's how well he says it. But I think in the long run Beckett is in for it. Because great writers tell the truth exactly—and get it right. A man can be a brilliant writer who writes wonderful lines, and still say what is just not so; like Sartre, Beckett—and in his lapses, Faulkner. Faulkner's sentimentality in the bad moments—every reader knows he's missing a little. I like Dilsey. I believe Dilsey really exists, but I just don't believe that Faulkner understands her or really cares. He's more interested in Dilsey as a symbol than as a person. Everything that Faulkner says about Dilsey is no doubt true . . . it's just all those things he didn't say, the things that make her fully human, not just a symbol. Mythologizing her—or accepting the standard mythology of his age—he slightly skews the inevitability of his story. He does the same thing every time he turns on his mannered rhetoric—distorts the inherent emotion of the story and thus gets diverted from the real and inevitable progress of events.

INTERVIEWER: You've said there are exceptions to your thesis on moral fiction. Could you mention a few?

GARDNER: First, there's fiction that's neither moral nor immoral—minor fiction, pure entertainment. I'm accused of not valuing it, but actually all I say is that it's trivial: I'm not at all against it except when some critic takes it seriously. I favor it as on a hot day I favor ice cream. Second, there's fiction I'd call moral only in the earnestness of its concern. This kind of fiction I would *not* call trivial. There's one man whose name is Ernest Finney. He's a wonderful writer. He sent me his fiction, he's been writing for years, unpublished. He writes grim, frightening stories. But I would certainly publish them if I had a magazine. Absolutely no question. One is about a lower-class guy, tough; he's got a good car, a T-Bird, third-hand. He marries this beautiful girl who's kind of a whore. She finally gets his money and disappears. He's making his money stealing. He goes to prison. All the time he's in prison, he plans on killing her. That's all he cares about, that's all he thinks about. His idea is to put a shotgun up her and blow her to smithereens. You understand exactly why he feels the way he does. It's a very powerful, terrifying story. Because you become the character. You would do it too.

INTERVIEWER: How does this fit any standard we've talked about?

GARDNER: Well, I think it's moral fiction, but in a tricky way. Finney does honestly describe a situation. He's not looking for ways that we could live better—the highest way—but he's describing exactly, and with original genius, how it feels to want to kill your wife. Terribly difficult. It's moral fiction of the third degree. Moral fiction can exist in only three forms. The highest form is moral fiction in which you see absolutely accurate description of the best people; fiction that gives you an idea how to live. It's uplifting: you want to be like the hero. You want to be like Jesus, or Buddha, or Moses, whatever. Tolstoy does it. Everybody wants to be like Pierre in *War and Peace.* Everybody wants to be like Levin in *Anna Karenina.* In the next form of moral fiction you see an evil person and you realize you don't want to be like that. Like Macbeth. You see there's an alternative. You don't have to be like Macbeth. It's kind of negative moral fiction, or moral fiction in the tragic mode, where you want to be different than the protagonist—you want to be better. Then there's the third form, wherein alternatives don't exist. Not for fashion's sake or for the cheap love of gruesomeness, but from anger and concern, you stare into the smoking volcano. That's the world of Ernest Finney's fiction, or Constance Urdgang's. You understand exactly why a wife would want to kill her husband, saw up the body, and put it in a suitcase. We've all read the newspaper stories about this kind of thing. It happens. But only a great artist can show it happen so that you feel that you saw it, and saw it from inside the murderer's mind: you understand. That doesn't tell you what you should do. It doesn't tell you, I don't want to be like that. But it makes you understand and, understanding, hunger for a world not like this. It's obviously the least uplifting of the three kinds of moral fiction, but it's morally useful. Mostly what we get, it seems to me, is "serious" fiction not in any of those three categories. People kill people, we don't understand why they did it, we don't care why they did it, we read it because it's cheaply thrilling, an escape from the common decency we sometimes feel trapped in. Blood drips, people piss on people or live their boring "lives of quiet desperation." It's at worst a kind of sick daydream, at best useless actuality, not morally worth reading.

INTERVIEWER: What effect do you think your writing has had?

GARDNER: I think it has given a few readers pleasure. And I suppose it may have depressed a few. I hope it does more good than harm.

PAUL F. FERGUSON
JOHN R. MAIER
FRANK MCCONNELL
SARA MATTHIESSEN
Spring 1979

Notes on the Contributors

DR. PAUL F. FERGUSON *(Interview with John Gardner)* has long been associated with the Brockport Writers' Forum under whose auspices this interview was conducted in 1977. A specialist in medieval literature with interests in modern fiction and detective fiction, he is a visiting lecturer at the State University of New York at Geneseo.

DAVID HAYMAN *(Interview with Kurt Vonnegut, Jr.)* is a professor of comparative literature at the University of Wisconsin at Madison. He has published interviews in *TriQuarterly, Contemporary Literature,* and *The Iowa Review.* His books include *Ulysses: The Mechanics of Meaning* and *A First Draft of Finnegans Wake* (edited with Clive Hart).

JANNIKA HURWITT *(Interview with Nadine Gordimer)* is a free-lance writer. Her work has been published in *The Paris Review,* the *Village Voice,* the *Soho Weekly News,* and *Yankee Magazine.*

ALFRED MACADAM *(Interview with Carlos Fuentes)* teaches Latin American literature at Barnard College and Columbia University. His most recent book, *Modern Latin American*

Narrative: The Dreams of Reason, was published by the University of Chicago Press.

J. D. MCCLATCHY *(Interview with James Merrill)* has published a collection of poems, *Scenes From Another Life* (Braziller, 1981). He teaches at Princeton.

FRANK MCCONNELL *(Interview with John Gardner)* is associate professor of English at the University of California, Santa Barbara, and author of *The Spoken Seen: Film and the Romantic Imagination* (Johns Hopkins University Press), *Four Postwar American Novelists: Bellow, Mailer, Barth and Pynchon* (University of Chicago Press), and a book on film from Oxford.

JOHN R. MAIER *(Interview with John Gardner)* teaches English at the State University of New York College at Brockport. He is the author of a number of works on medieval and Renaissance English literature, the literature of the ancient Near East, literary criticism, and the interplay between literature and philosophy. One part (Tablet XII) of his translation of *The Epic of Gilgamesh,* a project with John Gardner and Richard Henshaw, has appeared in *MSS* magazine; the complete work will be published in the near future.

SARA MATTHIESSEN *(Interview with John Gardner)* is a writer currently reporting for a Vermont television station.

DAVID MICHAELIS *(Interview with Kurt Vonnegut, Jr.),* a contributing editor of *The Paris Review,* is the author of *The Best of Friends: Profiles of Extraordinary Friendships,* and co-author of *MUSHROOM: The Story of the A-Bomb Kid.*

ROBERT PHILLIPS *(Interview with William Goyen)* is a writer and critic whose previous ten books include his story collection, *The Land of Lost Content,* and two poetry collections, *The*

Pregnant Man and *Running on Empty*. He is a contributing editor of *The Paris Review*.

GEORGE PLIMPTON *(Interview with Kurt Vonnegut, Jr.)* is the editor of *The Paris Review*. His most recent book is *Fireworks: A Celebration*.

DOTSON RADER *(Interview with Tennessee Williams)* has most recently published a novel, *Beau Monde*. His other books include *Blood Dues* and *Government Inspected Meat*, and he is currently at work on a series of articles about presidential families.

RICHARD RHODES *(Interview with Kurt Vonnegut, Jr.)* is a novelist and journalist. He has published four novels and many essays. He is currently at work on *Ultimate Powers: A History of the Bomb*, to be published in 1984.

CHARLES RUAS *(Interview with Carlos Fuentes)* was a contributing editor at the *Soho News*, and has done literary interviews for *The Paris Review* and the *The New York Times*. He is currently finishing a book on contemporary trends in American fiction.

ELIZABETH SPIRES *(Interview with Elizabeth Bishop)* published her first book of poems, *Globe*, in 1981. Currently she is completing a second collection, tentatively titled *Letter from Swan's Island*. She has been the recipient of grants from the National Endowment for the Arts and the Ingram Merrill Foundation. She lives in Baltimore, Maryland, and is a lecturer in English at Goucher College.

DANIEL STERN *(Interview with Bernard Malamud)* is a novelist, critic, and playwright. His ninth and most recent novel, *An Urban Affair*, was published in 1980. He lives in New York and Amagansett with his wife, who is a literary agent.

PETER STITT *(Interview with Stephen Spender)* is a regular poetry reviewer for *The Georgia Review*. His work has also appeared in *Poetry, The New York Times Book Review, Parnassus, The Southern Review, The Sewanee Review,* and elsewhere. He is the author of *The World's Hieroglyphic Beauty: Essays on and Interviews with Six Contemporary Poets.* Work in progress includes *Engagements with Reality: Postmodernism and the Traditional in Contemporary American Poetry* and the authorized biography of James Wright.

PETER H. STONE *(Interview with Gabriel García Márquez)* is a New York freelance writer. His work has appeared in the *Atlantic, The New York Times Magazine, The Nation, Newsday,* the *Village Voice,* and other publications. He is a former editor of *Ramparts* magazine.

MARINA WARNER *(Interview with Rebecca West)* is a British journalist, novelist, and biographer. She is the author of *Alone of All Her Sex: The Myth and Cult of the Virgin Mary* and *Joan of Arc: The Image of Female Heroism. The Skating Party,* her most recent novel, was published in 1983. She is currently working on a study of the female form in allegory.